Minding the Gap

Why Integrating High School with College Makes Sense and How to Do It

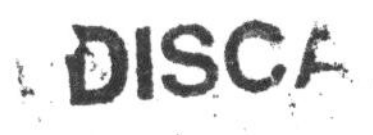

Minding the Gap

Why Integrating High School with College Makes Sense and How to Do It

Edited by

Nancy Hoffman

Joel Vargas

Andrea Venezia

and

Marc S. Miller

HARVARD EDUCATION PRESS

Cambridge, Massachusetts

Library of Congress Control Number 2007928175

Paperback ISBN 978-1-891792-45-8
Library Edition ISBN 978-1-891792-46-5

Published by Harvard Education Press,
an imprint of the Harvard Education Publishing Group

Harvard Education Press
8 Story Street
Cambridge, MA 02138

Cover Design: Alyssa Morris

The typefaces used in this book are ITC Stone and Stone Sans.

Contents

Acknowledgments ix

Introduction 1

PART I WHY INTEGRATE GRADES 9 THROUGH 14? **13**

1 – Confessions of an Education Fundamentalist: Why Grade 12 Is Not the Right End Point for Anyone **15**
Anthony P. Carnevale

2 – Doing the Math: What It Means to Double the Number of Low-Income College Graduates **27**
Susan Goldberger

PART II ONE SYSTEM ACROSS 9–14: THE STATE OF THE STATES **43**

3 – Common Ground **45**
Andrea Venezia, Joni Finney, and Patrick M. Callan

4 – The History of the Separation of K–12 and Postsecondary Education **55**
Michael W. Kirst and Michael D. Usdan

5 – A College-Ready Nation: An Idea Whose Time Has Come **65**
Kristin D. Conklin and Stefanie Sanford

6 – Raising Expectations for Academic Achievement **73**
Stan Jones

PART III ALIGNMENT AND INTEGRATION OF STANDARDS, ASSESSMENTS, AND CURRICULUM ACROSS 9–14 **79**

7 – Alignment of High School Expectations to College and Work **81**
Christine Tell and Michael Cohen

8 – All One System: The Promise of O*Net **87**
Anthony P. Carnevale

9 – Challenges in the Transition from High School to College 93
David Conley

10 – Sending Signals to Students: The Role of Early Placement Testing in Improving Academic Preparation 105
Bridget Terry Long and Erin K. Riley

11 – The California Early Assessment Program: Implications for States in Developing Readiness Agendas 113
David Spence

PART IV PATHWAYS ACROSS 9–14: PRACTICES IN PLACE **121**

12 – Lessons from the Field: A Tale of Two Early College High Schools 123
Cecilia Cunningham and Roberta S. Matthews

13 – Another Route to College 133
Terry Grobe

14 – Combining Middle and High School to Improve College Success 139
Dan Restuccia

15 – CUNY College Now: Extending the Reach of Dual Enrollment 143
Tracy Meade and Eric Hofmann

16 – Academic Identity Development: Student Experiences in Two Early College High Schools 151
Michael J. Nakkula and Karen C. Foster

17 – Secondary-Postsecondary Learning Opportunities: Some Promising Practices 159
Jennifer Brown Lerner and Betsy Brand

PART V PATHWAYS ACROSS 9–14: EMERGING POLICIES **165**

18 – Creating Pathways for Struggling Students within a 9–14 System 167
Adria Steinberg and Cheryl Almeida

19 – State Policies that Support the Integration of 9–14: The Case of Early College High Schools 175
Joel Vargas

20 – Return on Investment Analysis of Integrating Grades 9–14 183
Robert Palaich, John Augenblick, and Margaretha Maloney

21 – Using Dual Enrollment to Build a 9–14 System 191
Nancy Hoffman

22 – Evolution of an Innovation: A Commentary on the State of Accelerated Learning 203
Travis Reindl

23 – Exploring Education Reform Systemically: The United Kingdom's Nuffield 14–19 Review 211
Geoff Hayward

PART VI WHAT COMES NEXT? ACCOUNTABILITY, DATA SYSTEMS, FINANCING 219

24 – Postsecondary Numerical Goals as Catalyst for P–16 Reform: Texas Sends a Message 221
Michael Collins

25 – Assessing and Reporting Progress: Florida's Integrated Data Systems 227
Jay Pfeiffer

26 – Data Requirements for a Coherent P–16 System 233
Chrys Dougherty and Lynn Mellor

27 – Seamless Data Systems to Promote Student Progression 239
Peter T. Ewell

28 – Developing a P–20 Budget Tool: Giving Direction to Oregon Public Education 249
Jill Kirk, John Tapogna, and Duncan Wyse

29 – Financing Higher Aspirations and Better Preparation 259
Arthur M. Hauptman

30 – Integrating Public Finance into Strategies for Improving Preparation, College Enrollment, and Persistence 269
Edward P. St. John

Notes and References 279

About the Editors 301

About the Authors 303

Index 313

Acknowledgments

We are grateful to the Bill & Melinda Gates Foundation for its generous support of new schools and better education policies, many of which are described in this book. In addition, the foundation's support for Jobs for the Future made this book possible. We would also like to acknowledge the wise counsel of our JFF colleagues—especially Marlene Seltzer, president of JFF, and Richard Kazis, senior vice president—in the shaping of this book. And, finally, we would like to express our thanks to our intrepid and patient authors, who responded graciously to our requests that they trim their pieces—a difficult task because each one had so much of importance to say.

Introduction

Most Americans believe that education is the great equalizer, the engine of opportunity, and the best route to careers with family-supporting wages. But that belief is eroding as postsecondary education becomes the baseline requirement for success in today's economy. With the new requirement of "some college" for all, education is in danger of becoming an "unequalizer"—yet another force widening the gap between the rich and the poor. Postsecondary opportunity flows to more affluent young people, given the mutually reinforcing combination of better preparation in high school, the expectation of earning both a high school diploma and a college degree, the ability to pay for college, and the advantages of social class.

Young people from the middle and upper ends of the socioeconomic spectrum are almost five times more likely to earn a two- or four-year college degree than those from low-income families. As for earning a place in higher education through excellent academic achievement, high school graduates from poor families who score in the top testing quartile are no more likely than their lowest-scoring, affluent peers to attend college. The former enroll at rates of 78 percent; the latter at 77 percent (Advisory Committee on Student Financial Assistance, 2001).[1] And then there are the many young people who do not get a real chance at college: Nearly half of our nation's African American students and nearly 40 percent of Latino students attend high schools in which graduation is not the norm. In the nation's 900 to 1,000 urban "dropout factories" that serve primarily African American and Latino students, completing high school is a 50:50 proposition at best (Balfanz & Legters, 2004).

It is not just because young people want some assurance of an adequate standard of living that a postsecondary credential is in high relief. From many a bully pulpit, our leaders argue that the country needs a better-educated workforce to stay competitive. The argument is well known: Economists predict that job growth in the United States will be substantial for workers with college and graduate-level degrees but will decline for all others. At the current rate of degree production, there will not be enough educated workers to fill these positions. To ensure the nation's economic future, the argument says, our postsecondary systems must produce millions of additional college degree holders.[2]

Some speakers point as well to the moral and political risks to our society of a shrinking middle class and a growing divide between the very rich and the many poor. If the speaker is an educator, the argument goes, we need to reduce the number of high school dropouts, raise the standards represented by the high school diploma, and staunch the leaks in the "pipeline" to and through postsecondary education.

The going gets rough, though, and the conversation less predictable when it comes to the steps needed to address a problem for which the country is unprepared. As Anthony Carnevale has pointed out:

> The essential fact that the architects of the modern education system didn't foresee was that access to a mass system of postsecondary education would become the threshold requirement for middle-class status; that the only purpose of high schools would be to send people to college; and that employability would become the implicit standard of educational adequacy. And it is this set of facts that raises the longer-term questions about efficiency and equity in American education.[3]

WHAT WE ARGUE

Minding the Gap takes to heart the threshold requirement of some postsecondary education for all along with questions about equity. Because one in two students from middle- and upper-income families are already attaining a postsecondary credential whatever their high school achievement levels, compared with one in ten students from the lowest economic quintile (Advisory Committee on Student Financial Assistance, 2001),[4] it asks, "What policies and practices would most quickly, cost effectively, and successfully produce a higher number of postsecondary credentials among low-income and first-generation students whose attainment rates remain so low." It joins the many voices advocating for improved high school education to decrease dropout rates and ensure that all students graduate from high school ready for further education or well-paying, flexible work. But *Minding the Gap* goes several steps further.

If everyone needs an education through two years of college or the equivalent, then the nation has an obligation to provide a far more certain pathway for postsecondary success than it does now. Because so many young people fail to complete the final years of high school, graduate but do not apply to college, or begin postsecondary education only to drop out within the first few semesters, the book focuses on these high school / college transition years, the period in which young people are most vulnerable to the educational failure that will severely limit their life chances. The book advocates for *an integrated secondary/postsecondary system, one in which a post–high school credential is the default end point, and in which the transition between sectors is eliminated to the greatest extent possible. In other words, if low-income students disappear in the transition between high school and postsecondary, rethink and restructure the transition and build the structures needed for a seamless system.* By "post–high school education," we mean the quotient of educational attainment that provides choice and flexibility in work and life, such as a career certificate or an associate's or bachelor's degree. By *integrated*, we mean a system with the following characteristics:

Secondary/postsecondary shared responsibility:

- K–12 and postsecondary standards, assessments, curricula, and expectations for student academic effort are aligned to first-year, college-level, academic expectations at broad-access higher education institutions—thus reducing the need for remediation.

- K–12 and postsecondary share responsibility for successful student transitions between levels of education, including transitions for the most vulnerable youth.

Multiple pathways to a postsecondary credential:

- K–12 and postsecondary work together to provide well-defined curricular pathways to a postsecondary credential for all students. The number need not be large, but one or two pathways are insufficient to meet the diverse backgrounds and learning styles of the nation's young people.
- Most students—not a select few—have opportunities to accelerate their education and to undertake college credit-level work while in high school.

Seamless accountability, finance, and governance systems:

- A state's accountability system follows students across sectors through linked data collection systems, and states can hold high schools and postsecondary institutions accountable for improving their course- and degree-completion rates.
- A single state education finance system distributes funds equitably, from kindergarten through college, and it creates incentives for an integrated system.
- Collaborative or joint governance structures plan, set goals, and monitor results across all the education systems.

This book addresses the secondary/postsecondary gap at multiple levels—from the misalignment of high school and college curricula and pedagogy, to separate and disparate funding mechanisms and formulas for K–12 and higher education, to disconnects in data systems across K–16. A number of essays build on the alignment work currently going on to establish standards and assessments across high school and college that move students from college readiness at high school graduation to nonremedial college work. Others build on the dual enrollment activity that is enabling an increasing number of students to gain college-level credit in high school.

Minding the Gap shows that pieces of an integrated system with the characteristics above exist now, but not all in any one state or district, and in no state are they organized for maximum effect. However, the evidence that there *is* momentum toward an integrated system is as follows: States are asking public schools and postsecondary institutions to come to agreement about the meaning of "college- and work-ready" at the end of high school. This challenge is calling into question both high school and postsecondary expectations. A number of states are already providing free postsecondary education through grade 14 for students completing the associate's degree in high school, although most do not advertise the opportunities as such. Many states allow students to replace high school requirements with equally or more-challenging college courses at no cost. Much of this integration remains under the radar and is not yet seen as the backbone of a K–16 or 9–14 system.

STRATEGIES FOR INCREASING THE PROPORTION OF YOUNG PEOPLE EARNING POSTSECONDARY CREDENTIALS

Starting with the GI Bill, and accelerating in the 40 years since the civil rights movement and the influx of women into higher education, the face of postsecondary education has been changing. Indeed, U.S. postsecondary education is far more diverse than it was in the 1950s, and some of that diversity is the result of the development of effective strategies for ensuring that a greater number of young people prepare for and enter postsecondary education. But the perplexing fact is that since the 1980s, growth in degree attainment has slowed, reaching a plateau in the 1990s,[5] and the number of 18- to 19-year-olds entering higher education has grown only 4 percent.[6] At the same time, approximately 90 percent of high school students say they intend to go to college. Clearly, the strategies that worked so well for decades to prepare young people for postsecondary opportunity and provide for their success are no longer enough to produce the number of degree completions the nation needs (Venezia, Kirst, & Antonio, 2003).

What do young people need to complete a postsecondary credential? In brief, three resources are essential and must exist across 9–14: a rigorous academic program that sequences and scaffolds academic demands in a trajectory that moves without break from high school through college-level work; dependable financing for higher education promised at least by ninth grade; and a web of support—school-based, familial, and community—through high school and into postsecondary. Some schools, families, and communities can supply all three types of resources, but many cannot, and in the United States at the dawn of the twenty-first century, the major responsibility falls to the 50 states to attempt to equalize opportunity and prepare all citizens to meet the needs of today's economy. Indeed, state policymakers are coming to realize that they must attend to postsecondary attainment rates just as they do to success in the first 12 years of education.

In regard to the first essential resource, academic rigor, a number of states are boosting the academic requirements for high school graduation. As a first step, many are instituting a core curriculum that ensures that the default high school pathway *is* a college preparation sequence. Going further, a substantial number of states are aligning high school graduation standards with the standards required to advance directly into nonremedial, college-level work. For example, 29 states are at work on such alignment through the American Diploma Project Network of Achieve, Inc. Some states use tenth- or eleventh-grade assessments to provide students with information about their readiness for college while there is still time to address deficiencies, and some states and school districts are mounting programs to recover high school dropouts and students who fall behind in earning credits. These students also need intensive academic work to meet the more-rigorous standards required to complete high school or enter a community college.

The steps are smaller toward providing dependable financial resources. Some states promise financial aid, including tuition-free college for low-income students who complete core academic requirements. Others provide free college credits in high school through dual enrollment and other accelerated-learning options for students who meet those academic standards.

The third category—the web of school-based, familial, and community support—is less well developed across states and school districts, but a number of schools and communities are promoting postsecondary education as an attainable future for their young people. They provide informational counseling, help with completing college and financial aid applications, one-on-one mentoring and tutoring for students, and visits to college campuses. Faith-based and community organizations particularly are active in this arena, and states do provide some financial support for such ventures.

All of these strategies have a role to play; this book's platform rests on research-based evidence that high school-related strategies *alone*, however powerful and appropriate, will not get the results needed.[7] The systems that support and mold K–16 education—state-level financing, data collection, accountability, and governance mechanisms—must work in tandem. Secondary and postsecondary sectors need to be financed more efficiently and collaboratively; state K–12 and higher education administrative bodies and legislative committees need to operate together; and accountability systems, data collection, and analysis tasks must follow students substantially beyond age 18.

HOW THIS BOOK CAME ABOUT

We asked each contributor to *Minding the Gap* to carry out a thought experiment in his or her particular areas of expertise: "What would it take to create a 9–14 system incorporating the characteristics set out on pages 2–3 above?" This was not a theoretical question. All the authors are either implementing programs or policies that align and integrate 9–14, or they carry out research and analysis about policies and programs already in place. The result is that from their various positions—provost or school developer, commissioner or funder, researcher or advocate—each writer took stock of an aspect of the 9–14 integration agenda.

There is remarkable vitality in the reports from the field, but not surprisingly, the pieces do not line up with the ideal characteristics cited at the beginning of this introduction. Even so, readers will find a unique snapshot, documenting practices and policies existing in 2007 that could be the foundations of an integrated system, with the speculation of some authors reaching far beyond what currently exists. The core of *Minding the Gap* describes and analyzes work at the seams between high school alignment and the integration of standards, assessments, and curriculum; pathways in place across 9–14; and emerging 9–14 policies. Two sections address systemic issues writ large. These are about the structural and political disconnects in our education system and how they might be fixed: why there has been only modest progress in developing K–16 schooling since the concept first gained currency 25 years ago, and how finance, governance, data, and accountability systems might look if they were to produce the results we need. Each section begins with a brief note setting the context and pointing to themes in each essay.

There are inevitable gaps in what any one book of manageable length could take on. One immense challenge to practice and policy in creating an integrated system is faculty (teacher and professor) preparation and professional development. A second is the question of what to do about career and technical education—namely, can it be used as a mechanism to engage more students in high school and prepare students well for life after high school, both college and career? The first of these issues is not addressed, and the second, only briefly.

PROGRESS ON 9–14: REFLECTIONS ON SCALE, QUALITY, AND EQUITY

The arguments and propositions in this book are tentative. No 9–14 system as proposed yet exists in a single state or school system. Nonetheless, as the essays suggest, activity is taking place on a number of fronts. The work is deepest in the provision of college-level learning in high school, in the creation of longitudinal data systems, and in the alignment of math and English high school exit standards with nonremedial, postsecondary entrance standards—activities that build a foundation for integration. But not all states have engaged. As of early 2007, 18 states have the ability to match student records between the P–12 and higher education systems. Twenty-nine states are working on alignment through the American Diploma Project network, and six states had enacted college-ready standards. Thus, it is not easy to estimate the scale of 9–14 activity, its quality or depth, or for whom.

These questions matter a great deal for the propositions here, and most authors do not address them because they focus on a specific state or aspect of the education system. Thus, the following sections are an attempt to look *across* the 9–14 terrain, with attention to whether 9–14 activity is actually affecting student learning. Because 42 states have dual enrollment legislation, and many have longstanding programs, reasonable indicators of 9–14 activity are the extent of college-level work in high school, the direction of revisions to state dual enrollment policies; and the level of interest in such new models as early college high schools. Such policies and practices require that students, faculty, credits, and dollars cross between the sectors. Accordingly, while it is at best a proxy for integration, dual enrollment is the gauge we use here.

We raise three questions about dual enrollment:

- *Scale:* What is the scale of current activity? Do the rate and nature of the increases in activity justify optimism about the integration of 9–14?
- *Quality:* How should one characterize the quality of practice and policy being produced in 9–14 configurations? What capacity exists to monitor or evaluate these efforts?
- *Equity:* What challenges and benefits does an integrated 9–14 system pose to the agenda of greater equity of outcomes for low-income, underrepresented young people in our education system today?

Scale

The essays raise issues of scale and demand for integration in three areas: students, policies, and programs. In 2006, the National Center for Education Statistics published the first national study to attempt to capture the number of students participating in exam- and course-based, college-level learning in high school. The quantitative report followed on studies of dual enrollment undertaken by the Office of Vocational and Adult Education, as well as an increasing number of studies of dual enrollment from scholars, researchers, and observers of higher education. The attention itself was an indicator that the dual enrollment phenomenon was growing. Among key NCES findings were the following for the 2002–03 school year:[8]

- There were an estimated 1.2 million enrollments in courses for dual credit.[9]
- Overall, approximately 813,000 high school students took college-level courses through postsecondary institutions, either within or outside of dual enrollment programs. This represents about 5 percent of all high school students.[10]
- Most public high schools offered dual credit or exam-based courses. Overall, 71 percent of public high schools offered courses for dual credit.
- Ninety-eight percent of public two-year institutions had high school students taking courses for college credit, compared to 77 percent of public four-year institutions, 40 percent of private four-year institutions, and 17 percent of private two-year institutions.

The NCES data establish a baseline for measurement of the extent of college-level learning in high school, aggregated for all 50 states. However, dual enrollment opportunities vary dramatically across states, so an aggregate of all high school students in the country gives a limited account. While useful, the NCES data blend states that have large, long-standing programs with those lacking any formal mechanisms for dual enrollment.

To understand the increase in college-level course-taking requires looking at those states that have a history of providing such opportunities and keeping data. The data signal growth trends within states (even if they are not comparable across states due to the inconsistent ways the data are collected). For example, Florida and Utah, with long-standing, well-known programs, had increases in participation, respectively, of 20 percent between 1998 and 2003, and 100 percent between 1995 and 2003. Utah's increase helped prompt the state to promise to pay 75 percent of upper-division college tuition for students graduating from high school with an associate's degree.[11] The Illinois Community College Board reports that between 2001 and 2002, when the state began awarding Accelerated College Enrollment grants to community colleges to support all or part of the college tuition and fees of participating high school students, enrollment increased 100 percent and was ten times greater than in 1991–92 (Andrews & Barnett, 2002). Enrollment growth almost doubled in Kentucky (from 9,321 in 2001–02 to 18,291 in 2004–05), most of it in the Kentucky Community and Technical College System (Kentucky Council on Postsecondary Education, 2006).

The single district with a substantial integrated K–12 and higher education system is New York City. From the 2001–02 academic year to the 2005–06 academic year, college credit enrollments in City University of New York's College Now program increased by 49 percent to reach over 20,000 completed courses taken by high school students.[12]

A second indicator of scale is the number of states that enable dual enrollment through their policies. Forty-two states have dual or concurrent enrollment policies, and some states (e.g., Pennsylvania) are now setting policy for the first time (Western Interstate Commission for Higher Education, 2006). Also, a number of states are revising policies that were originally crafted as entitlements for gifted and talented students in order to support broad high school reform goals. In addition to the states noted above, Maine, North Carolina, Ohio, Texas, Virginia, Washington, and several other states are considering or already have broad access. These states are signaling that dual enrollment can boost the college success rates of a wide range of students, including those headed into career and technical programs. Here, too, the trends are toward greater opportunity through policy.

In terms of scale, the least-developed programs are those that coherently align and integrate course sequences across the sectors with the goal of promoting postsecondary completion. To qualify as a true integrated pathway, students would graduate from high school with anywhere from one to four semesters' worth of college credit. Early college high schools currently serve over 20,000 underrepresented students in such integrated pathways, and they are expanding rapidly; middle colleges similarly build pathways, as do some tech prep programs.[13]

North Carolina is the lead state in this area, constituting 75 nationally recognized "Learn & Earn" early college high schools, each partnered with a community or four-year college. If coherent pathways like these increase in number in other states, it would be a robust indicator that 9–14 has taken hold in practice.

Only state policies can enable such 9–14 activity to grow to scale, and because states compete with one another, they can spread popular innovations across the country. States are putting in place the high school foundations for an integrated system: default college preparatory curricular and alignment activities, including such innovations as early assessments of student readiness for college-level work. Whether a substantial number will build true pathways remains to be seen.

Quality

As pressure on states and institutions grows—from educators and from families—to offer more opportunity for college-level work in high schools, stakeholders are raising issues about the quality of 9–14 approaches. Quality issues are characterized in two ways: in terms of the rigor of teaching and learning in specific courses and, less frequently but just as importantly, the comprehensiveness of the experience offered. That is, for college-level work to promote college success for underrepresented students, quality is synonymous with adequate academic support and advising, properly sequenced high school and college courses, appropriate academic content, and thorough, engaging instruction.

Neither policies nor practices to ensure quality in either individual courses or programs are well developed. Yet, as several essays illustrate, increased demand is raising—although not yet satisfactorily answering—questions about quality, and fast on the heels of such questions are others about accountability, incentives, and capacity-building. Indeed, if secondary and higher education take joint responsibility for student success, the collaboration must be buttressed by K–16 governance, including an accountability system that crosses sectors. And K–16 accountability, or even higher education accountability alone, does not yet exist. The accountability measures required by No Child Left Behind have little in common with the National Survey of Student Engagement or the Collegiate Learning Assessment, both of which figure prominently in the higher education debate about assessing the results of student learning.

As for individual courses, quality was not a major problem when only a handful of advanced students earned credit for college calculus, biology, or literature. But the picture changes as greater numbers of high school teachers provide college credit for courses taught in high schools, and postsecondary institutions hire adjunct professors to meet the course demands of younger students both on their campuses and in schools. States, schools, and postsecondary institutions are beginning to address this contentious issue. Evidence on both sides of the high school/college divide challenges received wisdom that college standards are necessarily higher and nonremedial college courses more intellectually challenging than high school courses. Beyond knowledge of the statistics on remediation rates of students entering postsecondary institutions, there is little systematic data about the confusing overlap of standards, content, and intellectual demand between the offerings of the final years of high school and the first years of college—especially when considering community colleges and the broad access, four-year sector of postsecondary. Indeed, *Minding the Gap* offers perhaps the first detailed look on a micro level at the attempts of high school and college teachers to collaborate to build sequences of courses in specific institutions, and at small programs as they compare requirements at the high school and postsecondary levels.

While it is seductive to say that all students should graduate from high school ready for work and college, to ensure quality demands entering the black box of the classroom. Both teachers and students must understand what it means to be a successful college student. Policies at the state level yield quality only to the extent that they can promote capacity for secondary/postsecondary collaboration locally. This means a state or higher education system role in supporting, funding, and encouraging professional interaction and professional development across high school and college. It means as well such measures as establishing faculty qualifications and credentials, auditing syllabi, administering standardized assessments instituting end-of-course examinations, and visiting classrooms and reviewing student work.

At this point, it would be irresponsible to generalize about course quality: far too little is known. We do acknowledge, however, that course titles alone are inadequate to gauge the level of rigor a course might attain. The College Board's decision to audit all Advanced Placement courses is a first step toward calibrating course quality against explicit external standards. This may be a harbinger of future efforts to ensure that the content of high school courses is at least consistent with the course title and, in the case of college prep courses, at the level of challenge necessary for the student to succeed in college.[14]

In regard to the quality of integrated programs, early college high schools—the best-developed model—are only now graduating their first classes with substantial college credit. These schools provide adequate academic support and advising, properly sequenced courses, and thorough, engaging instruction, and some appear to be succeeding in building well-aligned postsecondary partnerships. But the numbers are small, and here, too, a vision of good practice exceeds examples on the ground.

Equity

About equity, there is much more to say. *Minding the Gap* begins from the premise that the high school "dropout factories" in our major urban centers are a shame to the nation. They undermine the goals of the long struggle for civil rights that began half a century ago. And every essayist here starts with the underlying assumption that high school graduation and rigorous, relevant curricula are the major immediate barriers that low-income, underrepresented students face in attaining a postsecondary education. Every writer is concerned to make the transition seamless; most sign onto the proposition of providing a semester or more of college-level work in high school free of cost to families. This promise of free college courses signals a public pledge to help young people attain the minimum skills and knowledge they need to enter the workforce, and it acknowledges that high college costs and lack of academic support through the transition are hurdles that must be surmounted.

Consideration of equity inheres as well in state policies that have a goal of ensuring that students graduate from high school "college- and work-ready," whether through a default college preparatory curriculum, incentives for students to enroll in AP classes and take AP exams, dual enrollment, or the early promise of financial aid in return for adequate performance. On the cutting edge are states implementing policies that establish numerical goals, timetables, and public reporting structures for increasing the number and percent of underrepresented students attaining postsecondary credentials, and states drafting and passing legislation to recover students who have dropped out of high school.

It is important to acknowledge that much of this confrontation with the inequities of public schooling are the result of both the adoption of standards-based reform in K–12 and the implementation of No Child Left Behind requirements for the disaggregation of data by population groups within schools. Whatever one's view of NCLB, were there no assessments and no data, much of the country would still be able to deny the inequities in resources and results of public education. In fact, as a number of essayists point out, public data across K–16 will show the continuation of inequities within postsecondary education—a phenomenon that is only now beginning to appear on the public screen as data demonstrate the channeling of low-income students into the least-well-resourced, least-competitive higher education institutions, while the selective public "flagships" and private colleges and universities court students in the upper-income brackets who can pay tuition and are potential contributors to their coffers.[15]

That said, the explicit challenges to the equity agenda and the unintended consequences of moving to a 9–14 system are many. The number of dropouts can increase as high schools raise standards. Marginal students enrolling in college-level courses in high school without adequate support and preparation can reinforce their unfitness for postsecondary education. Larger numbers of students entering and aiming to complete postsecondary education can drain a higher education system with limited resources and capacity, prompting institutions to become more selective rather than more welcoming.

In regard to the challenge posed by young people who disengage from high school, as the authors of one essay argue, state policy and opinion leaders have a critical moment in which to integrate the conversation about dropouts with discussions of a seamless 9–14 education. And as opportunities for college-level work in high school increase, it is incumbent upon high school/college partnerships not to implement "college-level lite." That is, as a transition-to-college strategy, permitting more students to take one randomly selected college-level course is likely to fail. Needed are sequenced pathways to general education and career preparation designed with individual student needs, capacities, and interests at the forefront. While early and middle college high schools are at the radical end of the continuum of integrated 9–14 programs, the emerging data from these schools will soon be able to answer the question: What is the right dosage of college-level work in high school for any single student to ensure the completion of a postsecondary credential?

Finally, an issue that *Minding the Gap* hardly alludes to: the consequences for postsecondary systems if a greater number of and better-prepared students arrive on college campuses. While this would, of course, be good news, higher education has barely begun the conversation about how to help a greater number of students succeed. Without more resources, higher education will have to run more productive and streamlined operations to meet the country's need for a much greater number of credentialed and highly competent young people. The country is just beginning to address the waste of time, talent, and money that comes with the "revolving door" prevalent across so much of postsecondary education.

CONCLUSION

It is fair to say that *Minding the Gap* raises more questions than it answers. Is the nation ready to make a quantum leap to align and better integrate high school and postsecondary education? Will integration increase the number of young people succeeding in postsecondary education? Are *Minding the Gap* authors reading the tea leaves accurately? While there remain many reluctant and resistant players—particularly in the postsecondary sector—and there are gaps in our ability to figure out what an aligned system will look like, *Minding the Gap* points to governors, state education commissioners at the K–12 and postsecondary levels, chancellors of state higher education systems, and state legislators who "get it." The country needs a much better educated workforce and a community of well-informed citizens. And our state leaders understand that their state's well-being depends on an education "fix" to achieve fiscal health for the long term. Especially, for low-income young people, aligning and integrating the systems is a first right step to achieve better results.

PART I

Why Integrate Grades 9 through 14?

The United States is not doing well in educating our low-income young people. With a diminishing middle class, we are increasingly a society divided by years and quality of education. We can do better, but not without a clear understanding of the intersection of education and the global economy, and precision about which young people we are failing, how many, and where they are falling out of the education pipeline.

Economist Anthony Carnevale argues that our education systems are not designed to supply the education that young people need today, particularly at the secondary level. In high school, disparities based on social class begin to magnify into vast differences in future earnings. Rather than continue tracking low-income young people into dead-end jobs, high school should be the place to start these students on paths to careers that require postsecondary education. Although economists disagree about the extent to which the U.S. labor market will expand its need for college-educated workers and how fast, Carnevale argues that if college-level jobs do not come into being, the best investment the country could make is to create them. This is good politics, good for the economy, and critical for the survival and growth of the middle class. He then presents a vision of secondary/postsecondary pathways that blend liberal arts and applied learning in ways that would provide better career preparation than the structures now in place.

Susan Goldberger looks at the high school and postsecondary outcomes for a cohort of American eighth graders in order to target interventions that would "double the number" of low-income students who complete college. Her analysis identifies four transition points at which the education system loses substantial numbers of low-income students. While the findings confirm those of others—improving attainment requires better academic preparation and alignment between high school and college standards, along with improved second-chance pathways—her thought experiment puts real numbers in place. Goldberger takes as a target moving from the approximately 90,000 low-income young people earning an associate's or bachelor's degree per year to 180,000 within the next ten years. For example, she argues that "if the approximately 1,500 small schools . . . in underperforming urban districts . . . were able to achieve 90 percent graduation rates and 80 percent college-readiness rates among their 67,500 graduates each year, this . . . would add over 17,000 new low-income degree earners."

1

Confessions of an Education Fundamentalist

Why Grade 12 Is Not the Right End Point for Anyone

Anthony P. Carnevale

For most of the twentieth century, high school was enough for a shot at middle-class status and wages. Nowadays, no one goes anywhere in the American job market unless they go to college first. The notion of "college for all" is a controversial idea among elites but not among American families. Nowadays, more than two-thirds of us go on to postsecondary education or training after high school. Consequently, access to college has become the essential goal for K–12 education. And middle-class employability is now the penultimate standard for K–16 educational adequacy.

The increasing importance of education beyond high school in allocating economic opportunity results from the following factors: the rise of the global knowledge economy; the slow and painful death of the American blue-collar economy, in which workers, mostly white males, earned good wages with a high school education or less; the weakening of the social safety net; and the emergence of a society where men, women, and youth are fully mobilized at work.

College has become the tipping point that determines persistence in the middle class and the gateway to the upper three income deciles.

Data from the Current Population Survey show that since 1967, families headed by workers with bachelor's degrees or better are either staying in the middle class ($28,000 to $81,000 per annum) or moving beyond the $81,000 threshold into the top 30 percent of family incomes, increasing their share in the top category from 32 percent to 56 percent over the period.

The share of middle-class families headed by workers with some college but no bachelor's degree has fallen from 68 percent to 55 percent since 1967. The decline in middle-class membership among these families is equally divided between those who have risen above the $81,000, upper-income threshold and those who have fallen below the $28,000, low-income threshold.

The middle-class cohort among those with high school or less is steadily melting into the bottom 20 percent of family incomes, below $28,000 per annum. In 1967, almost half of families headed by high school dropouts, and 70 percent headed by high school graduates, were in the middle class, with earnings between $28,000 and $81,000 in current dollars. By 2004, only a third of dropouts and half of high school graduates were still in the middle class, and virtually all of those who left had fallen below the $28,000 family income threshold, into the bottom 20 percent of family incomes.

Since the 1970s, the wage advantage of a college degree over a high school diploma has increased from 36 percent to 76 percent, a cool million dollars over a working life. And the wage gap between high school and college-educated workers has grown even as the supply of college-educated workers has increased dramatically. Since 1979, college wages have risen, even though there has been an increase of about 117 percent—about 33 million people—in the supply of new job seekers with at least some college.

A college education has become a prerequisite for access to jobs with employer-provided benefits. According to data from the Current Population Survey, almost 95 percent of employees with a college degree have employer-provided health care coverage, compared with 77 percent of employees who are high school graduates and 67 percent who are high school dropouts. Almost 90 percent of employees with a college degree have access to employer-provided pension plans, compared with 81 percent of high school graduates and 53 percent of dropouts.

If the past is any guide, the future promises more of the same. Projections that my colleague Jeff Strohl and I prepared for the U.S. Senate Committee on Health, Education, Labor and Pensions, using both U.S. Census and Bureau of Labor Statistics data, show that, altogether between 2002 and 2012, there will be 24 million brand-new jobs for workers with associate's, bachelor's, and graduate degrees, a 30 percent increase—almost 10 million new jobs for bachelor's-degree holders alone, a 37 percent increase.

Will we be able to meet the future demand for college workers if we rely on America's own college workforce? Not easily. Baby-boom retirements should create a steady stream of replacement openings for college-educated workers. By 2020, for example, there will be 40 million college-educated baby boomers between the ages of 55 and 75. Census data show that, at current enrollment, persistence, and graduation rates, we aren't producing college-educated workers fast enough to replace retiring baby boomers. Between 1980 and 2000, we increased the share of workers with college by a hefty 20 percent. At current rates of college-going, the share of workers with at least some college will only increase by 3 percent between 2000 and 2020.

That's a big part of the reason why our projections show that as early as 2012 there will be a surplus of more than three million workers with high school or less and a shortage of about seven million workers with at least some college.

Will shortages of college workers actually occur? It all depends. Competition for college workers could increase wages and encourage college-going and graduation. But rising college wages over the past 30 years have not resulted in supply catching up with demand. And in the future, the increasing size of the global college workforce could hold college wages down in the United States, blunting incentive effects, as it already has in engineering and information technology. We could move toward a skill-based immigration strategy to import more college workers, especially from Eastern Europe, Russia, China, India, and Brazil. But that would mobilize significant opposition among those with international family ties, especially among Hispanics. We could delay retirement for baby boomers. But political opposition would be significant. Besides, delaying retirements will mostly affect noncollege workers, who are dependent on government retirement benefits. Aggressive offshoring of existing college jobs is another strategy that carries negative political risks.

The wild card in the future role of college education as the arbiter of economic opportunity is the global economy.

With the addition of Brazil, Russia, India, and China, the size of the earth's capitalist workforce doubles, reducing our share of the world's college-level workers from about 30 percent to 15 percent. And foreign college workers will be a lot cheaper than American workers for decades to come.

So far, offshoring has been a trickle—a few hundred thousand jobs a year, at most. That's relatively small in an economy that includes almost 150 million jobs and creates and destroys millions of jobs every month. But more than 70 percent of offshored jobs have required at least some college. And as many as 40 million American jobs are theoretically vulnerable to offshoring.

We also need to keep our eye on the invisible offshoring of college jobs that follows along behind the global flows in financial capital. Our ability to attract and retain financial capital and focus investments on new college jobs is just as important as keeping the college jobs we already have. Financial capital tends to follow the path of least resistance, merging downhill toward the lowest cost. No one will miss the college jobs we never had and the raises we never got.

A loss of college jobs and a decline in wages are critical because they threaten the survival and growth of the American middle class. Ultimately, we need enough college jobs to maintain and expand access to the middle class, while allowing employers to compete freely in the growing, global talent pool of college-educated workers.

The real American future for college jobs likely lies somewhere between the sunny shortage narrative and the dark side of globalization and offshoring. The nation will most likely be a crazy quilt of local labor markets, some with shortages and some with surpluses of college-educated labor. Wage growth among those with postsecondary education may slow or even decline in some cases, although the relative wage advantages of college over high school will remain high and probably grow.

But it is important to understand that there is a way to reconcile the sunny shortage vision and the darker view of the runaway train of college-wage and job decline associated with globalization. The keystone for connecting these alternative narratives is the addition of growth strategies targeted on the creation of good jobs that require postsecondary education and training.

A proactive economic strategy targeted on creating college jobs trumps the dark view of globalization.

In the ideal case, effective, college-led growth strategies maintain strong and growing demand for postsecondary skill at home and allow American employers to compete for postsecondary talent through immigration and offshoring. In addition, growth in labor demand, especially in demand for skilled labor, reduces the negative pressure on immigration, in general, and on skill-based immigration, in particular. With strong demand for skilled workers, policies that emphasize inclusion also become viable, as do family services like child care, because they encourage female labor force participation.

We know we need targeted strategies because the last two recessions ended with "jobless recoveries" that brought disappointing job growth and even more disappointing growth in college jobs. There were two reasons that the old-time religion of tax cuts and printing money does not create more college jobs: A lot of the new spending leaks overseas, and, even if the demand is there, from an employer's point of view, creating new college jobs is a lot more expensive and risky than creating low-wage service jobs. By adding targeted strategies that promise to create good jobs, the college-worker-shortage narrative becomes less naive and the globalization narrative becomes more positive.

If protecting and growing the American middle class is our goal, then college-level job creation becomes the proper measure of success in judging our economic strategies, and employability in middle-class jobs becomes the accountability standard for measuring educational adequacy.

Economics aside, there are cultural and political reasons to stick with a "college for all" strategy.

There's more than money involved in the American love affair with college. "College for all" is good politics, in part because all the alternatives are widely regarded as second best, at least through high school. Polls show that people want their own kids to go to college, although they will support alternative vocational tracks in high school for other people's children. But the notion of a high school vocational track as an alternative to college is the policy wonks' version of fool's gold. Ultimately, there are no "other people's children." All children have parents, and all parents want their kids to go to college.

The economic and political path of least resistance is more college jobs, not the development of an alternative vocational track in high school. Vocationalism is fine as long as it happens in "college." Right now, we have only one education track that works—the college track. The last thing we need in the interest of economic and racial justice is two education tracks that actually work—college education for our own kids and high school vocational training for other people's children.

The combination of college-for-all and college-led-growth strategies as the predicate for economic success and growth and inclusion is not just good economics; it's good politics. Our growing reliance on access to college education as the arbiter of individual opportunity results from mutually reinforcing economic trends and cultural biases.

The American public regards the beneficence of education as gospel. As Norton Grubb and Marvin Lazerson (2004) point out in *The Education Gospel*, education has long since become the basic American text for reconciling democratic equality, in principle, with the inevitable differences that arise in individual talent, striving, and economic outcomes.

In the American case, the taproot to the growing college consensus reaches deep into the electorate's individualistic cultural biases. We Americans welcome our increasing reliance on education through the college years as the arbiter of economic opportunity because, in theory, education allows us to expand merit-based opportunity without surrendering individual responsibility. After all, we each have to do our own homework to make the grades and ace the tests that get us into selective colleges and in line for the good jobs.

The education consensus complements our other key preferences for an open economy and a limited government. It has become the nation's preferred "third way," between the economic instability that comes with runaway world markets and the individual dependency that Americans associate with big government and the welfare state. For Americans, the economic power of education has become both an economic and a political miracle. It allows us to anchor economic opportunity in a merit-based system driven by individual responsibility, without actually laying our hands on the economy or the labor market.

We have flirted with an alternative "second chance" education and training system dedicated to workforce development and retraining for economic adjustment. But all we learned from the second-chance system is that it's the first chance at K–16 education that counts. For now, the second-chance system has been all but abandoned. Federal funding in real 2003 dollars has declined from $27 billion in the last Carter budget to about $3 billion in the 2007 Bush budget. In the meantime, postsecondary education, especially community college, has become the nation's real workforce development system, both by design and by default.

Those of us who support an education-led economic and social policy need to avoid the temptations of education fundamentalism.

It's not hard to deconstruct the American education gospel. Treating education as a panacea can make too much of a good thing. Our increasing reliance on education sometimes borders on educational fundamentalism—the tiresome notion that the remedy for every economic and social problem is the mantra: education, education, education!

When support for education solutions overreach, it allows the nation's elites to offer education bromides instead of remedies on hard issues like trade, unemployment, immigration, race, income dispersion, and access to pensions and health care. Clearly, there is a vacuum in the nation's economic and social policy that education alone cannot fill.

Education seems fair in a society that prefers to reward individual merit and character. But in a society where people start out unequal, educational success measured by test scores and grades can become a dodge—a way of laundering the found money that comes with being born into the right bank account or the right race.

There are lots of ways to start out unequal. Gender is one of them. Because our labor markets are segregated by gender, women have to get at least one more degree than a man to earn as much. That's one reason why young women go to college more and stay longer than young men do.

Among all the ways to start out unequal, race is still the worst. American racism persists even without racists. The lingering effects of Jim Crow still haunt our institutions, isolating minorities in ghetto neighborhoods and in decrepit schools that don't send kids to college.

Race, gender, and economic class often go together, but class is the common coin of the realm when it comes to limiting college opportunity. The extraordinary work of Eric Turkheimer at the University of Virginia shows that the majority of talented, lower-income youth don't develop their innate abilities by the time they are ready for college. They don't get the chance to be all they can be. By way of contrast, Turkheimer finds that the best predictor of the developed abilities of the children of middle class and affluent families at college age is their innate abilities measured when they were children.[1]

Many look at findings like Turkheimer's and conclude that the real problem lies in childhood and K–12 education, well beyond the reach of postsecondary education. But that's another dodge. While the odds are stacked against low-income and minority students, many beat the odds only to be turned away at the college door. Data from the National Education Longitudinal Survey (NELS) show that among equally qualified high school students, youth from low-income families go to four-year colleges at half the rate of their academic peers from middle- and upper-income families. And youth from low-income families in the top quartile of high school test scores go to college less frequently than affluent youth in the lowest high school test quartile.

In addition, there are basic inefficiencies in American education in that most youth who beat the odds against becoming college-qualified get ignored. These students are the low-hanging-fruit for increasing access, persistence, and diversity in postsecondary education. They can be found in large numbers in the upper half of the test-score distribution from working-class families and low-income families that make less than $83,000 per year, with a median income of about $40,000. Affluent students get the college support they need from their advantaged families, schools, and peers. But lots of working-class and low-income students who are college-qualified fall between the cracks. They aren't rich enough to get the support that comes with being born into the right bank account, and, because they are so successful, programs like NCLB ignore them. More than a million of these college-qualified students get lost along the way to their high school senior year.

Our analysis of NELS data shows comparable failures of persistence among high-performing high school students eight years after high school graduation. Among U.S. students in the top half of the test-score distribution in the nation's high school graduating class, 17 percent (559,000) either do not go to a two- or four-year college (94,000), or go but will not graduate within eight years (465,000).

Of these 559,000 top students who do not make it:

- 23 percent (129,000) come from families in the top income quartile (earning $83,001 and above in 2005, with a median income of $145,000);

- 33 percent (85,000) come from families in the second-highest income quartile (earning $50,280 to $83,000 in 2005, with a median of $65,512);
- 25 percent (140,000) come from families in the third-highest income quartile (earning $26,730 to $50,279 in 2005, with a median of $38,306); and
- 19 percent (106,000) come from families in the bottom income quartile ($26,729 or less in 2005, with a median of $15,000).

Our leaky education pipeline is unlikely to get fixed anytime soon. Most states and schools do not even have student record systems that would allow them to track individual student performance effectively between grade school and college, let alone intervene to help students who get lost or lose their traction along the way.

The K–16 education pipeline is "all one system" only in concept. We are a long way from operational transparency and alignment in K–16 education. And the great divide between the K–16 system and the competencies required for twenty-first-century labor markets and democratic citizenship in our runaway world is profound.

The disconnect between the culture of higher education and the culture of K–12 education becomes more obvious all the time. The K–12 system mandates universal access and strives toward a universal adequacy in the opportunity to learn. Unlike the K–12 system, college access is selective, and resources tend to flow toward the most successful students. Like reserving beds in the best hospitals for the healthiest people, we reserve seats in the best colleges for the best students. As a newly arrived mass democratic institution, postsecondary education will ultimately have to meet mass democratic standards of accountability.

American education is front-loaded in the individual life cycle. It works best for mobile youth with long-term career horizons, but less well for relatively immobile adults who have accumulated lots of human capital in particular careers. Besides, while lifelong learning is a line in everybody's speech, it never gets a line in anybody's budget.

And, of course, education cannot solve a jobs problem all by itself. In the short term, education does not create jobs, except for educators. In the short term, jobs create demand for education. When college jobs are not there, or when they disappear, growth strategies are required to complement the supply of educated workers.

There used to be at least three roads to college; now they are converging into one.

Parental education and income are strong threads in the complex weave of social and economic forces that influence academic readiness for college, as well as the choices academically qualified students make among the more- and less-selective colleges.

In the early post–World War II era, there were three kinds of parents whose kids went to college: parents with high school or less who had good jobs that brought high incomes; parents with postsecondary education; and parents with both good jobs and high education levels. High school–educated men with blue-collar jobs, often in unions, earned enough to live in neighborhoods with good schools and other forms of supportive social capital, such as libraries, public safety, and peer support among similar students from upwardly mobile families. Many of the children in these families went to college, even though their parents had a high school education or less.

At the same time, there were families with relatively high levels of parental education but less income. The children of schoolteachers, for instance, went to college more because of high parental education and expectations than because of their family income. And the children of parents with both high education levels and high income—the children of doctors and lawyers, for instance—almost always went to college.

Youth in higher-income families with college-educated parents are doubly advantaged. They find college, especially the more expensive, highly selective colleges, more affordable. More importantly, their childhood and adolescent development are nested in neighborhoods, high-quality schools, and home environments that provide the necessary social support, information, and encouragement for academic readiness for college. Many low-income and minority students are not afforded an equal opportunity to learn, and many who are qualified for four-year colleges do not attend for want of information, support, and money.

As the strength of the relationship between education and income grows, families with the highest incomes are increasingly likely to be parents with the highest level of educational attainment. Conversely, low-income families increasingly have parents with low education levels. We are increasingly clustered into families with both high parental education and income and families with neither. As a result, two roads to college are converging into a single, narrower pathway.

High schools are the right place to start aligning education and careers.

High schools are the mediating institution among education, college, and careers. At this juncture, education supply and economic demand begin to interact in complex ways. Individual education and career expectations begin to motivate behavior. Universal standards give way to multiple pathways to college, job training, and careers. Differences in educational opportunity that are only implicit in K–8 education become explicit, tracking students into college and career trajectories that will ultimately determine lifetime opportunity. Marginal differences in the opportunity to learn in high school magnify over a working life into vast differences in lifetime earnings and wealth.

When viewed through the prism of workforce development, it is difficult to disentangle high school and postsecondary learning except as three roughly distinctive education and career tracks that have emerged in high school in the midst of standards-based reforms:

- Roughly a third of high school students take the high road to college and are poised for attaining bachelor's or graduate degrees. These students, primarily from upper-middle-class homes, follow the "early college" pathway, enrolling in college-credit curricula leading to admissions into selective four-year colleges and ultimately into managerial and professional careers in the private sector. Almost three-quarters of the nation's high schools now have various versions of these "early college" programs, including AP, International Baccalaureate, and dual enrollment, and most require minimum grade points or test scores for entry. These students are driven by the admissions requirements of selective colleges, rather than by public K–12 standards.

- Students from "working families" follow the muddy middle path guided by standards-based high school curricula and go on to the less-selective, public, two-year and four-year colleges that provide pathways to careers as technicians, as rank-and-file professionals (e.g., K–12 teachers, nurses, public administrators), and in the uniformed services. As the competition for seats at college increases and prices rise, these students, the nation's public workforce, are continually bumped down the hierarchy of selectivity and completion rates.
- Students in the bottom tier of the middle school and high school continuum follow the low road through middle school and often drop out of high school. Dropout and push-out rates climb to almost half of African American and Hispanic students. Many eventually complete or get GEDs but are ultimately consigned to the low-wage, low-skilled workforce. Their earnings losses begin in high school and accumulate as a result of their limited access to learning and empowering technology on the job.

Within high schools and postsecondary institutions, the connection between education and work is implicit but not explicit in accountability regimes. Academic curriculum content and assessments are increasingly aligned in high schools, but they still do not align more broadly with college and career requirements. As a result, the current standards and the assessments that accompany them beg the question: "Standards for what?" Among policymakers, parents, students, and employers, the most common answer is: "Standards to assure access to postsecondary education, training, and viable careers."

The path of least resistance for reform is the current trajectory from high schools up the education pipeline toward postsecondary institutions. Postsecondary reforms are most likely to be achieved by melding high schools and postsecondary institutions using the concept of education and career pathways that mixes academic and applied learning. The widely supported notion of expanding "early college" programs beyond elite students would be a good place to start. High schools are the best platform for postsecondary reform because they are more cohesively governed, and they are already committed to democratic standards of accountability characteristic of mass education. Postsecondary institutions are highly fragmented and, compared to high schools, governed by a more elitist competition for prestige and a more aggressive sorting by income class and race. If mass democratic standards are to include going to college, those standards will have to come from the high schools.

We need to be careful that the increasing economic value of education does not turn education into job training.

As access to postsecondary education increasingly becomes the arbiter of middle-class status and earnings, we need to be careful that the increasing economic value of education doesn't turn education into job training. The temptation to provide narrow vocational training rather than more general learning is strong in a market economy, especially in our current resource-poor environment.

Turning robust education into narrow training is not only bad education—it's also bad economics. Resorting to a narrow vocationalism will result in an underinvestment in the economic value of postsecondary education. The economic value of general competencies exceeds, and is growing faster than, the value of job-specific competencies. While specific occupational skills have greater short-term economic value, skills that are more general, have long-term, latent value. General competency leavens all subsequent learning and practical experience. It is the educator's version of what financiers call "patient capital" or long-term investment. The longer-term latent value of general skills learned in college is one reason why engineers start out way ahead but fall behind managerial generalists in middle age.

Most jobs now require preparation that sounds a lot more like liberal education and professional education than narrow job training. For example, occupational data from the U.S. Department of Labor shows that the differences in earnings between people who perform in the bottom and top quintile of problem-solving and critical-thinking skills is almost $50,000 per annum. And general competencies increasingly drive earnings differences among people with the same education levels. Among those in occupations that require some college but no bachelor's degree, for example, those in the bottom quintile of problem-solving skills earn $22,000 per annum and those in the top quintile earn $48,000. Differences between the bottom and top quintile in problem-solving skill at the bachelor's level are $26,000 and $67,000. At the graduate level, the parallel differences balloon to $35,000 and $90,000.

We also need to aspire to a pragmatic balance between education's growing economic role and its cultural and political roles. As the economic value of education increases, we will need to remember that education, especially higher education, is about more than dollars and cents. It should do more than provide foot soldiers for the American economy. Education has intrinsic as well as extrinsic value. Higher education, for instance, is a crucial anchor for the professions in their struggle to maintain their values and standards in a world increasingly driven by the narrow valuation of cost efficiency and direct earnings returns; the medical professionals are the most obvious case in point.

Moreover, educators have cultural and political missions to ensure that there is an educated citizenry that can continue to defend and promote our democratic ideals—at home and abroad. Streams of inquiry that trace back to various sources from Theodor Adorno to Seymour Martin Lipset demonstrate convincingly that once nations achieve a basic level of wealth, tolerant political attitudes and political participation depend more on education than on economic class. Moreover, the same streams of research suggest that more general forms of education, as opposed to narrow vocationalism, tend to promote tolerance and undermine the development of authoritarian personalities.

But the educators' economic role has become pivotal. If educators cannot fulfill their economic mission to help youth and adults become successful workers, they also will fail in their cultural and political missions to create good neighbors and good citizens. The inescapable reality is that ours is a society based on work.

Education that leads to good jobs empowers Americans to do work on the world, rather than retreat from it.

A decent job is the price of admission to America's middle-class culture and polity. Those who are not equipped with the knowledge and skills necessary to get, and to keep, good jobs are denied full social inclusion and tend to drop out of the mainstream culture, polity, and economy. In the worst cases, they are drawn into alternative cultures, political movements, and economic activities that are a threat to mainstream American life.

There's no doubt that a lot needs fixing if education is to continue in its increasingly powerful role as the principal arbiter of opportunity in America.

The risk and the effort are both worthwhile. The education consensus represents most of the common ground that remains in the American political dialogue—and the only polite conversation that remains between red and blue America. The interface between education and economic opportunity has become the maximum point of consensus and political leverage in the American public dialogue. The strengthening of the relationship between education and economic opportunity does not ensure equal opportunity, but it does provide new possibilities for economic and social progress.

Because of its broad acceptance, the education consensus provides the most legitimate and compelling context for promoting racial and economic justice. Educational opportunity carries unique face validity as the authentic indicator of fairness among American institutions.

The widely shared collective interest in access to education—ultimately, access to postsecondary education and training—encourages political solidarity across the broad spectrum of working-poor, working-class, and middle-income families.

The globalization of college labor markets is likely to broaden the current education consensus. The diffusion of risk and downward wage pressures across the full spectrum of educational attainment will foster growing support for education and adult retraining among the full spectrum of working families and political leadership.

Moreover, support for education as the cornerstone for domestic policy will continue to be reinforced by the business community and financial interests, which are universally vocal in their view of education as a key economic asset for ensuring the nation's global competitiveness. The business and financial community prefers support for education to an expanded welfare state and limitations on trade and capital flows that will arise as globalization increasingly threatens American jobs. If there is to be a grand bargain on trade between American business and American workers, greater access to postsecondary education and retraining is bound to be part of the deal.

"College for all" became an inevitable populist cause when the high school–educated, blue-collar economy began closing down for white men. Now the sons of blue-collar men are crowding the college gates alongside women and minorities who had already asserted their rightful claim on the American promise of upward mobility. Ironically, when access to college became the primary arbiter of opportunity and the primary pathway to the American dream, we got a step closer to the merit-based society we have always wished for. Now we have to figure out how to make it work for a lot more of us. It's not working yet. PreK–16 education is still a very leaky pipeline to the American middle class, especially for racial minorities and working-class and lower-income youth. And college selectivity looks like a fig leaf for race- and class-sorting in a system where only 3 percent of the students in the top 16 colleges come from the bottom income quartile.

Of course, there has always been a gap between the reality of life in America and this meritocratic ideal at the heart of the American dream. But it is an article of faith in our culture that the gap between merit and opportunity closes inexorably. Putting meat on the bones of the populist notion of "college for all" is the new frontier in meeting the equally cherished goals of merit and opportunity. If we can't operationalize the notion of "college for all" in a way that balances our commitment to merit and opportunity, education risks becoming a passive participant in a system that fosters the intergenerational reproduction of economic and cultural elites. And the intergenerational reproduction of elites offends our democratic ethos, denies our claim to exceptionalism in the history of nations, and weakens our legitimacy in the global contest of cultures.

2

Doing the Math

What It Means to Double the Number of Low-Income College Graduates

Susan Goldberger

In October 2003, Jobs for the Future convened practitioners and policymakers from across the K–12 and higher education divide to address the need to improve college-going and college completion in the United States, particularly for lower-income individuals. Titled *Double the Numbers*, the conference rallied participants to take on the goal of doubling the number of low-income individuals who earn college credentials.

Since that gathering, the idea of "doubling the number" of college graduates has bubbled up in a surprising number of places. Single institutions have embraced the concept, as have state college systems. Charles Bantz, chancellor of Indiana University–Purdue University Indianapolis, told his institutional leadership and its supporters, "We must invoke the power of two and double the number of bachelor's degrees completed at IUPUI so that we will graduate 5,000 undergraduates by 2010. This is an audacious goal, but one worthy of the IUPUI family." Northern Virginia Community College's ten-year strategic plan includes the goal of doubling the college-going rate of historically underrepresented populations.

States have also taken up the call. In 2004, Michigan governor Jennifer Granholm announced the formation of a blue-ribbon Commission on Higher Education and Economic Growth, chaired by the lieutenant governor, to identify strategies for the state to double the number of college graduates and ensure they have the skills needed to succeed in the modern workplace. That same year, Florida's university presidents announced a plan to more than double the number of BA degrees granted, from 40,000 to 86,000 a year, so that the state would move up to the national average of 1,375 degrees per 10,000 residents, ages 18 to 44. Most recently, District of Columbia school and municipal leaders commissioned a report prepared by the Bridgespan Group entitled *Double the Numbers for College Success: A Call to Action for the District of Columbia.*

Doubling the current production of college completers has obvious appeal, especially in the context of educational equity. Based on recent data, 1 out of 2 students from middle- and upper-class families can be expected to earn a college degree, compared with only 1 in 10 students from the lowest socioeconomic quintile.[1] Closing the gap in college attainment rates is nothing short of a moral imperative for a society committed to equal opportunity for all. But practically speaking, improving the academic success rates of low-income youth at critical junctures of the education pipeline will also yield the greatest increase in the number of degree earners.

The goal of this chapter is to estimate what it will take to double the number of low-income young people earning an associate's or bachelor's degree within the next ten years, from approximately 90,000 to 180,000 a year. Specifically what numeric improvement targets must we set along each stage of the education pipeline (e.g., increase in high school graduation rates, increase in college readiness levels of these graduates) to achieve that goal?

To answer this question, we use an existing database—the National Education Longitudinal Survey (NELS), a survey of approximately 25,000 students who started eighth grade in 1988 that has been used by many researchers to understand patterns of progress to and through high school and college—to identify the order of magnitude of improvement in low-income students' attainment of particular educational milestones that will be needed to double the numbers.

We begin with some questions that others have explored using this data set: At what points along the educational pipeline are low-income students particularly prone to falling out and failing to persist? How does this compare with the progress of their more-affluent peers?

Where our analysis differs is in the effort to specify the magnitude of improvement needed at key points along the way if the goal of doubling the number of low-income students who earn AA or BA degrees is to be met—reduction of dropping out and recapture of dropouts into programs that prepare them for college; increased levels of college readiness among high school graduates; improvement in college completion rates among college-ready low-income high school graduates; and effective support for inadequately prepared students who enroll in college.

While our focus is on improving college completion rates for the most vulnerable students, the actions outlined here will benefit all students, particularly moderate-income youth, who share many academic and personal challenges with low-income youth. Targeting the most critical transitions, the chapter points the way for practitioners and policymakers alike who are trying to reduce pipeline leakages and improve the efficiency and equity of our educational institutions.

BARRIERS TO SUCCESS: IDENTIFYING LEAKS IN THE EDUCATION PIPELINE

Despite the national push to raise the academic achievement of high school students and increase the flow of students going to college, the percentage of young people earning a college degree remains disappointingly low. Since the standards-based movement began its transformation of K–12 education in the early 1990s, the percentage of 18- and 19-year-olds enrolling in college has only increased about 4 percent, and degree completion rates have remained flat. The bachelor's degree completion rates of 25- to 29-year-olds grew less than 1 percent, from

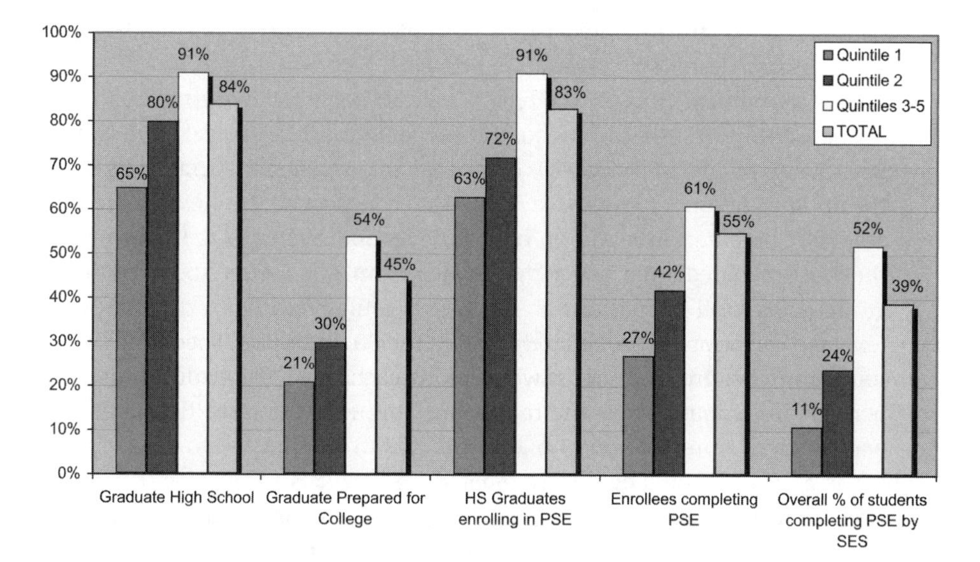

Figure 1. Percentage of Eighth Graders by SES Status Who Attain Different Levels of Education. The college completion gap between low-SES and high-SES students is the cumulative result of gaps in achievement along every step of the education pipeline.

27.8 percent to 28.6 percent, between 1997 and 2005, the most recent year for which data are available.[2]

As with many other education issues, the inability to increase postsecondary degree attainment significantly is inextricably bound up with the deeper failure of our society to bridge the academic divide between the haves and the have-nots. Our analysis of data from the National Education Longitudinal Study pinpoints the problem: Students from the middle and upper end of the socioeconomic spectrum (i.e., quintiles 3–5) are almost five times more likely to earn a college degree than their least-advantaged classmates.[3] While 52 percent of students from the middle and upper levels of the socioeconomic ladder complete college and earn a postsecondary degree, only 11 percent of students from the lowest group attain a degree. Students from the second-lowest group fare better, with 24 percent earning a college degree, but still significantly worse than their more-affluent peers (see figure 1).

This chasm-like gap in college completion rates between students from low-income families with limited formal education and their peers from upper-income, more-educated families is the cumulative result of significant differences in achievement along every step of the education pipeline. Our analysis has identified differences in four major areas:

- *High school completion:* Only 65 percent of students from the bottom of the socioeconomic ladder earn a high school diploma, compared to 91 percent of students from the middle and upper levels (see figure 1). Another 13 percent of students from the lowest socioeconomic group earn a GED (General Educational Development) certificate, while 7 percent of students from the middle and upper levels earn a GED. (See more on GED holders on page 33.) But a significant achievement gap remains: 78 percent of students from the lowest-income families hold some kind of high school credential (traditional diploma or GED), compared to 98 percent of students from middle- and upper-income families.

- *College preparation:* Only 21 percent of high school graduates from the lowest socioeconomic quintile are adequately prepared for college-level work (somewhat, very, or highly prepared), compared to 54 percent of graduates from the middle and upper levels (see figure 1).[4] As expected, the lack of adequate academic preparation relates to high college failure rates. Just 15 percent of the least-prepared high school graduates from the lowest socioeconomic group who enroll in college earn a degree (see figure 2).
- *College enrollment:* Only 63 percent of high school graduates from the lowest socioeconomic group enroll in a postsecondary institution, compared to 91 percent of graduates from the middle and upper groups (see figure 1). The poor academic preparation of many students from the lowest-income families is a clear factor. The more prepared a student is for college, the more likely that student is to enroll. But even among similarly prepared students, a gap remains: While 83 percent of somewhat-prepared high school graduates from the bottom of the socioeconomic spectrum enroll in college, 96 percent of somewhat-prepared students from the middle and upper groups enroll (see figure 5 on page 35).
- *College persistence:* The gap in college achievement rates cannot be explained fully by the college enrollment gap or the college readiness gap, however. There are significant differences in college completion rates even among similarly prepared college enrollees: Only 40 percent of somewhat-prepared high school graduates from the lowest-income families who enroll in college eventually earn a college degree, compared to 65 percent of somewhat-prepared students

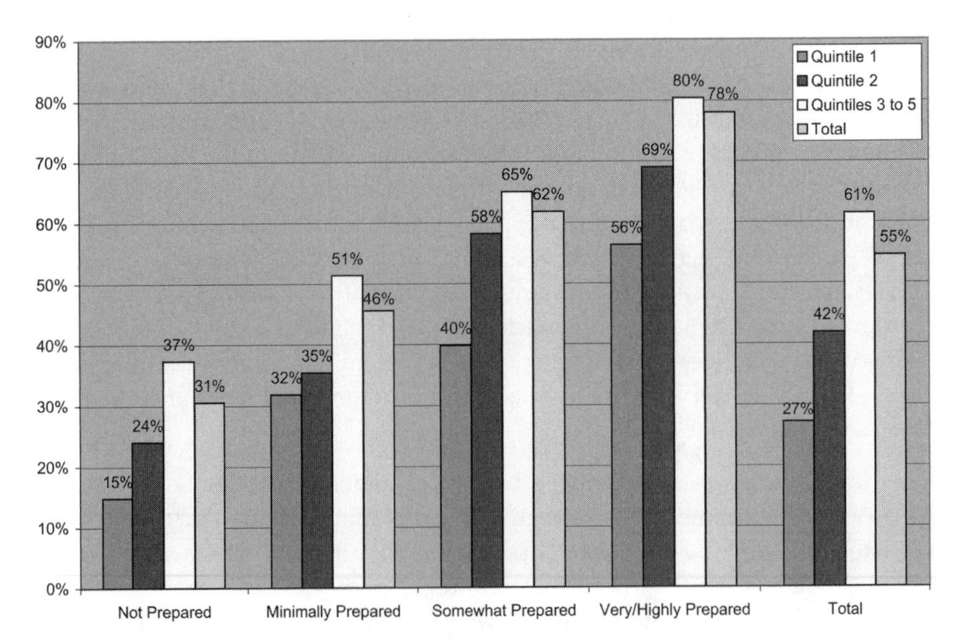

Figure 2. Degree Attainment of High School Graduates Who Attended College, by SES Category and Academic Preparation Level. The gap in college achievement rates by SES is not explained fully by the college enrolllment gap or the college readiness gap.

from the middle- and upper-income groups (see figure 2). The gap is similar among the *best* prepared: Some 56 percent of very- or highly prepared students from the bottom of the socioeconomic ladder earn a college degree, compared to 80 percent of very- or highly prepared from the middle- and upper-income groups.

SIZING THE PROBLEM: ESTIMATING THE CURRENT NUMBER OF LOW-INCOME COLLEGE DEGREE EARNERS

Developing effective strategies for increasing college attainment rates for low-income youth first requires a clear understanding of the size of the problem. However, such figures are not readily available on a national scale. In order to estimate the number of low-income young people currently earning college degrees compared to their more-affluent peers, we applied the results we obtained from the National Education Longitudinal Study to the approximately 4 million students who were eighth graders in the fall of 2001—the high school graduating class of 2006.[5,6] For the purposes of this analysis, we divided the students into five socioeconomic groups of equal size (800,000 each) and compared the expected educational outcomes of the lowest socioeconomic group with the average of the three highest groups, or top 60 percent of students.

Of the estimated 800,000 eighth graders from the lowest socioeconomic level, we can expect that just under 90,000 (11 percent) will earn a college degree by 2014—eight years after their scheduled high school graduation (see figure 3).

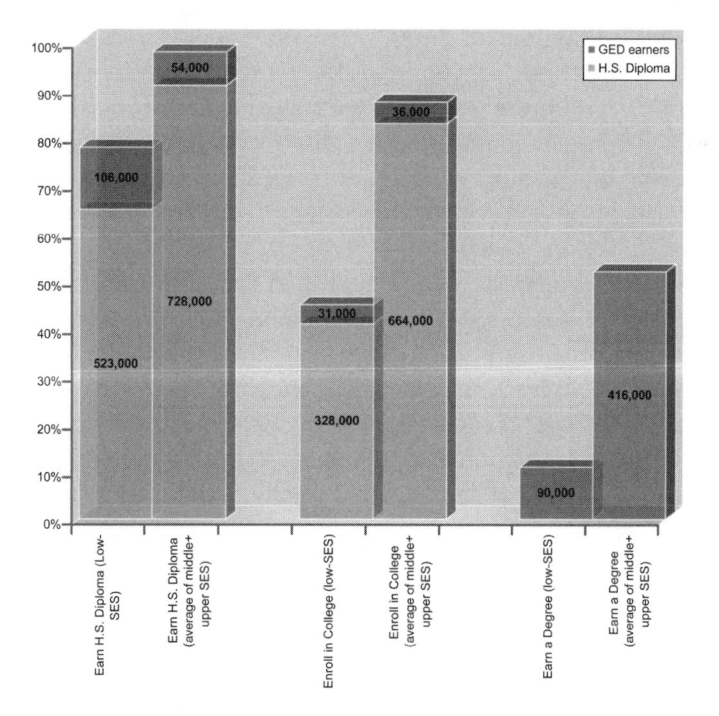

Figure 3. Degree Attainment for Eighth Graders by SES (800,000 Low-SES and 800,000 Mid- and Upper-SES). Of approximately 800,000 eighth graders from the lowest socioeconomic level, about 90,000 are estimated to earn a college degree by 2014. Far more middle- and high-SES students, 416,000 of 800,000, are projected to do so.

As figure 3 illustrates, the problems begin before high school graduation. Only 523,000 students are expected to earn a high school diploma by 2014 (65 percent of the original 800,000 low-income eighth graders). Only 328,000 high school graduates are expected to enroll in college (41 percent of low-income eighth graders). Only 88,900 of these college enrollees are expected to earn an associate's or bachelor's degree by the year 2014 (11 percent of low-income eighth graders).

Another 106,000 students are expected to take the alternative route of earning a GED (13 percent of the original 800,000 low-income eighth graders). But only about 1,500 of them will earn a college degree by 2014 (0.2 percent of low-income eighth graders).

Taking GED holders into account brings the projected total number of postsecondary degree earners from the lowest socioeconomic group to approximately 90,000.[7]

More-affluent students are expected to fare significantly better. Slightly more than half (52 percent) of the students enrolled in eighth grade in 2001 who belong to the middle and upper parts of the socioeconomic spectrum will likely attain a college degree by 2014. If the lowest socioeconomic group performed at the average level of the top three groups, 326,000 more would earn college degrees.

DOUBLING THE NUMBERS: HOW TO MAKE THE BIGGEST IMPACT IN INCREASING THE NUMBER OF LOW-INCOME COLLEGE DEGREE EARNERS

Closing the college attainment gap between young people from the bottom of the socioeconomic spectrum and their middle- and upper-income peers will require targeted action to stem the loss of students all along the education pipeline. In this section, we identify four actions that each would make a significant contribution to doubling the number of disadvantaged students who earn college degrees. We explain the rationale for focusing on each area and estimate the numeric impact of action in each area.

Success with any one of the approaches would significantly increase the number of college graduates from low-income backgrounds, yielding an additional 20,000 to 80,000 low-income degree earners per year. Success with just two or three of the approaches would reach the goal of doubling the number of low-income college graduates, yielding an additional 90,000 each year. Success in all four areas would actually "triple the numbers"—or more—yielding more than 200,000 additional low-income college degree earners each year. The approaches are:

1. Increase high school graduation rates and improve the college preparation of students in GED and alternative diploma programs. (Estimated Annual Yield = 43,300 to 88,000 additional low-income degree earners a year)
2. Increase the number of low-income high school students who graduate prepared for college-level work. (Estimated Annual Yield = 53,700 additional low-income degree earners)
3. Increase the number of college-ready low-income high school graduates who enroll in college and earn a degree. (Estimated Annual Yield = 31,500 additional low-income degree earners)

4. Increase the success rate of low-income high school graduates who enroll in college underprepared. (Estimated Annual Yield = 58,800 additional low-income degree earners)

Lever 1—Increase high school graduation rates and improve the college preparation of students in GED and alternative diploma programs

More than one-third (35 percent) of low-income eighth graders never make it to high school graduation, let alone to college. Of the 800,000 students from the lowest socioeconomic level who started eighth grade in 2001, we estimate that 277,000 will leave high school before graduating—almost as many as the 328,000 low-income high school graduates who will enroll in college. Therefore, any serious effort to double the number of low-income college degree earners must recapture these marginalized youth and put them back on a path to success.

A significant portion of disadvantaged youth who leave high school show remarkable persistence in continuing their education through the alternative route of earning a GED. Nearly 40 percent, or 106,000, of low-income students who leave high school without graduating eventually earn a GED, and almost one-third (29 percent) of those GED earners eventually enroll in college. Unfortunately, only a small fraction (5 percent) of those GED earners who go on to college actually complete a postsecondary degree. Thus, of the 106,000 low-income students who earn a GED, only 1,500, or about 1 percent, complete a college degree (see figure 4).

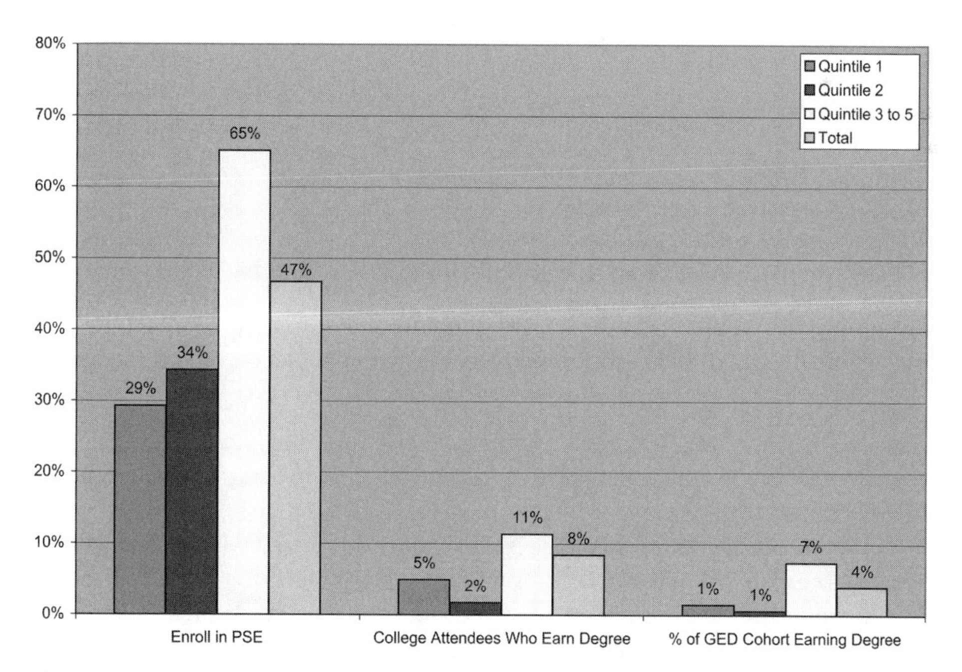

Figure 4. College Enrollment and Success Rates for GED Holders by SES Category. A substantial portion of low-income youth who leave high school earn a GED and enroll in college, but only a small fraction complete a postsecondary degree.

Policies that focus on the two related goals of recapturing dropouts and preparing them for college by the time of their high school graduation—and improving college-preparation and transition supports for GED earners—would result in an estimated increase of up to 88,000 additional low-income degree earners each year. Slightly more than half of these new degree earners would come from the ranks of GED holders, while the rest would be former dropouts who return to high school. This approach would require the following actions:

- Increase college enrollment and completion rates of low-income GED holders to the rates achieved by minimally prepared, low-income high school graduates (74 percent enroll and 32 percent earn a degree). This would result in 23,400 new degree earners each year. Achieving the more-ambitious target of increasing the college enrollment and completion rates of low-income GED holders to the rates achieved by minimally prepared high school graduates from middle- and upper-income backgrounds (91 percent enroll and 51 percent earn a degree) would result in 48,200 new degree earners each year.
- Retain or recover 50 percent of low-income students who now leave high school and help them to graduate at least minimally prepared for college-level work. This would result in 19,900 new college degree earners each year. Achieving the more-ambitious goal of raising the college enrollment and completion rates of these recovered dropouts to the rates achieved by minimally prepared high school graduates from middle- and upper-income backgrounds (91 percent enroll and 51 percent complete a degree) would result in 39,800 new degree earners each year.

Lever 2—Increase the number of low-income high school students who graduate prepared for college-level work

Several recent research studies demonstrate that the level of students' preparation for college-level work is highly correlated with their likelihood of earning a postsecondary degree.[8] Our analysis confirms these findings. We found a large gap in degree completion rates between prepared and unprepared students across all levels of the socioeconomic spectrum (see figure 2 on page 30). Only 15 percent of high school graduates from the bottom of the socioeconomic ladder who enter college academically unprepared eventually earn a degree, compared to 56 percent of their very- or highly prepared peers from the same socioeconomic group. Among more-affluent college students, the difference in completion rates between unprepared and highly prepared students is similar. Only 37 percent of unprepared high school graduates who attend college from the middle and upper socioeconomic levels complete a degree, compared to 80 percent of their very- or highly prepared peers.

Academic preparation for college is also highly correlated with college enrollment. More than 80 percent of high school students from the lowest socioeconomic group who are adequately prepared (somewhat, very, or highly prepared) enroll in college compared to 53 percent of their unprepared peers (see figure 5).

Increasing the number of students who graduate high school at least minimally prepared for college-level work would significantly improve the degree completion rates of students from all economic backgrounds. But it would have

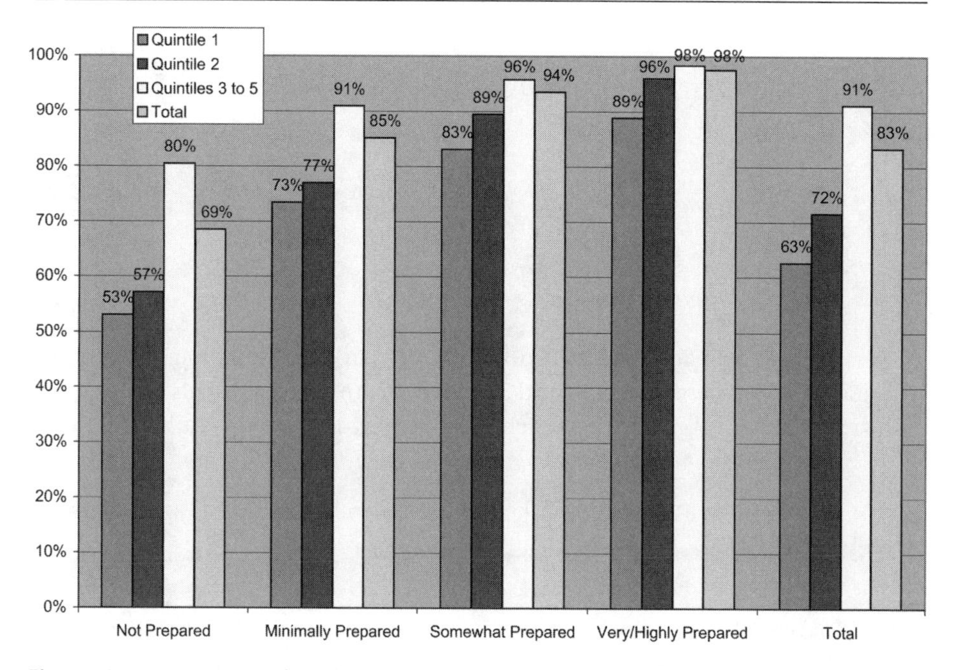

Figure 5. Percentage of High School Graduates Who Enroll in a Postsecondary Institution by Academic Preparation Level. Academic preparation for college is highly correlated with college enrollment.

the greatest impact on low-income students since they comprise a disproportionate percentage of unprepared graduates. Approximately two out of three high school graduates (66 percent) from the bottom of the socioeconomic ladder are unprepared for college work, compared to just one out of three graduates (32 percent) from the middle- and upper-income groups. Only 21 percent of low-income high school graduates are adequately prepared (somewhat, very, or highly prepared) for college work, compared to 54 percent of their peers from the middle- and upper-income groups (see figure 6).

Policies directed at increasing the college readiness of high school students from the lowest socioeconomic group could yield huge increases in the number of degree earners. Producing the following incremental improvements in their level of academic preparation could yield approximately 53,700 new low-income degree earners a year:[9]

- Raise the academic skills of 50 percent of low-income high school students who now graduate unprepared up to the next preparation level of minimally prepared for college work. This would yield approximately 26,850 additional degree earners each year.
- Raise the academic skills of 25 percent of low-income high school students who now graduate unprepared up two levels, to somewhat prepared for college work. This would yield approximately 21,700 additional degree earners each year.
- Raise the academic skills of 75 percent of low-income high school students who now graduate minimally prepared for college work up to the next preparation level of somewhat prepared for college work. This would yield approximately 5,100 additional degree earners each year.

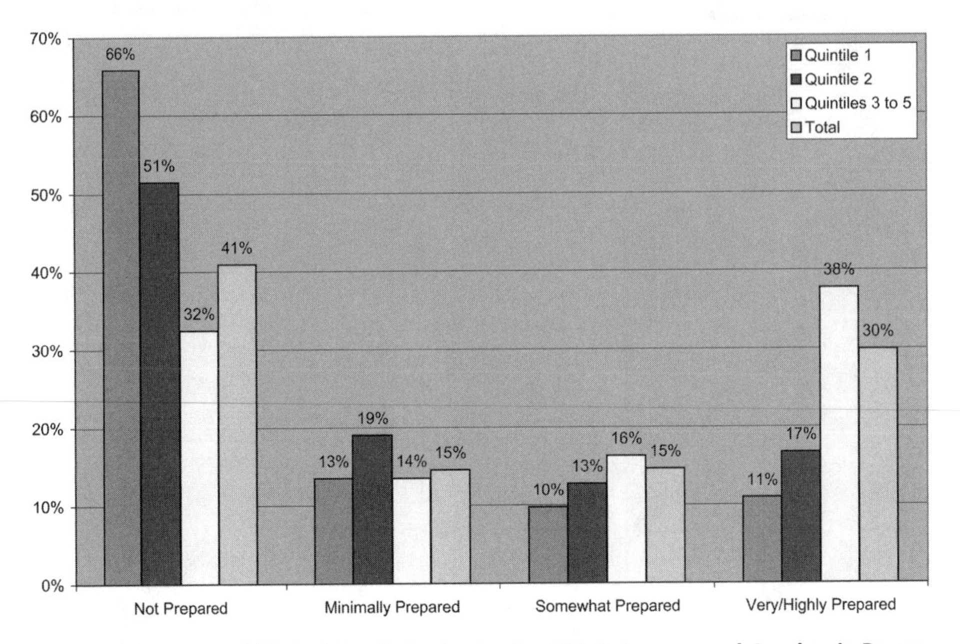

Figure 6. Percent of High School Graduates by SES Category and Academic Preparation Level. Low-income students comprise a disproportionate percentage of unprepared high school graduates.

Lever 3—Increase the number of college-ready low-income high school graduates who enroll in college and earn a degree

While the difference in the academic preparation of low-income students compared to their more-affluent high school classmates accounts for some of the difference in degree achievement rates, it doesn't account for it all. Even academically prepared high school graduates from the lowest socioeconomic group are less likely to enroll in college—and much less likely to earn a degree—than their middle- and upper-income counterparts.

The average college enrollment rate for adequately prepared high school graduates (somewhat, very, or highly prepared) from the middle- and upper-income groups is 97 percent, compared to 86 percent for similarly prepared low-income graduates (see figure 7). The gap in degree completion rates is even larger and more troubling. Only 49 percent of prepared low-income college enrollees eventually complete a degree, compared to 75 percent of similarly prepared middle- and upper-income students.

Adopting policies to close the gap in college enrollment and completion rates of academically prepared low-income high school graduates with those of their middle- and upper-income peers would make a substantial contribution to doubling the number of low-income degree-earners. The following actions would yield an additional 31,500 low-income graduates a year:

- Increase the college enrollment of academically prepared low-income high school graduates to those achieved by their more-affluent peers (from 83 percent to 96 percent for somewhat prepared students, and 89 percent to 98 percent for very/highly prepared students). This would add 11,900 new col-

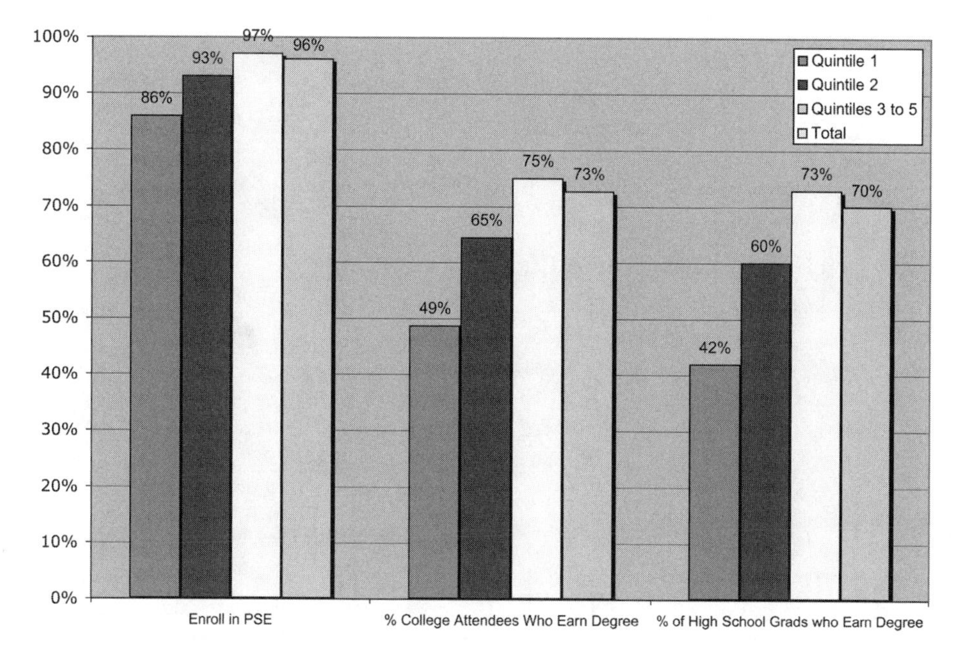

Figure 7. Outcomes of "Somewhat to Highly Prepared" College-Ready High School Graduates by SES. Even academically prepared high school graduates from the lowest SES group are less likely to enroll in college—and much less likely to earn a degree—than their middle- and upper-income counterparts.

lege enrollees to the estimated 93,000 somewhat to highly prepared low-SES high school graduates expected to enroll in college.

- After equalizing college-going rates among low-income prepared students and their more-affluent peers, increase the college completion rate of academically prepared low-income college enrollees to the rates achieved by their more-affluent peers (from 40 percent to 65 percent for somewhat prepared students and 56 percent to 80 percent for very/highly prepared students). This would add 31,500 new degree earners.

Lever 4—Increase the success rate of low-income high school graduates who enroll in college underprepared

Many high school graduates from the bottom of the socioeconomic ladder enroll in college but are not adequately prepared for the academic challenge. Close to three out of four (72 percent) of all low-income high school graduates who go to college—an estimated 227,000 students—are not ready for college-level work (56 percent not prepared and 16 percent minimally prepared; see figure 8). In contrast, only 42 percent of middle- and upper-income high school graduates are unprepared or underprepared (29 percent not prepared and 13 percent minimally prepared).

While inadequately prepared students from all socioeconomic backgrounds are much less likely to earn a degree than their more-prepared peers, low-income students are at particularly high risk of dropping out. Only 15 percent of unprepared

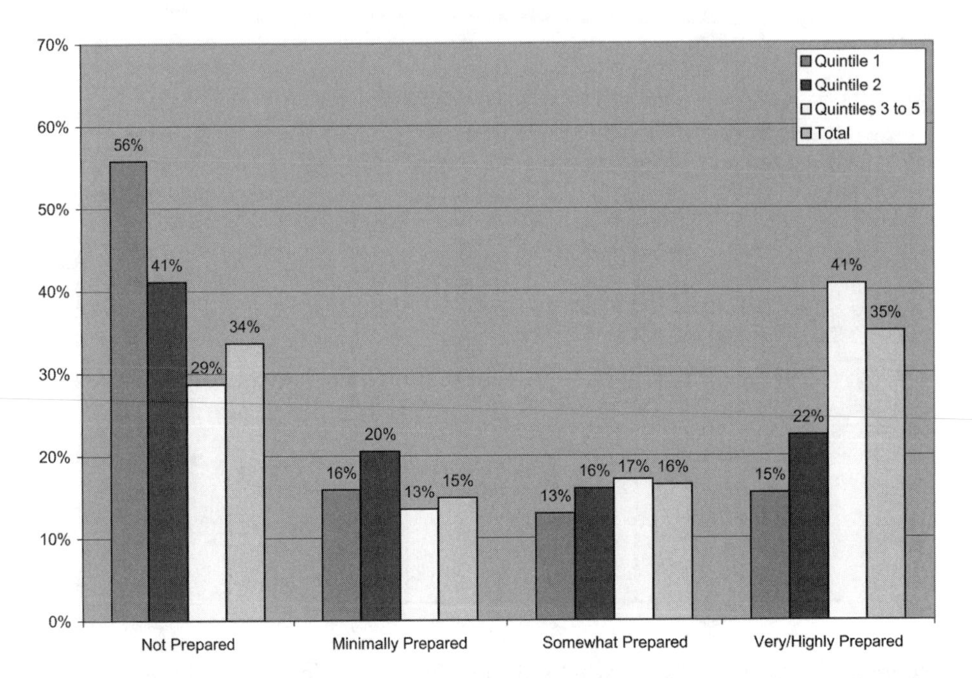

Figure 8. Preparation Levels of High School Graduates Who Enroll in College by SES. Many high school graduates from the bottom of the SES ladder enroll in college but are not adequately prepared for the academic challenge.

and 32 percent of minimally prepared low-income college enrollees eventually earn a degree, compared to 37 percent and 51 percent of unprepared and minimally prepared college students from middle- and upper-income families (see figure 2 on page 30).

While the long-term goal of education policymakers is for all students to be college-ready by the time they leave high school, improving schools enough so that all low-income students receive a high-quality secondary education will take many years to accomplish. In the meantime, most low-income high school graduates who aspire to a postsecondary degree will continue to enter college without adequate preparation. Finding more effective ways to support the academic, financial, and social needs of these college students is critical to achieving the goal of doubling the number of annual low-income college graduates.

The goal of improving the academic skills of unprepared and minimally prepared college freshmen up to grade-level standards within their first few semesters is ambitious, but appears within reach, based on research in Florida. A study of the Florida community college system, one of the country's higher-performing systems, found developmental education programs to be effective in moving many underprepared first-time college students up to college-level standards. Approximately 45 percent of the students who had failed the reading or writing portion of the college entrance exam and were placed in special classes to improve their skills later passed the highest-level college preparatory course in that academic area, qualifying them for college-level work. About 45 percent of the students who had failed the math exam later completed the required college preparatory sequence.[10]

Upgrading the academic skills of underprepared college freshmen through improved developmental education and other academic support programs would have a major impact on increasing the degree completion rate of students from the bottom of the socioeconomic spectrum. Providing additional financial, counseling, and social supports to struggling low-income college students also would help close the gap in degree completion rates between these students and their more-affluent peers. Implementing policies to achieve both of these goals could yield an additional 58,800 low-income college graduates a year. Achieving this target would require the following actions:

- Raise the academic skills of 50 percent of unprepared low-income college enrollees and 75 percent of the minimally prepared low-income college enrollees up to the somewhat prepared level during their initial semesters in college through improved developmental education programs. This would result in 130,300 more low-income students ready for college-level work by the end of their freshman year.
- After upgrading the academic skills of these 130,300 low-income, underprepared freshmen to a college-ready level (i.e., somewhat prepared level), support them to complete college at the same rate as somewhat prepared college students from quintiles 3 to 5 (i.e., 65 percent completion rate). These combined actions would add 58,800 new degree earners.

SUMMARIZING THE NUMBERS

Table 1 summarizes the increases in the number of low-income college degree earners that we project would result from each of the four approaches outlined above, for a total of 187,300 to 232,000 new college graduates a year.

It is important to note that adopting any of these approaches would not only help our least-advantaged students; these actions would also have a profound effect on improving the college completion rates of moderate-income youth—those from the second-lowest socioeconomic quintile—about 24 percent of whom currently earn postsecondary degrees. Many barriers to college completion that frustrate the aspirations of low-income students also stand as obstacles to moderate-income students. Students from both groups often sit side by side in large urban schools with inadequate college preparatory programs.

Doubling the degree completion rate of moderate-income youth as a result of the interventions recommended in this chapter would increase the annual number of degree earners from moderate-income families from 194,000 to 388,000. The combined impact of doubling the number of students from the lowest two SES quintiles would result in 284,000 new college graduates each year.

CONCLUSION

The analysis shows that doubling the numbers is a matter of simultaneously fixing multiple leaks in the pipeline for low-income and other students. While academic preparation at earlier phases is crucial to academic success in later phases, better early preparation alone is no panacea, and must be combined with better supports at each critical education transition.

Table 1. Targeted Actions to Improve College Success Rate of Low-Income Students

	Additional Degree Earners per Year	Annual Increase
Lever 1a (GED holders) Increasing the college enrollment and completion rates of low-SES GED holders to the rates achieved by low-SES minimally prepared high school graduates, or more ambitiously, to the average rates achieved by middle- and upper-quintile minimally qualified high school graduates.	23,400 to 48,200	26% to 54%
Lever 1b (Dropouts) Recovering 50% of high school dropouts, with those new high school degree earners enrolling and completing college at rates comparable to those achieved by low-SES minimally prepared high school graduates, or more ambitiously, to the average rates achieved by middle- and upper-quintile minimally qualified high school graduates.	19,900 to 39,800	22% to 44%
Lever 2 Improving the college readiness of high school graduates (i.e., moving 50% of unprepared to the next rung of minimally prepared; 25% of unprepared to somewhat prepared; and 75% of minimally prepared to somewhat prepared).	53,700	60%
Lever 3 Equalizing the college enrollment and degree completion rates between college-prepared low-SES high school graduates and their middle- and upper-income peers (quintiles 3–5).	31,500	35%
Lever 4 Raising the academic skill levels of unprepared and underprepared low-SES college enrollees their first year in college (i.e., moving 50% of unprepared to the next rung of minimally prepared; 25% of unprepared to somewhat qualified, and 75% of minimally prepared to somewhat prepared through effective developmental education and other academic supports) and equalizing the degree completion rates between these better-prepared low-SES college freshmen and their middle- and upper-income counterparts from quintiles 3–5.	58,800	65%
TOTAL	187,300 to 232,000	208% to 258%

The numeric targets suggested by our analysis—such as producing 53,700 new low-income degree earners by increasing college readiness levels of high school graduates—are ambitious but not unrealistic. For example, if the approximately 1,500 small schools created in underperforming urban districts in recent years were able to achieve 90 percent graduation rates and 80 percent college readiness rates among their estimated 67,500 low-income graduates each year, this reform alone would add over 17,000 new low-income degree earners. If the goal of establishing 500 early colleges in which students complete up to two years of college credit while still in high school were achieved, this reform could add 12,000 new low-income degree earners.[11]

While there is no "silver bullet" solution that can double the numbers, there are several promising approaches that, taken together, make the goal an achievable one. These solutions include creating new small secondary schools and programs that provide multiple pathways to college readiness and success for struggling and out-of-school youth, aligning high school curriculum and standards to college requirements, creating more supportive pathways into college for first-generation, low-income college students, and improving academic, financial, and social supports once these students reach the college campus.

By sizing the problem and its component pieces and then sizing the impact of reducing leakages at four key points in the education pipeline, this chapter presents a case for giving priority to certain kinds of interventions. The remainder of this book addresses the kinds of changes in practice and in policy that can help turn this thought experiment into a real program for educational efficiency and equity for the 21st century.

APPENDIX: METHODOLOGY

This chapter analyzes data from the National Education Longitudinal Study (NELS), which tracked the educational progress of approximately 25,000 eighth graders over 12 years, from 1988 to 2000. The base-year respondents were resurveyed in 1990, 1992, 1994, and 2000, regardless of whether they dropped out of high school. Based on 1988 demographics, whites represent 71.7 percent of the NELS student sample, blacks 12.9 percent, and Hispanics 10.5 percent. The results presented in this chapter are based on the NELS 88/00 student-level data, with a total sample size of 12,144. A weight is applied to the data such that only respondents who participated in each of the five waves of data collection were included in the various analyses.

The analysis combined variables from the NELS student survey and high school and college transcript data files. The student survey files contained variables measuring basic student demographic characteristics, student aspirations, and student work history. The various transcript data files contained variables measuring student high school courses, college enrollment history, and degree completion history.

The restricted-use version of the NELS data was used in this analysis to allow linkage between student survey records and transcript records.

The analyses were conducted by Optimal Solutions Group LLC under contract to Jobs for the Future. Optimal Solutions is a nonpartisan economic and social policy research firm with offices in Baltimore, Maryland, and Washington, D.C. The group offers rigorous public policy research and technical assistance to government agencies, corporations, nonprofit organizations, and foundations. Its expertise includes education policies, workforce development and social policies, health policies, and housing, economic development, and transportation policies.

PART II

One System across 9–14: The State of the States

State policy is the foundation for integrating grades 9–14 on a broad scale. These authors address the *realpolitik* of achieving the dramatic systemic and policy changes needed to integrate grades 9–14. One challenge is that no single policy lever will accomplish integration; multiple policy levers must be pulled together, including the alignment of secondary-postsecondary standards and the use of integrated systems for finance, data, and accountability. Collaborative or joint governance structures across K–16 are another desirable precondition, but, as Andrea Venezia, Joni Finney, and Patrick Callan attest, all of these changes would have to overcome significant resistance. For example, there is no consensus among the public and educators that readiness for postsecondary education should be the goal for all high school students. There is also institutionalized self-interest in maintaining long-standing organizational arrangements based on the separation of K–12 and postsecondary policy.

But there is also cause for optimism in the headway some states are making on parts of an integrated 9–14 agenda. Such states have identified priorities, set realistic goals, and developed strategies and models that others might adopt or adapt. Kristin Conklin and Stefanie Sanford describe reforms under way in a number of states, spurred by the support of the National Governors Association's high school reform initiative. Stan Jones describes Indiana's history of aligning pathways and providing low-income students with financial incentives to prepare for postsecondary education. These and other accounts lend credence to the observations of Michael Kirst and Michael Usdan, based on their case study of New York State's long-established single K–20 system and other states: in order to coordinate successfully, political, education, and business leaders must "advocate for inter-level coordination in much the same focused manner in which they drove efforts to implement standards-based reform."

3

Common Ground

Andrea Venezia, Joni Finney, and Patrick M. Callan

The country's population is undergoing major changes, and the fastest-growing student populations are ones that are traditionally underserved throughout the education pipeline—underrepresented in elementary, secondary, and postsecondary education—and they have the least-skilled jobs in the workforce. There are large educational gaps between low-income and economically well-off students—and between different ethnic groups—in postsecondary preparation, postsecondary program completion, and successful entrance into the workforce.

On the population change side, the minority segment of our population is projected to double (from 18 percent to 37 percent) between 1980 and 2020, and the Latino portion almost triple (from 6 percent to 17 percent). During the same period, the white working-age population—comprised largely of baby boomers—is projected to decrease from 82 percent to 63 percent. On the educational disparity side, whites aged 25 to 64 were twice as likely as African Americans, and almost three times as likely as Latinos, to have a bachelor's degree in 2000. In many states, these gaps are widening. Furthermore, approximately 50 percent of Latino and African American K–12 students do not finish high school (National Center for Public Policy and Higher Education, 2005).

If policies do not address these challenges, the college-educated portion of America's workforce will decline. If the educational gaps persist or widen, there will be a projected reduction in personal income per capita, which could decline by almost $400—from $21,591 in 2000 to $21,196 in 2020—in direct contrast to 41 percent growth between 1980 and 2000. In addition to harming individuals and families, this reduction would lower the tax bases of the nation and of states (NCPPHE, 2005).

Without improvements in the share of our young population from all income levels and ethnic groups completing high school and finishing at least some college, the United States may see its first substantive, sustained drop in the educational attainment of its citizens (National Center for Higher Education Management Systems, 2005). Such an unprecedented decline would affect the country's capacity to compete economically; states' abilities to provide basic services; and individuals' abilities to support themselves and their families. At a time when we need a greater proportion of our population to complete some form of education after high school, we may indeed be producing a less-educated populace.

This chapter explores the policy strategies that would link high school reform to college readiness and completion to significantly bolster reform efforts and dramatically raise the educational attainment of all young adults. We draw on our work with *Claiming Common Ground,* a collaboration among the National Center for Public Policy and Higher Education, the Institute for Educational Leadership, and the Stanford Institute for Higher Education Research (Callan, Finney, Kirst, Usdan, & Venezia, 2006).

The *Claiming Common Ground* report, which we coauthored with Michael Kirst and Michael Usdan, identified three state policy dimensions for improving postsecondary readiness opportunities for all high school students:[1]

- *Alignment of course work and assessments:* States should require K–12 and postsecondary education to align their courses and assessments. Currently, the K–12 standards movement is not connected to efforts to improve access and success in higher education. By alignment, we mean integrating the expectations of one education system into the other and connecting course work, pedagogy, curricula, and assessments.
- *State finance:* States should develop financial incentives and other supports that stimulate K–12 and postsecondary education to collaborate to improve postsecondary readiness and success. Most existing state finance systems perpetuate the divide between K–12 and postsecondary education.
- *Statewide data systems and accountability:* States should develop the capacity to track students across educational institutions statewide. Currently, few states collect adequate data to address the effectiveness of K–12 reforms in improving student readiness for college. States should publicly report on student progress and success, from high school through postsecondary education. Schools, colleges, and universities should be accountable for improving student performance, from high school to college completion.

LINKING HIGH SCHOOLS TO COLLEGES

Throughout the country, high school reform has become a major focus in an overall effort to raise student achievement. Postsecondary education and work readiness are the driving forces behind these efforts.[2] For these high school reform efforts to succeed, however, they must expand beyond the boundaries of K–12 school systems to encompass the less well-defined terrain of postsecondary readiness for all students. High school reform and changes in postsecondary education are interdependent. Some of the largest problems encountered in raising student achievement take place between our K–12 systems and our colleges and universities—a disjuncture that reform efforts have, to a large extent, ignored.

Because secondary schools and postsecondary institutions have divergent histories, institutional boundaries, and governance and policy structures, there are no widespread practices or traditions in the United States for these two levels of education to work together effectively, much less to resolve the many problems that occur between them. There are no postsecondary readiness lobbies in state capitals and no postsecondary readiness accountability systems within schools or colleges; no one is held responsible for the students who fall between the cracks of the two systems. Moreover, there is an outdated perception that only an elite group of students goes to college—that only a relatively small portion of high school students needs to be prepared for postsecondary education. In reality, almost 90 percent of high school students report that they plan to attend college, and approximately 70 percent of high school graduates follow up on that goal by enrolling in some form of postsecondary education directly after high school (Mortenson, 2004). And many more students enroll in some form of postsecondary education a few years after high school.

The vast majority of our nation's college students (about 80 percent) attend public institutions that do not have highly selective admission requirements (Venezia, Kirst, & Antonio, 2003). However, once students enter college, far too many learn that they are not ready to handle college-level course work. Forty percent of students in four-year institutions take some remedial education, as do 63 percent at two-year institutions (U.S. Department of Education, 2001). In addition, postsecondary completion rates are abysmally low at the institutions that serve most of our nation's college students. States ranged from 65 percent of first-time, full-time students completing a bachelor's degree within six years of college entrance in Massachusetts to 40 percent in Alaska (NCPPHE, 2004). Students who do not attend college full-time have even lower completion rates.

As these outcomes suggest, gaining admission to postsecondary education is not the most daunting challenge facing high school graduates (even if many students think that it is), and most postsecondary preparation efforts focus on admissions. The more difficult challenge facing high school graduates is to become academically prepared for college credit–level course work. Because getting into college is relatively easy at most postsecondary institutions, the de facto standards for college are embedded in the placement tests students take once they enroll in college. However, the college placement exams are not connected to what students learn in high school. Students may have a high grade point average on their high school transcript—and may have taken the prescribed college preparatory curriculum—but many still perform poorly on the placement tests once they are admitted. Surely, this lack of readiness to successfully complete college-credit courses helps account for the low persistence rates between the first and second years, as well as the overall low college completion rates.

COLLEGE-READY STANDARDS ARE CONFUSING

From the student perspective, the divide between high school and postsecondary education is very real. This is true for all postsecondary sectors, including community colleges, which enroll about 44 percent of our nation's undergraduate college students (National Center for Education Statistics, 2002). Community colleges have multiple missions, and most admit any student over age 18 who applies and can benefit from instruction. High school students know that community colleges do not have stringent admission requirements, so many view them as institutions that require no academic preparation. Few students understand that community colleges and other broad-access institutions *do* have academic standards (Kirst & Venezia, 2003). Students can enroll in such institutions quite easily, but that does not mean that they will be able to take college-level courses, enroll in their desired major, or complete their certificate or degree program. Once students enter college, they find out that they are required to take placement exams to determine if they must take remedial courses before enrolling in college-level work. About half the college students in the United States need to take remedial education (U.S. Department of Education, 2001).

Disjunctures between high school and postsecondary education manifest themselves in many ways. For example, high school assessments usually stress different knowledge and skills than do college entrance and placement requirements. College mathematics placement standards often include Algebra II, while standard college entrance exams rarely exceed Algebra I (The Education Trust, 1999). In addition, the course work from high school is not connected to postsecondary education. Students graduate from high school under one set of standards, and then must meet a whole new set of standards in college. For example, a recent ACT study found that college instructors believe that grammar and usage skills are the *most* important writing skills needed by incoming students. The study also found that these skills are considered to be the *least* important by high school teachers. Only 69 percent of high school teachers reported that they teach grammar and usage.[3]

The disjunctures are not limited to academic issues. States appropriate funds separately to K–12 and postsecondary education, creating turf battles and territorialism while providing those on each side of the divide with little or no incentive for collaboration. State accountability and data systems stop at grade 12 and begin anew at grade 13, with little or no connection between the levels. Current state information systems are generally more useful for supporting budget allocations to institutions than for assessing student transitions and policy efficacy. States are often incapable of determining, for example, the effects of policy interventions in high school on college attendance and completion. And there are few rewards or incentives for placing students into college-level work or for graduating college students in a timely fashion.

RECOMMENDATIONS: STATES MUST LEAD THE WAY

While the federal government, local schools, and postsecondary institutions have important roles in educational policy and practice, college-ready reform is primarily a state-level policy responsibility. States shoulder the major funding and policymaking responsibilities for *both* public K–12 and higher education. Fulfilling the promise of postsecondary opportunity requires states to create structural and procedural connections that improve student preparation for college. Too often, the connections between K–12 and higher education have been voluntary, piecemeal, local, and dependent upon ad hoc leadership commitments. If reforms to establish common ground between K–12 and postsecondary education are to succeed, they must extend well beyond local or regional collaborative efforts. They must reach farther than joint meetings, new memoranda of understanding, or statewide course-numbering systems.

If states are not focusing on connecting their systems across at least these dimensions—alignment of course work and assessments, state finance, and data systems and accountability—they are unlikely to increase the proportion of high school graduates who are ready for college-level work.

Alignment of Course Work and Assessments

States should require K–12 and postsecondary education to align their course work and assessments.

Requiring K–12 and postsecondary education to work together to align their course work and assessments is a key step to improving postsecondary readiness. This recommendation, a consistent theme for this book, is often called "integration." By alignment, we mean embedding standards from one system into the other—not just deciding upon a certain cut score on, for example, a high school assessment that purports to meet proficiency expectations for college-level work. Currently, the K–12 standards movement and efforts to improve access and success in higher education are operating on different tracks. For example, a widespread K–12 reform strategy is to increase enrollments in college preparatory courses. Yet despite some success in this area, remediation rates in postsecondary education remain high and college completion rates remain low.

This approach may be necessary, but it is not a sufficient strategy to improve college readiness. The number of courses that high school students take, and the units and names assigned to them, are often inadequate proxies for whether or not high school graduates are prepared to succeed in college-level work. The quality and level of the course work and instruction, and their level of alignment with postsecondary expectations, are the key elements of reform. Making improvements in these areas requires that colleges and universities participate in the new wave of high school reforms, so that new standards and curricula in high school are linked to what students need to know and be able to do in college.

High school assessments are another example of the multiple ways students receive mixed messages about the skills they need to develop for college. High school graduation tests in most states are benchmarked at the levels of the eighth, ninth, or tenth grades. There are few standards developed for the eleventh or twelfth grades or connected to the academic expectations of college. Students should receive diagnostic information through assessments at key intervals in high school—well before entering college—concerning their preparation for college-level academic work, so that they can change their course-taking patterns and improve their postsecondary readiness.

A promising example of collaboration and alignment is the Early Assessment Program between K–12 and postsecondary systems found in California. This program is a partnership of California State University, the State Board of Education, and the California Department of Education. Its goal is to ensure that high school graduates who attend CSU are prepared to enroll and succeed in college-level courses. It was initiated by CSU to give high school juniors opportunities to measure their readiness for college-level math and English, and to help them improve their knowledge and skills during their senior year.[4]

There are many anticipated benefits to the Early Assessment Program. For the first time, a large-scale, statewide program is providing students with information about their level of preparedness for college. If the program succeeds, students who participate will have the information and support they need to plan and improve during their senior year. CSU, in turn, will have enrollees who will need fewer remedial classes and who will graduate more quickly.

State Finance

States should create financial incentives and support that stimulate K–12 and postsecondary education to collaborate to improve postsecondary readiness and success.

Budget and finance incentives can stimulate collaboration between K–12 and postsecondary education. This will require legislative committees that oversee the budget processes for K–12 and postsecondary education to work together closely to find common goals in advancing postsecondary readiness and success. Currently, however, most states have separate legislative committee structures to oversee K–12 and postsecondary education. To the extent that these legislative oversight functions remain isolated from each other, they can, and often do, perpetuate the divide between schools and postsecondary education systems.

No state has fully aligned state budgets, financial aid, and other policies to provide incentives for K–12 and postsecondary education to support college readiness. However, Oregon and Indiana provide promising examples of how such alignment can take place.

In Oregon, state political leadership has set concrete goals for improving K–12 and postsecondary education collaboration to advance student success, which is described in more detail in chapter 28.[5] A brief explanation of this effort shows the importance of finance linkages across the education sectors.

The Oregon Business Council has taken the lead in developing an integrated statewide budget and finance model that would span the sequence of education from preschool to graduate school. According to Duncan Wyse, the council's president, the state's public education system is, as in most states, "composed of distinct sectors, budgeted and governed separately. There are no consistent [high school] exit and [postsecondary] entrance standards for students. Student movement through the system is organized by time rather than by achievement" (Wyse, 2005).

The governor has set concrete goals in the areas of high school graduation and college completion. In addition, joint boards—comprised of members from the state board of education and the state board of higher education—have recommended changes in linking the education sectors, including developing a unified and transparent state budget. The budget project tracks state expenditures for all major functions of K–12 and higher education. These expenditures are clearly illustrated by line items in the state budget. Rather than simple votes on annual spending levels for K–12 or postsecondary education as discrete budget categories, policymakers can see past expenditures by function and set priorities accordingly across the educational system. Further, changes in performance, such as graduation and completion rates, are reported annually to help determine the efficacy of such changes.

Another example is Indiana's Twenty-first Century Scholars Program, a national model in both broadening access to college and improving college readiness. Initiated in 1990, the program was the first state financial aid program to promise the future payment of college tuition for middle school students who qualify for the federal free and reduced lunch program. The Scholars Program targets low-income students in the eighth grade and requires each participating student to complete a pledge to finish high school, apply for college and financial aid, and enroll in an Indiana postsecondary institution within two years of completing high school. In return, Indiana encourages the Scholars to pursue a college preparatory curriculum; provides support services to them and to those who fulfill the pledge; and pays all or a portion of their tuition and fees at a public institution in Indiana (after other financial aid awards), depending on the rigor of their college preparatory curriculum (Evenbeck, Seabrook, St. John, & Murphy, 2004).

Statewide Data Systems and Accountability

States should develop the capacity to track students across educational institutions statewide and publicly report on student progress and success from high school through postsecondary education.

Robust statewide data and compatible accountability systems are needed to determine the effectiveness of programs and reforms in improving student achievement. Currently, the data derived from state information systems are generally more useful for supporting budget allocations to institutions than for examining student progress across multiple institutions. At the K–12 level, few state databases can track students who leave one school district and enroll in another. Many cannot accurately determine the percentage of students graduating from high school each year.

State databases are even more deficient in examining student transitions from high school to college. In most states, one data system stops at grade 12 and another begins anew at grade 13, with little or no connection between them. As a consequence, these states lack information needed to address the effectiveness of their public schools, their colleges and universities, or—the most critical assessment—the combined sectors.

As states seek to align and expand their information systems across K–12 and postsecondary education, they need to better understand the relationship between student readiness in high school and student success in college. Currently, 18 states do not even collect data on the courses taken by high school students (NCPPHE, 2004).

In most states, it is not possible to identify and analyze completion rates for students who enter college from the workforce, students who attend part-time, or students who attend multiple institutions. In short, without databases that connect educational institutions, it is difficult—if not impossible—to assess needs accurately, identify where the most substantial problems are, and design appropriate interventions. In tracking student progress across educational institutions and systems, state information systems need to standardize and report data on: high school academic courses and assessments; high school graduation; postsecondary education and work readiness; transitions between high school and college; transfers between colleges; student progress while in college; and completion of postsecondary education and training programs.

For example, the databases should be designed to answer questions related to postsecondary readiness:

- How do high school students who take college preparatory courses perform in postsecondary education?
- How do high school students who pass (or earn a proficient score on) state assessments perform in college?
- Considering those students who require remediation in college, what percentage took a college preparatory curriculum in high school?
- Given their students' performance in college, how can high schools strengthen their curricula and instruction to improve student readiness for college?

Two recent national efforts focus on the collection of education data across the education sectors:

- *The Data Quality Campaign* provides support for state policymakers to improve the availability, collection, and use of high-quality education data; the goal is to use data to improve student achievement. Created in 2005 with support from the Bill & Melinda Gates Foundation, it provides both resources for states to develop longitudinal data systems and a national forum for promoting greater coordination and consensus around data-related issues.[6]
- *The National Education Data Summit*, supported by the U.S. Department of Education, the Bill & Melinda Gates Foundation, the Alliance for Excellent Education, and Lumina Foundation for Education, was a two-day gathering in February 2006 that focused on "the importance of building effective, comprehensive K–12 student data systems so policymakers can use data to develop policies and improve educational outcomes."[7]

The public reporting of student progress and achievement across educational levels is crucial to the development of collaborative efforts to improve student readiness. However, requiring educational institutions to report data to state departments of education will not suffice in making the systems more accountable for student achievement. States need to work with educational leaders to develop clear student achievement targets that will require collaborations by K–12 and postsecondary systems to meet them. Ultimately, the primary outcomes for state accountability systems should be postsecondary readiness (the percentage of the young population completing high school prepared for college), participation and access (the percentage enrolling in postsecondary education), persistence (the percentage staying in college), and completion (the percentage graduating). In addition, useful indicators at various stages can include, for example, high school graduation rates and transfers from community colleges to four-year institutions.

Accountability is, in many ways, the least developed of the policy levers. High-quality data systems are a key element in the development of connected accountability systems. Although no state has instituted comprehensive data and accountability systems focused on improving postsecondary readiness and success, Kentucky's accountability system for postsecondary education offers a promising example.

In 1997, the Kentucky legislature passed the Postsecondary Education Improvement Act (House Bill 1). In addition to establishing goals for the state's system of postsecondary education, the legislation charged the Council on Postsecondary Education with creating an accountability system to "ensure institutions' compliance with the strategic plan and to measure educational quality and student progress in the postsecondary education system; research and service opportunities; and use of resources by institutions."[8] To address this charge, the council drew up a public agenda focusing on accountability, degree completion, and affordability of postsecondary and adult education through 2010.

The state's accountability system derived from key questions:[9]

- Are more Kentuckians ready for postsecondary education?
- Is Kentucky postsecondary education affordable to its citizens?
- Do more Kentuckians have certificates and degrees?
- Are college graduates prepared for life and work in Kentucky?
- Are Kentucky's people, communities, and economy benefiting?

The council developed state-level indicators for each question and outlined related benefits. For example, to answer the first question regarding postsecondary readiness, the council has required that the following data be collected (Callan, et al., 2006):

- K–12 student achievement (average ACT);
- The percentage of high school students scoring a three or higher on Advanced Placement exams;
- The percentage of incoming Kentucky high school graduates not requiring remediation in math and English; and
- The number of Kentuckians earning general equivalency diplomas (GEDs).

By including indicators for postsecondary readiness in its accountability system for postsecondary education, Kentucky set high expectations for collaboration across K–12 schools and colleges and universities to improve student achievement.

Data suggest that the reforms are working:[10]

- Undergraduate enrollment increased from 160,926 in 1998 to 205,832 students.
- By 2004, 81.8 percent of adults 25 or older had a high school diploma or a general equivalency diploma, up from 77.9 in 1998.
- The six-year graduation rate from Kentucky's public universities rose from 36.7 percent in 1998 to 44.3 percent in 2004.
- After the development of the Kentucky Community and Technical College System, enrollment grew from 52,201 in 2000 to 81,990 in 2004.
- The Research Challenge Trust Fund spent $350 million on postsecondary education between 1997 and 2003, enabling the University of Kentucky and the University of Louisville to hire dozens of new professors.

Ultimately, postsecondary persistence and graduation data are the central outcomes for accountability systems. Each state's system of accountability must be unique, however, for each should account for the distinct and diverse educational needs of its population, the mix of educational institutions in the state, and the history and context of its educational enterprise. There is a need for further innovative thinking about policies that could address this underdeveloped area, especially given how limited improvements are thus far.

SUBSTANTIVE CHANGE

The three policy levers discussed here are not the only areas of promise for states interested in college-ready reform. For example, K–16 governance commissions that include both K–12 and postsecondary leaders and that build on these levers can be an important step toward necessary reforms. These bodies, however, should be charged with specific responsibilities, and they must have enough resources, influence, and authority to make real change. And they must be accountable for performance. State agency collaboration is essential—both in terms of the content of work and the organizational structures supporting that work. Having components of readiness reform in statute appears to be useful but not sufficient for creating change.[11]

Yet even a K–16 entity is in itself insufficient to engage the depth of reform that is needed. In fact, these structures sometimes deflect attention from policy changes. Sometimes they exacerbate tensions between school and postsecondary leaders. And sometimes they become discussion forums rather than drivers of change.

Likewise, some state reform efforts focus on technical issues, such as those involved in alignment. For example, some states are analyzing the relationships between their high school exit assessments and their college entrance and placement exams; 25 have signed on to such work under the aegis of the American Diploma Project.[12] Granted, this is very important work, but it is ineffective absent real action to address the organizational, political, and financial issues that are often the real obstacles to alignment between the sectors. It needs to be accompanied as well by mechanisms to get the higher standards into schools and classrooms.

In short, if states do not accomplish substantive changes in each of the areas outlined above, they should not be surprised to find that their K–12 and postsecondary education systems continue to operate along separate orbits. And if a state implements changes in more than two areas, there will be interactions among them; states should be aware of this and monitor how reforms affect one another. Engaging in policy reform almost always involves political challenges. Every state undertaking such reform will struggle with such issues, including how to involve the governor or the appropriate legislative committees in reform and how to sustain the reform after leaders leave office. Although each state is unique, no state's political or educational context creates insurmountable hurdles to this kind of work. Challenges await, but the work must be done, and it must be done state by state.

4

The History of the Separation of K–12 and Postsecondary Education

Michael W. Kirst and Michael D. Usdan

The profound organizational, political, and cultural chasms that have historically divided the systems of K–12 and postsecondary education in the United States are beginning to receive attention in professional networks and associations. Nonetheless, the two educational levels largely remain self-contained universes. Inter-level initiatives are barely visible in most jurisdictions, and many tinker at the edges of reform, leaving the central pieces untouched. This bifurcation has a long history and many causes, yet a variety of issues and forces will, we believe, compel closer inter-level relationships in the years immediately ahead, despite the long history and tradition of separation.

Historically, few connecting mechanisms or institutions have enabled the levels of education to cooperate on issues of mutual concern. Inter-level issues are on the margin in most places and remain nobody's direct responsibility, nor do they have an immediate constituency. Such concerns commonly fall through the cracks between the two systems. The history, tradition, and legal structure of the dual system so deeply perpetuate and institutionalize the separation that the leverage for sustaining inter-level issues most likely will require the intervention of external forces—prestigious business leaders and elected officials—in much the same way as such influential leaders spawned the national accountability or standards-based reform movement in K–12 education.

Some 40 years ago, one of the coauthors with two colleagues published an analysis of the developing relationship between elementary-secondary and higher education in 12 geographically and demographically diverse states (Hurwitz, Minar, & Usdan, 1969). Our main questions were: What was the status of inter-level relationships, as of the summer of 1967? Were changes in relationships taking shape? If so, through what processes and institutions? How did patterns of change differ among states, and why? In what circumstances did either conflict or cooperation between levels appear to be taking shape?

We discovered that, in most cases, the relationship was virtually nonexistent. The inter-level issues had barely surfaced in most states. However, three sources of social pressure were causing more attention to be centered upon the division of elementary-secondary education from higher education. One was the expanding cost of education of all types, the result of population growth, heightened aspirations, new technologies, and generally mounting prices. A second was the increasing tendency to question established educational forms and procedures, including obstacles to individualization and flexibility in the education process. A third pressure was the rising demand for educational services, which overlapped or fell between the customary spheres of the collegiate and secondary school systems. This last factor was variously the product of new occupational skill needs, expanded leisure time, and economic demands that the entry of young people into the labor market be delayed.

Open political conflict between elementary-secondary and higher education was scarcely to be found on any broad scale in any state, though in a few instances there had been friction over specific issues. However, there was some cooperation, which again tended to be ad hoc (as it is today), and particular to given events or special functions. Only a handful of efforts were being made to institutionalize relationships across the levels within state policy structures or processes, a reality that remains all too true today in most jurisdictions.

These findings remain largely valid today, despite growing interest in interlevel issues. Despite the profound political, economic, technological, and demographic transformations that have reshaped our nation and world, the historical pattern of cultural and institutional isolation and separation between the education levels has persisted. Why has this relationship remained relatively impervious to change in a larger environment in which change is the only constant?

LOOKING BACKWARD: THE EVOLUTION OF THE K–16 DISJUNCTURE

The origin of this fissure between K–12 and postsecondary education stems, in part, from the laudable way the nation created mass education systems to deliver curriculum for both systems. In the 1890s, there was no organized system or common standards for college admission. Nearly half of colleges had either low entrance requirements or none at all (Ravitch, 2000). Some colleges accepted students from preapproved secondary schools or used their own exams. High school educators wanted a more uniform and less-haphazard system. In 1892 the National Education Association appointed the nation's first blue-ribbon education commission to recommend secondary school academic standards. The "Committee of Ten," as it was called, included five college presidents, three high school principals, a college professor, and the U.S. commissioner of education; it was chaired by Charles W. Eliot, president of Harvard (Ravitch, 2000).

The committee envisioned that only a tiny proportion of high school graduates would go to college. Nevertheless, the report recommended that all pupils be prepared for any path in life by "melding the objectives of liberal education (i.e., a curriculum of rich content) and mental discipline (i.e., the training of the mind)" (Ravitch, 2000). The committee supported adding to the high school curriculum subjects like history, the sciences, and classical languages (e.g., Latin) that would be taught through active learning instead of memorization. The report was attacked for its support of an academic education for all students, and some critics praised the European approach of different schools based on career choices of preteens.

The Committee of Ten's report influenced education policy and led to the creation of the College Examination Board, with its common college examination for diverse colleges. In 1900, the College Board set uniform standards for each academic subject and issued a syllabus to help high school students prepare for college-entrance, subject-matter examinations. Soon after, the University of California began to accredit high schools whose curricula were adequate for university preparation. As the number of high schools grew rapidly, however, universities could no longer do accreditation. And after the number of postsecondary institutions expanded greatly as well, the regional high school accrediting associations split with higher education accreditation to lessen the workload, but doing so deemphasized K–16 alignment.

At the same time, changes in teacher education forced the levels apart. Elementary teachers were originally prepared in two-year postsecondary normal schools—"normal" meaning according to rule, model, or pattern. In 1910, there were 264 normal schools, enrolling 132,000 students (Dunham, 1969). But teachers colleges began to prepare not only secondary teachers but elementary teachers as well. These institutions were linked to K–12 schools, and interactions across K–16 levels were frequent. Then, as demands for more spaces in higher education grew, the functions and enrollment of teachers colleges expanded, and these became multipurpose state colleges, often governed (like normal schools) by K–12 state boards of education. This growth caused recruitment of arts and sciences professors who sought higher academic prestige, but education schools or departments were typically viewed by the colleges' more diverse faculties as having low prestige. Thus, the final step would transform former normal colleges into universities where only the education school connected with K–12 teachers and students.

In terms of curricular expectations, in 1918, the Cardinal Principles of Secondary Education appeared, introducing a very different vision from the Committee of Ten report. High school enrollments were expanding and the student bodies becoming more diverse, and many students were viewed as incapable of learning the traditional academic curriculum (Tyack & Cuban, 1995). The Cardinal Principles were to be a blueprint for social efficiency: Students should be offered vocational training and courses on family life, good health, citizenship, ethical character, and the worthy use of leisure. Schools began to give students intelligence tests to put them in the appropriate academic track. The expanded and differentiated curriculum might help to retain more indifferent secondary students and better adapt them to a changing society. Traditional academic subjects and pedagogy were deemphasized, but courses multiplied to provide something practical and engaging that would retain students in high school.

This influential report helped spawn a shopping mall high school that lacked both coherence and a focus on college preparation for most students, resulting in the high school as we know it today.

The American comprehensive high school was thus designed for many—often conflicting—purposes, and it did not focus primarily on college preparation. In the years after World War II, the notion of academic standards shared across the sectors vanished. "Aptitude" tests like the SAT replaced subject-matter standards for college admission, and secondary schools placed more emphasis on elective courses in nonacademic areas.

RECENT TRENDS

The politics of elementary-secondary education in more recent decades has been heavily influenced by the professionalization and institutionalization of the educational function. The development of education as a functional specialty and the establishment of qualifications for entry have promoted a sense of identity among practitioners and served as a basis for the creation of strong professional groups. These have tended to behave in "responsible" ways and to use a rhetoric oriented to public service. Thus education came to be a recognized and respected profession, with strong coherence and much influence in the conduct of the elementary and secondary schools. Until quite recently, the politics of public schools have been dominated from inside by the administrators and teachers, along with their allies in other parts of the society. In the nature of things, the organized forces of education have had few natural political enemies and much social support.

There are widespread indications that these traditional patterns are breaking down, a trend with important implications for the relationship between levels. Some reasons for this shift are obvious. Professional educators have lost much of their influence as business and political leaders have driven the national accountability movement. In many states, elementary-secondary education itself no longer seems to present a united political front, and some of its old allies have drifted away. Furthermore, the entire range of public school aims and practices has been called into question more frequently in recent years. To a greater or lesser degree, throughout the country the traditional professional dominance of educational politics has broken down and been replaced by a "new politics of education," with presidents, governors, mayors, and corporate chieftains providing leadership in efforts to reform education.

A major consequence of this "secularization" trend is an increasingly fluid political situation. Where formerly the elementary-secondary education establishment was a sort of rock upon which all else was founded, there is now much less structure and certainty. In some cases a vacuum exists; in nearly all cases adjustments are taking shape. Out of this situation grows the probability of new political relationships between the levels of education. Given the symptoms of disarray in elementary-secondary education, the prospects seem to be increasing for higher education to fare relatively well when stronger relationships do develop.

The generation of new relationships between the levels of educational systems is also intertwined with the condition of educational governance. The formal and informal structures in the education field reflect the operation of political forces and in turn affect the shape and use of those forces. Some of the differences among states in the political relationship between educational levels can doubtless be accounted for by structural variations. Three points of organizational structure are pertinent: those that govern elementary-secondary education; those that govern higher education; and those that are designed to bridge the two.

Any analysis of inter-level relationships must be predicated upon an understanding of how these three points of organizational structure interact within the unique political and cultural context of any given state.

CASE STUDY: NEW YORK STATE

New York State provides a particularly interesting focal point because of its historical traditions—particularly the long-standing structure of the Board of Regents—a board that governs all of education in New York.[1]

Structurally, education in New York has a long-established, unified governance structure and historical context that should provide a national prototype for inter-level articulation. However, a persuasive case can be made that it might have been easier to establish K–16 relationships 200 years ago than it is today. Despite rather recent efforts by the New York State Board of Regents and the commissioner of education to bridge the levels, the centrifugal forces separating the educational levels have transcended the long-established, quite credible, centripetal governance and legal structure.

In New York, as in most other states, the cultural and operational deterrents to closer relationships between the educational levels have transcended structural arrangements that could potentially promote closer inter-level linkages. Ironically, the K–12 and postsecondary systems that at one time were closer together often have grown further apart in the last century.

The Regents, embedded constitutionally since 1784, is the nation's oldest education governing board, and it is viewed in many quarters as the most influential state board of education. However, the inability of the Regents to bridge the inter-level chasm more effectively illustrates how complex and deeply embedded are the factors that deter stronger linkages between the education sectors. Thus, New York is of particular interest to policymakers concerned with building more coherent K–16 systems.

Structurally and in theory, the Regents are responsible through the University of the State of New York infrastructure for all educational and cultural institutions, including elementary-secondary education, higher education, museums, libraries, public broadcasting, and the licensing of some 40 professions. As a result, the issue of K–16 reform is perceived not as a new, recent, evolving, or discrete concern, as it is viewed in other states, but as a matter that has been an integral part of the responsibility and role of the Regents and its staff, the state education department, for literally hundreds of years. For example, the statewide Regents exams have been embedded in the state for more than a century. In most states, of course, statewide standards and accountability systems are very recent, and the increased influence of statewide policymakers is a new phenomenon. The Regents also have extensive responsibilities that are unique among state education agencies, such as broad authority to charter and accredit all institutions and academic programs. Every program concerned with teacher or administrator certification must be sanctioned by the Regents.

The Regents have been much more involved in K–12 than in higher education. In K–12, they have traditionally set specific standards and expected outcomes, exerting a great deal of centralized control. Higher education has enjoyed much more freedom and independence from state constraints. There are a number of reasons for this, not the least of which is the unusual influence of private or independent higher education in New York. The 138 private institutions enroll approximately 40 percent of the students, award almost 60 percent of the bachelor's degrees, and about 70 percent of the first professional degrees like law.

Paradoxically, the Regents structure, while impressive in providing a mechanism for greater K–16 collaboration, may be rather seductive and dysfunctional in that many may believe somewhat complacently that structure alone is sufficient to promote inter-level cooperation. When interviewed in 2004, many education leaders in the state—while granting that the Regents could compel greater K–16 cooperation if they had the will—believed that strong policy momentum in that direction is unlikely because of volatile K–12 issues, such as testing, finance, and the achievement gap (see Venezia, Callan, Finney, Kirst, & Usdan, 2005). K–12 in New York, as in other states, is "under siege," and there is policy turmoil and overload. Some observers contend that despite the Regents structure, communication and interaction between K–12 and higher education are still minimal. For example, a chasm allegedly still exists between the standards set for students and teacher education at the two levels. Numerous interviewees testified that the K–16 relationship is poorly crafted and unrecognized, and that the need to bridge the levels remains a serious issue.

The power of the Regents is limited in important ways. They cannot appropriate resources, although they can make fiscal recommendations. Their recommendations frequently create hostility among elected officials, who must bear the political onus of raising the revenue to pay for increased educational services.

A major issue driving closer inter-level coordination in New York and other states is concern about the adequacy of the academic preparation provided in elementary and secondary schools. About 80 percent of New York's secondary graduates now enter postsecondary education. As a result, there is greater interest on the part of higher education in what students know and have to know in order to succeed in college. High postsecondary dropout rates reflect inadequate high school preparation. It is increasingly difficult at all educational levels to calibrate high standards with reasonable expectations of an increasingly demographically diverse, multilingual student body. Thus, higher education has become much more involved and concerned with the quality of K–12 schools.

Higher education, in turn, is increasingly viewed as the linchpin of efforts to attract more high-value jobs to New York, particularly in upstate areas, where the decline in manufacturing has had particularly negative effects on the economy. Recent efforts by the New York State commissioner of education to play a more proactive role in supporting and building closer linkages of secondary with higher education reportedly are attributable at least partially to the identification by the legislature and the business community of higher education as the core of economic development.

The commissioner has actively supported regional economic development initiatives by collaborating with the regionally based Boards of Cooperative Educational Services (BOCES), New York State's intermediate districts. The BOCES are under the direct control of the state education department. This illustrates the potential of the Board of Regents and its staff to promote K–16 cooperation at the regional as well as state level.

There appears to be a general consensus that the Regents structure can leverage greater cooperation. There also was articulated the common belief that K–16 planning should flow from specific issues that span the educational levels—issues like libraries, teacher education, administrator preparation, finance, and special education. In other words, coordination should be predicated on specific priority issues and mutual common interests and needs, rather than forced structurally.

There also are a number of significant disincentives to improved inter-level coordination. There is a widespread lack of understanding throughout the state of the Regents' structure and authority. The board's independence is a liability as well as an asset because it is viewed by the governor and other elected officials as unaccountable to the taxpaying public. New York has a strong executive budget system, and the state's governors have been frustrated by the Regents' autonomy as a "fourth branch" of state government. Governors on a bipartisan basis have sought to curb its powers.

The influence of the Regents on K–16 or any other major policy issue is significantly affected by its detachment from the powerful executive branch and other elected officials. The commissioner of education must walk a fine line between the Regents to whom he reports and the governor who can make his life miserable on budgetary and other major issues. Recently, for example, the executive branch froze positions in the education department, thus weakening the latter's capacity to meet new responsibilities with regard to standards setting, accountability, and implementation of the federal No Child Left Behind legislation. Some observers regard the significant reduction in the number of education department employees as political payback because the Regents allegedly are uncooperative and too independent.

Another deterrent to moving the K–16 agenda is that, despite the K–16 structure, each education entity is entrenched, massive, and powerful. Although the legislative and executive branch leaders might talk about changing the existing structure, the current entities are very powerful and quite adept at preserving their own interests and the status quo. In essence, everyone is a "prisoner of the existing structure" and locked into current policies and practices.

This problem is exacerbated by partisan political realities that have become institutionalized over three decades. The State Senate has been controlled by Republicans and the Assembly by Democrats since 1974. The Regents are selected by the legislature, with each legislator having one vote, regardless of which house he or she serves in. Because the Assembly is a much larger body, the Democrats control the selection of Regents. This procedure is held in such disdain by the Republicans that they reportedly have walked out at times during the selection process. As a result of this partisan rift, the Regents and its staff were resented and often opposed by long-serving Republican governors and senators prior to the 2006 elections.

Thus, there is no center of political authority for determining educational policy. The responsibility is unclear and diffused. The detachment of the Regents from the state's political mainstream might have been positive in a different era, but the body's reported remoteness and inaccessibility may not be sustainable in the contemporary turbulent educational environment, in which expectations are so high and the issues are so volatile and significant to the electorate.

Some New York commentators were wary about stronger K–16 connections for somewhat different reasons. The evidence is unclear as to whether efforts to bridge K–16 and span boundaries are sustainable or worthwhile. While such efforts certainly are useful in realms like teacher education, the problems facing K–12 are so immense that efforts to focus on K–16 might not only complicate matters but also serve as a dysfunctional diversion from central K–12 concerns like quality and closing the achievement gap. Thus, there is an undeniable need for more congruity between the educational levels, but strategies to achieve this laudable goal should be implemented very carefully.

POLICY IMPLICATIONS FROM HISTORY

This historical overview and the New York case study reveal a deeply rooted and long-lasting separation between K–12 and postsecondary education. The chasm includes structures, policies, habits of mind, and professional relationships and interactions. The two levels simply do not believe that they have much in common. College professors do not view K–12 secondary school teachers as their colleagues. K–12 school administrators rarely attend meetings with postsecondary leaders. This situation exists even between high schools and community colleges in close proximity. There are separate state legislative committees for K–12 and postsecondary education. There are few forums where K–20 policy can be enacted. In sum, it will take very powerful policy levers to impact professional cultures and structural impediments. We have only begun to explore potential K–20 policy levers and incentives. Can new policies overcome this historical K–20 disjuncture?[2]

The lessons of K–20 history suggest that the lack of relationships between K–12 and postsecondary policymakers, journalists, and professionals may not be overcome by small-scale initiatives or by convening the key influential players around a meeting table. History has shaped a divided K–20 ecology, and even large amounts of money may do little to change it.

Each sector has its own reasons for keeping distance from the other. Prestige in postsecondary education does not come from close identification with K–12. College teachers, even in community colleges, have distanced themselves from K–12. California community colleges were initially part of the K–12 system, but they now operate in a separate orbit. In another example, Western Michigan University has a respected education school, but its relationship with K–12 is much different than it was when it was called Western Michigan State Teachers College.

K–12 leaders have been wary of letting colleges exert too much influence. Not every high school student attends college, and there are strong lobbies for career and technical education. Secondary school educators feel challenged by their system's own problems, so linkage with postsecondary education is often not a major objective. Many states embrace local control of K–12. This inhibits coordination with postsecondary education. Public university trustees are rarely chosen for their knowledge about K–12 transition issues. The public views higher education as being in much better shape than K–12, and does not want any major overhaul (Immerwahr, 1999). Large-scale remediation efforts increasingly occur in higher education, but the sector remains ambivalent about closer integration with K–12.

GAINING TRACTION

Despite the aforementioned difficulties inherent in developing closer inter-level relationships in New York and elsewhere, K–16 issues undeniably are gaining traction throughout the country (*Chronicle of Higher Education*, 2006). A number of national organizations and foundations have been developing initiatives that are designed to connect the levels more meaningfully. The following provides only a sampling of these efforts to catalyze closer coordination.

The National Governors Association, for example, has joined with a number of education groups and foundations in national efforts to improve high schools, with a focus on postsecondary readiness. NGA joined with Achieve, Inc., an organization of national political and business leaders, in jointly sponsoring an education summit in 2005 that focused on the urgency of improving the nation's secondary schools.

This summit meeting produced the "Action Agenda for Improving America's High Schools," a report that urged states to create mechanisms that would more effectively bridge the K–12–postsecondary divide. Colleges, which all too frequently have been recalcitrant about engaging in K–16 discussions, were urged to define their academic and admissions expectations more explicitly. This meeting, which was keynoted by Bill Gates, attracted widespread attention in the media and among influential business and political leaders.

Entities such as Achieve, the Education Trust, Jobs for the Future, the Pathways to College Network, the Western Interstate Commission for Higher Education, and a growing number of other groups also are focusing attention on the need to make high school curricula more demanding. The Education Trust has been a forceful voice in advocating for improved and more equitable teacher recruitment and placement practices, the expansion of dual credit approaches, the need for stronger incentives and sanctions to compel greater higher education involvement, and other initiatives designed to close the K–12–postsecondary disconnect.[3]

A number of the aforementioned organizations have joined forces in efforts to promote greater K–16 collaboration and integration. The American Diploma Project, for example, reflects an impressive and ambitious partnership between Achieve, the Education Trust, and the Fordham Foundation to work with about half of the states to connect college requirements with high school standards, strengthen the secondary school curriculum, and develop college readiness instruments.

Approximately 35 states are working to align high school standards with postsecondary admissions requirements. The escalating attention being paid to interlevel issues is in large measure attributable to the financial support recently being provided by a wide array of both private and corporate foundations. Foremost among these funders is the Bill & Melinda Gates Foundation, which is spending approximately $800 million to improve high schools and increase the number of youngsters prepared for postsecondary education through varied early college and scholarship programs. One of the earliest foundations to take an interest in this field was the Pew Charitable Trusts. The GE Foundation has invested $100 million to support education, business, and community collaborations to strengthen college readiness for K–12 students in localities in which GE operates. The Ewing Marion Kauffman Foundation has initiated a multiyear $70 million program in Kansas City, Missouri, and Kansas City, Kansas, designed to assist low-income youngsters prepare for college. Lumina Foundation for Education has created networks of volunteers in 25 states to help students fill out student-aid forms. Numerous other funders, such as KnowledgeWorks in Ohio, the W. K. Kellogg Foundation, the Nellie Mae Education Foundation, and Sallie Mae Funds recently subsidized programs designed to overcome financial and other deterrents that preclude low-income youngsters from contemplating or attending postsecondary education.

Despite this undeniable and encouraging growth of interest and action on inter-level issues, the laudable efforts thus far still remain woefully inadequate. The tempo and profundity of political and economic changes have been so rapid that mere ad hoc projects to reform our disconnected education systems will no longer suffice. Hundreds if not thousands of disparate activities and programs designed to close the continuing K–12–postsecondary chasm (while well intentioned and often effective within their limited realms) are insufficient. The K–16 movement, despite the aforementioned positive escalation of interest and commitment, is still in an embryonic stage of development, yet students' education needs cannot be met through traditional, glacially paced, decentralized patterns of reform and change in our diffused and fragmented education systems.

We have no illusions about the political complexities of effecting basic policy changes that fly in the face of education culture and decades of history and tradition. Indeed, we are skeptical about educators driving or endorsing such changes and would contend that they will occur only if influential political and business leaders become engaged and advocate for inter-level coordination in much the same focused manner in which they drove efforts to implement the standards-based reform movement in K–12 education.

5

A College-Ready Nation

An Idea Whose Time Has Come

Kristin D. Conklin and Stefanie Sanford

In 1983, *A Nation at Risk* paid equal attention to elementary and secondary problems and solutions, but since then, the "standards movement" to improve American public education has largely ignored high schools. As recently as 1996, the nation's governors resolved at the first National Education Summit to place a priority on the early grades.

Since then, though, the political calculus has changed entirely. No Child Left Behind, the 2002 reauthorization of the Elementary and Secondary Education Act and a signature bipartisan domestic policy achievement, focused attention on schools and the achievement gap between different population subgroups. National concerns about economic competitiveness and rising college costs (along with high levels of remediation for students entering higher education) brought college readiness issues to the fore. In 2005, these forces converged and then culminated with Bill Gates's speech at the third National Education Summit, which focused on high schools. He christened the American high school "obsolete," an adjective that reverberated through state-of-the-state addresses and legislative debates across the nation.

Today, philanthropic, state, and federal leaders have coalesced around the idea that all high school students should graduate on time and ready for college and work. We bring a certain bias to this observation. Our organizations—the National Governors Association (NGA) and the Bill & Melinda Gates Foundation—have worked together over the past three years to advance this idea and focus attention on this most-neglected component of the American educational system. Some proactive state boards of education and state education agencies have set public benchmarks for high school graduation rates, and governors in all 50 states have committed publicly to improving the accuracy of graduation rate measurements. The federal government has dedicated a new revenue stream to supporting high school graduates who complete a college preparatory curriculum. And, just as important, most Americans, including most high school students, recognize that a postsecondary education is necessary to take part in the American middle class.

To understand this progress—and to accelerate it so that 90 percent of high school students graduate prepared for college, and the nation doubles the number of adults with a postsecondary credential—it is useful to reflect on how the problem, solution, and political streams converged and which strategies within these strands were most significant.

The sinewy path of streams, the rush of political opportunity and leadership, the window of opportunity sliding open: political scientist John Kingdon used all these metaphors to explain how an idea's time has come. His seminal book, *Agendas, Alternatives, and Public Policies*, appeared within a few months of *A Nation at Risk*. Its construct is salient today to help policymakers, educators, and advocates understand how the idea of universal college readiness came to frame the public policy agenda in education.

First, data, research reports, and powerful anecdotal evidence came together to illuminate the need to reframe high schools' mission to college readiness. At the same time, a high-profile event, a hard-hitting speech, a broad state policy blueprint, and a complementary list of concrete, short-term strategies helped coalesce decisionmakers around a set of policies for improving the alignment of standards, assessments, and incentives for students across grades 9 through 14. Flowing alongside these problem and solution streams, the political stream includes middle-class angst about a changing economy, business campaigns for increased science and technology capacity, and bipartisan, dynamic leadership for the 9–14 solutions, coming from former Virginia governor Mark Warner and the President himself.

The efforts described here are now in play to varying degrees in about 35 states, although some states still pay little attention to college readiness issues. That said, the traction of these approaches, supported through our organizations and the related work of others, such as Achieve, Inc., Jobs for the Future, and the Education Trust, has created a level of momentum seldom found around complex public policy issues.

DEFINING THE PROBLEM: A LACK OF COLLEGE READINESS

Before an idea is woven into the fabric of the public policy agenda, experts, politicians, and the general public must agree on both the nature of the problem and its urgency. A Supreme Court decision, state-level indicators of college readiness, and a growing body of empirical evidence about changing economics and demographics have helped decisionmakers and the public coalesce around a pressing national problem: the lack of college readiness among high school students.

In the 2003 Supreme Court decision *Gratz v. Bollinger*, Justice Sandra Day O'Connor called for colleges to gradually move away from race-based decisions in undergraduate admissions. This ruling forced the nation to look at the depth of its pipeline of college-prepared youth. Shortly before the *Bollinger* decision, Jay Greene, a prolific researcher, released simple, startling statistics from a fresh analysis of federal longitudinal data. Across the 50 states, less than 20 percent of all African American and Latino ninth graders graduated on time and ready for college. Greene has updated his 50-state analysis twice since his initial report, and, in each instance, the indicators underscore the significant gap between the nearly universal aspiration of high school students to attend college and their academic readiness to do so. His indicators have been cited across the ideological spectrum.

In the first years of this new century, policymakers awoke to the twin-barreled reality that economic and demographic changes necessitate dramatic increases in the number of adults with college credentials. On the economic front, empirical reports have prompted policymakers and opinion leaders to focus on America's international competitiveness, especially as fueled by innovation. Researchers at ACT, the Educational Testing Service, the U.S. Department of Education, the Manhattan Institute, Achieve, and the Fordham Foundation have presented solid evidence that the requirements for middle-class jobs are comparable to the skills needed to succeed in college. Also, educational advocates widely disseminated analyses of Bureau of Labor Statistics data, state standards, and work applications in high-growth industries and handed them directly to policymakers through channels such as the National Governors Association. The reports and analyses helped create a bipartisan consensus that the mission of high schools to prepare students for life after high school needed to change to a new common purpose: graduating all students ready for college.

READINESS IS THE GOAL: WHICH SOLUTIONS ARE ON THE PUBLIC AGENDA?

Once a particular problem definition gains traction among policy elites, a public agenda can be advanced based on a set of high-level solutions. In 2005, state and national policymakers agreed that too few high school graduates were ready for college. At the same time, state and federal policymakers agreed in principle on policy solutions articulated in two national reports issued by NGA and Achieve: *An Action Agenda for Improving America's High Schools* and *Getting It Done: Ten Steps to Improving America's High Schools.*

The *Action Agenda* was endorsed by the nation's governors and business and education leaders at the 2005 Summit on High Schools. Rather than providing a one-size-fits-all solution, the *Action Agenda* provides a concise set of "9–14" recommendations, and it advocates for system-wide changes to significantly improve the college-ready rate. Some of these changes include: restructuring how high school policies are made; how standards and assessments are benchmarked; how data and accountability systems are constructed; how high school educators and leaders are prepared and rewarded; and how secondary and postsecondary curricula and instruction can be blended to improve college completion rates.

Getting It Done, part of former NGA chairman Mark Warner's initiative, Redesigning the American High School, listed ten actionable steps for state policymakers, and it included a compendium guidebook that matched each solution with practical tips, such as enabling legislation, estimated costs, and evaluation results in states or districts with strong (or promising) track records implementing the policy. *Getting It Done* offered relatively low-cost, easy-to-implement solutions that also introduced the public and policymakers to the broader *Action Agenda.* Success on any of the steps in *Getting It Done* can help build the political will to advance the *Agenda*'s longer-term, more-systemic solutions.

These two reports set a common framework for policymakers, not just because they captured the need to be both broad and discrete with solutions, but because they became the starting point for teams of policymakers and educators to jump-start this agenda. The core recommendations became commitments that policymakers and business leaders agreed upon when they joined the American Diploma Project Network (now 29 states strong).

At that point, the greatest impetus drawing the attention of policymakers to the *Action Agenda* and *Getting It Done*'s solution set was the NGA Honor States Grant Program. With $23 million in direct, discretionary funds available to launch high school improvement projects (the only such funds currently available for statewide leadership), 35 states completed lengthy applications. A comprehensive state audit—known as the *Blueprint for an Action Agenda*—required state teams to evaluate their own state policies and data to assess the extent to which they were implementing the *Action Agenda* and *Getting It Done*'s Top Ten. The *Blueprint* helped states set priorities, and it gave all key decisionmakers a common understanding of which policies they needed to move first and what solutions their state would have to pursue to raise high schools' college-ready graduation rates.

GETTING TRACTION ON THE PUBLIC AGENDA

To judge progress across the country, Achieve's report, *Expectations Gap 2006*, provides a helpful cross-sectional analysis. Also helpful are the 35 states' responses to the *Blueprint for an Action Agenda*, as well as grant-reporting documentation submitted to the NGA Center for Best Practices. These sources point to four successful entry points that have been proven effective for states. These high-traction solutions either increase transparency around the need for universal college readiness (i.e., linked student unit record systems, stronger graduation requirements) or strengthen the incentives for student preparation (i.e., college-level learning in high school, hybrid financial aid programs).

These solutions have become public policy because they are concrete, actionable within a single legislative session, and build political ownership and public momentum for universal college readiness. Each strategy is logically and politically attractive as a starting point for the broader *Action Agenda*. And each of these high-traction solutions addresses a fundamental challenge—and therefore provides the real "win" that all policymakers need—while also helping stakeholders "own" future policy changes that will improve college readiness.

Increasing Transparency: Linked Student Unit Record Systems

The move to transparency—clearer, more-accurate information about student achievement (test scores) and student attainment (graduation rates)—has proven to be one of the most catalytic outcomes from the Summit/*Action Agenda* work, both nationally and within states. Education data have been notoriously slippery and wracked with ideological bias. When governors and business leaders were unable to get clear answers to their most basic questions, pressure built to bring to the field of education the technological innovations that increased business productivity. Simultaneously, Greene's graduation-rate data provided ample momentum for change: the first step to bringing the American high school into the 21st century would have to be data systems that tell the truth about system performance and allow for real evaluation of interventions. In the words of former Michigan governor John Engler, states needed "a system that knows where each student is every day and how they do over time." Not a sexy issue, but one that resonates with governors, business leaders, and the public. It also sets the stage for real improvement over time.

Increasing Transparency: Requiring the College Preparatory Curriculum for Graduation

Transparency in data, revealing low college readiness, has in turn created demand for broader access to college preparation. For state policymakers, requiring a college preparatory curriculum is an intuitive blunt instrument to broadly increase college readiness. Policymakers can easily argue that if all youth take a college prep curriculum, then all graduates are college ready. Graduation requirements (something real and measurable) can be changed within a single legislative session, and consequences can be phased in over four to six years.

Compared to changing college-ready standards (not a real change in the minds of the public) or calibrating high school assessments (necessitating deep collaboration between the K–12 and higher education sectors), this policy change is relatively easy to implement. And as *Getting It Done* notes, it can be relatively inexpensive to implement in the short term.

Since 2005, eleven states have enacted college-ready graduation requirements: Delaware, Indiana, Kentucky, Michigan, Minnesota, Mississippi, New Mexico, New York, Ohio, Oklahoma, and South Dakota. Sixteen states have plans to upgrade their requirements in the next few years. What remains to be seen is the expense of this strategy in terms of teacher professional development to teach higher-level courses and the student supports necessary to assure that all students meet the new standards.

This policy option is obviously more complicated in execution and requires commitment to increase student supports, yet it leads naturally to a more logical, linear, and accountable execution than other *Action Agenda* elements. For one, it reiterates the need for linked student unit record systems that contain student-level transcript information and college readiness scores. The policy also creates an incentive for stronger collaboration between K–12 and higher education. Finally, it illuminates very specific demands for teacher quality and capacity, especially in math and science.

Indiana was the first state after the *Action Agenda* was published to require that all students graduate with a college preparatory curriculum. Prior to a statewide mandate, Indiana voluntarily encouraged students to complete its Core 40 curriculum. A strong local control state, Indiana built statewide political will for the policy change with data. Ten years of voluntary implementation showed that Hoosier graduates were more likely to enroll and persist in and complete college if they had taken the Core 40 curriculum.

To achieve its goal, Indiana has identified gaps in the preparation and supply of high-quality math teachers. College presidents, provosts, and deans are voluntarily looking at aggressive ways to improve teacher training and the math teacher pipeline, and the state board of education is developing a statewide assessment policy that will include a college-ready assessment of all students. Most notably, stakeholders, from mayors to principals to parents, are coming together to describe what a redesigned high school needs to be to assure that all students graduate with the Core 40—ready for college. Furthermore, in 2006, the legislature mandated universal access to college-level learning, with a guarantee of free tuition for low-income students who ready themselves in redesigned high schools that blend grades 9–14. All of these activities are supported by Indiana's NGA Honor States Grant.[1]

Promoting Readiness: College-Level Learning Opportunities

Problem streams also converge around concerns of college access and affordability. The rising costs of college, along with demands for increased rigor in high schools, have led to considerable interest in "college in high school" opportunities, including dual enrollment, increased access to Advanced Placement courses, and more boldly, schools that actually blend high school and postsecondary, such as early college high schools.

These interventions are broadly appealing in a number of ways. For students, they allow the opportunity for acceleration and help build a sense of confidence and motivation to tackle college-level work. For parents, the options provide some potential relief from the ballooning costs of college. And for policymakers, they offer a compelling entry point for making fundamental changes regarding the purposes of high school: to create the mission of college readiness for all. This dynamic is most at play in North Carolina, where Governor Mike Easley's "Learn and Earn" initiative will launch early college high schools in every county. Each school will be tied to a specific career theme designed to prepare a high-quality workforce as a key economic driver for the state.

Promoting Readiness: Student Financial Assistance

Hybrid student financial aid programs, which serve needy students who graduate on time and prepare themselves for college, represent another solution that has gained traction across states. This policy is recommended in both the *Action Agenda* and *Getting It Done*. Since 2005, Colorado, Massachusetts, Michigan, and Maine have adopted this solution, and at least four more states are considering it (New York, North Carolina, Mississippi, and Washington). Notably, the federal government has authorized a new Academic Competitiveness Grants program, which provides bonus Pell Grants to students who complete a rigorous course of high school study. During 2006–07, a total of $790 million will be available for these new grants, with a total of $4.5 billion available over the next five years.

The Arkansas story of increasing college readiness—one that Achieve and NGA recognize as "front of the pack"—began with its Academic Challenge Scholarship. The Challenge Scholarship is available to any student whose family income is less than $60,000 and who completes a college preparatory curriculum: four units of English; four units of math, including Algebra I, Geometry, and Algebra II; three units of science with a lab; and three units of social studies. These students are guaranteed admission to most public colleges in the state. The scholarship pays up to $2,500 the first year, increases annually, and is renewable for a total of four years, provided the student maintains a cumulative college grade point average of 2.75 on a 4.00 scale.

Before Arkansas created the Challenge Scholarships, only 47 percent of entering freshmen took the college-core classes in high school. Today, 75 to 78 percent of college freshmen have taken the college-core classes. Students receiving scholarships are also much more likely to stay in college and complete a degree. Of the students from the Class of 2003 who went to college, only 68 percent have stayed in college so far. But 81 percent of those with Academic Challenge Scholarships have remained in school and are working toward their degrees.

Financial aid policy has given Arkansas entry to other important policy changes. The course work requirements of the Challenge Scholarship became the Smart Core curriculum, which will be required of all high school graduates beginning with the Class of 2010. Implementation of the mandatory Smart Core has required the governor and state education officials to address the end-of-course assessment and data-systems policies that are needed to increase the uniformity of course offerings throughout the state. It also requires constant attention to nurturing public will for universal college readiness through an active, student- and family-focused communications campaign. All of these longer-term strategies are supported by Arkansas's Honor States grant.

The multistate structure of the NGA Honor States work and Achieve's American Diploma Project are structured to foster both intrastate collaboration *and* competition—sharing what works and providing national political cover for bold state action, and also providing momentum for more rapid progress as chief executives vie with one another for policy achievements and economic development wins.

CONCLUSION

While a series of events have come together to create national and state momentum around refocusing the mission of high school to increasing college readiness, it is incumbent upon each state to translate its commitment into implementation and results. The trajectory of college readiness from problem to solution serves as a good proof point for how states and organizations can insert an issue into the public agenda, build public will, and generate the commitment and follow-through that generate results.

Below are several recommendations to help states and policymakers build momentum, increase commitment, and ensure enactment:

Set a bold, audacious, public goal such as college readiness for all. A publicly acknowledged and accepted goal encourages policymakers and other stakeholders to honor their commitments. Additionally, regular public reporting on progress makes the process transparent and facilitates community engagement and support, making implementation more effective and long-term.

Keep solutions concrete. The *Action Agenda* and *Getting It Done* outlined systemic yet discrete remedies that provided policymakers with options for reform that could be implemented within one legislative cycle. Both were part of larger, systemic frameworks, and small, concrete actions laid a foundation for future programmatic and policy changes.

Build consensus for a broader agenda and road map. NGA and Achieve worked with a variety of national partners to build consensus around the *Action Agenda* and the *Blueprint* and used them as the broader agenda and framework for high school redesign. They strengthened existing P–16 councils, leveraged the creation of new ones, organized field trips of teams of policymakers, and the creation of networks to build the foundation for buy-in at policymaking, implementation, and community levels.

"Find your Bono." National spokespeople can provide the spark that brings the political, policy, and solution streams together. Strong advocates can help to maintain national and state momentum *and* help to build the political will to implement some of the more-challenging reforms.

Finally—and perhaps this is both implicit and obvious—changes in policy and increased pressure from the public are necessary for fundamental change but by no means sufficient for changing teacher practice and effectiveness at the classroom level. Focused and aligned professional development (preparing teachers to execute at a new level) combined with data transparency (confirming that improved practices improve college readiness) will be the ultimate indicators of this agenda's success. We believe that these activities and their sequencing have laid the foundation for this transformation. Much work remains to be done.

6

Raising Expectations for Academic Achievement

Stan Jones

In the past, when many states, particularly in the Midwest, enjoyed a thriving manufacturing base, high-wage employment was readily available to workers whose relatively low level of skills was compensated by a willingness to work hard and perform physical labor. As a result, a low proportion of high school graduates pursued higher education. However, with dramatic shifts in the economic foundations of these states, efforts over the past two decades have focused—with much success—on increasing the number of students pursuing a college education.

Today, more Midwestern students are enrolling in collegiate programs than ever before as families recognize the importance of a college education to their children's future. Unfortunately, though, college graduation rates have not kept pace with the growth in enrollment. Only 55 percent of full-time students in Indiana seeking a bachelor's degree complete that degree within six years. The reality is that many students may leave college without the educational credentials that lead to better jobs and higher wages. As a natural progression, most state-level discussions are shifting the dialogue and their efforts toward expanding college access specifically in ways that also lead to increased college success. One of the most prominent discussion topics is the rigor of the high school curriculum for all students.

The U.S. Department of Education study, *The Toolbox Revisited: Paths to Degree Completion from High School through College*, showed that a rigorous high school curriculum is the best ticket to success in college (Adelman, 1999). Based on a longitudinal study of a representative group of students from the 1992 high school class, *The Toolbox Revisited* found that 90 percent of students who took a demanding academic program in high school went on to earn a college degree by the year 2000.

Yet only a handful of states require high school students to pursue advanced courses in core subjects like math and English in order to graduate. According to *Closing the Expectations Gap*, a recent survey of all 50 states, more than two-thirds of the states report that they are aligning their high school standards with college and workplace expectations (Achieve, 2006). However, the report, conducted by Achieve, Inc., an organization set up by the nation's governors and business leaders, indicates that only five states have completed that process. Similarly, 20 states are moving to enact graduation requirements that include four years of rigorous English and mathematics through at least Algebra II.

Even with these efforts, there are still many students who simply are unsuccessful in their educational pursuits. Nationally, out of every 100 ninth graders, 32 will not graduate high school, and 82 will not graduate college. In nearly every state, students can do all that is asked of them to earn a high school diploma yet still be unprepared for success in college or work. Now more than ever, a state's economic vitality depends on an educated workforce. Success will only be realized if the state's entire education system is geared to prepare and enable all students to achieve at high levels.

The states moving the farthest and the fastest to close the expectations gap are those that have effectively overcome the traditional barriers between the K–12 and postsecondary worlds. If we expect high schools to better prepare young people, we need to be clear about what it takes to succeed in higher education and communicate it widely.

In Indiana, we have made huge strides in this respect by strengthening four key areas: expectations, alignment, accountability, and incentives. As commissioner of higher education, I was among the many stakeholders who strongly advocated for significant efforts to change how we prepared our young people for college and work. Our experience points to a number of recommendations about how states can bring key leaders together to initiate change.

Mobilize key state leaders

For Indiana, the vehicle for change was enhanced by the creation of the Education Roundtable. Composed of equal representation from the business and education communities, the roundtable is cochaired by the governor and the superintendent of public instruction. Key to its success has been bringing together all stakeholders—some of whom have been in direct opposition to one another on issues related to education and other areas—to collaboratively work for the best interests of students and the state. Recognized by state legislation, this bipartisan business/education coalition has made improving high school academic achievement a central focus of its current P–16 reform initiative.

The roundtable includes two primary groups of stakeholders in education. The first group is comprised of individuals representing the K–12 and higher education communities (university presidents, faculty, teachers, principals, superintendents, school boards). They must buy in to and help develop the standards and assessments. The second group includes individuals or organizations that can influence the general assembly, the public, and the education community: key legislators, the governor, the state superintendent, and leaders from the state chamber of commerce, the state manufacturing association, and the building trade unions.

Align high school requirements with college expectations

In most states, the focus on raising high school graduation requirements has emerged primarily to address economic concerns. In Indiana, business and education leaders recognized more than a decade ago that the state and its citizens would face severe economic hardship unless more young people were ready for college and the demands of the global workplace. Officials were aware that low-skilled, high-paying jobs in manufacturing would become extinct, and that the middle-class dream of finding good work with good wages was on the decline. We also recognized that the "new economy" jobs we wanted to bring to Indiana demanded a workforce with greater skills and knowledge—advanced math, as well as science skills, mastery of writing, and the ability to analyze and communicate effectively.

As a result, Indiana introduced the "Core 40" college preparatory curriculum—a statewide initiative. Even though the curriculum was voluntary for students, the percentage of Indiana young people graduating from high school with the "Core 40" diploma skyrocketed from 13 percent to 65 percent in ten years. Over that same period, the state moved from 34th to 10th in the nation in the percentage of high school seniors going to college.

Core 40 is not a new invention: It is a classic college prep curriculum that every public high school has offered for at least the last four decades. The college prep curriculum was expected of students when we sent one-third of the high school seniors on to college, and it is what should be expected for the two-thirds we now send to college. The key component is math through Algebra II, preferably including a rigorous, senior-year math course. Three years of science are required, including biology and physics or chemistry, as are four years of English, including speech, writing, and literature. A foreign language is recommended but not required to lessen the resistance to a curriculum required for all students.

Make the college prep curriculum the default curriculum for all high school students

A rigorous academic curriculum is the single most important factor in determining a student's success in college.[1] Too many students are counseled away from a college curriculum based on the assumption that they are not college material. This becomes a self-fulfilling prophecy, without even giving the student a chance to succeed. Rather than have students opt into a challenging college preparatory curriculum, automatically enroll them into this important preparation. This communicates a very clear expectation for what courses students should take to prepare for life after high school, and it removes many of the obstacles that students encounter in seeking access to those courses.

After 12 years of offering Core 40 as a voluntary curriculum, the Indiana legislature made it the default curriculum beginning with students entering high school in the 2007–08 academic year. It is now assumed that students will "opt in" to Core 40. In the future, to opt out will require a parent/student/counselor conference; all three parties must meet and agree to an opt-out decision. This effort helps Indiana families of first-generation college-goers understand what is required for success, and it empowers them to raise expectations for their children.

Align the standards to the high school courses and assess student performance

Aligning what goes on in the classroom to state-mandated standards is a key to providing consistency, quality, and rigor to courses. In Indiana, the goal is to be "clear, concise, and jargon-free" in the state standards—and to provide teachers with examples and definitions of how to align their course work to those standards.

The Education Trust, the Fordham Foundation, Achieve, ACT, and the College Board have provided critical assistance to our efforts. Independent third parties bring credibility to the dialogue, which strengthens participation and acceptance from a variety of key stakeholders. Additionally, the specific knowledge brought by outside experts elevates opportunities for enhancing the proficiency and creativity of the state-level experts.

Achieve, in particular, has been instrumental in our success. Indiana is one of 29 states working with Achieve's American Diploma Project on aligning expectations, data systems, and accountability across K–12, higher education, and business.

Another approach that puts great education theories to a real test is the use of end-of-course assessments. States should assess high school students before the senior year to provide signals and additional supports that ensure students graduate college-ready. End-of-course assessments allow a state to determine whether students have acquired the standards in key college preparatory courses. Not surprisingly, Indiana's end-of-course tests in Algebra II and eleventh-grade English have revealed widely uneven proficiency levels across the state, as well as unacceptably poor performance. These early indicators provide additional opportunities for schools to ensure that students have the necessary skills required for success in college.

Align high school exit standards with college entrance standards

The problem is not with high schools alone. College faculty members and administrators regularly complain about the lack of student preparation, but their institutions continue to accept unprepared students and to enroll them in remedial courses—basically high school algebra and English classes. One of the hardest challenges Indiana faced in implementing the Core 40 was getting higher education to actually use the curriculum as a minimum college admission standard. This first happened voluntarily and then by law for all public four-year colleges and universities in the state.

Although the higher education community enthusiastically supported Core 40 as the high school exit requirement, it took time and persuasion for them to see the wisdom of adopting Core 40 as a minimum course requirement entrance standard. Such alignment is critical to ensuring consistency across the educational sectors.

Align financial aid with rigorous course-taking

Cost continues to be a factor in college participation. Approximately 47 percent of graduates from families in the bottom income quartile will continue immediately to college (compared to 85 percent of graduates from families in the top income quartile) (Mortenson, 2006). However, financial aid alone will not guarantee college success. Indiana has enhanced its need-based financial aid policy by promising additional assistance to low-income students if they graduate with the Core 40, and even more aid if they do so with Academic Honors.

Not only are Core 40 students enrolling and succeeding in college at higher rates, but the combination of financial aid incentives and the required enrollment in Core 40 has also allowed us to reach more and more first-generation students. Beginning with the 2006–07 school year, the federal government has enacted a similar program called the Academic Competitiveness Grants, designed to provide low-income college freshmen and sophomores who have completed a "rigorous" high school program with grants of $750 to $1,300 a year.

In 1990, Indiana also created the 21st Century Scholars program as a way of raising the educational aspirations of low- and moderate-income families. Income-eligible seventh and eighth graders who enroll in the program, fulfill a pledge of good citizenship to the state, graduate from high school, and maintain a 2.0 grade point average, are guaranteed the cost of four years of tuition at any participating college or university in Indiana. The first group of Scholars headed to college in 1995, and since then, nearly 15,000 Scholars have received scholarships. In addition, Scholars receive a host of wraparound support services (e.g., tutoring, mentoring, academic counseling) in both high school and college. A recent study conducted by the Indiana Education Policy Center indicates that ninth-grade students participating as 21st Century Scholars were significantly more likely than non-Scholars to enroll in college. Of the 2,202 students in the study, nearly 80 percent enrolled in an Indiana college within one year of high school graduation (St. John, Musoba, Simmons, & Chung, 2002).

Provide incentives for students to take advantage of college preparation tools

In addition to ensuring that students take a rigorous college prep curriculum, a number of supplementary tools can assist both students and schools. For instance, an ongoing Indiana program pays the test fees for students who take the PSAT. When it was first implemented, the goal was to use this program to supplement other efforts aimed at increasing early planning for and access to college. As a result of this support, about 60 percent of each graduating class now takes the PSAT prior to graduation. As expected, the percentage of Indiana students taking the SAT has also increased, to about 62 percent.

Recently, the College Board developed tools that enable schools to utilize the PSAT as a way to identify students who would be well served by Advanced Placement programs. Such efforts feed directly into another of Indiana's incentive-based programs, one that funds AP tests taken in mathematics and science. Previously, Indiana's participation in the AP program had been dismal. Since 2000, Indiana has experienced an 80 percent increase in AP test-takers and an 89 percent increase in tests taken. AP tests are often an indicator of a state's success with its best and brightest students; just as important, they can qualify students to receive college credit dependent on the scores received.

Create a deliberate and ongoing communications effort

Students and families need a consistent message from business, higher education, and K–12 about what is expected. Paramount to Indiana's efforts to improve both college-going and success in college has been explaining the necessity for a drastic shift in the state's high school academic program. Most of the state's high school and college counselors—and many parents—believed that some students did not have the skills to succeed in Core 40. We argued that students who were not part of this curriculum were inevitably on a track toward low wages and dead-end jobs. We explained that young people would be more engaged in school and motivated to learn if high schools wiped out low-level remedial academic courses that reinforced low expectations and contributed to behavioral problems. Over the past 12 years, as the percentage of students receiving Core 40 diplomas has grown to 65 percent, resistance and skepticism have given way to support and enthusiasm.

Publicly report progress and take greater responsibility for the performance of the students

It is essential to inform the public on how well high schools are preparing students for college and how well colleges do with the students they admit. Higher education should report back to high schools on how their graduates perform in collegiate courses, so they can use that information to strengthen the academic experience of the next class of students. Similarly, states should publicly report remediation, persistence, and completion rates for all higher education institutions and work to improve these rates.

In Indiana, we have advanced our public reporting of K–12 and higher education indicators of progress. However, we have yet to realize the goal of a systematic approach for linking indicators across the systems. New efforts, such as an electronic high school transcript initiative, hold great promise in making such connections and cross-sector reporting possible.

Drastic changes must be made if the next generation of students is to succeed. Continued transformation into a global economy demands that states prepare students for a highly competitive market. The reason is not only to link between education and high-quality jobs; all state stakeholders have to recognize that higher levels of education can elevate quality of life as well. By investing early in a young person's life, a state is well positioned to cultivate long-term benefits.

PART III

Alignment and Integration of Standards, Assessments, and Curriculum across 9–14

In building a standards-based education system, educators have faced a hard reality: It takes only an eighth-grade level of achievement to pass most high school "exit" exams. Despite improvements in the K–12 system, then, large numbers of high school graduates are not "college- and work-ready." In response, a number of states have joined the American Diploma Project led by Achieve, an organization formed by governors and business leaders in 1996 to raise academic standards and achievement levels. Here, Christine Tell and Michael Cohen describe the challenges and successes of the ADP in guiding the 29 states in the network as they analyze their achievement gaps in English and math, align their English and math standards to Achieve's benchmarks, and undergo quality reviews of their improved standards. For the ADP states, the step after alignment is to embed the standards in high school curriculum.

As Tell and Cohen note, for employers, ADP's standard-setting is a particular struggle because the skills required in the workplace often take an applied form that does not line up with academic disciplines. Picking up on this issue, Anthony P. Carnevale describes the potential of the U.S. Department of Labor's O*Net data set to provide fine-grained analyses of the knowledge, skills, abilities, and work values related to a wide range of careers. He argues that this new data could "connect the dots" between K–16 education and the real demands of work.

David Conley describes a second approach to alignment: Standards for Success worked with faculty and administrators from across the country to specify expectations in entry-level general education courses at U.S. research universities. From this work, Conley established not only course content descriptions and standards, but also habits of mind and dispositions that distinguish the high school learning environment from that of college. In his essay, he goes beyond alignment to propose a new academic sequence of study for the senior year of high school and into the first year of college that would effectively integrate grades 12 and 13 at the classroom level.

The two final pieces describe what have come to be called "early assessment programs"—tests that give high school sophomores or juniors and their teachers prognoses of students' readiness for college-level work, accompanied by information on areas needing improvement. Bridget Long and Erin Riley look at Oklahoma, Ohio, and California, which illustrate three options for implementing early placement testing. David Spence describes the California Early Assessment Program (EAP), of which he was a key architect. EAP embeds items in California's standard tests for eleventh-grade English and Algebra II to measure students' readiness to begin nonremedial work in the California State University System. It also fosters professional partnerships between college teachers and high school faculty—relationships required to design an integrated system.

7

Alignment of High School Expectations to College and Work

Christine Tell and Michael Cohen

On the surface, it would seem to be a simple conversation: align the expectations for students exiting high school with the expectations for their entry into the first year of college and work. The result might be a consensus document that could create an understanding of what students need to know and be able to do in order to succeed in their next steps after high school. In some states, these conversations have actually occurred (though rarely statewide) over the past 10 years, under the K–16 and/or P–20 banners among various groups of K–12 educators and postsecondary faculty, along with an occasional employer. However, these conversations alone, though worthy starting points for alignment, have proved insufficient to "double the numbers" of students prepared to meet the demands of college and work. And they certainly have not been systematic enough to allow any state to sequence curricula and assessments into a coherent, integrated 9–14 continuum.

Since the National Education Summit in February 2005, a group of states belonging to the American Diploma Project (ADP) Network formed by Achieve, Inc., has taken the alignment conversation into the statewide arena of public policy.[1] Entry into this arena requires the commitment and participation of a state's governor and its leadership of all three sectors—K–12, higher education, and employers. The result is cross-sector, co-owned *Academic Standards for College and Work* that ultimately align high school standards, assessments, and courses required for graduation with college placement tests, course descriptions, and student outcomes for first-year credit-bearing course work—and with requirements for entry-level employment.

For the ADP Network states, the alignment of high school expectations with the demands of college and work is the first step in a public policy action agenda that has the goal of preparing *all* students for postsecondary education and employment, and holding high schools and postsecondary institutions accountable for their success.

THE CASE FOR ALIGNMENT

When the nation's governors gathered in 2005 for the National Education Summit, cosponsored by Achieve and the National Governors Association, they were confronted with a litany of data that documented the failure of the American high school to prepare students for the demands of college and work.

- Three-quarters of high school graduates go on to college, yet nearly a third immediately require remediation because they lack basic reading, writing, and math skills.
- One out of every four students enrolled in a four-year college and nearly half of all community college students do not return after the first year, and far fewer earn two- or four-year degrees in a timely fashion.
- Surveys of recent high school graduates reveal that some 40 percent of those in college, and 45 percent of those in the workforce, recognize they have significant gaps in the skills they need to succeed (Peter D. Hart Research Associates, 2005).

Achieve findings from five years of research as part of the American Diploma Project further confirmed Bill Gates's opening Summit declaration that "our high schools are obsolete."[2] Specifically, Achieve learned from colleges and employers across states that the expectations for what high school students must learn do not reflect the knowledge and skills they will need to succeed in college and work. What it takes to earn a high school diploma is largely disconnected from what it takes for graduates to compete beyond high school—either in the college classroom or in the workplace. Further, because academic standards for high school students do not reflect college admissions and placement requirements, students often get conflicting signals from high schools and colleges about what constitutes adequate preparation.[3]

The ADP Benchmarks in English and mathematics that emerged from this research represent a convergence around the core knowledge and skills that both colleges and employers require. They are also ambitious, but colleges and employers regarded these rigorous benchmarks as essential skills for *all* high school graduates. In mathematics, the ADP Benchmarks reflect content typically taught in Algebra I, Algebra II, and geometry, as well as data analysis and statistics. The English benchmarks demand strong oral and written communications skills that are staples in college classrooms and most 21st-century jobs. They also contain analytic and reasoning skills formerly associated with advanced honors courses in high schools.

When the ADP findings were published in 2004, no state required all students to take Algebra II to graduate, and few state high school assessments measured the essential skills suggested in the ADP Benchmarks.[4] Clearly, the high school diploma has lost meaning as a symbol of preparation for life beyond high school, and states are facing an imperative for post–high school preparation that produces results. In a word, states must take policy actions that *align* their high school exit standards with the demands of college and work so that students can:

- enter into credit-bearing course work in two- or four-year colleges, without the need for remediation and with a strong chance for earning credit toward their program or degree; and
- gain entry-level positions in quality job and career pathways, which often require further education and training.

THE ALIGNMENT INSTITUTES: A COLLABORATIVE PROCESS

Twenty-nine states, representing more than half of all public school students in the United States, joined the ADP Network between 2005 and the end of 2006. From these, thirteen ADP Network states committed to a 10- to 15-month formal process of alignment. Cohort I states (Arkansas, Colorado, Georgia, Louisiana, Massachusetts, and Pennsylvania) began in November 2005, and Cohort II states (Idaho, Maryland, Michigan, Minnesota, North Carolina, New Jersey, and Oklahoma) in February 2006.

Prior to entering this formal process of alignment, many of these states had included college faculty and employers on committees that draft K–12 standards, and some states had held focus groups to see how well draft standards comport with the real-world demands of college and work. None, however, had conducted deliberate, thorough analyses or scrutinized the extent to which their current or emerging state standards aligned to these demands.

Leaders in these 13 states represent K–12, postsecondary, and employers, and they echo the same needs and anticipated benefits of collaboration. Achieve establishes the sequence of events, sets benchmarks for products, provides data and analyses, develops models and tools, organizes activities, facilitates conversations, shares best practices, and provides external checks to ensure quality results. For its part, each state forms an Alignment Team that uses the strategies and tools learned in three "Alignment Institute" sessions to work with colleagues in its state to produce *Academic Standards for College and Work* in English and mathematics that are:

- adopted, endorsed, or otherwise recognized by state postsecondary institutions as defining the knowledge and skills necessary for placement into credit-bearing courses;
- adopted by the state board of education or other appropriate governing body as defining the knowledge and skills in math and English that all students should meet by the end of high school; and,
- verified or endorsed by employers and the business community as constituting skills necessary to enter and succeed in the 21st-century workplace.

States also commit to incorporating these standards into a range of policies and practices, such as high school graduation requirements, course descriptions, high school assessments, and postsecondary placement policies and assessments.

The first of three institute sessions began with an analysis provided by Achieve. A side-by-side comparison of the state's high school standards with the ADP Benchmarks allowed states to begin identifying gaps in expectations from high school to college and work. Each State Alignment Team also identified gaps in student performance in math and English, using data provided by the College Board and ACT, as well as state assessment and National Assessment of Education Progress results compiled by Achieve. Teams began to work with colleagues back in their states to draft *Academic Standards for College and Work* in math and English. As they returned to subsequent institutes, they reported their progress and shared effective strategies and tools.

Achieve conducted an in-depth Quality Review of each state's draft, asking panels of national content experts to provide feedback on the relative rigor, focus, coherence, specificity, clarity, and measurability of the standards compared to the ADP Benchmarks. State teams then planned statewide outreach to postsecondary and employers to communicate results and solicit input to ensure that the standards are benchmarked to ADP's national perspective and that they also reflect the unique needs of the state.

While all state teams "graduated" at the third institute with a "diploma" for having completed the technical assistance portion of the institutes, Achieve continues to work with state teams to refine standards. A second Quality Review, already completed in some states but not in others, provides final external validation and paves the way for adoption by the state board of education and, in some cases, the governing body for higher education.

Throughout this process, Achieve has been building recognition among its state teams that moving from adoption of standards to implementation of policies governing high school graduation requirements and placement in credit-bearing college course work will require yet another round of planning and deeper work in partnerships between high school and postsecondary leaders and faculty.

RESULTS AND EMERGING LESSONS

Presently, 10 of the 13 states have produced *Academic Standards for College and Work* and completed the Quality Review I process. Four additional state boards of education adopted college- and work-ready standards linked to graduation requirements.[5] For all 13 states, we anticipate completing the alignment process, from our initial side-by-side analysis to board adoption, by November 2007.

While Achieve continues to work with states to produce results in this alignment initiative, lessons are emerging:

Unified leadership at the state level matters.

In states with a public postsecondary system, the leadership and staff (boards of regents and/or state higher education executive officer or CEO) can unify faculty vision, coalesce engagement efforts, and implement consistent statewide policies. In Georgia, for example, every public two- and four-year institution has standing faculty committees that have actively participated in the drafting and review of the *Georgia College and Work Readiness Standards in Mathematics and English*. In Louisiana, an alignment team representing two- and four-year postsecondary institutions worked with academic deans across all campuses to vet their proposed alignment of high school standards with levels of performance required for success in first-year college courses. In Indiana, postsecondary leaders not only helped shape the high school standards, but they all now require students to take the Core 40 curriculum (which is based on those standards) for admission to four-year colleges.

These are promising signs, but historically postsecondary institutions and their leaders have been unable to sustain partnerships with secondary educators; the benefits have not been self-evident. The states noted above are on the leading edge of acknowledging the benefits of the 9–14 or K–16 approach.

In a few states, the governor has made the alignment of expectations across K–12, postsecondary, and the workforce a state priority that in effect, mandates state-level K–16 conversations. In Colorado, then-governor Bill Owens signed an executive order creating the Colorado Education Alignment Council in 2005. Co-chaired by the commissioners of K–12 and higher education and a business leader, this council was charged with a major review of high school and college academic standards. Their recommendations include specific remedies for closing the "expectations gap," so that high school graduates will be prepared for entry into both postsecondary and the workforce.[6]

In Michigan, the Lieutenant Governor's Commission on Higher Education & Economic Growth, created by Governor Jennifer Granholm in 2004, brought together key leaders, including university and college presidents, lawmakers, state department directors, and other individuals representing business, labor, recent college graduates, skilled trades, and K–12 education. This commission was charged with developing a plan to double the number of Michigan residents who obtain college degrees. Final recommendations, later enacted into legislation, included the development of rigorous high school standards, graduation requirements, and college-ready assessments aligned with the "competencies necessary for post-secondary success and readiness for work."[7]

Whether collaboration is voluntary or mandated, alignment efforts tend to move forward faster when state-level leaders become publicly engaged in initiatives that recognize the critical need for high school graduates to be prepared for college and work.

Employers are willing to engage in results-driven alignment activities.

Most ADP State Alignment Teams struggle with finding an appropriate way to engage their employers in the standards-setting process. Unlike postsecondary institutions, businesses and business organizations have expectations that may not relate well to academic standards. Employers can describe the skills young people need to be successful in their workplaces, but those skills often take a more-applied form than that of academic standards.

The states that have been most successful have found a way to elicit samples of workplace tasks that show the levels of reading, writing, and mathematics problem solving that employers demand. The Maryland Business Roundtable launched a website for high school students that illustrates the state's rigorous standards by identifying the academic skills, course work, training, and tasks that promote success in a wide range of entry-level quality jobs. The Colorado Alignment Team (coordinated by the Fund for Colorado's Future) launched a statewide employer outreach effort using local chambers of commerce. Surveys of the importance of a subset of ADP skills in math and English in entry-level, high-quality jobs were collected, along with sample resumes and typical tasks. This provided a rich data bank for policymakers to consider more-rigorous graduation requirements and for department of education staff to revise high school standards.

The *Academic Standards for College and Work* must be embedded in the high school curriculum (specifically, in descriptions of courses required for graduation) to ensure that college and employer expectations are addressed.

Quality Reviews by Achieve content experts indicate that state standards may be typically lacking in one or more areas valued by both employers and faculty in English (logical reasoning, working in teams, reading informational text, oral presentation, workplace writing and research) and in mathematics (advanced reasoning, tasks requiring more than procedural knowledge, and data and statistics).

While high school senior English courses are heavily literature-based, entering college freshmen encounter writing composition as their first required course. Many high school seniors complete their math requirement prior to the twelfth grade and are unprepared for entering college algebra, even though they completed the sequence required for high school graduation. State Alignment Teams are now beginning to align or embed their *Academic Standards for College and Work* into model course descriptions that may be both traditional (e.g., Algebra I, II, geometry, data and statistics) or integrated (e.g., Integrated Math I–IV) and include capstone projects or studies that are intended to prepare students for the rigor of postsecondary and the workplace. These activities point to future work for all states, and suggest that the course and curricular sequencing that David Conley proposes will be most effective in states that have participated in ADP.[8]

CONCLUSION

The alignment conversation has changed from 2004 when the ADP benchmarks proposed a new, more-rigorous consensus around college- and work readiness. Today, eleven states have put into place policies that require students to meet similar rigorous benchmarks for high school graduation: Arkansas, Delaware, Indiana, Kentucky, Michigan, Minnesota, Mississippi, New York, Oklahoma, South Dakota, and Texas.

By building cross-sector consensus about the knowledge and skills that prepare students for college and work, states in the Achieve Alignment Institutes are learning that they are more likely to ensure support for more-rigorous standards, assessments, high school graduation requirements, and postsecondary placement policies, which are needed to make the vision of college- and work-ready students a reality.

8

All One System

The Promise of O*Net

Anthony P. Carnevale

Since 1983, when *A Nation at Risk* equated educational adequacy with national competitiveness and individual employability, rhetoric has justified reform in the interest of career objectives. However, with the emergence of education beyond high school as the dominant arbiter of economic opportunity, the interests of both efficiency and equity call for greater alignment between education and occupational knowledge, skills, abilities, interests, and values.

In the past quarter century, we have moved from "high school for all" to "college for all" as the prerequisite for middle-class jobs, and it is now widely accepted that access to college begins in preschool. Yet over the same period, it has become equally apparent that we cannot afford to continue to satisfy the growing demand for education efficiently or fairly by simply adding more years of universal schooling at both ends of the education pipeline. Thus far, the response to the core problems of efficiency and equity in education has been broad support for aligning teaching and learning with education standards, but largely ignored has been the alignment of education and career opportunities.

Today, this alignment seems to be an obvious step to take along the path of reform. Moreover, it also seems intuitively obvious that if we could better understand how teaching and learning in school relate to the diverse kinds of knowledge, skills, abilities, values, and interests that lead to successful careers, we could open up career pathways to the diverse talents of our youth, thereby expanding choices and distributing economic opportunity more equitably.

Granted, the education system and the labor market have been gradually aligning since industrialization began, yet there is still a profound disconnect between academic content and the occupational knowledge, skills, abilities, values, and interests required for economic success. As a result, there are two separate labor markets in America, paralleling the separation of content taught in the K–16 system from the actual competencies required in workplaces: (1) a labor market in experienced workers rewards proven *competence* as observed by employers and peers; and (2) a labor market in entry-level workers uses education as the marker of *potential* for further learning on the job.

America's education system and labor markets are likely to remain separate as the developmental needs of individuals and employers simultaneously expand and diverge. The demand for entry-level preparation will continue to grow as learning requirements escalate on the job in response to the blurring pace of economic and technological change. More-robust knowledge, skills, and abilities will be required for individuals to get a fast start up the learning curve in entry-level jobs, to keep up on the job, and to expedite transitions from job to job. Professionalism will need to take new forms as individuals pursue occupational interests and protect occupational values initially nurtured in educational institutions.

As a result, we will obviously need strong bridges between education and work, but the heavy construction will have to occur on the education side of the gap. Governments, educators, and individuals will have to take increasing responsibility for providing students with occupational knowledge, skills, and abilities, as well as for nurturing occupational interests and values as employers continue to recede as the incubators for developing human capital.[1]

THE MISMATCH BETWEEN CURRICULA AND COMPETENCIES

The most profound disconnect of schools from careers lies in the apparent discontinuity between academic disciplines and 21st-century occupational competencies. This evident lack of fit raises obvious questions as to whether the current curriculum, which is the focus of hard-won reform in American high schools, is the most effective way to deliver those competencies for all students. To begin with, the current college prep curriculum does not provide an obvious transition to the more-applied focus of postsecondary education and training. In postsecondary education, the vast majority of students avoid the academic silos of math, science, and the humanities in favor of curricula that have a stronger career focus, with the business major leading the pack.[2]

For a very long time, employers have asserted that jobs actually require a complex set of competencies that are neither reflected in academic credentials nor nurtured through academic pedagogy. Until very recently, our ability to observe and measure these skills and their distribution among occupations has been largely anecdotal. All of that has changed with the recent completion of the O*Net database, which allows us to measure the value of these competencies, and to at least begin a dialogue over the appropriate roles of educational institutions and employers in providing core 21st-century competencies.

LINKING EDUCATION AND OCCUPATIONS: A STATE-OF-THE-ART TOOL

The O*Net database specifies the full set of occupational competencies required for success in particular occupations and related clusters of similar careers. Operated by the National O*Net Consortium and funded by the U. S. Department of Labor, the database includes occupational knowledge, skill, abilities, work values, work contexts, and work interests, as well as key performances (tasks and activities). Its primary use so far has been as a counseling tool for career planning, delivered online through a user-friendly interface.[3] With the exception of occupational knowledge, though, very few of the O*Net competency domains look like words one finds in a course catalog or a K–12 content model.

O*Net's occupational data are anchored in a tripartite set of cognitive competencies: knowledge, skill, and ability.

- *Knowledge classifications* are content domains familiar to educators, from math and the sciences, to the humanities, to knowledge in more-applied disciplines like accounting.
- *Skills* are competencies that promote further learning. They are divided into content, processing, and problem-solving skills. Content skills are fundamental skills needed to acquire more specific skills in an occupation. These include reading comprehension, active listening, speaking, writing, math, and science. Processing skills are procedures that contribute to the more-rapid acquisition of knowledge and skill. These include critical thinking, active learning, learning strategies, and monitoring. Problem-solving skills involve the identification of complex problems and related information required to develop and evaluate options and implement solutions.
- *Abilities* are defined as enduring and developed personal attributes that influence performance at work. In the parlance of education psychology, these closely approximate "aptitudes." O*Net divides abilities broadly into creativity, innovation, mathematical reasoning, and oral and written expression. Each of these broad abilities is subdivided into component elements. For example, innovative abilities include fluency of ideas, problem sensitivity, deductive reasoning, and inductive reasoning.

In addition to the cognitive competencies, O*Net classifies competencies that are tied to personality traits that are markers for success in particular occupations. These key competencies are work style, work values, and interest.

- *Work style* is a personal characteristic that can affect how well someone does a job. Some of these characteristics are creativity, leadership, analytical thinking, attention to detail, integrity, social orientation, stress tolerance, teamwork, independence, and adaptability.
- *Work values* are individual preferences for work outcomes. Important outcomes for individuals include recognition, achievement, working conditions, security, advancement, authority, social status, responsibility, and compensation.
- *Interest* is defined as individual preferences for work environment. Interests are classified as realistic, artistic, investigative, social, enterprising, and conventional.

The O*Net data also measure particular work contexts in which occupational work and learning occurs.

- *Work context* is defined as the physical and social factors that influence the nature of a job. These factors are interpersonal relationships, physical work conditions, and structural job characteristics. Interpersonal relationships refer to competencies required in contact and interaction with others and the ability for group work. The level and intensity of interpersonal relations is high in jobs like doctors, dentists, firefighters, teachers, barbers, and policemen.
- *The physical working condition* refers to one's physical environment.
- *Structural job characteristics* refer to the responsibility and level of independence one has on the job.

The O*Net database includes tasks and activities associated with individual occupations and occupational clusters. Tasks and activities represent key performances that combine occupational knowledge, skills, abilities, values, and interests. As such, they point toward authentic teaching opportunities and key opportunities for assessment. Once specified, these broad competencies can be taught and assessed more self-consciously and, hence, more equitably.

CONNECTING THE DOTS

Connecting the dots between the K–16 education system and "the real demands of work" is more easily said than done. There are notable exceptions, especially in vocational and professional education, but as a rule, school and work in the United States are characterized by separate experiences, separate curricula, and separate modes of learning. Academic and occupational learning also tend to be separated sequentially. There is a tendency to provide general education first, then to put an occupational point at the end of each student's academic pencil, increasingly in the postsecondary years. By way of comparison, the European apprentice system mixes academic and applied learning.

However, while linking education and careers is a complex and ongoing project, the first steps are actually easy. We can already link student records and employment records, as a handful of states have done. Student records tied to wage records, available for all workers since in the 1930s, tell us about the employment and earnings returns to education programs, all the way down to the individual course and instructor level. Eleven states already link student records and wage records, at least in part.

On that foundation, the development of a deeper alignment and transparency between education curricula and competencies can begin with O*Net, which can throw open the mysterious black box at the interface between education and the economy.

While O*Net cannot tell us exactly how to teach key competencies, it can:

- track career competencies back to academic curricula and translate particular academic disciplines into applied forms as career competencies;
- measure the extent to which career competencies are learned on the job or in school, and track the transferability of competencies and academic knowledge among different occupations;
- show how academic knowledge and competencies combine as recipes for success in particular occupations and occupational clusters;
- calculate the earnings returns from academic knowledge and career competencies;
- show the current and projected demand for academic knowledge and career competencies; and
- provide key tasks and activities in occupations that are the true venues for learning a particular set of competencies and the true basis for assessing mastery of any combined set of competencies.

O*Net could become the golden spike that joins education and career tracks. As such, it would serve to clarify and expedite transitions from school to work, as well as transitions form job to job. Tools like O*Net can also be used to promote upward mobility. With O*Net, we can begin to understand the full set of knowledge domains, skills, abilities, values, and interests that lead to career choices. Once these are understood, we can develop these competencies across the full range of economic classes.

Of course, education cannot succeed in meeting its cultural and civic responsibilities simply by providing foot soldiers for the advancing armies of global capitalism. But the O*Net data suggest that it is a mistake to view the economic, cultural, and civic value of education as a zero-sum game. The knowledge, skills, abilities, values, and interests required for 21st-century careers codified in O*Net are broad and diverse enough to serve the educators' cultural and civic missions as well as individual employability.

9

Challenges in the Transition from High School to College

David Conley

The past 15 years have seen the proliferation of initiatives and research designed to connect high school and college more directly. These activities include studies of ways to: identify entry-level college knowledge and skills; reorganize high schools to better prepare students to succeed in college; better integrate grades 9–14; and show how colleges can support improved alignment with high schools. This research has produced significant findings related to improving the transition from high school to college, and these findings point to a number of ways that high schools and colleges can improve the alignment between the secondary and postsecondary education sectors.

INITIAL EFFORTS AT SYSTEMS ALIGNMENT

With the development of state high school content standards and assessments, interest emerged briefly in the mid-1990s in the use of proficiencies developed by college faculty to determine who gets into college (Conley, 1996). Higher education systems in Oregon (Conley, 1994), Wisconsin (Competency-Based Admission Pilot Project, 1995), Nebraska (University of Nebraska, 1993), and New York (City University of New York, 1992) developed performance statements that specified the knowledge and skills incoming freshmen needed if they were to succeed in entry-level courses.

However, few of these statements had a substantive effect on state standards-based high school reforms. States never adapted their secondary-level testing programs to connect with college readiness, nor did they revise high school content standards with an eye toward aligning them with postsecondary expectations (Brown & Conley, 2007). Almost without exception, the reforms of the mid-1990s focused on knowledge and skills benchmarked to expectations and exams at an eighth- to tenth-grade level (Achieve, 2004).

Two states did launch extensive experiments with what was called *competency-based* or *proficiency-based admission*. For several years, the University of Wisconsin System ran a pilot program of competency-based admissions. Data from the pilot indicated that students admitted on the basis of competency rather than grades did slightly better in first-year courses and were more likely to stay in college (Garb, 1998).

The second higher education system to experiment in this arena was the Oregon University System. Beginning in 1993, the OUS developed a comprehensive process to admit students to college based on the proficiency they could demonstrate in specified key areas related to college success, including measures required by the state high school assessment system (Conley, 1994). Under this model, known as the Proficiency-Based Admission Standards System (PASS), high school students could use results from state standards-based exams and national college entrance tests in addition to collections of classroom-based work to demonstrate requisite knowledge and skills. Research conducted on PASS found that the measures employed to gauge proficiency predicted success in freshman college courses as well as or better than similar and more-traditional measures (Tell & McDonald, 2003). Oregon piloted PASS in 52 high schools that enrolled over half the students in the state. However, full implementation of PASS was tied to the state's twelfth-grade Certificate of Advanced Mastery, which was never fully implemented. Thus, PASS is an option for admission to public universities in Oregon, but it is not a requirement. Several Oregon districts and a number of individual high schools currently include PASS assessment information on their student transcripts. Many others utilize PASS as the common reference point in the school or district for college readiness and for a program of study that prepares their students for college.

Another effort worth noting is the American Diploma Project, a national initiative to detail not only college readiness skills but also preparation for community college and work (Achieve, the Education Trust, & the Thomas B. Fordham Foundation, 2004). Many states have utilized the ADP standards in English and mathematics as a frame of reference for analyzing and revising state high school standards and exams.

Overall, few, if any, states have designed academic content standards to challenge all students to reach for college readiness. Yet students who aspire to be the first in their families to attend college depend almost completely on the state (along with their local school district and high school) to establish policies and programs that will enable them to be college-ready (Venezia, Kirst, & Antonio, 2004). In the absence of appropriate state standards and exams keyed to postsecondary success, college readiness is defined as a prescribed sequence of courses, an approach that is ineffective for first-generation college-goers due to the tremendous variation in course rigor between high schools and within any given high school. Schools serving the largest concentration of poor and minority students tend to have the lowest expectations for students and the fewest students in college prep courses, ensuring that students at these schools are more likely to end up in remedial courses upon admission to college, which limits their probabilities of graduating (Adelman, 1999, 2006). State standards and exams do little to help students gauge their college readiness.

In other words, those most dependent on state tests to give them information on college readiness receive little useful guidance. A score of "proficient" or even "advanced" on a state test says little about how well the student is actually prepared for college success. Even worse, the test may convey to students that they are doing quite well, regardless of their actual level of preparation, leading some students to choose not to take a full academic load their senior year. Some states seek to remedy this by requiring all students to take a national admissions examination, such as the ACT or SAT. However, these exams may be poorly aligned with state standards and exams or without any clear connection to scores on state exams. This then leaves students with two potentially conflicting interpretations of their academic preparation level.

COLLEGE READINESS KNOWLEDGE AND SKILLS

To help address these issues, the Center for Educational Policy Research (CEPR) launched in 2000 a large-scale project to define the specific knowledge and skills that are required to succeed in entry-level university courses. Known as Standards for Success, the effort specified in detail, at a national level, what is expected of students in entry-level general education courses at leading U.S. research universities. In 2003, every high school in the country received a copy of the findings in the publication *Understanding University Success* (Conley, 2003), which noted that foundational capabilities (e.g., critical reading, reasoning and logic, interpretation, analysis, a spirit of inquiry) are as important as any specific piece of content knowledge. The report's detailed descriptions of core content knowledge and habits of mind in English, mathematics, the physical sciences, the social sciences, second languages, and the arts created a clear framework for connecting state standards with college readiness expectations and for designing high school programs to prepare students to meet college expectations.

The summaries that follow are derived from *College Knowledge: What It Takes for Students to Succeed and What We Can Do to Get Them Ready* (Conley, 2005), which presents both the full set of knowledge and skills for university success generated by Standards for Success and descriptions of how high schools can be organized to promote college readiness for all students.

College Readiness in Reading, Writing, and Critical Thinking

Proficiency in reading and writing is fundamental to college success. To succeed in college, students need to be active, strategic readers who employ such techniques as summarizing and paraphrasing material, critiquing what they read, and taking notes that capture the most important issues in what they read. They need to be able to identify when a text requires especially close attention, and then to adjust reading speed accordingly. Once in college, students will routinely be expected to express and even defend positions on material they have read. This requires the ability to cite supporting evidence and construct logical arguments. They will be expected to realize that a piece of writing can be interpreted in a variety of ways and that a writer's point of view and personal experience influence the way a piece is written.

Students who are familiar with a range of traditions in world literature will be adequately prepared for an introductory literature course. They will also benefit from being aware of major U.S. and British authors—both men and women—and of representative literary works from a variety of cultural traditions.

Students also benefit from familiarity with literary forms and genres. They should be able to recognize the forms (e.g., novel, poem, play, essay, short story) and to know, for example, what makes a biography different from a novel, a short story, or an essay. To understand the purposes and possibilities of the various forms, students need to be able to distinguish among genres: comedy, epic, tragedy, romance, and others. They should be able to recognize that all literature is embedded in historical and social contexts that influence authors' choices of language, theme, message, and assumptions.

However, literature is not the only important form of literacy. In fact, college students likely will encounter nonliterary works more frequently, such as textbooks and related materials. The ability to read and interpret tables, graphs, charts, and other visual figures is crucial.

Writing is another pillar of college success, in part because it is the means by which performance is judged in many courses. Writing is also important because it forces a certain cognitive development to occur, one that requires logical and orderly reasoning and precise decisions about word choice, sentence structure, and considerations of style.

Students should be able to capitalize, punctuate, and follow the basic rules of the language to write clearly and convincingly. But beyond mastering proper usage, successful students can communicate ideas, concepts, emotions, and descriptions. To do so, they employ a range of techniques and strategies associated with good writing, including focusing on a topic, understanding how to construct and use a thesis statement, being able to use a variety of forms of logic to formulate and defend arguments presented, and knowing how to be persuasive and expressive without abandoning logic.

Editing, in particular, is an important skill. To edit, a student must be reflective, self-analytical, and able to apply general rules of language to the specifics of a particular piece of writing. Finally, editing requires both persistence and a certain amount of preplanning to allow enough time to pass for a "finished" piece to be viewed with a fresh set of eyes.

In contrast to these diverse aspects of college readiness, the current program of high school English/language arts instruction can be characterized by a lack of systematic development of the full range of literacy skills needed for college success. Writing fares poorly in high school, in part because large class sizes limit teachers' ability to pay the required careful attention. For example, evidence suggests that 75 percent of students never receive writing assignments in social studies or history courses, subject areas in which extensive writing is required in college (National Commission on Writing in America's Schools and Colleges, 2003). Many high school teachers eschew instruction in grammar and conventions, either because it does not interest them or it is not their strong suit in the first place.

The typical English/language arts "sequence" in most high schools permits great latitude in what is taught and is not really a sequence at all. Even though most colleges require four years of English courses, variation in the high school English curriculum results in a paucity of entering students with well-developed reading and writing skills. A well-sequenced English/language arts curriculum with progressively greater challenge in what students read and how they write will help more students be ready for entry-level college courses, essentially all of which require sophisticated reading and writing skills.

College Readiness in Mathematics

College mathematics encompasses the interaction of principles, techniques, and knowledge with ways of thinking about mathematical ideas and phenomena. Knowing how to "do" math is not enough. Students must be able to "think" mathematically as well—both conceptually and procedurally.

Problem solving is at the heart of math and becomes increasingly important in college, not only in math but in an ever-increasing range of subject areas, such as business, economics, and the physical sciences, where courses employ basic and more-advanced math. Students should understand math as a symbolic language-and-thought system that helps us understand the natural world. The most fundamental element of math is logical thinking, combined with a modicum of common sense. Mathematical thinking leads to greater familiarity with the logic of scientific experimentation and the notion that reaching a solution may require multiple steps. Students who learn to think mathematically come to understand that some problems have more than one correct answer, and that many of the most-interesting problems have no correct answer at all. Mathematical thinkers have high degrees of fluency with the basic algorithms, conventions, symbols, and rules of mathematics.

Students must know how to record accurately and precisely the results of symbolic manipulations and be able to apply mathematical notation with fluency. However, math stymies many students because they cannot manage the basic manipulations required to solve problems or reach more complex and conceptual aspects of mathematics.

Algebra is a key building block for college math. Without a deep understanding of basic algebraic concepts and techniques, students will struggle with much of the math they encounter in other subjects. Some key elements of algebra are the abilities to manipulate polynomials; compose and decompose functions; understand exponents, roots, and their derivatives; understand basic theorems of exponents and roots; understand logarithms and their properties; solve linear equations, including quadratic equations; distinguish between and among expressions, formulas, equations, and functions; understand the relationship between equations and graphs; and use all of these understandings and techniques to solve a range of common problems.

College-level math also expects students to be familiar with basic trigonometric and geometric principles. Students should understand solid, plane, and analytic geometry, as well as the basic relationships between geometry and algebra.

While a number of states make an effort to include math through mid-level algebra on their exams, and a number of exams do have a problem-solving component, few contain the level of algebra necessary to measure whether a student has mastered this key area thoroughly. However, the brevity of most state (and national) tests of all types and their broad scope mean that they cannot provide meaningful measures of knowledge on subtopics, and so cannot be used to diagnose strengths and weaknesses or be aligned with college readiness standards. End-of-course exams, which are in use in less than a dozen states, can be quite useful for identifying at least a basic understanding of key content knowledge taught in a course. Advanced Placement and International Baccalaureate examinations are the exception. They measure in-depth content knowledge and mathematical thinking and provide good indications of college readiness.

Crosscutting Skills and Dispositions

Some important skills and dispositions cut across subject areas. For example, the ability to understand research results and to conduct a variety of types of inquiry is increasingly important in higher education. To conduct such investigations, students must be able to formulate and refine a research question, identify major issues or competing points of view, understand the degree to which evidence supports an opinion, distinguish the line between opinion and evidence, distinguish between primary and secondary sources, and identify information that supports or refutes their point of view.

College expects students to use a wider range of sources than a simple Internet search yields. This requires them to be familiar with a range of databases and library resources. They will be expected to determine the credibility and biases of sources. Increasingly important is the ability to understand what constitutes plagiarism, as well as to know how to cite works properly, when and how much paraphrasing is appropriate, and when and how to quote a source.

Another important crosscutting skill is critical thinking. Students who can think critically make connections between what they study, their personal experiences, and what they learn in other subject areas. They make connections within a subject area between the parts and the larger whole that is the structure of that particular discipline. Students who are confident critical thinkers are willing to state a point of view and to defend the logic and present the evidence that support it. They are not afraid to challenge an assumption. They are aware of the weaknesses of their own arguments and gaps in their logic, and they can accept feedback that points out those flaws in their reasoning and argumentation.

ADDITIONAL STUDIES OF ENTRY-LEVEL COLLEGE COURSES

Some may argue that the preceding descriptions apply to a subset of American postsecondary institutions, those that accept the best-prepared students. Interestingly, this does not seem to be the case. The Center for Educational Policy Research and the Educational Policy Improvement Center, a not-for-profit organization that works in partnership with CEPR, have now conducted several studies that analyzed hundreds of entry-level courses at a wide range of postsecondary institutions nationally. The EPIC studies asked instructors to identify the content that was most important to success in their classes, the habits of mind they sought to develop in students, and the most effective instructional practices (Conley, Aspengren, Gallagher, & Langan, 2006; Conley, Aspengren, & Stout, 2006).

The findings from these studies are striking in the degree to which they reinforce what emerged from our initial work with research universities. The importance of the habits of mind was abundantly evident, as was the emphasis on learning key concepts and content well. Faculty repeatedly comment on what they perceive to be the intellectual immaturity of incoming students and the inability of these students to express themselves orally or in writing. Faculty state that students often become defensive when their opinions are challenged and seem not to understand that college is a community where information is exchanged and questioned.

THE DIFFERENCES BETWEEN HIGH SCHOOL AND COLLEGE

Our research has led us to conclude that high schools and colleges are fundamentally different learning environments. The disconnect is not merely structural; it is deeply rooted in cultural and functional differences. The two institutions think about the nature of knowing differently, with high schools focusing primarily on transmission of content and colleges on utilizing content as a means to stimulate ways of thinking and knowing. High school and college really do not represent two points along a continuum, but two potentially orthogonal views of education and its purposes.

Although high schools do prepare many students successfully for college each year, high schools as learning environments have a very different focus, organization, and belief system than do colleges. This must be fully understood and acknowledged before policies designed to align high schools and colleges are attempted.

The modern comprehensive high school provides students with a learning environment that is largely incoherent intellectually. In attempting to be all things to all students, high school often fails to achieve any single goal for any single group of students. The lack of a clear outcome measure or criterion for a successful high school education means that any education a student receives is acceptable, so long as it leads to a diploma. The course title and course credit system reinforces the lack of coherence, as students pile up credits from courses that do not function as a sequence to develop intellectual maturity and coherence.

High schools, as currently designed, have great difficulty providing focused, coherent programs of study. They can neither specialize nor generalize effectively. Courses are not sequenced in a meaningful fashion, and requirements can be met in so many different ways that they do not result in any predictable knowledge and skill mastery in a subject area. The daily schedule, in which classes operate in isolation from one another, leads to a fundamental fragmentation of knowledge in the minds of students. Some teachers are well grounded in the subject matter and its ways of thinking, while others may have less understanding of the content they are teaching and about the habits of mind or the foundational principles and concepts of the subject area.

While colleges are far from perfect, they differ from high schools in several important ways. Colleges by design lead toward specialization. They are surprisingly adaptive to new developments in academic fields, and even to new pedagogical innovations. Witness how quickly much of higher education has integrated technology within and outside the classroom. Each year, a large university may initiate and terminate new programs and majors in several academic areas. This enables them to specialize more effectively and to meet a wider range of student goals with relative efficiency. Colleges also generalize through what are called "breadth" or "general education" requirements. While the specific courses used to meet the requirements are varied, the courses tend to share an emphasis on developing habits of mind crucial to mastering the subject area and necessary for subsequent college success. In this sense, colleges are able to generalize and specialize in a coherent, sequential fashion.

Content Overlap between High School and College

One additional striking finding from our research on the differences between high school and college courses is that college instructors teach as new material much of what high school instructors also teach as new material (Conley, et al., 2006). For example, a course entitled College Algebra will likely cover many of the same topics as a comparably titled high school course. However, the first-year college student may be startled to learn that seemingly familiar material comes at a much faster pace and is much more conceptual in nature. In college, it is more important to draw inferences or apply principles than to repeat what has been memorized.

This may be a "good news / bad news" finding. The good news is that it does not seem to be the content itself that limits high school student success when doing college-level work. It may be the ability of students to handle the work flow and, most important, to think in different ways about what they are being taught. If this is so, dual enrollment programs may be much more feasible for a wider range of high school students, if high school courses develop the work habits and thinking skills expected in the college course.

CONNECTING HIGH SCHOOL AND COLLEGE

That said, projects such as Standards for Success suggest what can be done to build relationships between high schools and colleges and to redesign the educational programs of both at two key intersection points: the senior year of high school and the first year of college.

Aligned Courses

At CEPR, we have been bringing together high school, community college, and university faculty to address this challenge by developing courses that are fully aligned between high school and college (Conley & Ward, 2006). Those courses are created through a systematic process that engages high school and college faculty as collaborative partners who calibrate their expectations, then develop materials and assignments geared to those expectations. Aligning high school and college courses requires careful, deliberate planning and communication between faculty at both levels. This begins with agreement on the exit-level skills for high school in the subject area and the corresponding expectations found in entry-level college courses.

The next step is to compare course documents. High school course syllabi contain much less information about what the course teaches, its goals and learning objectives, and the habits of mind that students are expected to develop in the course. The high school syllabi often dwell upon classroom discipline and procedures, barely mentioning content to be learned, means of assessment, or other substantive aspects of the course.

The college syllabus, by contrast, is more detailed and focused on what is to be learned and the ways of knowing upon which the course is predicated. Many college and universities impose consistent requirements for minimum content for course syllabi. By contrast, few high schools seem to have any such requirement. Getting some agreement between secondary and postsecondary on what constitutes an acceptably detailed syllabus is key to organizing aligned courses.

Once instructors reach some agreement about what they are teaching, they can then develop sequenced expectations. This is perhaps done most easily in writing, where a common scoring guide for analyzing writing assignments can be employed in a senior-level English class and then again in an entry-level college composition course. If high school and college students see their writing being scored using the same criteria at both levels, they are more able to generalize what they learned in high school to the new setting of a college writing course.

Senior Seminar

The most elaborate and complex outcome of our research on high school–college alignment has been the senior seminar, a high school course designed to prepare seniors for what they will encounter in college, without actually teaching college-level material in the class. Rather than introduce new material, the senior seminar focuses on the habits of mind described previously and consolidates and deepens student understanding and mastery of material taught previously in high school. Students are expected to engage actively with the material, to participate in class, to think about what they are doing, to consolidate prior learnings, and to develop intellectually. They are challenged to document or support assertions and opinions. Their writing must meet high technical standards, and they are always expected to edit what they write. The pace of the senior seminar approximates an entry-level college course, thereby allowing high school students to gauge their readiness for what they will experience in a few months when they enter college.

Most important, the senior seminar is designed not for the highest-achieving students but for all those who may go on to some form of postsecondary education. This is a large group in most high schools and consists of students who are in the greatest need of being challenged more. These students often take less than a full load of classes during their senior year or take less-demanding courses, and they subsequently struggle in entry-level college courses or are placed into remedial courses. The senior seminar helps these students continue to develop the knowledge, skills, and work habits necessary for success in college rather than taking their senior year off.

MEETING THE NEEDS OF THE ECONOMY AND SOCIETY

Our research at CEPR and EPIC leads us to several conclusions about what is needed to improve students' college readiness.

Students must know how to think, reason, and use their minds beyond simply repeating what they have been told.

Students must be comfortable with engaging actively in learning and sharing in responsibility for their own education. They should have a spirit of curiosity and inquiry, rather than viewing education solely as a path to financial reward or a job. The spirit of inquiry and joy of learning can be nurtured through the judicious use of stimulating projects, interdisciplinary seminars, field-based studies, and learning situations where students can exert leadership and find creative solutions to challenging tasks and complex problems.

High school studies should be progressively more challenging, with the senior year being the most challenging of all.

One of the first steps to take along this road is to agree upon high school exit standards that include the habits of mind that will be developed in every high school class. Another is to create true sequences in high school subject areas in order to foster intellectual growth in addition to covering new content. At the very least, all students should take yearlong classes in English, math, science, and social science during their senior year. Ideally, senior seminars should be an integral part of the twelfth-grade curriculum.

High school course syllabi must meet high, consistent standards for quality and content.

High school faculty should agree to construct and publicize syllabi that contain common elements. These syllabi should define key course content, prerequisites, and outcome skills, how the course fits with other courses in a sequence, how the course prepares students for college readiness, and, perhaps most important, which habits of mind are developed in the course. All syllabi need to contain explicit information on how grades will be determined, how performance is assessed, and what is expected in key assignments. These syllabi should be compared to college readiness standards to determine how well the high school program of study as a whole aligns with college expectations.

High school subject areas should be sequenced more coherently, and all students should be expected to take a challenging program of study.

The incoherence of the current high school program of study makes it difficult for all except the most motivated and well-supported students to succeed. High schools must change drastically if they are to ensure that students cannot make bad decisions and that all students are engaged in a challenging program of study for which postsecondary readiness is one possible outcome. This implies the sort of "default" scheduling for incoming ninth graders that has become accepted as state policy in Texas and Indiana and is becoming more prevalent in high schools with large populations of students who will be the first in their families to attend college. These default schedules should be composed of a sequence of courses that impart key knowledge and skills and develop critical habits of mind.

High school teachers and college faculty must communicate directly with one another.

Ultimately, system articulation is built upon concrete understandings and negotiations among faculty in high schools and colleges. Each partner should be willing to commit to a set of college readiness standards that define the goal the high school seeks to attain by the end of the senior year and the challenge level the college institutes in its entry-level courses. To achieve this, high school and college faculty need to meet regularly, compare assignments, and discuss student work. This activity should occur at the local and the state levels.

Colleges need to communicate better with high schools regarding placement methods, standards, and tested content to promote better alignment between the exit-level high school course and the college placement test.

Colleges need to become much more active partners by providing better information to high schools on how placement and remediation decisions are made. This information can help high schools make better decisions about what to review with students, particularly during the senior year. In addition, data on how well students from each high school perform in entry-level general education courses during their first year in college and how many end up in remedial courses will help high schools determine with greater precision what they need to change so that more students enter college ready to succeed.

Entry-level college courses will then have to be much more explicitly aligned with these expectations.

Such courses must not teach as new material content that students should be expected to have mastered in high school. The challenge level should be appropriate, and syllabi from these courses should be widely distributed to high schools. The entry-level college classes must set the tone for the intellectual development of students that is the hallmark of a college education in the United States.

States should be prepared to establish the policy frameworks that support or even mandate the types of interactions, negotiations, and agreements across institutional and system boundaries described here.

Perhaps most important for states, their standards and assessments should have some reasonable relationship to postsecondary success, even if every student is not expected to be college-ready in order to pass a state high school exit exam. It is now time for states to undo what they have done previously by instituting standards and tests disconnected from postsecondary success, and to create policy mechanisms that replace the existing system with one that truly aligns grades 9–14 to enable the vast majority of students to emerge from high school fully ready to succeed in college once admitted. This is what students and their parents expect and what in large measure will determine the future success of the U.S. economy and society.

10

Sending Signals to Students

The Role of Early Placement Testing in Improving Academic Preparation

Bridget Terry Long and Erin K. Riley

THE HIGH SCHOOL PREPARATION PROBLEM

Although two-thirds of recent high school graduates enter college each year, many of these students are academically unprepared for college-level material (Greene & Foster, 2003). With the costs of remediation estimated at $1 billion or more nationally at public colleges alone, many states are looking for other ways to address academic preparation (Breneman & Haarlow, 1997).

Early placement testing offers a possible solution. Such programs administer exams to high school students in order to provide them with early signals that they may lack competencies critical to success in a postsecondary institution. The tests are designed to improve the information high school students have regarding their preparation for college and encourage those who fall short to take additional course work in their senior year. Ohio estimates the cost of improving a student one level higher in college math using an early testing program is $17 (Laughbaum, 2003). With costs considerably less than college remediation, early placement testing programs may be a much more affordable way to address the problem of preparation for some students.

Oklahoma, Ohio, and California illustrate three options for implementing an early placement testing policy. They differ, in particular, in the degree of cooperation between K–12 and higher education, an aspect that has significant implications.

EARLY PLACEMENT TESTS: CONNECTING 9–14

The large numbers of students placed into remediation soon after graduating from high school are a signal of the ineffectiveness of many secondary school systems. Indeed, the need for remediation in college is closely tied to a student's high school curriculum. A study by the Ohio Board of Regents (2002) found that students who had completed an academic core curriculum in high school were half as likely to need remediation in college compared to students without this core.

Similarly, Adelman (1999, 2006) emphasizes the importance of academic preparation in high school for success in college.

However, completion of a high school core curriculum does not ensure that a student will avoid remediation in college. Many students who complete upper-level math courses in high school still require math remediation courses or need to repeat subjects in college. For example, 25 percent of Ohio high school graduates with a known core curriculum required remediation in either math or English (Ohio Board of Regents, 2002). The need for supposedly "academically prepared" students to complete remediation suggests that the problem is larger than just poor high school course selection or the lack of a college prep curriculum at some schools.

In fact, the misalignment between the material defined as necessary by high schools, as well as the level of rigor of some of these courses and the competencies colleges require, has been well documented (McCabe, 2001). Venezia, Kirst, and Antonio (2003), for instance, detail how the standards for high school courses are entirely different from those for college classes. Moreover, assessments administered in high school often emphasize knowledge and skills that differ from those that are tested in college entrance and placement exams.

The use of college placement exams as diagnostic tools in high school is one promising policy aimed at better connecting student high school preparation with the requirements of postsecondary courses. For example, several states administer the same remediation placement test that is ordinarily given to college freshmen to students in grades 10 or 11. High schools share the results with the students and their parents as a way to inform all parties of the competencies that remain to be mastered. With their teachers and counselors, students can then determine what courses to take while still in high school in order to avoid college remediation.

A FRAMEWORK FOR COMPARISON

State-level early placement testing policies take a variety of forms and differ in several important ways, depending on how the policy was developed and a state's mission or goals. (See table 1 for a summary of these key elements for several of the nation's larger programs.)

- *States use different testing instruments.* The exams range from standardized tests, (e.g., ACT's Plan) to exams closely resembling those that colleges give to entering freshmen. The colleges may develop the placement exams themselves or buy them (e.g., from ACT, which authors the COMPASS exam).
- *States differ in the timing of the exam.* Some policies target high school juniors; others test high school sophomores or even eighth graders.
- *States differ in the degree of school participation.* Some states require all high schools to participate, while others make involvement voluntary at either the school or classroom level.
- *The governance of programs differs in terms of the level of coordination between high schools and colleges.*

Among the states profiled here, there is a great deal of variation in these four factors. In terms of the exam instrument, Oklahoma uses a ready-made product from

Table 1. Summary of Select Early Placement Testing Policies

Program	Degree of Participation	Level of Coordination
OKLAHOMA EDUCATIONAL PLANNING AND ASSESSMENT SYSTEM (EPAS) *Exam Instrument:* ACT Explore and ACT Plan *Grade Level:* Explore is administered to eighth-grade students; Plan is administered during the fall of the tenth grade year.	Schools elect to participate and must use both assessments if serving both eighth and tenth graders, and they must assess all students.	Oklahoma State Regents for Higher Education developed the program with ACT to help ensure equitable college preparation.
OHIO EARLY MATHEMATICS PLACEMENT TESTING (EMPT) *Exam Instrument:* Exam is similar to mathematics placement exams offered at large, four-year, state universities. *Grade Level:* Exam is usually given to eleventh graders or students currently taking Algebra II, trigonometry, or precalculus.	High schools elect to participate, but there are no requirements about which students are tested.	Developed by a high school teacher and professor at Ohio State University, today the program is supported by the Ohio legislature and overseen by the Ohio Board of Regents.
CALIFORNIA EARLY ASSESSMENT PROGRAM (EAP) *Exam Instrument:* Items added to the end of the state-required California Standards Test. *Grade Level:* The test is administered during the spring semester of eleventh grade.	All students have the option of completing the EAP in addition to the California Standards Test.	The program was a joint effort of the California Department of Education, state board of education, and the California State University system. Additional input from the postsecondary sector came from the University of California's Academic Senate and faculty.
ILLINOIS PRAIRIE STATE ACHIEVEMENT EXAM (PSAE) *Exam Instrument:* State developed assessments as well as the ACT and ACT WorkKeys. *Grade Level:* Test is administered during the spring semester of eleventh grade.	All public school students are tested.	The Prairie State Achievement Exam was established by the Illinois General Assembly to comply with the requirement for a high-quality, yearly student assessment at the high school level.
NORTH CAROLINA EARLY MATHEMATICS PLACEMENT TESTING PROGRAM (NCEMPT) *Exam Instrument:* Placement exam created by NCEMPT closely matches the college placement exam students would face when entering the UNC system. *Grade Level:* Students enrolled in and close to completing Algebra II or upper-level math courses.	High schools elect to participate in the program, but there is no mandatory level of participation for students or grade levels.	The program is funded by the University of North Carolina Office of the President. An advisory committee for the program consists of representatives from each of the 15 state universities, the Department of Public Instruction, the community college system, the governor's office, and the UNC-General Administration.
KENTUCKY EARLY MATHEMATICS TESTING PROGRAM (KEMTP) *Exam Instrument:* Online mathematics test designed by Kentucky college and high school math teachers to assess math preparation level. *Grade Level:* Test is administered to tenth and eleventh graders.	Test may be taken at the convenience of teachers and students. A single student or an entire class may participate.	House Bill 178, the legislation that governs KEMPT, was passed unanimously and signed into law by the governor. The program is funded by the Kentucky Council on Postsecondary Education and represents a partnership between Northern Kentucky University and the University of Kentucky.

Sources: ACT (2003a), ACT (2003b), EMPT (2006a), CSU (2006), NGA (2005), KEMTP (2005), and Bernhardt and Hilgoe (2005).

ACT, while Ohio wrote an exam that closely resembles the test students would take when entering college. California's instrument combines a state-mandated high school exam with questions from a college placement exam.

Grade level of testing and the degree of school participation also distinguish the programs. Oklahoma tests eighth and tenth graders, in order to provide planning information well before students leave high school, but Ohio and California target eleventh graders to alter their senior-year course-taking decisions. While both Oklahoma and Ohio target high schools rather than students, Oklahoma mandates that all students within a participating school must be tested, and high schools participating in Ohio's program may test one Algebra II class or an entire cohort of juniors. California is the only one of the three states that leaves the decision about participation up to the student. In addition, California's program demonstrates the highest level of coordination between K–12 and higher education.

THE IMPLICATIONS OF DESIGN

Beyond the basic framework, a comparison of programs suggests that policymakers must weigh heavily the implications of design. The size, scope, and governance structure of a program, as well as the policies developed beyond the test to support the program's intentions, are key dimensions to consider. The degree of participation and the chosen testing instrument will affect the program's size and the scope. A program limited by a high school's (or even a teacher's) initiative to participate, such as in Ohio and Kentucky, may not reach all students who would benefit.

Moreover, the testing instrument may limit the effectiveness of the signal the test is meant to provide. While a broad-based, standardized test (e.g., PLAN) covers more subjects than a math test designed to reflect a placement exam, can it provide precise information regarding the match between college readiness and current skills? Or is it a measure of general academic aptitude? If the latter is true, the test may not contribute anything substantially different from other K–12 standardized tests, crippling its ability to serve as a signal to students, parents, and teachers regarding the transition to college. Finally, while expanding the number of students taking the ACT has important implications for access, it, too, may serve as a measure of how well students have performed in high school, rather than a reflection of their college preparedness.

Program governance is another key design dimension of early placement testing polices. Shared governance is reflected by the level of coordination between stakeholders of a policy, but it may be more appropriately measured by a program's ability to meet students' needs. Involvement by educators and administrative bodies (e.g., the department of education, boards of higher education) in all phases of the program shows great promise for improving transitions in 9–14. One possible benefit of shared governance is the ability to increase the stakes for the test in a positive way. For example, when stakeholders across 9–14 were included in California's design process, colleges placed enough credence in scores from the early placement exams to exempt students from testing again at college entry. This provided an incentive for students to take the necessary course work to pass the first time.

Finally, states must consider what occurs after scores are reported. The evidence suggests that taking a test and receiving a score report falls short of providing many students with a clear signal. Students must be supported after the test with counseling to encourage additional course enrollments. Governance plays a key role in this stage as well. Consideration should be given to the gaps in student preparation, and, as occurred in California, new courses should be developed to fill those areas that are responsible for the breakdown of successful transitions.

THE OHIO EARLY MATHEMATICS PLACEMENT TESTING PROGRAM

Ohio's Early Mathematics Placement Testing Program (2006a), launched in 1978, began as an experimental program between one high school in Columbus and an Ohio State University math professor. The founders hoped that high school juniors, when informed that their math skills did not measure up to the skills needed to succeed in Ohio State math courses, would take additional courses in their senior year, reducing the need for remediation. The year following the implementation of the program, the high school's enrollments in senior mathematics courses increased 73 percent.

The EMPT, also known as the Algebra test, is usually administered to high school juniors. As part of the test, students name the public college or university they would like to attend, as well as their first and second choices for college majors. Students receive more than a simple score report: a personalized letter details how each test score translates into a college placement level. Based on this level of placement, the letter informs the student whether or not he or she needs remediation and encourages the appropriate math course work while still in high school. However, students must still take placement tests when they arrive on college campuses the following year, regardless of their EMPT scores. The letter also provides information about the course work typically required in the majors that interest the student. Participating high schools receive a summary report, helping them consider their overall performance and possible responses.

The EMPT program is supported by the Ohio Board of Regents, with funding from the Ohio legislature. It remains closely tied to the Ohio State University math department, although all Ohio state-supported, four-year universities and some two-year and private colleges have been incorporated into the program. On the other hand, there is little connection with K–12 systems, and participation by high schools is voluntary, limited, and fluctuates from year to year. For example, between the 2003–04 and 2004–05 school years, participation fell from 261 to 231 high schools.[1]

Since 1978, 12 states have followed Ohio's example and implemented similar programs, including North Carolina and Kentucky.[2]

THE OKLAHOMA EDUCATIONAL PLANNING AND ASSESSMENT SYSTEM

Oklahoma's early placement testing results from actions taken by the State Regents for Higher Education. During the early 1990s, college remediation rates exceeded 60 percent in some parts of the state (ACT, 2003a). Because many Oklahoma high school students were unprepared for college, the Regents decided to raise college admissions requirements from 11 to 15 units of high school core course work. However, the Regents recognized that this would burden some groups more than others, so they also initiated the Educational Planning and Assessment System (EPAS) to assist K–12 systems in providing equitable preparation for all students. EPAS, developed in collaboration with ACT, is a voluntary student assessment and instructional support program, designed to provide feedback to both high schools and individual students regarding their preparation.

In 1993, Oklahoma piloted EPAS in four school districts. Today, participation is left up to the high school, yet EPAS reaches 95 percent of Oklahoma's eighth and tenth graders in 489 districts (ACT, 2003a).

EPAS is comprised of two early placement exams from ACT: Plan and Explore. Eighth graders in private and public schools are accessed with Explore, an instrument that includes the four academic areas—English, mathematics, reading, and science reasoning—as well as career exploration and planning components to encourage students, parents, and teachers to think forward to college or career. The Plan assessment, administered in the fall to tenth graders, includes the Unisex Edition of the ACT Interest Inventory (UNIACT), an interest inventory to help students consider career and educational options, as well as the same academic subjects covered by Explore.

In some respects, EPAS is more like a standardized testing program than a placement program. The testing instruments provide general information about preparation, but they are unlikely to provide specific details for students regarding the match between their skills and college-level courses. As a signal, EPAS provides a measure of preparation and skill level for high school students, which may help encourage completion of the core or other college preparatory work. However, it may not be targeted or timed to inform students of specific skills they would need prior to entering college in order to avoid remediation.

THE CALIFORNIA EARLY ASSESSMENT PROGRAM

California's desire to provide a signal to students regarding college preparation resulted in a program that differs dramatically from those in Ohio or Oklahoma. In the 23-campus California State University system, more than 60 percent of first-time freshmen require remediation in English, math, or both, despite statewide requirements of a college preparatory curriculum and at least a B grade point average.[3] In 2003, the California Department of Education, the state board of education, and the CSU system launched the Early Assessment Program. Input from the postsecondary system came from the CSU chancellor's office and representatives of the CSU Academic Senate, as well as the University of California System office, its faculty, and an Inter-segmental Coordinating Committee (National Governors Association, 2005).

The broad collaboration of stakeholders from K–12 and higher education is not the EAP's only distinguishing factor. The EAP was designed to include three components: early testing, opportunities for additional preparation in the twelfth grade (including specially designed courses), and professional development for high school math and English teachers. Each component combines both K–12 and postsecondary efforts, linking success for students to success for high schools and colleges. Aside from the primary goal of aligning the CSU placement standards with K–12 standards in math and English language arts, the program hopes to increase the proficiency of CSU freshmen and reduce the remediation rates of incoming classes to 10 percent by 2007.[4]

California has attached its voluntary early placement testing program to an existing mandatory test. The EAP is administered during the eleventh grade as part of the required California Standards Test. The EAP has two parts: the Early Assessment of Readiness for College English and the Early Assessment of Readiness for College Mathematics. Each part adds an additional 15 items to the California Standards Test, and the English exam also includes a 45-minute essay. Scores are computed from a subset of relevant CST and EAP items.

Students are notified whether their score meets CSU requirements; if so, it exempts them from future CSU placement testing. If their scores do not meet the requirement, students may use online math diagnostic tools to identify strengths and weaknesses.[5] Diagnostic tests are also available to teachers, who can give them in class to determine where students are struggling. In addition, many high schools have developed courses to provide seniors with skills they need, while incorporating remedial work (Mills, 2004).

In the first two years of the program, participation among students grew, with 185,695 students taking the English exam and 119,338 students taking the math exam in 2005.[6]

DO EARLY PLACEMENT TESTING POLICIES IMPROVE ACADEMIC PREPARATION?

There has been no systematic study of the effects of early placement testing policies on high school preparation or college outcomes. However, states have provided encouraging summary statistics. Oklahoma's early placement testing program appears to provide students with a viable signal regarding the importance of taking the core (ACT, 2003a). The percent of students taking a high school core curriculum increased, especially for minority students: the proportion of African American students taking the core rose from 38 percent in 1993 to 51 percent. Average ACT scores also increased, even as a higher percentage of students took the exam. Moreover, between 1997 and 2002, the college-going rate increased from 51 to 58 percent.

In Ohio, an evaluation found that participation in the Early Mathematics Placement Testing program had a significant effect on mathematics placement at the college level; the evaluation further concluded that the program effectively reduced remediation (Zuiker, 1996). Students who participated in EMPT were more likely to place higher in math upon entering Ohio State University and less likely to require remediation. However, the program's effect was due in part to the fact that participants were more likely to take a twelfth-grade math course. This suggests that the test itself is only one component of the signal, and that an early testing program may also need a counseling component.

In California, it is too early to know if EAP will reduce remediation rates in the CSU system, yet the state is encouraged by students' increased interest in the program. In 2005, 21 percent more students took the English test than the year before, and 3 percent more students took the math test.

CONCLUSION

Preliminary statistics like these may not convince many policymakers that early testing programs are a viable tool to address preparation for college. Studies that compare program participants to nonparticipants are needed, with some recognition of whether or not the program is voluntary. Also, it would be beneficial to compare remediation and other college outcomes in states with and without an early placement program.

That said, the programs profiled here all seek to better prepare students for college-level work, and they provide information regarding the skills students need to transition to postsecondary study. Early placement tests designed to signal to students what they know—and to varying degrees, what they *need* to know—are one possible way to reduce remediation by encouraging additional course work prior to college.

Policymakers in both K–12 and higher education should carefully consider the implications of particular program designs on the signaling strength of such efforts. Will the program reach all students? Does the test provide enough information, and is there enough counseling support to impact high school course decisions? Does the program help bridge the gap between K–12 and higher education?

Furthermore, states may consider how additional elements added to an early placement testing program could help close the secondary/postsecondary divide. As demonstrated by California's EAP, collaboration does not have to end after the placement test is devised. Professional development and new high school courses designed in joint collaboration can be integrated into a larger program to reduce remediation and increase college-level proficiencies.

11

The California Early Assessment Program

Implications for States in Developing Readiness Agendas

David Spence

From 2001 to 2005, I helped lead a major effort to connect the college readiness standards and related tests of the California State University System precisely with those of the California public schools. Since its inception with the first statewide tests in spring 2004, the Early Assessment Program has made the readiness standards for CSU's 23 campuses, enrolling 400,000 students, explicit for high school teachers. The program also has provided a clear and early signal about student readiness for college-level work—giving students an opportunity to improve their preparation during their senior year of high school.

This description of the development of the Early Assessment Program and its status in 2006, along with the key decisions and issues that I and others addressed during its creation, may be helpful to other state policymakers as they build programs with similar aims.

THE EARLY ASSESSMENT PROGRAM

The Early Assessment Program consists of three components:

- The high school–based assessments;
- Help for students during their senior year; and
- Professional development for high school teachers.

The Assessments

The founding of the EAP was rooted in CSU's need to assess students during high school to help more of them strengthen their reading, writing, and mathematics skills before entering college. CSU faced a plight common among state higher education systems: 60 to 70 percent of incoming freshmen needed considerable remediation after admission. Years of extensive freshmen feedback reports to high schools and the statewide distribution of CSU's common set of readiness standards in English and mathematics had yielded meager gains, leading CSU to seek approval to administer its college-placement (or readiness) tests to high school juniors. However, state legislators and K–12 school leaders opposed such a change amid concerns that students faced too much testing already and that educators might find another set of academic standards confusing alongside the existing state-adopted public school standards.

CSU then turned to the existing California Standards Tests (CSTs)—specifically, the end-of-course tests in Algebra II and eleventh-grade English that all students took as part of the state's testing, school accountability, and reporting system.

With the assistance of the Educational Testing Service, CSU and public school faculty and staff analyzed the CSTs and their underlying performance standards. In some cases, they found, CSU's discrete placement standards were not identified as specific CST test items. Thus, the CSTs were revised by adding about 10 to 12 questions derived from CSU placement standards to the 50-item test. The new items were part of the state-adopted school academic standards, but they had not been test items on the CSTs. A 40-minute writing exercise also was added. (There are plans to rotate more items into the CSTs based on the CSU readiness standards and, in the process, reduce the need for further augmentation.)

The multiple-choice tests yield two scores: a core CST score and a CST-augmented score indicating CSU readiness. The readiness score is the combination of a subset of the related core CST readiness items and the added items. Students, families, and schools receive test results in August, before the fall semester starts. Including the readiness assessments as part of the CSTs heightens the impact of these tests and their standards. Previously, the tests held low stakes for students and high stakes for schools, but students now have reason to take them seriously as well. Teachers also have clearer ideas about which school standards to stress as they work to ensure that all students are well prepared for college.

Better Use of the Senior Year

As state leaders and educators revised the high school tests, it became clear that the tests needed to be offered far enough into high school that students had been exposed to the college readiness standards, but early enough to permit time to strengthen their academic preparation before graduating. Practically speaking, this meant administering the tests late in the junior year. By then, most students have nearly completed Algebra II and three years of high school English.

The CSU mathematics and English faculties developed activities aimed at strengthening areas specifically related to the CSU placement standards. For mathematics, CSU faculty and staff revised an online tutorial program, complete with a teacher-advising component, and offered it to seniors who needed additional preparation. But English/language arts presented a very different challenge in that college preparatory students would take another English course in the twelfth grade; math beyond Algebra II was optional, although more courses were recommended. English also posed the bigger challenge because expository reading was at the heart of the remediation problem. Not only did a much higher percentage of students score poorly on post-admission placement tests in English than in math, but students also fared much worse on the reading components than on the writing portion. Indeed, the first statewide administration of the CST, in 2004, showed that less than a quarter of the high school juniors tested met CSU's English-readiness standards.

This led to a wholly different approach for some twelfth-grade language arts classes. CSU faculty and staff came to recognize that the fundamental reading problem lay in students' limited capacity to read and understand academic texts with more-advanced comprehension, contributing to their limited understanding of math and other disciplines. Given the importance of this strategic skill, CSU faculty and their public school counterparts developed a twelfth-grade course to replace (or augment) the traditional, literature-based English course. This new course is based on a series of modules designed to help students better comprehend and explain academically dense texts, such as those found in textbooks, analytical essays, and more-advanced newspaper editorials and opinion columns.

Called the 12th Grade Expository Reading and Writing Course, the course was developed by a task force of CSU faculty, high school teachers, and content specialists. Course assignments emphasize the in-depth study of expository, analytical, and argumentative reading and writing. Designed to prepare students for college-level English, the course also includes an assignment template and an accompanying series of primarily nonfiction texts.

The academic standards it covers are aligned with the official California school content standards. However, the substance of the course—and especially the related professional development for teachers—extends teachers' understanding beyond the simple description of a standard (what needs to be known or done) to the actual level of expected student performance (how well something is known or done).

Ultimately, the development of this course and its evaluation rubrics have provided a rich opportunity for CSU faculty and public school teachers to reach consensus on the precise level of student performance that is expected on a series of reading and writing standards that signify students' readiness for CSU.

Professional Development

Some of the most important components of the Early Assessment Program are its activities that help California's high school teachers know the CSU readiness standards well and use them effectively for classroom instruction. The foundation of the EAP is to help high school teachers make the readiness standards a priority in the classroom so that their students become progressively more proficient in language arts and math.

Given that the development of more-effective reading and writing skills posed the most urgent and fundamental challenge, the EAP's professional development components include two initiatives: the preparation of teachers for the new expository reading and writing course, and additional help for high school teachers through CSU's Reading Institute for Academic Preparation program.

Begun in 2002, the Reading Institute for Academic Preparation is offered through CSU campus and school partnerships. High school teachers from all subject areas take part in the training. The RIAPs have focused on eleventh- and twelfth-grade teachers, but there are plans to extend professional development to teachers in earlier grades so that they understand the performance levels their students eventually will be expected to reach.

CSU staff report that the RIAPs help teachers know the expectations for college-level English, see how these standards are part of California's English content standards, and develop instructional strategies to build reading comprehension skills and how they relate to literacy. Teachers learn and practice specific instructional strategies to build reading competency, including vocabulary development, comprehension, content-specific reading demands, critical thinking, and reading/writing connections.

Several features make these professional development activities effective.

- Their focus on a common and targeted set of standards intensifies the attention of participating teachers and keeps the activities tightly aimed at specific outcomes.
- Great care is taken to emphasize that the CSU readiness standards are subsets and discrete components of the existing California school standards. To assert that the readiness standards are aligned with the school standards understates the relationship, because these readiness standards are one and the same with a subset of the school standards. The objective of the professional development is to stress the existing school standards that need to be taught and highlighted more effectively by classroom teachers.
- The activities go beyond surface descriptions of a standard's content to generate a grounded and deep understanding of the kind and level of performance expected. CSU faculty and staff familiar with the level of student work that signifies readiness for CSU interact directly with their public school counterparts to seek shared understandings. Frequently based in the examination of case studies of college-bound students, these joint activities have proven to be personally and professionally intensive but tremendously effective in developing common expectations of the meaning of college readiness.
- Teachers identify specific ways they can help students reach the expected levels of performance. Through the activities, teachers identify course work, assignments, and teaching strategies that have proven effective in helping students meet the readiness standards.

OBSERVATIONS ABOUT THE EARLY ASSESSMENT PROGRAM

By fall 2006, California had experience with two years of statewide readiness assessments, the most recent tests involving nearly 210,000 high school juniors in English (about 50 percent of those eligible) and more than 134,000 in Algebra II (72 percent of those eligible). The senior-year assistance programs are established statewide, and increasing numbers of high schools offer the new twelfth-grade English course. Professional development activities have spread, and CSU leaders continue to work to ensure that the university system's readiness standards are centerpieces in its teacher-preparation programs.

All of these components undergo robust evaluations. The most telling program evaluation, of course, will examine whether more students succeed on the eleventh-grade tests and are ready for CSU, and whether students who do not succeed on the tests get the help they need during their senior year and become ready for college-level work upon admission to CSU.

My work with many other states seeking to establish programs with similar purposes suggests the following observations and conclusions about the EAP:

- The EAP's ends and means are in the right order. Adjusting teacher and classroom priorities and practices reflects the true purpose of the program; testing is simply a means or tool for galvanizing these actions.
- The EAP's design and process are comprehensive and structurally sound, supporting the program's goals.
- The EAP's ultimate success will depend on the extent to which professional development penetrates statewide and teacher-preparation programs embrace the readiness standards.
- Success also will depend on whether schools and districts are held accountable for results.
- Key to bringing the CSU readiness standards into high school classrooms was a set of interrelated decisions: to focus on the state public school standards; to ensure that the exact CSU readiness standards were embedded in them; and to highlight these standards as integral components in the state accountability tests.

IMPLICATIONS FOR OTHER STATES

As the president of the Southern Regional Education Board, a nonprofit organization with 16 member states, I work with state leaders and policymakers as they wrestle with the college readiness challenge as part of the board's mission to improve K–12 and postsecondary education. From my past experiences, and more recent observations of how other states are approaching this challenge, two thoughts stand out.

First, no state program can or should be wholly replicated in every state. Not only is "ownership by creating" critical to program success, but state academic standards, assessments, professional development, governance, political environs, and accountability structures differ tremendously as they apply to public schools and higher education.

Second, while the details will vary from state to state, several key issues and decisions need to be addressed by all states as they build readiness initiatives. The results of these key decisions will determine the form and effectiveness of these state efforts.

That said, the following are observations and, in some cases, conclusions about the directions states should take.

A fundamental observation is that the consideration of all of these issues should be couched in the context of how best to guide high school classroom teachers toward helping students achieve college readiness.

Improving college readiness can only happen in the classroom. Our high school teachers certainly can and want to prepare more students for postsecondary study, but many states currently lack the conditions that would enable teachers to make college and career readiness their highest priority. All decisions about how to advance a state's readiness agenda should be targeted toward supporting a teacher-based focus on readiness.

What are these key decisions for state policymakers as they look to design state readiness programs?

Teachers need one set of college readiness standards to follow in reading, writing, and mathematics.

State policy leaders need to insist on the identification of these common standards, who sets them, and how they are applied. K–12 and postsecondary education sectors together need to develop these statewide readiness standards. In addition, all of postsecondary education needs to agree on these standards and apply them in their post-admission placement (readiness) decisions. A shortcoming of the EAP is the absence of California's 108 community colleges, which did not adopt the readiness standards and tests. Without the standards, high school teachers will continue to be confused by absent or differing definitions of readiness from various colleges. States also need to clarify that readiness is not about admissions and that access will not be reduced. As of early 2007, no state had met this challenge of developing one set of readiness standards.

The exact, discrete readiness standards created by postsecondary education and the public schools should be embedded in the state curriculum and adopted by the state K–12 and higher education boards.

This issue concerns the relationships of the college readiness and school standards. Teachers should not be forced to sort through overlaying or correlating (if not competing) sets of academic standards.

In this era of school accountability, teachers focus on these state-adopted standards and tests more than ever. A key decision during the EAP's development was to use the official state school standards as the base, and then to ensure that CSU's specific placement standards were part of the school standards. The practice of only aligning or correlating these standards was rejected. The nature and performance expectations of school standards across states will vary. Some states will need to upgrade, revise, supplement, or substitute current school standards to ensure that the exact readiness standards are embedded and that they reflect the readiness-performance expectations. It is worth the effort.

The election to use an existing state school assessment as the base for college readiness testing constituted perhaps the most critical decision made by CSU.

This key decision for state policymakers concerns the choice of tests used in high school to indicate students' level of readiness. CSU wanted to have its exact readiness standards assessed. The selection of an existing school-based test not only connected the high school and CSU readiness assessments, but it also made these elements virtually one and the same. CSU decided virtually to merge its readiness standards and readiness test items into the school tests, rather than use separate tests—one for CSU and a different one for the schools—and developing correlations that would indicate how scores on one test predict scores on the other. CSU and California's public schools chose the direct approach: identify those school standards that were identical to CSU readiness standards, adjust the school tests to fully include these joint school- and college readiness standards, and then rely on these school tests to assess achievement of the standards.

There are other reasons to use state-originated school tests, even though they may need to be revised. For one, this strategy minimizes the amount of testing students face—a practical and political concern for many educators and state leaders. Second, teachers give priority to tests that are central to state, school, and student accountability. To the extent that these state tests can be adjusted to include the full range of readiness standards, they will rise to an even higher level of priority for classroom teachers. Notably, most of the graduation tests now offered by many states do not range high enough in their standards to measure college readiness. Third, state tests by their nature must be based on the state-adopted standards and have the advantage of being closer to the classroom (especially end-of-course tests), thus facilitating the connections among standards and tests and classroom instruction.

Testing is a core issue to be resolved in crafting state readiness initiatives. States have other options, including the use of admissions and norm-referenced tests such as the ACT and SAT. These options are tempting because of their availability and familiarity, and it may be possible to make them work as readiness assessments. However, for the ACT or SAT admissions tests to be effective for state college readiness initiatives will require assurance that these tests contribute constructively to the principles outlined earlier, namely that:

- The ACT or SAT standards become the recognized statewide college readiness standards.
- The standards on which these tests are based become the officially recognized statewide public school standards—not correlates or additions.
- These tests become the state tests for assessing both college readiness and high school achievement of the school standards (and are factors in the state school accountability process).
- The ACT or SAT standards are made transparent enough so that they can be conveyed to classroom teachers in performance terms.

The more straightforward choice, though, is for states to identify one set of readiness standards agreed to by the schools and colleges statewide, integrate them into the state-adopted school standards, and then revise the state tests to measure performance on these exact standards.

A SHARED ENDEAVOR

I have been asked on several occasions what I thought was the single most valuable part of readiness programs like the EAP. Without reservation, not only the most valuable but also the one indispensable component is the bringing together (in person) of higher education faculty and public school teachers, both for standards and test construction and for professional development to convey the standards statewide. More important was why they were brought together and their method of work, which, in short, was to make college readiness performance standards-based—a concept well known and practiced since the 1990s by many public schools, but virtually unknown in higher education. Without this process for taking readiness standards beyond mere descriptions of content to what they mean in terms of student performance, they will not be useful to classroom teachers, the capable professionals who hold the keys to improving student readiness.

Defining explicitly how well and at what levels a student needs to be reading, writing, or doing math to be ready for college can be accomplished by having postsecondary and public school teachers (with the technical assistance of experts on setting and testing performance standards) interact to develop a shared understanding of expected performance levels. This can be done only by postsecondary and K–12 teachers jointly evaluating student work and negotiating a shared view of acceptable levels of performance. It will be painstaking, detailed work, but it can yield invaluable results—a clear sense of exactly how well students must perform. Indeed, this interactive process will help convey powerfully the readiness standards to classroom teachers through professional development, and to prospective teachers in preparation programs. State readiness initiatives need to be capped by such a process or else all of the standards-setting and testing will have limited value in helping more students become well prepared for postsecondary education.

PART IV

Pathways across 9–14: Practices in Place

In almost every state, high school students can take college courses through the vehicle of partnerships between high schools and local postsecondary institutions. Most of these dual enrollment programs are geared to students who are getting a head start on college but would attend in any case. However, some states have begun restructuring dual enrollment to serve as a bridge to college for low-income students and those whose parents did not go to college—young people for whom college is not a given.

Cecilia Cunningham and Roberta Matthews describe two such partnerships established between the City University of New York (CUNY) and the New York City Public Schools. These dual enrollment programs are in the form of early college high schools—small schools designed so that at-risk students can complete high school with up to 60 college credits. Cunningham and Matthews get down to the micro-level: the sustained human interaction between high school and college faculty that must exist if students are to learn in a setting in which high school and college courses are sequenced across the sectors, and students get the academic and social supports they need to succeed.

Terry Grobe describes a different secondary-postsecondary partnership for students who have failed to pass the Massachusetts Comprehensive Assessment. Another Route to College, in Holyoke, Massachusetts, places these students on a community college campus, where they take a blend of high school and college courses in a more-adult environment.

Drawing on the example of University Park Campus School in Worcester, Massachusetts, Dan Restuccia argues for an extended grade 6–12 design that does away with middle school. The 6–12 design makes a rigorous college preparatory curriculum and college-level courses accessible to all, goals that are a stretch for schools that begin in ninth grade.

These interventions are modest. In comparison, the most extensive dual enrollment partnership between two institutions, CUNY's College Now program, provided New York City public high school students with 40,000 college courses in 2005–06. Drawing on one of the few data sets tracking students in dual enrollment courses, Tracy Meade and Eric Hofmann explore what happens when a long-standing program attempts to open multiple pathways to college participation for students who are off track in their education.

Two chapters ask key questions about integrated high school/college programs for at-risk students. To answer the first question—What can research tell us about the psychological impact on students in integrated programs?—Michael Nakkula and Karen Foster have been following the "academic identity development" of students in two early college high schools. To address the second question—What does evaluation research tell us about program results?—Jennifer Lerner and Betsy Brand have identified and analyzed the common characteristics of a variety of secondary-postsecondary learning options. They also have captured preliminary outcome data and pose questions for further research.

12

Lessons from the Field

A Tale of Two Early College High Schools

Cecilia Cunningham and Roberta S. Matthews

Since 2002, we have been deeply involved in the development of two very different early college high schools in New York City—the Middle College Early College High School at LaGuardia Community College in Queens, which converted to an early college, and the Science, Technology and Research Early College High School, created in association with Brooklyn College. Both colleges are part of the City University of New York. Along the way, we have learned valuable lessons about the thorny issues associated with blending two institutions and the complex pedagogical issues that arise in preparing high school students, many from low-income backgrounds and with no history of higher education in their families, for college success.

Although each new early college high school has a unique and local developmental story, organizers find many common challenges in their attempts to break down long-standing barriers that separate high schools and colleges. Not only is it difficult to integrate high school students smoothly into college life, but it is often tricky to integrate two separate institutions and their faculties. Our experiences provide entry points for other school developers to design and implement integrated experiences.

A TALE OF SCHOOLS

In the 2003–04 school year, Middle College Early College High School (MCECHS) at LaGuardia was already 30 years old when it started an early college pilot. That same year, Science, Technology and Research (STAR) Early College High School opened as a new school, with a small number of students primarily from low-income backgrounds and with high expectations for their college success. As early college high schools, both MCECHS and STAR offer an integrated academic plan for completing a diploma and an associate's degree (or 60 transferable credits)—the equivalent of two years of college work—within five or fewer years of starting high school. Enrollment in college classes, for which students may earn both high school and college credit, is a requirement. Students move forward into college classes in some subject areas, while completing high school work in others. The schools strive for at least 60 percent of the students to acquire 24 to 30 credits by the end of the senior year in high school. These goals—and the eventual completion of a bachelor's degree—are visible to all in recruitment literature, class sessions, and student talk, and they are facilitated by a comprehensive support structure from ninth grade through graduation.

MCECHS, which is located on the LaGuardia Community College campus, already had a long tradition as a middle college high school of working with students who had experienced a lack of academic success in junior high, and it shared with its host college the mission to serve underprepared students. In 2002–03, with funds from the Ford Foundation, leaders started to plan the transition from a Middle College to an early college high school. Middle Colleges are high schools on college campuses for underserved youngsters, and every student can earn college credit. Middle College Early College students must take college classes, up to 60 credits, to earn a high school diploma. Middle Colleges and the Middle College Early Colleges have the same design principles; the only difference is the amount of college course work expected.

Because of prior experiences, many MCECHS students resisted committing to intensive academic work. Rather than risk losing their current students or shifting their demographic focus, organizers decided to use the first two years of high school to engage students, and then offer them the option, but not the requirement, of joining the early college for the eleventh and twelfth grades. Initially, 60 percent of the students chose early college during the three-year pilot, which ended successfully in 2006 with the permanent establishment of the early college.

The school then decided to develop structures to ensure that all students have a minimum of twelve college credits (the equivalent of four college courses) by the end of the twelfth grade. Many students earn an additional eighteen credits by the end of their fourth year of high school. Those who choose to may stay for one more year to complete an associate's degree along with their high school diploma. In 2006–07, there were 480 students, equally female and male, 64 percent Hispanic, 10 percent black, and 17 percent white; 67 percent are free-lunch eligible. As of the 2005–06 school year, 60 percent of the early college students had earned a high school diploma and an associate's degree (or 60 transferable credits) by the end of the fifth year in high school.

STAR emerged at the same time, but entirely from scratch. In November 2002, the Gateway Institute—a pre-college program in New York City public high schools to prepare minority and low-income students for medical careers—invited Brooklyn College to partner with it and the Woodrow Wilson National Fellowship Foundation to found a science/math high school for inner-city students. By May, there was a principal and a commitment among many key college faculty and administrators, particularly in the sciences, to support the program. This made it easier to convince others from the college to cooperate as time went on. In fall 2003, STAR opened with 5 teachers and 76 students and a space in the former Erasmus High School, approximately one mile from campus.

STAR students are primarily children of color, including many from Afro-Caribbean backgrounds who would have been zoned for Erasmus High School when it was a comprehensive high school. Many are the first in their families to go to college. Today, STAR has 448 students (including 69 sixth graders who are launching STAR Middle School). The 377 early college students are equally male and female, 80 percent black, 10 percent Hispanic, 6 percent multiracial, and 4 percent Asian and white. Overall, STAR has an attendance rate of 94 percent and expects to graduate 100 percent of its first senior class in June 2007.

LOGISTICAL LESSONS ON BLENDING TWO LEVELS OF EDUCATION

Since 2002, when the national Early College High School Initiative was launched, the model has been introduced on a large scale to public postsecondary institutions; it requires new ways of thinking for both the colleges and the high schools.[1] Both may resist the idea of fully integrating high school students into the college environment. Professors and staff are concerned that high school students will flounder or bring behavioral problems; some worry that students are too young for some of the mature themes discussed in college classes. High school administrators and teachers need to accept that they will be sharing, if not "losing," their students at some point to another institution, and that all the usual challenges of programming students to complete requirements for graduation will be complicated by association with a college. Success depends on taking advantage of a combination of the strategic, the expected, and the serendipitous; what these may be will vary, but the combination is essential.

Gradual Approach Smoothes the Way

Both MCECHS and STAR entered collaboration through "porous points" that would enable participating institutions to gradually accept the model. As school developers, we tried to find entry points into the college where our students would be welcomed and their experiences—successful or not—would be used as "teachable moments" to move the experiment forward. We did not make the mistake of trying to do it all at once.

For MCECHS, the critical decision was making the developmental (remedial) course sequence at LaGuardia Community College the entry point for all students. Faculty who teach developmental courses are accustomed to working with challenging learners and helping them advance to credit classes. All students began with an "express" developmental reading class during the summer prior to the eleventh grade, without taking the placement exam. The college had designed this weeklong intensive for those who scored just below the passing entrance exam score, and it proved successful with MCECHS students. Ninety percent of the first cohort of early college students passed the assessment test administered in the fall by the City University of New York.

This high success rate showed that the high school students were being adequately prepared for college classes; it gained trust and allies among the college faculty. Subsequent years saw an improvement in the pass rates in the reading class and on the entrance exams as the requirements for the entrance exam became visible to the high school teachers, and strategies used in the college classes were easily incorporated into high school instruction.

An entirely different approach set the entry point for STAR at Brooklyn College. During the winter of 2003–04, science faculty and administrators, whose support would be critical, met to explore what they and the college had to gain from partnering with a science/technology early college high school. They immediately saw how the project would address a number of shared goals. With the buy-in of key stakeholders, involvement followed naturally from other chairs, programs, and departments, including the School of Education, whose support was critical. Now there is an assumed commitment to STAR at Brooklyn College.

An annual summer retreat for Brooklyn College faculty and STAR teachers, first held during the summer before STAR opened, drives the collaboration. This overnight event provides a venue for sustained conversations about curriculum and students, an opportunity to share what works, and the possibility of developing new approaches and moving in new directions. Follow-up takes place through discipline-focused meetings (although these are held less often than they should be).

Through the retreat and follow-up sessions, relationships have developed around mutual interests, shared curriculum development, and team teaching. The participation of retired faculty has been a potent force for the integration of Brooklyn College and STAR. In mathematics education and in science, two key faculty members have worked with STAR teachers (many of whom came to STAR as brand-new teachers with little or no experience in the classroom) to develop curriculum materials, hands-on activities, course syllabi, practice examinations, laboratory experiments, Regents examination test-prep materials, team teaching, and the coordination of college students tutoring high school students for the Regents exams. A moment of pride for one of the retired faculty members (who as a member of the chemistry department at Brooklyn College had a long track record of reaching out to high school chemistry and physics teachers and students) came at the beginning of the second year of STAR. He was walking down the hallway past the science teacher he had mentored the year before and overheard this now "veteran" teacher say to the new science teacher, "You see that older guy over there? That's George. Listen to him."

In sum, at both MCECHS and STAR, interpersonal connections and shared concerns supported the introduction of—and continue to facilitate—cooperation and communication.

Overcoming Physical and Logistical Barriers

Integration is easier if the high school and college share a space, academic calendars, and schedules. This "power of place" happens at MCECHS, which is located on the LaGuardia Community College campus, and where the high school students are treated like college students and assume the persona of college students. But this is not so for STAR, which is a mile from Brooklyn College. However, when STAR students arrive on the college campus, they quickly assume a new persona, shedding their uniforms, arriving as individuals and not as a cohort, and insisting on buying lunch at the college cafeteria.

To accommodate the physical separation between the institutions, sections of college courses offered entirely or partly for STAR students at the college are all scheduled on the same two days. These extended periods of time on campus also maximize the number of college courses that STAR students can take. In addition, once college courses and schedules are set, usually six months to one year in advance, STAR acknowledges that whatever scheduling changes are needed after students begin registering for courses, it is the high school that must make the necessary adjustments. There are more physical and logistical barriers to be overcome when the power of place is the power of places.

College Standards Take Precedence

While the success of the high school students is paramount, college departments must control the standards, the placement of students, and the hiring of faculty to teach college courses. Further, the chairs of college departments must be actively involved in all aspects of course scheduling. The oversight of professional and accrediting organizations, and the general vigilance on college campuses that standards must be maintained, make such control essential to garnering support. On the other hand, college courses may be taught by college faculty, high school teachers, or both as teams, and their associations yield unanticipated partnership models that evolve between institutional structures and people.

PEDAGOGICAL LESSONS

From the beginning, both of us had planned to prepare high school students to adjust to the demands of college classes by offering a variety of experiences: summer workshops, advisory hours, and well-orchestrated introductions to college-level work and expectations. Nevertheless, our experiences in very different venues showed that the extent of the need is much greater than we anticipated.

At both MCECHS and STAR, the goal during the eleventh and twelfth grades is to "scaffold" the transition from high school to college, thereby smoothing the transition to postsecondary life. College work is more difficult and the pace faster, and students must be much more responsible for their own progress. Feedback from instructors is less frequent and less formal. It is each student's responsibility to seek assistance from the instructor and to ask for clarifications, a dramatic departure from the high school norm in which teachers check to see if students understand what is expected of them. Learning to function within these new norms needs to be systematically taught to students and addressed in formal structures—often several years earlier than usual.

Rigorous academic work for younger students must be coupled with strong academic supports until the students develop the habits of mind and work needed to do college work independently. The power of early college lies in doing this work with high school students, when they are more malleable to the demands and influences of their teachers and positive peers.

Several approaches have proven effective in helping students succeed as they enter the world of college—in the areas of pre-college preparation, extra supports for students doing college work, and new structures for college courses themselves.

Pre-college Experiences

STAR students have the opportunity to develop a sense of connection to Brooklyn College through a series of noncredit experiences during their first year of high school. Beginning in the first semester, a Brooklyn College librarian offers introductory library orientations to STAR teachers and students. During subsequent semesters and as the need arises, the librarian then works with STAR teachers to develop structured library visits that support subject-based class research projects.

During the second semester, STAR students take six-week, noncredit seminars developed by college faculty and STAR teachers. These seminars, taught by college faculty, expose students to various campus facilities and laboratories so that they experience the rigors of college course work before actually taking a college course. The seminars are linked to the students' high school courses and offered in such areas as anatomy, anthropology, and archaeology.

Tenth-grade students enroll in seminars that support and reinforce high school courses. They also participate in specialized tutorial seminars that are aligned with the New York State Regents exams. These seminars are provided by Brooklyn College faculty, working with STAR teachers and Brooklyn College student tutors.

Grouping High School Students Together in College Classes

At MCECHS, the decision to put high school students together in college classes, ideally in groups of eight or fewer, was informed by experiences with the power of high school guidance groups and the power of positive peer pressure and support. The high school students in each group support one another in college classes. They also provide multiple sets of notes that the high school teacher can use to teach note-taking and ensure that students have access to missed notes or homework assignments. Most importantly, students learn to meet the demands of the college class by working together. And we wanted no more than eight students in a group so the college classes would not be overwhelmed by our younger students.

We also wanted to ensure that early college students have a real college experience. To accomplish this, the MCECHS early college coordinator, a high school teacher who undertakes this responsibility, works with the college department chairs to set up the schedule of classes. This requires that the high school do more long-range planning. Arrangements must be made to ensure that there are enough sections of any given class, and the high school schedule has to coincide with the college schedule.

Co-requisite Classes

At MCECHS, students who do not pass the developmental reading or writing courses are not left behind. The first college course they take in the fall of the eleventh grade is a "co-requisite" course that does not require passing either placement test. At the community college, co-requisite classes may be taken at the same time as developmental classes, and they provide students with real college experiences. By moving all MCECHS students forward together as a group, those who have not passed the test can spend more time working on their skills while continuing to progress with their cohort. Classes like art, computer science, and foreign languages provide opportunities to gain college credit as the students improve their skills. The first college classes have proven to be very motivational for high school students—to do better in all of their classes, high school and college.

Seminars to Support College Work

MCECHS seminars are held daily, taught by a high school teacher, and provide academic assistance and guidance support for students enrolled in college classes. The seminars focus on helping students understand college expectations and learn how to "work the system," from deconstructing assignments to forming positive relationships with professors. Seminar leaders coach students to advocate for themselves, teaching them when—and how—to ask for additional help, and to understand that their need for assistance does not communicate academic or intellectual inadequacy. They also learn how to find various college resources, such as tutoring and the library, manage multiple assignments, read college texts, take effective notes, and manage their time. Peer groups work together on college assignments. Through facilitation by the seminar teacher, students can literally compare notes and review what took place in the college classroom. Seminar teachers can then help students understand how to take better notes by determining what information is central and what is tangential. In the beginning, seminar teachers are in contact with college instructors to ascertain how students are progressing. Assistance is not limited to academic issues. Students think of seminar as a supportive space where many types of problems are solved, including those that might occur within their families.

Bridge Classes

MCECHS and STAR both offer "bridge" classes (which sometimes serve as dual-credit classes) during the regular school day. At MCECHS, the classes are taught by a high school teacher jointly chosen by the corresponding college department and the high school (although sometimes they are team-taught by high school and college faculty). These semester-long classes meet five times a week, two sessions more often than the corresponding college class, in order to meet the high school seat requirements and also to offer additional support for all students to complete the course successfully. At STAR, courses are taught by college faculty on the college campus.

At both campuses, students who comfortably meet high school requirements but not college requirements can, through several mechanisms, receive just high school credit. Thus, high school students are not penalized for pushing themselves into the unknown world of college classes.

Stretch Courses

Because Brooklyn College does not offer developmental or remedial courses, STAR students must take regular college courses. One helpful strategy has been to offer the STAR students the opportunity to take "stretch" courses, which run over two semesters instead of one, to slow the academic pace and provide necessary support.

For example, STAR students, beginning in their freshman year, may take dual-credit foreign language courses to move toward fulfilling the three-semester college language requirement. But each course runs over a full year instead of a single semester. At Brooklyn College, a few such courses (generally in science and math) were offered already; providing such an opportunity to early college high school students eased the apprehensions of both high school and college participants. The "stretch" courses in foreign language have been very successful, with pass rates hovering around 99 percent.

In some cases, stretch courses serve as a transition to regular semester courses and provide the necessary scaffolding for both teachers and students to test student skill sets and course-delivery modes. Based on the strengths of the students who were placed in and completed the college composition course, the English department at Brooklyn College has decided that the students who qualify for the course are quite capable of completing it in one semester; beginning in fall 2006, English 1 was offered as a regular, single-semester course.

Stretch courses do cost more than traditional courses; however, the benefits involved more than offset the expense. We need the vision and the accounting practices to capture these efficiencies and make them operational.

JUMP-STARTING RESPONSIBILITY

Both of us had anticipated and planned for the transition from high school to college by offering summer workshops, advisory hours, and well-orchestrated introductions to college-level work and expectations. With the foresight of much experience, we began with all of this in place. However, we learned from the intense early college experience that students need even more emotional and social support than we had anticipated. The key to success was fine-tuning our application of what we already knew about students' developmental stages and consciously building upon known strengths, while also identifying and shoring up undeveloped areas.

When early college students do not succeed, they do not succeed for the same reasons that traditional or nontraditional older students do not succeed: They underestimate the amount of work expected and the degree of self-responsibility necessary to succeed. The success of high school students in college depends on jump-starting their ability to accept the responsibilities of being college students, several years earlier than usual. Success in college for younger students depends as much on the affective as the cognitive, as much on attitude as preparation, as much on willingness to step up to a different set of expectations as it does on academic prowess. And, in some cases, high school students may successfully begin accumulating college credits as early as their first year.

The early college structure should help students grow to see themselves as powerful learners, capable of success in college courses, and, in fact, real college students. For this to happen, we need:

- academic and affective support systems that start in high school and extend through college participation;
- visible articulation between the high school and college that keeps student experience at the center of all decisions;

- enhancement and expansion of peer group relationships for high school students who have increasingly more college students as peers (e.g., peer learning communities that have no age barriers); and
- enlargement of the professional educational community responsible for high school students to include college faculty and staff.

Successful integration depends on creating models that aggressively address and ameliorate the concerns of the principal players, on learning from experience, and on reversing or modifying initial approaches. Integration occurs when there is flexibility, creativity, and openness to what one learns along the way. How the barriers come down and who brings them down is a local adventure. While our examples can provide images of how it might be done, ultimately, every college and early college partnership must create the right local combinations for success.

13

Another Route to College

Terry Grobe

Another Route to College is an alternative, senior-year program for youth who have not passed the Massachusetts high-stakes graduation test. Operating at two sites, ARC is unique in Massachusetts, where few programs are experimenting with high school/college "blends" that improve the postsecondary transitions and overall academic trajectories of young people. ARC restructures the senior year of high school for a group of predominantly low-income youth and fuses it with college access and preparation services.

Launched in 2003–04, the ARC in Lawrence, Massachusetts, is a small program serving the needs of a special group of English-language learners who need intensive support to pass the Massachusetts Comprehensive Assessment System (MCAS). The students generally take ELL or study skills classes at Northern Essex Community College in order to build the language and soft skills they need to succeed in college.

The ARC in Holyoke, Massachusetts, in contrast, is going much further in using the concept of high school–postsecondary integration to serve at-risk youth. With funding from the Bill & Melinda Gates Foundation, the program is being reconstituted into a variation of an early college high school model serving young people in grades 11–12.[1] The promise of this expanded pilot program, including the issues and opportunities that have informed and driven its growth, holds lessons for a broader set of 9–14 configurations in Massachusetts and other states.

THE ORIGINS OF ARC

ARC was developed and is supported by the Commonwealth Corporation, a quasi-public state workforce development agency. The program is modeled on the senior year component—the Plus Phase—of Diploma Plus, an alternative school design for young people at risk of not completing high school, or those who have already dropped out.[2] Evaluation results were quite positive for youth in the Plus Phase: 75 percent earned a "C" or better in college course work; 80 percent went to college.[3] Early evaluation results convinced CommCorp of the efficacy of this model for helping at-risk or disengaged youth finish high school and transition to college.

The impetus for ARC came in 2001, when the level of concern rose in urban communities over the numbers of seniors who might not "get over the bar" during the first years of implementing a high-stakes graduation requirement. Massachusetts was one of the first states in the country not only to develop and implement a rigorous standards and assessment system but also to provide remedial funds for school systems with large numbers of youth who failed MCAS in the target grades (fourth, eighth, and tenth). These state remedial funds enabled school systems to fashion their own support programs or partner with other institutions to create new and innovative programming. In Springfield and Lawrence, entrepreneurial staff in the school systems and at the local community colleges built on their existing partnership efforts to help develop and launch *Another Route to College* programs, using a combination of this state funding, school system dollars, and in-kind college contributions.

PROGRAM DESIGN

In Springfield, the early college high school is a competency-based program that provides a rich mix of academic work, MCAS support, and college transition activities for youth who elect to finish high school at Holyoke Community College. In the first year of operation, 2002–03, the ARC program served approximately 30 seniors. By the fall of 2006, ECHS was serving 125 juniors and seniors.

In ARC's first year, programming consisted of senior-level humanities and math classes, remedial or for-credit work using PLATO (an online instructional system), small-group and individualized test-preparation workshops, and a senior seminar to provide career-preparation and college-transition experiences.

Now that the program has evolved into a two-year experience, students are involved in a broader mix of academics. Teachers have developed an interdisciplinary set of core courses that embed the standards and academic content students need in order to graduate from high school, and students also receive intensive help to prepare for and pass the MCAS. In year two, students continue their academic work and take the Senior Seminar that involves them, as a cohort, in career development and college planning. Students take one or two college courses as part of Senior Seminar, and complete an internship or community action project in a field of interest.

The Holyoke ARC program (now the early college high school) has encouraged students to integrate into the life of the college. Seniors have college IDs and can attend any campus sports, performance, or political event. They use college facilities, including the library, computer labs, the Career Resource Center, and the Bartley Athletic and Recreation Center.

In the spring, each senior presents a graduation portfolio to a review team comprised of program staff, college and school system partners, and other stakeholders. The portfolio contains all key documents—a professional resume, letters of reference, and college financial aid forms, applications, and acceptance letters necessary to enable students to take the next steps after high school.

WHO THE EARLY COLLEGE HIGH SCHOOL SERVES

ARC was initially designed to serve high school seniors who failed either or both sections of MCAS—English language arts and math—after one or two subsequent retakes. The Holyoke early college high school expanded the population to include juniors who need a stronger and more-supportive academic experience and more exposure to and guidance in transitioning to postsecondary education.

Both sites serve students who could be considered "underserved" in their home high schools. For example, in FY 2005, Holyoke served 27 twelfth graders and 10 eleventh graders. The largest percentage was Hispanic students at 24 percent, followed by African American youth at 18 percent. The program included roughly equal numbers of male and females. Nearly 30 percent of these youth qualified for free or reduced-price lunch, and nonnative English speakers comprised the same percentage of students. In the Lawrence site, nearly all students were nonnative speakers of English.

THE EARLY COLLEGE HIGH SCHOOL EXPERIENCES

Many Holyoke ARC students considered themselves adequate students before enrolling in the early college high school, yet most reported having bad experiences in their home high schools. Although passing the MCAS was often their main motivation to join the program, students quickly realized that, in a sense, they had "reached the end of the road" in their high school experience and needed something more. Being on a college campus and experiencing college life was exciting and challenging. Some young people felt that being on a campus actually enabled them to become more responsible and "grown-up."

Youth saw their relationships with the early college high school staff as very positive, in contrast with those they'd had with teachers in their home schools. Students perceived their teachers as "helpful, supportive, and respectful," and they felt they really benefited from being taught by such "caring and committed adults." Students also appreciated the ability to focus on a small number of academic areas, rather than a slew of courses, and most believed they got the most out of the individualized support they received in math. Students perceived their course work to be easier than work in their home high schools, but they were clear in explaining that this was because they had received extra help and support to understand the work, not because the content was easier or less demanding. Finally, many early college high school students said the program changed their views of the future. Students began to see college as doable, and then went on to formulate very specific post–high school education plans (Brigham Nahas Research Associates, 2004).

OUTCOMES

ARC has demonstrated strong outcomes at both sites; in fact, results were positive even in the first year of operation, and they have continued to improve since then. In the 2003–04 school year, over 95 percent of youth involved in the program passed the MCAS in their first or second attempt. Eighty percent of the students earned a "C" or better in their first college courses, and that same proportion of students reported that the program raised their educational aspirations.[4]

In the fourth year of operation, 2006–07, over 95 percent of young people now pass the MCAS (100 percent in the Lawrence site on the first retake), compared to

84 percent of youth statewide who passed both exams after the second attempt (64 percent of African Americans and 65 percent of Latino youth passing after the first retake) (Massachusetts Department of Education, 2004). More remarkable is that roughly 90 percent of the first cohort of early college high school youth transitioned to two- or four-year colleges.

SUPPORT FROM PARTNERS

To plan and launch the ARC program, an oversight group of school and college partners met monthly at Holyoke Community College. This group still meets on a quarterly basis to resolve issues and work on developing and expanding the early college high school model. Early on, this group finalized budgets, leveraged their institutions' resources, and secured classroom space. They also addressed a number of other critical issues, such as how to award and report "dual credit" for college courses, and how to arrange schedules and meet transportation needs, including how to reconcile the college and school system schedules and breaks. In addition, the group created staff job descriptions, interviewed and recommended finalists for staff positions, planned and conducted orientations for students and parents, and managed all phases of student recruitment and intake.

One initial concern for partners was how to secure adequate funding for this small but intensive program. Partners funded ARC through short-term support from the state Department of Education and contributions from the local school systems, each of which initially provided a teacher and additional funds for materials. Holyoke Community College provided space, student IDs, the use of its facilities, and partial support for expenses associated with use of the PLATO lab and Career Resource Center, as well as passes for the Pioneer Valley Transit Authority busing at no cost to the students during the college semester.

With program start-up under way, partners struggled with one particular and unanticipated issue: Few youth passed the college placement test on entry, a benchmark they needed to meet in order to enroll in credit-bearing college courses, rather than noncredit developmental courses. Initially, partners solved the problem by placing seniors in developmental classes with teachers who could engage them around the content and build in study skills and other college readiness strategies. Ultimately, the Holyoke ARC partners decided to admit high school students in their junior year in order to create more focused academic time before young people took their first college courses.

THE "VALUE ADD"

The early college high school at Holyoke Community College has provided a strong educational option for discouraged students, many of whom are at risk of not completing high school. By locating the program on a college campus, staffing it with supportive high school teachers, and using college resources and support staff, students get the best of both worlds. They can experience a more-adult environment where they are challenged to be responsible, while receiving the support and guidance appropriate for seniors in high school. By enrolling in dual-credit courses at the college, students get a chance to interact with a diverse group of students of various ages, benefit from their perspectives and experience, and get a start on a college career.

Because early college high school teachers work closely with the Holyoke professors in dual-credit courses, students get the support they need to succeed, and options are in place in case students appear unlikely to pass a particular college course. Because of the vigilance of the early college high school staff and college partners, students either do well in their first college classes, or they withdraw in time to avoid getting failing grades (and try again the next term). These early experiences convince a majority of students, most of whom are the first in their families to be college-bound, that they can indeed go on to college and succeed.

College preparation is integral to the Senior Seminar at Holyoke. The seminar leader builds authentic activities directly into her classes. In the fall, students use the college Career Resource Center to explore various career areas. When feasible, they choose their first college courses to reflect their individual interests. During the second semester, students participate in job shadows or internships, also related to a career field of interest. In addition, all students conduct online research to find colleges or universities with related degree programs. They visit colleges, complete financial aid forms, and, as a requirement, apply to Holyoke Community College and at least one other college of their choice. At the end of the year, seniors present graduation portfolios.

IMPLICATIONS AND OPPORTUNITIES FOR BLENDED EDUCATION

The small, pilot ARC programs have experienced a modicum of stability because of their novelty and their success in improving student outcomes. Perhaps even more important are the lessons these programs hold regarding the efficacy of blended models for struggling students and the opportunities for doing this work at greater scale.

Lawrence, a small but specialized program, provides an important educational option for youth who need intensive English-language support to pass the MCAS, graduate from high school, and transition to college or postsecondary training programs. And, in addition to ARC, Lawrence sponsors a Diploma Plus program that offers youth a longer-term high school program option. Taken together, Lawrence has begun to broaden the number of choices available to earn a high school diploma and thereby better serve youth who are discouraged or off track for graduation.

In Holyoke, partners are using the ARC experiment to think about how they might reconfigure high school using a blended design for youth who need extra support to graduate and go on to college. As the partners faced the fact that entering seniors were rarely ready to take college courses and that a solely at-risk support program was a very expensive proposition, they expanded to serve both entering juniors and seniors and renamed it "early college high school."

Significantly, when the Springfield ARC closed for part of a semester in 2005–06 because of school system budget shortfalls, the partners were determined not to lose a program that had demonstrated high school completion and college readiness value for so many youth. At midyear, they reopened with restored school system funds and funding from the Bill & Melinda Gates Foundation. Currently, the partners are developing the early college high school as a larger regional "college readiness" option; neighboring urban districts will be able to "buy slots" in the program using average daily attendance (ADA) dollars.

While the expansion of this program is to be celebrated, there is still a need to collect and study student data on college persistence. There is anecdotal evidence that ARC graduates who went on to Holyoke Community College relied on their former early college high school teachers for help and advice as they navigated their freshman year and attempted to pass the all-important "gate-keeping courses." If local practice mirrors the national trends, students are likely to need more structured and ongoing academic and counseling support into their first college years, such as an 11–14 configuration that offers a high school diploma and an associate's degree. Such a "2+2" configuration might better ensure the postsecondary success rates of these urban young people.

The Holyoke experience also illustrates how partners can grow a fully blended model from the beginnings of a small pilot program. A program like Holyoke's could operate as a small 11–14 school, located on a campus with strong Tech Prep linkages, connections with Science, Technology, Engineering, and Mathematics (STEM) initiatives, and a well-developed technology infrastructure, and taking full advantage of a recent expansion of new building space. Hypothetically, the early college high school could be sustainable with a combination of remediation and dual enrollment dollars, STEM funds, and ADA dollars from neighboring urban systems, as well as a local Job Corps Program seeking greater college access for the young people they serve.

14

Combining Middle and High School to Improve College Success

Dan Restuccia

As states and school districts seek to make dual enrollment opportunities a reality for all students, they run into the challenge of making a rigorous program of study accessible to students who enter high school already behind in their academic skills. The magnitude of this challenge cannot be overstated, particularly in urban districts. In New York City, for example, less than one-third of incoming ninth graders are reading at grade level.[1] College NOW, a program of the City University of New York (CUNY) that offers dual enrollment for juniors and seniors in the New York City public schools, has begun to take on this challenge by offering remediation supports to students through its *multiple pathways* program.[2]

Another option that CUNY—through its six early college high schools—and other innovators are pursuing is to extend high school downward to create new small secondary schools that span grade 6 or 7 to 12. Starting in the middle-school years gives educators the extra time they need to bring struggling students up to grade level and prepare them to tackle college-level course work in high school.

The case can be made for this idea—using an extended-grade design to make a rigorous college preparatory curriculum accessible to all students—at the University Park Campus School, a grade 7–12 neighborhood public school in Worcester, Massachusetts, where three-quarters of the students are low-income and two-thirds do not speak English at home. The school, which serves as a clinical training site for practitioners starting early college schools for underserved students, has had extraordinary results educating students who enter secondary school well below grade level, and catapulting them on to college. In its ten-year history, all students but one at this open-admission school have passed the tenth-grade MCAS test on the first try, and every graduate, 95 percent of whom are first-generation college-goers, has gone on to seek a higher education degree. Over half of juniors and seniors at UPCS take courses for credit at the school's partner, Clark University, a selective liberal arts institution, and 80 percent take at least one AP course. A key element of the school's success is a coherent, vertically aligned curriculum that clearly maps backwards from the standards and expectations of AP or college-level work to skill levels of incoming seventh graders. At UPCS, students learn the critical analytic thinking skills of each discipline even as they are still shoring up their basic skills.

Small grade 6–12 schools are gaining momentum nationwide as school developers search for ways to make college course work accessible to all students in high school. The College Board was funded by the Bill & Melinda Gates and Michael & Susan Dell foundations to establish up to 18 schools in New York State that would provide low-income and minority students with a rigorous, grade 6–12 or 7–12 curriculum geared toward the successful completion of college. Along with CUNY, the National Council of La Raza has adopted a grade 6–12 structure for its early college schools. A number of high-profile charter school operators have adopted the 6–12 or similarly structured model for their schools as well, including Aspire Public Schools in California, YES College Preparatory Schools in Houston (whose Southeast campus was ranked as the 88th-best high school in the nation by *Newsweek* because of its strong Advanced Placement program), Uncommon Schools in New York, and the SEED Foundation in the Washington, D.C., area.[3]

Getting an early start in preparing students for the rigors of college-level work is not the only advantage of grade 6–12 designs. Schools like UPCS, College Board Schools, and early colleges that have an explicit college preparatory mission start drumming the idea of college into students at an early age. Many—such as CUNY's early colleges and UPCS—are on or near college campuses, and others start taking students on visits to area colleges as soon as they enter. Extending the culture of college to children as young as 11 years old creates an aspirational environment, where students are motivated to persevere through the academic and personal challenges they may face. Further, mentoring between successful older students and younger ones is vital in forging a school culture that is both caring and focused on college.

While innovative school developers have led the way in championing schools that combine middle and high school grades, the idea is beginning to gain traction in systemic reform efforts. Manuel Rivera, the former superintendent of public schools in Rochester, New York, has led what is probably the most ambitious effort in the United States to adopt the upper-grades model. Rivera, who was named Superintendent of the Year in 2006 by the American Association of School Administrators, launched a wholesale reconfiguration of the city's schools into a system in which most students will attend grade 7–12 schools. Rivera cited the dismal performance of the district's middle schools and the challenges of the ninth-grade transition as the drivers behind his decision to implement this reform (Jonas, 2007).

Emphasizing the need for students to master basic skills in earlier years, and the importance of focusing in the upper grades on continuing education into college or other training, Rivera divided the schools into a "foundation academy" for seventh through ninth grades and a "commencement academy" for tenth through twelfth. At the same time, the district is aggressively pursuing college partners for each of its schools. Several secondary schools in the district are planning to convert into early college high schools. Other schools operated by the College Board require that students take at least two AP courses in order to graduate.

Early college high schools and other designs that integrate college courses into the high school curriculum seek to improve the alignment of the high school curriculum to college requirements, creating a smoother transition from high school to college. By providing a coherent grade 9–14 program of study, the early college design uses culminating college courses and standards in the upper grades to drive the high school curriculum and provide a seamless and well-structured ladder to college-level work.

But for such a seamless college transition to succeed, students need to enter grade nine ready to begin a rigorous program of study that leads to college-level work. For that, preparation needs to begin earlier, and another transition—from middle school to high school—needs to be made just as seamless. Combined middle/high schools eliminate altogether the transition in ninth grade, where many students fall off track on their path to graduate. These new small secondary schools are uniquely positioned to align the middle school curriculum to an end goal where all students are enrolling in AP or college courses by their senior year, and graduating from high school with college credit already on their transcripts.

15

CUNY College Now

Extending the Reach of Dual Enrollment

Tracy Meade and Eric Hofmann

Since the launch of the Advanced Placement program in 1955, opportunities for students to begin college while in high school have increased dramatically, with many colleges and universities now offering a variety of AP and other credit-based transition options. Most of these programs are no tall educational order: college-ready students are eligible for them; all other students are not. Some college-sponsored efforts—such as Middle Colleges and early college high schools—are specifically designed to serve these other students. They demonstrate that significant secondary-postsecondary overlap is not only possible but necessary for student success.

Less tested is the idea that *limited* interaction with a college through traditional dual enrollment can equip underprepared students for postsecondary success.[1] Research and data have provided few clues about the actual versus the theoretical capacity of dual enrollment programs to set the more-ambitious curricular goals of reaching less-prepared students because the numbers remain small: only an estimated 5 percent of institutions with dual enrollment programs serve students "at risk of educational failure" (Kleiner & Lewis, 2005).

A close look at one dual enrollment program—College Now of the City University of New York—begins to provide some answers. After several years of collecting and reporting on program data, we came to see the need for a new program model that would extend dual enrollment's reach to underprepared students. The experiences and evolution of this particular program highlight the institutionally short-sighted design of the traditional dual enrollment model vis-à-vis students equally deserving of, but deemed ineligible for, a quality university curricular encounter.

UNDERPREPARED STUDENTS SHUT OUT OF DUAL ENROLLMENT OPPORTUNITIES

College Now began in 1984 at Kingsborough Community College in Brooklyn, and it expanded in 2000 to all 17 colleges of the City University of New York (CUNY). This voluntary program provides free college-credit and preparatory courses and activities to more than 30,000 students from 280 New York City public high schools.[2]

The program is offered before and after school, both on college campuses and in high schools across the city, and it has a well-developed summer component. College Now is the largest dual enrollment program in an urban public school system in the nation, and its mission has always been twofold: to help students (1) meet high school graduation requirements, and (2) prepare for success in college.

A dual enrollment program designed in part to help students meet high school graduation requirements is a departure from a traditional model serving those who are already bound for college and want a head start. Even so, enrollment in college-credit courses continues to be College Now's main attraction. Between 2001–02 and 2004–05, enrollments in this core program activity increased by 48 percent, from 13,800 to 20,400 (see figure 1).

The answers to the most basic questions about participation and student outcomes in College Now tell a straightforward story:

- Qualified high school students are enrolled in college course sections.
- There are as many students enrolled as program coordinators estimated would participate.
- In large part, participants are doing well in their classes. In 2004–05, about 14,600 (15 percent) of the 95,300 juniors and seniors in New York City public high schools took at least one college-credit course through College Now. The program met 96 percent of its target registrations in these courses, and 81 percent of students completed them successfully.[3]

For some students, the benefits clearly last beyond their College Now course work. Conducting a multivariate analysis of students who participated in *any* type of College Now activity and entered CUNY in fall 2003, the coordinator for evaluation and research in CUNY Collaborative Programs recently found that these students had a statistically significant 5 percent increased probability of being retained into the third semester of college compared with their public high school colleagues who did not participate. Anecdotal evidence had always suggested that students felt better prepared for college because of their College Now experience;

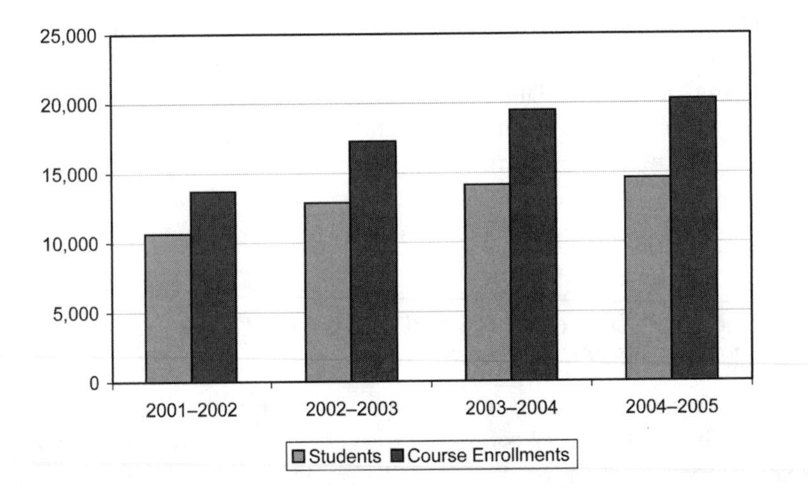

Figure 1. College Now Students and Enrollments in College-Credit Courses

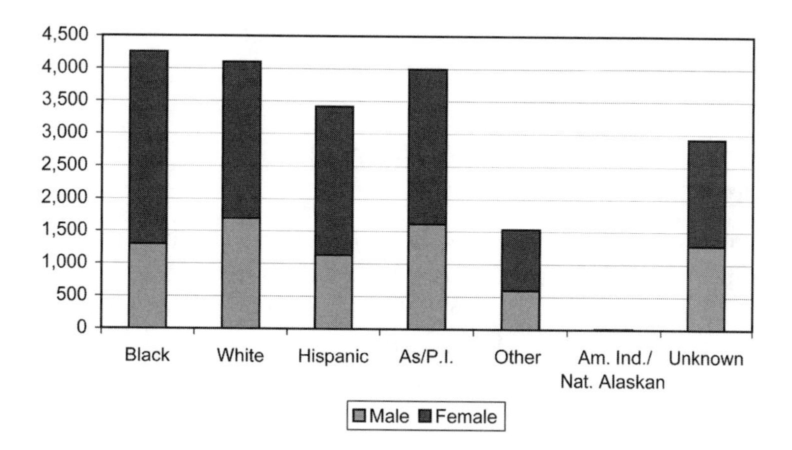

Figure 2. College Now Enrollments in College-Credit Courses by Race/Ethnicity and Gender, 2004–2005

we were encouraged to find that College Now participation also proves significant in the quantitative analysis.

Despite this and the program's many other important accomplishments, demographic data reveal that College Now does not serve a representative population of New York City eleventh and twelfth graders in courses offered for college credit. Many students cannot take advantage of credit offerings—the traditional goal for students in dual enrollment—because they do not meet CUNY eligibility requirements for these courses. Longitudinal data show familiar patterns of participation in college-credit courses and reveal significant gaps in the categories of race/ethnicity, gender, and race/ethnicity and gender combined. For example, according to statistics available from the New York City Department of Education, black male students represented 14 percent of eleventh- and twelfth-grade enrollments in 2004–05, but they accounted for only 6 percent of enrollments in college-credit courses that same year. Hispanic males represented 15 percent of eleventh- and twelfth-grade school enrollments, but they accounted for less than 6 percent of college-credit course enrollments in College Now (see figure 2).[4]

The students who enroll in the college-credit courses sponsored by College Now are those whom CUNY and its high school partners consider college-ready. In 1999, CUNY aligned its baccalaureate admissions requirements with a score of 75+ on the New York State English Language Arts and Math A Regents exams; a score of 75+ now demonstrates that a student does not need remediation at CUNY, and College Now eligibility for college-credit courses at the senior colleges, which no longer offer remedial course work, is based in part on students attaining these Regents scores.[5]

As important as this alignment is, it presently aligns only *successful* high school students with CUNY's baccalaureate programs and College Now, which is why coordinators of the 17 campus programs cite eligibility requirements as a major obstacle to enrolling a more-representative population in college-credit courses. And the other students? If and when they arrive at CUNY, many will spend time in remedial courses that carry zero credit, because a high percentage of incoming freshmen do not meet eligibility requirements in the area of reading, writing, or mathematics.

NEW PROGRAMS PREPARE UNDERREPRESENTED STUDENTS FOR COLLEGE WORK

While dual enrollment programs were never designed to fix high schools, the large number of students ineligible for credit courses in College Now or entering CUNY needing remediation has compelled the program to look for ways to reach these students earlier in high school. We believe a more comprehensive university response to bridging the secondary-postsecondary divide involves *first* understanding why so many students—and so many black and Hispanic males, in particular—are not sufficiently accomplished to access college-credit courses, *and then* providing opportunities to support their academic achievement.

To reach students who do not appear to be on track for participation in college-credit course work, College Now provides *multiple pathways* to participation. These include pre-college courses and activities for younger students to help prepare them for college-credit courses or other college-sponsored activities that keep them practicing for college. Through initiatives driven by CUNY's central office program administrators, as well as projects developed on the local campuses, College Now has developed several types of activities that serve ninth- and tenth-grade students, as well as those in eleventh and twelfth grades not eligible for college-credit courses.

Several types of recent college-influenced programming provide noncredit dual enrollment pathways for New York City public high school students. For example:

- Over the last four years, many of the College Now programs have built campus-based, daylong, four- to six-week summer programs anchored by college-credit courses, but we have stepped up funding for the development of summer programs for students ineligible for credit courses. A language arts program with rowing at the Borough of Manhattan Community College, a marine ecology program at Brooklyn College, and a Certified First Responders program at LaGuardia Community College are breaking into new dual enrollment territory by attracting students to rigorous programs that do not award college credit but demand a commitment commensurate to that of college-level study.
- In 2006, a Kingsborough Community College pre-college culinary arts course explored food cultures, food science, cooking, and entrepreneurship. Many of the students who enrolled had little knowledge of opportunities provided by technical education. One unexpected outcome was that four participants—all general education students—applied to and were accepted into the college's Culinary Arts Program. Remarkably, none of these students had even applied to college by spring of their senior year. Although this course was originally designed for tenth and eleventh graders, we found that the culinary arts theme holds promise for college professional training programs interested in reaching high school juniors and seniors who otherwise might not apply to college.

- At LaGuardia Community College, a college English teacher and a high school counselor with a psychology background collaborated to create an interdisciplinary tenth-grade course titled Oedipus on the Couch. Students study Greek tragedy through the lens of Freudian and Jungian psychology and other psychological theories. They engage in frequent writing activities and construct creative projects that enrich their understanding of the literature and theory. The instructors devote significant classroom time to probing discussions modeled on the college seminar format.

The impact of the new efforts is uncertain at this time because they are so new, but enrollment data are promising. Participation is slightly more representative of the city's high schools across each of the categories of race/ethnicity, with 15 percent selecting black or Hispanic males (compared to 12 percent in college-credit offerings in these programs). Likewise, participation by gender favors females less so. For example, male participation across the three summer 2006 courses listed above was 41 percent, compared to 34 percent in the college-credit courses offered in the respective programs in the 2005–06 academic year.

The noncredit dual enrollment options described above were not originally (or specifically) seen as part of a larger educational plan for College Now students. Their aim was simple: We wanted high-interest activities that would enroll a more-representative population of the city's students in College Now. But an opportunity was created where we could begin to imagine alternative pathways to college. As a result, we have begun closer scrutiny of this category of courses; this is in anticipation of providing a sequence of academically rigorous activities that prepare more students for college-credit courses or for a further enrollment in college-sponsored activities that keep high school students actively engaged with a college through diverse academic projects and campus experiences.

THE FOUNDATION COURSES PROJECT[6]

The major area of new programming is the development of College Now Foundation Courses. This is a curriculum and professional development project whose purpose is to prepare students primarily in tenth or eleventh grade for the academic demands of college through pre-college courses focused on learning in the disciplines. New York City high school teachers and CUNY college faculty design and teach academically rigorous, high-interest courses for high school sophomores and juniors, introducing these students to the skills and habits of a particular field, with the courses offered for high school credit (elective credit or in a subject area, as determined by the principal).

Foundation Courses begin with the question—"What are some of the important things experts do in a specific discipline?"—before exploring the processes that block student success in discipline-based practices. The purpose of these activities is not to give a content overview but rather to equip students with a set of skills that will build and expand their understanding and appreciation of issues within a discipline. Foundation Courses are being developed through participation in a semester-long workshop and designed around an engaging theme. Hands-on and experiential learning activities are a vital part of the developed curricula, with the syllabi driven by activities (including reading, writing, discussion, and problem solving), rather than by coverage of prescribed content typical of introductory survey courses.

The Foundation Courses model of curriculum development encourages the use of both low- and high-stakes assignments that provide evidence of student learning. Students receive ongoing oral and written feedback on their work, and teachers engage them in frequent "meta-conversations" about what and how they are learning and how that relates to college-level learning in a particular discipline. Some class time is set aside for reading, writing, laboratory, or problem-solving activities. While these courses often map onto general fields (e.g., English, math, science, or social science), some address standards across disciplines, focusing on literacy, numeracy, and scientific inquiry.

College Now's course design strategy considers the interplay among learning goals and activities, teaching methodologies, and learning standards. In developing this work, we have looked to the *Standards for Success* project developed under the direction of David Conley (*Understanding University Success*, 2003).[7] College Now Foundation Courses address a limited number of these standards and deepen support around the areas where students struggle most.

Faculty participants in the Foundation Courses project begin by asking the following questions:

- What prior understanding is most valuable for college courses in my discipline?
- Where do college students struggle the most in my field?
- What types of reading, writing, or numeracy activities would prepare students for study in my discipline?
- What is the proper balance of depth and breadth, or "coverage," in the initial contact with the discipline?
- What teaching strategies best serve high school students?
- What classroom technologies might enhance student learning in a particular discipline?
- What assessment approaches would be most appropriate to support student learning?

Since this project's inception in fall 2005, 33 college and high school instructors have worked with College Now to design Foundation Courses.

On another front, College Now is joining program efforts with other educational organizations and with several CUNY college initiatives funded by the National Science Foundation. These organizations and projects also are finding that high school curricula do not properly prepare capable students for postsecondary success. College Now is contributing a college preparatory component to these additional efforts.

For example, collaborating with New Visions for Public Schools, an education reform organization for improving the quality of public school education in New York City, College Now offers Foundation Courses that students in small schools in the Bronx may take to "recover" high school credits. These courses improve upon traditional credit-recovery programs, such as night school, by providing more engaging courses with a higher aim than fulfilling seat-time requirements. In summer 2006, six teachers from New Visions schools developed courses such as

Bio-Invaders, Statistics in the Bronx, Mythology, and The Sahara for implementation during the 2006–07 school year for students needing subject-area credits in order to remain on track for graduation.

In another collaboration, College Now and the Center for the Advanced Study in Education (at CUNY's doctorate-granting institution) are examining the distressingly high failure rate of public school students in Advanced Placement courses and exams. Doctoral "fellows" and high school math and science teachers are working together to identify the mismatch of college and high school math and science curricula. These curricular gaps will be filled with activities jointly created by the fellows and teachers, and the activities will then be placed in a sequence within a College Now Foundation Course. Such activities will push students to practice skills they presently arrive lacking when they enroll in college preparatory, Advanced Placement, and college-credit courses.

Students participating in these types of college-sponsored activities benefit from the early signals they receive about their preparation for doing college-level work, and they gain important exposure to academic disciplines and majors, including career majors. With effective planning and negotiations among high school and college administrators, these activities can generate course-taking sequences leading to appropriate college-credit opportunities. For students who do not participate in a capstone credit activity, at the very least they will gain some important tools for college success.

EXPANDING REACH

In hindsight, we recognize that a confluence of factors—including assumptions about the dual enrollment model—contributed to College Now's enrollment of a demographically unrepresentative slice of the New York City high school population. For example, the program's size led us, for a good three years, to increase college-credit course enrollments in response to the program's mission, without due attention to the uneven quality of the city's high schools or to whether the students we served were representative of the city as a whole. Furthermore, a program of this size requires management and accountability structures that take time to become fully operational. When these structures were in place, they provided the means to produce data reports that made it increasingly evident that a program for urban public high school students needs to provide pathways for students in *all* participating high schools, not only or predominantly those with substantial numbers of students eligible for college-credit courses.

Expanding our work in the area of pre-college activities presents real challenges. Initial analysis has revealed that course implementation will be a major obstacle without strong buy-in from high school administrators who are under pressure to show results on state-mandated tests. Moreover, whereas students who are eligible are participating in college-credit courses in large numbers, pre-college offerings are a much more difficult sell when we remove the carrot of college credit. Finally, College Now is often only one of many programs partnering with the schools, and these programs often compete for students' time and attention, reducing the number of available students for any given co-curricular program.

Given the practical challenges and the lack of national dual enrollment data in the area of balanced enrollment by race/ethnicity and gender, we believe that these programs must expand their reach earlier in school by continually engaging college faculty, creating noncredit opportunities, and, when possible, building supports for sixth, seventh, and eighth graders to produce intensely focused efforts to ensure representative participation. Moving to earlier grades means systems and curricular integration are necessary if we are to realize dual enrollment's greater potential. In time, the days of discrete sharing of successful high school students will be replaced by greater secondary-postsecondary collaboration that asks the institutions to create pathways for all students. As integration occurs, secondary and postsecondary institutions will not add disadvantage to the already-steep educational climb of urban public high school students.

16

Academic Identity Development

Student Experiences in Two Early College High Schools

Michael J. Nakkula and Karen C. Foster

There is a significant psychological complement to the larger curricular and policy issues associated with integrating grades 9 through 14. With attention finally being paid to the importance of curriculum alignment in the transition from the ninth grade in high school through the first two years of college, we must understand the experience of students participating in such curricular restructuring efforts. It should come as no surprise when successful high school graduates from underresourced and underperforming high schools struggle to experience a comparable degree of individual success in college. If high school does not adequately prepare young people for a relatively smooth transition to college, the degree of remediation needed in the freshman year can be demoralizing, even humiliating, particularly for young people who thought they were prepared when they arrived on campus.

Despite the gaps between the high school and college curriculums, most students have the intelligence to catch up and eventually earn a college degree. However, intellect plays a secondary role at best in this psychological scenario. The leading parts go to such psychosocial experiences as self-confidence or educational self-efficacy (confidence in one's educational abilities), pride, shame, motivation, and future orientation. All these psychosocial factors get wrapped together, forming what we commonly call "identity"—that is, a core, consistent sense of who we are.

To explore this psychosocial terrain in the context of the integration of high school and college, we and our colleagues have studied the experiences of students at two schools participating in the Early College High School Initiative, funded by the Bill & Melinda Gates Foundation and others. These schools have undertaken quite dramatic initiatives intended to make college success a reality for all students by making the high school-to-college transition more seamless. Within the context of efforts to integrate grades 9 through 14, this study examines the *psychological alignment* that is so important to the successful transition from high school to college.

THE EARLY COLLEGE HIGH SCHOOL INITIATIVE

Over the past three years, we have interviewed more than sixty students from the two schools, along with many of their teachers, advisors, and parents. Our goal has been to understand the ways in which students experience the opportunities presented in their schools, with a specific emphasis on what we call *educational identity development*. We want to understand how students in these schools come to see themselves as learners, and also to determine the impact of such self-perceptions on their views of the future, including how they perceive their ongoing education and career development.

The Early College High School Initiative centers on a higher education access model intended to support potential first-generation college students, particularly students of color, in the transition from high school to college by allowing them to earn up to two years of college credit or an associate's degree during high school. This core design feature is intended not only to address financial barriers to higher education but also to break down curricular disparities between high school and college course work that make the transition particularly difficult for students from low-performing high schools.

Early college high schools do not follow one particular model, but rather differ widely in their structural organizations and relationships with higher education partners. Nonetheless, the initiative expects the structures of all early college high schools to reflect features based in best-practice research, including smaller class sizes, individualized learning approaches, high academic expectations, and culturally relevant, experiential curricula.[1] Additionally, all early college high schools have a higher education partner, typically a two- or four-year college or university. The higher education partner makes college courses available to early college high school students, and it provides some level of support or consultation to improve college access and success.

With the guidance of Jobs for the Future, which manages the initiative, we selected for study two schools that reflect some of the diversity in student experiences as well as in school structures. The study began in fall 2003 and will continue at least through spring 2007, when many of the students will graduate.

The Wallace Annenberg High School in Los Angeles is part of The Accelerated School, a prekindergarten–grade 12 charter school that preceded the establishment of the early college high school. It is located in the heart of South Central Los Angeles and serves a largely Mexican American population, as well as a significant number of African American students. The school's higher education partner is California State University, Los Angeles. After their sophomore year, interested students can take college courses in chemistry and philosophy on the high school campus; during the course of the study, about 20 students completed one or more of these courses. In the summer after their junior year, approximately 60 students completed courses at the college in economics, history, and critical thinking. In addition, several Wallace Annenberg teachers are teaching college-level courses that earn the students credit at CSU, Los Angeles.

The Dayton Early College Academy in Ohio is a pilot school within the Dayton Public School District. It is located on the campus of its higher education partner, the University of Dayton, and affiliated most strongly with the university's School of Education and Allied Professions. Since DECA's inception, the higher education partnership has expanded to include Sinclair Community College, where some 50 early college high school students take credited courses toward an associate's degree. DECA is one of several model schools supported by the district in a larger campaign to attract students and families back to the public schools. DECA students are primarily African American, with smaller numbers of white students.

The philosophy of the Early College High School Initiative holds that most students, but certainly those who are at least average in academic aptitude, have the cognitive capacity to succeed in college. However, for low-income populations in general—and low-income populations of color, in particular—college is currently an option primarily for those students who are exceptional, either academically or motivationally. For middle-income populations and above, on the other hand, the average student is expected to attend and complete college. To confront this double standard, the initiative features particular facets of college *expectations*, college *exposure and experience,* and college-level *challenges*, all of which are scaffolded through ongoing advisor and teacher support intended to guide students to take advantages of such opportunities.

EXPECTATIONS, EXPERIENCE, CHALLENGE, AND TRANSFORMATION

College expectations are communicated in every facet of the early college high school experience, from application and placement interview, through ninth-grade orientation, and later in high school college-related advising. Students are expected to study college websites to learn what colleges look for in applicants and what they expect as adequate preparation. Leaders from both schools are clear that success cannot be based on a comparison of outcomes with public school systems or elsewhere; rather, it must be defined internally—within their own schools—according to a set of expectations that includes a college education for all participating students.

Early college high schools match their expectations for college success with exposure to a broad range of college-related experiences that begin in the ninth grade. Those experiences include field trips to college campuses, preparation for the college admissions exam, the planning of strategies for high school success leading to college, and discussions with guest speakers on college admissions processes and sources of financial aid, including scholarships. DECA initially eased everyday exposure by locating the classrooms for ninth-grade students on the college campus, although it has since secured its own classroom space adjacent to the campus. The high school itself was cofounded by the dean from the University of Dayton School of Education, which paved the way for meaningful partnerships with the university. By the time we interviewed them, at the end of the ninth grade, DECA students commonly spoke of "feeling like a college student"; they attributed this feeling to being a part of the college campus, including using the dining areas, classrooms, and the larger campus.

Implicit in the early college high school model is the conviction that high expectations and college exposure are insufficient if not accompanied by college-level academic challenges. Each school works to prepare students for taking college courses by the eleventh grade at the latest, although many start earlier. Preparation includes developing study skills, such as library research strategies, revising and resubmitting work, learning to use scheduling books for remembering assignments and planning for deadlines, and learning through lecture, as well as learning how to take notes on a lecture.

We have heard story upon story of the impact of success in college course work on the students' emerging view of themselves as learners and future college students. The following interview with Andrew, a tenth-grade student at the Wallace Annenberg High School, depicts the transformational impact that can ensue from the proper blend of expectation, exposure, and challenge:

Interviewer: How did you learn you were good in math?

Andrew: I was taking college calculus [in the tenth grade]. I think it was 101.

Interviewer: How did you do in it? . . . What grade did you get?

Andrew: I got an A in it.

Interviewer: Oh, that's doing very well! How did you become so strong in math?

Andrew: In middle school we had a great math teacher. . . . In sixth grade I was like a normal math student, but then in seventh grade, Ms. Stevens, she said—well, me and this other girl named Andrea, "You two are doing really well. Would you like to skip to algebra?" So that's when we went to algebra. And then it went on like that.

Interviewer: So how has this experience [of doing well in the college math class] affected the way you think about what you want to do down the road?

Andrew: Well, first I wasn't really thinking about my career or whatever, but seeing how I do good in math, I'm like—I want to be an engineer or something . . . when I get older.

Interviewer: Before you thought about that, what were you thinking?

Andrew: It wasn't too good. [laughs] I was going to be, I was trying to be a part-time garbageman.

Interviewer: [laughs] Okay. Well, this [being an engineer] is different from that.

Andrew: Yeah. This is way different. I was trying to be—because I heard they got good money. . . . You don't need a lot—like a lot of qualifications. . . . So I was going to take the easy way out, I guess.

Interviewer: Well, the easy way out in some ways, but it's not exactly easy work, right?

Andrew: Yeah, it's not easy.

Interviewer: What made you—how did you learn about being a garbageman?

Andrew: Well, I don't—I just . . . like seeing around, like, you know you see garbage trucks around. And my father told me they get paid—well, one of my father's friends, because he [Andrew's father] works for the city, not as a garbageman, but one of his friends is a garbageman and he gets paid like a good amount of money.

This interview captures classic features of the ways in which daily experiences shape longer-term identity development. At the same time, it captures a shift in functioning and perspective that is all too rare because the circumstances that supported the shift are commonly absent.

Regarding exposure, Andrew's development was proceeding along lines consistent with his view of the world. His father exposed him to a commonly seen occupation that pays a decent wage, even at part-time! In addition, he was a "normal math student" from his own perspective, until exposed to a more challenging teacher. Andrew's own expectations for himself likely began to shift after succeeding in his seventh-grade math class, but even then, he could only have conceived of himself as a good middle school math student. It was success in his college course as a tenth grader that opened up a different world of expectations, associated with the shift in aspirations from garbageman to engineer.

For students like Andrew, succeeding in a mainstream inner-city high school math class consistently results in a reduced payoff. The gap between such math classes and college course work often is extreme, and, as a result, many high school students are ill prepared for the challenges at the next level of their education. But as a student at WAHS, Andrew not only knows what those challenges look like; he has begun to meet them.

PSYCHOLOGICAL ALIGNMENT IN THE 9–14 TRANSITION

Andrew's example speaks to the importance of not only curricular alignment but psychological alignment as well. Core knowledge derived from early college high schools includes the knowledge that one can succeed in college.

Knowing is different from *believing*. Knowing for Andrew is rooted in experiential evidence. Whereas believing is largely an abstract, future-oriented phenomenon—"I believe I can succeed in college, based on my success in high school"—knowing has a stronger, immediately relevant, experiential foundation: "I know I can succeed in college because I have begun to do it."

College beliefs can be dashed when students experience a profound disconnection between college and high school course work. Genuine knowledge of college success—knowledge grounded in past success in challenging college course work—is more difficult to shake. There are exceptions, of course, such as those that occur when a student completes college course work early on that proves to be far less demanding than material encountered later on. Nonetheless, a psychological orientation toward college success, rooted in firsthand experiences of such success, is likely to be more realistic, more hardy, than one exclusively rooted in *imagining* what college will be like, based on reading about it or talking with others who have attended.

POSSIBLE AND EXPECTED SELVES

Several researchers have documented the discrepancy between underserved students' higher education plans and their school-related behavior and academic achievement. Yowell's (2002) study of students' "possible selves" found that although the "hoped-for selves" of many Latino students included attending college, their "expected selves" and "feared selves" indicated an underlying belief that they were unlikely to achieve these goals. Unlike depictions of hoped-for selves, which are founded on abstract aspirations, wishes, and fantasies, expected selves are associated with specific plans and strategies that are goal-focused and consistent with present behavior (Markus & Nurius, 1986, as cited in Yowell, 2002). Yowell argues that Latino students' comparatively lower academic achievement is more consistent with a future view of themselves that does not include higher education. Mickelson (1990) references an "attitude-achievement paradox" between the academic achievement and educational goals of African American students, noting their pattern of reporting that they plan to attend college even though their investment in school is inconsistent with that plan. Mickelson proposes that this discrepancy is due to such students' conflicting experiences about the value of education within a social context of low-income, ethnic-minority status.

Mickelson's findings are consistent with John Ogbu's (1986) influential and highly contested proposition that young African American students, males in particular, often develop an "oppositional identity" toward academic achievement, based on their linking of high achievement with white oppression. More recently, Chavous, Bernat, Schmeelk-Cone, Caldwell, Kohn-Wood, and Zimmerman (2003) have found an important caveat to Ogbu's findings that is relevant to the students in this study. They found that experiences and awareness of injustice and racism can foster academic motivation in underserved students by strengthening their resolve to refute negative expectations for their academic achievement.

The following quote, from an African American female student at DECA, is consistent with Chavous et al.'s findings:

> With math, I want to finish geometry, but I also want to start taking [courses] like precalculus and trig. I know it's going to be hard, but I want it to be hard. I want to be frustrated. So after I get it done, I can feel like, "Look what I just accomplished!"

To whom is this student speaking? She is speaking to herself, in part, but many of the students in our sample have communicated a strong desire to speak out to all doubters, particularly those who doubt them based on race or ethnicity. Part of the "expected self" for the African American and Latino students in our study is a person who is not only experienced in academic success and preparation for college, but also one specifically experienced in such matters as a student of color. Psychological alignment for many of these students includes linking academic success with perceived race-based expectations. As an African American boy at Wallace Annenberg put it so succinctly in his ninth-grade interview with our team:

> I might go to a historically black college. . . . I study black history [on my own]. It's important to know what my people have been through. I want to go on to make a difference in the world . . . and I need a college education to do that.

Psychological alignment for such students includes preparation for academic challenges, as well as race-based challenges. The *possible self* in this regard is one that anticipates such challenges abstractly; the *expected self* is one that has taken on these challenges in current encounters, thereby strengthening the student for similar challenges in the future.

FROM HOPE TO EXPERIENCE . . . AND BACK AGAIN

> I was an all-A student at [former school]. But supposedly I was on a sixth-grade level [when entering DECA as a freshman] when I took the test. I was, like, "No, this is not right." My mom was, like, "What is going on? [My daughter] has always been an A student." There was no way the test should show that I was on the sixth-grade level.
>
> —A DECA student

Psychological alignment for college success for students like the DECA student quoted above requires a great deal of restructuring, to say the least. In her case, the sixth-grade "possible self" held limitless possibilities. However, her new ninth-grade "expected self" suffered a dramatic blow. For some students and their families, experiences like these serve to motivate them for the extraordinary challenges ahead; for others, it can derail them permanently.

The Early College High School Initiative recognizes such starting points as common for many urban students in overcrowded public schools, and it takes action intentionally to restore the hope that can be dashed when confronting such realities. The work to be done requires full immersion—in the academic experiences needed for college success. The more closely those experiences approximate college-level work, the more effectively they prepare students for the realities ahead. Without such experiences, hope is likely to lead urban students to the fate of so many of their peers: college admission without graduation. With such experiences as a foundation, a college degree is much more than a possibility; it is an expectation grounded in the reality of experienced college success.

17

Secondary-Postsecondary Learning Opportunities

Some Promising Practices

Jennifer Brown Lerner and Betsy Brand

The debate about the need for higher standards in high school as a strategy to promote college access and success has gained significant traction in the last decade. One way states and districts have addressed the problem of preparation for college is to encourage high school students to take college classes for credit during high school. Such approaches help high school students learn about college, try out college-level classes, and experience the demands of college-level learning.

To better understand the impact and value of such programs, the American Youth Policy Forum (AYPF) engaged in an effort to identify program evaluations, especially of programs serving first-generation, low-income, and low-performing students, students with disabilities, and underrepresented minorities. The result is a compendium, *The College Ladder: Linking Secondary and Postsecondary Education for Success for All Students*, which profiles 22 programs and addresses questions about their effectiveness and viability.

AYPF coined the term Secondary-Postsecondary Learning Options (SPLOs) to encompass the following kinds of approaches:[1]

- *Dual Enrollment:* Provides opportunities for high school students to participate in college-level course work. Programs offered both on campuses of colleges or universities or in high schools. Includes Advanced Placement.[2]
- *Tech Prep:* A sequence of study in a technical field that offers students the opportunity to earn postsecondary credit toward a technical certificate or diploma. Funded under the Carl D. Perkins Vocational and Technology Education Act through grants to states.
- *Middle and Early College High Schools:* Autonomous schools located on or near the campus of a postsecondary education institution and integrating secondary and postsecondary courses for dual credit. Middle college high schools graduate students with a high school diploma and some postsecondary credit within five years of entry; early college high schools are designed so that students can earn both a high school diploma and an associate's degree or the equivalent within four to five years of beginning ninth grade.

- *Programs Serving Disadvantaged Youth:* Targeted at out-of-school or disadvantaged youth. Provides an opportunity for them to participate in challenging, college-level course work with appropriate support. Many programs operated by community colleges or community-based organizations in partnership with a postsecondary education institution and a school district.

OUTCOMES FOR SECONDARY-POSTSECONDARY LEARNING OPTIONS

The intent of *The College Ladder* project was to identify evaluations of Secondary-Postsecondary Learning Options within each of the four categories, and to report on their outcomes for various groups of students, particularly low-income and first-generation students. AYPF found that few programs have kept accurate data on student demographics. Few have longitudinal data or a control group, and many evaluated programs serve higher-achieving, more-advantaged students. Most have outcome data at a specific point in time, such as at high school graduation or after one semester or one year of postsecondary education. Thus, the evaluations summarized in *The College Ladder* provide a useful first step; we need a different kind of research to understand the long-term effects of SPLOs.

Within the limitations noted, the outcomes are generally positive, indicating that students receive some benefits from participating in SPLOs. For programs evaluated with a comparison control group, SPLO participants typically outperform their peers who do not participate. The evaluations did not address financial benefits or cost-savings.

The College Ladder looked at 9 outcomes and 22 studies, although no study considered all of these outcomes (see table 1).

Table 1. College Ladder Outcomes and Number of Included Studies that Look at the Outcome

Outcome	Number
College-going rates	15
Credits earned during high school	12
High school graduation, including other high school outcomes	11
College course grades/GPAs	9
High school standardized tests	7
College placement tests	6
Degree attainment/time to degree	6
College retention	5
Job market outcomes	5

SUCCESSFUL STRATEGIES

While the lack of data limits our ability to make conclusions about the overall effectiveness of Secondary-Postsecondary Learning Options, four strategies appear to help students succeed in these programs:

- Caring adult advisors;
- Academic assistance and tutoring support;
- College success class in pre-semester or first semester; and
- A safe environment and peer support network.

The examples that accompany each strategy described below only begin to demonstrate the creative means through which the SPLOs included in *The College Ladder* personalize their programs and closely align their approaches with youth development principles that have proven effective for serving low- and middle-achieving students.

Caring Adult Advisors

Research has demonstrated that with access to caring adults, young people will be more successful as adults themselves, and, at-risk youth, especially, will demonstrate significant benefits by being paired with a caring, competent adult over time (Jekielek, Moore, Hair, & Scarupa, 2002). The programs included in *The College Ladder* present a range of advising programs, from formal curricula interwoven into the school day, to more informal relationships based upon student needs. Guidance is particularly required in SPLOs because students must negotiate secondary and postsecondary systems simultaneously.

The Early College Program at Wells High School in Maine is a partnership with the York County Community College. The Wells Early College Program is part of Maine's statewide high school reform effort to ensure success and increase students' college-going rates. Recruitment targets students who are considered underperforming because they are not working to their full potential; they face financial barriers to college; they are uncertain about their aspirations and future; or they would be first-generation college attendees.

The Wells program was designed with a "high-touch" philosophy to engage students constantly with their adult advisors for extensive support and personalized contact, both at the community college and high school. Advisors also support the collaboration between the two institutions, supporting collaborations between their faculties. Program coordinators based at the community college are responsible for day-to-day operations: recruitment, admissions, orientation, and serving as primary advisors for student participants. The coordinators monitor students' academics and provide an outlet for them to raise issues or concerns, either academic or socioemotional. The high school advocate, typically a guidance counselor, assists with student advisement and also participates in the admissions decisions and serves as a resource for the high school faculty.[3]

Academic Assistance and Tutoring Support

There is a strong relationship between utilization of academic support services and persistence to program or degree completion (Churchill & Iwai, 1981). Students who receive academic support improve their scholastic performance and develop higher expectations for future educational success (Smith, Walter, & Hoey, 1992). Peer tutoring also affects student retention, especially for underrepresented and disadvantaged students who need to develop basic academic skills (National Academy of Sciences–National Research Council, 1977).

Many SPLOs have academic assistance programs to ensure that students succeed in college courses, but few such supports are integrated into the academic program design. Comprehensive academic assistance services include monitoring student progress throughout a course, creating plans to ensure that struggling students complete courses successfully, and offering intensive tutoring. SPLOs that are autonomous "blended" schools, such as middle and early college high schools, are most likely to include these intensive services.

Middle College High School at San Joaquin Delta College in California serves students in grades 9–12 who may be the first members of their families to attend college and have had difficulty affiliating within a large high school (e.g., students who would not feel comfortable in afterschool clubs or sports). Middle College High School focuses on preparing students to attend four-year colleges and universities. It recently converted to the early college high school model, which allows students, if they choose, to spend an additional year at the community college to earn either an associate's degree or additional credit transferable to a four-year institution.

To integrate incoming students into Middle College High School's elevated academic expectations, students must participate in the Academic Success Center (ASC), a proactive, early intervention program. The ASC provides structured, supervised, study hall time where teaching assistants—either community college students or Middle College students who have previously succeeded in a college course—work one-on-one with current students. Together, they complete homework, organize notebooks, or review note-taking and study skills as students adjust to the more-rigorous demands of college courses.[4]

College Success Class in Pre-Semester or First Semester

College preparatory programs play an important role in the preparation of at-risk and underrepresented students for college, but there is little empirical evidence related to the actual success of such programs (Swail, 2004). Many of the SPLOs require students to participate in "college success classes" before entering a college classroom. Such classes typically cover study skills, time management, and expectations of college-level courses. According to the student survey responses and program data we reviewed, these courses significantly contribute to student success in the college classroom.

The Gateway to College program of Portland Community College in Oregon serves students who have either dropped out or are considering dropping out of high school by providing an educational experience that allows them to earn a high school diploma while simultaneously earning significant college credit or an associate's degree. These students are defined by program admissions criteria as behind in high school credits based on age cohort, a GPA of 2.0 or below, or having erratic attendance patterns. During the initial semester, entitled Gateway Foundation, students participate in college survival and success classes that help develop effective study skills, acclimate them to college life, and introduce them to the facilities and services available at Portland Community College.[5]

Safe Environment and Peer Support Network

Research confirms that peer support has the power to promote student learning (McKeachie, Pintrich, Lin, & Smith, 1986). In addition, peer networks serve to develop the social skills that are essential for success in life after college (Cross, 1985). Students cite the environment created at SPLOs, particularly those that encompass the entire school day, as a key ingredient of success. They report that school is a place where it is "cool" to do well and that it provides opportunities to engage in lively discussions with classmates. The evaluations point to efforts by SPLOs to value these students as serious scholars. Student participants also comment on a culture of positive peer pressure that exists when their classmates challenge themselves and one another and when adults set high expectations for their performance.

Initially funded through the Charles Stewart Mott Foundation, Mott Middle College in Flint, Michigan, attracts students from diverse backgrounds who are unhappy or unsuccessful in their district high school. Located on the campus of Mott Community College, the school has established itself as an alternative school serving students with emotional problems who need help overcoming challenges, including balancing school and family life. Mott Middle College's guidance approach is based upon creating a relationship of mutual trust among all members of the school community and teaching students how to be autonomous individuals. The weekly "activity period" supplements this concept of mutual trust by allowing students to see teachers in a different light, outside of the classroom. During this time, students and teachers share activities and knowledge through informal activities, such as chess games or jam sessions.

Students meet twice weekly in focus groups of approximately 20 students and one faculty advisor. The groups discuss issues, academic or social, that prevent students from succeeding in school. Focus groups also serve as school governance committees; students use these as a forum to bring up ideas for school improvement. Faculty focus group leaders often use this time to introduce workshops on soft skills, such as conflict-resolution or study skills, to supplement the academic curriculum. Although classes are small—typically no more than 22 students—and often incorporate these skills, focus groups are an opportunity to personalize the school community by creating a family atmosphere. Students traditionally remain in the same focus group during their time at Mott Middle College.[6]

NEED FOR IMPROVED DATA

As all who have studied these programs know, there is a pressing need for better data collection. Typically, Secondary-Postsecondary Learning Options collect and maintain qualitative data that provide information on student attitudes toward programs, not quantitative data demonstrating student success in college-level course work or longer-term outcomes, such as enrollment and success in postsecondary education or job attainment and wages. In addition, few programs disaggregate data by race, ethnicity, income level, or other characteristics. Because the data, especially quantitative data, are so sparse, it is difficult to provide definitive answers on the benefits of SPLOs.

We are energized by promising new data collection efforts, such as the Early College High School Initiative's Student Information System. The system will contain data on student achievement prior, during, and after their enrollment in an early college high school, providing a longitudinal data sheet on participants. This will allow for the assessment of the long-term effects of student participation in SPLOs. In addition, the Student Information System will allow early college high schools to compare their outcome data with other high schools in their district. Comparison data will not only provide evidence of effectiveness of early college high schools, but will also help districts identify approaches that are successful in increasing persistence in high school and higher education.[7]

While data is of obvious value to researchers and policymakers as they seek to determine the effectiveness and value of these programs, there are other important reasons for programs to collect and review data. Data has immense value to the programs as a means for evaluating, assessing, and improving their own practice on a regular basis. While outcome data gathered by programs often merits celebration, it can also shed light on problem areas leading to program improvements. Recognizing that many practitioners view data collection as a burdensome chore, we encourage them to consider data as an important tool in program development and sustainability, and we encourage the funders of SPLOs to provide for data collection.

A NEW APPROACH

While we lack empirical data to make sweeping claims about the value of SPLOs, it is clear that they help students to complete high school, access more rigorous curricula, and think about college in their future. The strategies outlined here help explain why SPLOs are proving successful, particularly with low- and middle-achieving students. In some cases, it is a simple matter of providing more support, more adult guidance, and higher expectations to young people whose high school environment has lacked these essential ingredients.

Understanding the potential of SPLOs will promote a new approach to secondary education, one that breaks down the barriers between high school and college and involves youth earlier and more directly in the adult world. The structures and supports necessary to blend secondary and postsecondary education are continuing to be explored and tested. We strongly believe this is the right direction for high school reform. Youth need a broader view of their future than what high schools normally offer. Being on a college campus or accessing college-level course work may help them imagine a different and more positive future.

PART V

Pathways across 9–14: Emerging Policies

The first three essays here discuss the policies needed to build, sustain, and further develop pathways across 9–14. The policies are quite specific. Some were identified by practitioners who met barriers in their work, such as stringent eligibility requirements for participation in dual enrollment or a prohibition against using high school funds to pay for college course-taking. Others were developed through research: for example, Indiana is the first state to require schools to report on the number of ninth graders who do not have enough credits to be promoted. The legislation draws on research on early warning indicators—those factors that identify high schoolers not on track to timely graduation.

The authors also point to mid-level policy problems that must be solved in the long term to provide a true integrated 9–14 system. Joel Vargas discusses ways to reconcile K–12 per-pupil expenditures with flexible financing across 9–14. Flexible funding could open the doors of community colleges to older adolescents who have disengaged from high school. As Adria Steinberg and Cheryl Almeida note in writing about improving pathways for struggling students, the accessibility and relative affordability of community colleges make them a potentially powerful bridge into the education system or labor market. Robert Palaich, John Augenblick, and Margaretha Maloney suggest that states would gain long-term benefits by making short-term financial investments to promote the accelerated advancement of low-income and first-generation students into college-level work while still in high school.

This section also focuses on ways the developing state policy agenda could reshape the educational experience in grades 9–14. Nancy Hoffman argues that dual enrollment can serve as the foundation for a 9–14 system; it already requires formal, permanent structures for the flow of students, dollars, and credits across the high school/college divide. Using the frame of an "adaptive innovation," Travis Reindl recommends the next steps to figure out whether and how accelerated learning options (Advanced Placement, International Baccalaureate, early and middle colleges) can reshape the 9–14 landscape to get better results.

In the United Kingdom, as in the United States, the participation of young people in education beyond the level required by statute has stagnated over the last decade. And both countries have fallen behind the best-performing OECD countries. The sole non-U.S. contributor to the book, Geoff Hayward describes a comprehensive, unconventional, and long-term policy development exercise, the Nuffield 14–19 Review, from which the United States could learn much. Launched in 2003 and now developing an advocacy agenda, the Review engages a wide network of people from schools, higher education institutions, unions, the private sector, government, and voluntary organizations. Among the most important factors in the Review's analysis of the "push and pull [of young people] into and out of the education and training systems" is their decisionmaking process.

18

Creating Pathways for Struggling Students within a 9–14 System

Adria Steinberg and Cheryl Almeida

The rising aspirations of young people are evident in the growing percentage who identify "going to college" as their goal and expectation, and in the growing percentage who, in fact, enter a two- or four-year college directly after graduating from high school. Less evident is the fact that college aspirations and educational persistence also characterize a growing percentage of the young people who struggle to make it through high school in five or six years or who leave before achieving a diploma.

Emergent data revealing that 30 percent of our young people are not on track to graduate from high school in four years, if at all, have driven renewed attention to struggling and out-of-school youth (Olsen, 2006). While this group of young people is no longer invisible, policy and practice leaders continue to underestimate them—not just in sheer numbers, but also in motivation and capability.

Although many states are undertaking efforts to address the dropout problem, these efforts tend to remain separate from those aimed at K–16 integration or college and career success. By maintaining this bifurcation, state leaders are reinforcing the view that college is the expected destination only for some, and that for those who fall off track at any point during high school, a satisfactory outcome of policy is to increase the number who achieve a high school diploma or alternative certificate (most frequently the General Education Development certificate—the GED) and, perhaps, an entry-level job.

As "keen economists," young people themselves are well aware of the limitations of these outcomes.[1] It is only marginally easier for GED holders to get a job than it is for high school dropouts, and their lifetime earnings are not substantially higher than those of their dropout counterparts.[2] Neither the GED nor an entry-level job suffices as an end goal.

The renewed attention to the scope of the dropout problem, and the growing commitment to a more seamless pathway for students in grades 9–14, offer state policy and opinion leaders a critical opportunity to integrate these two conversations around a unified policy goal: helping all young people to obtain the postsecondary skills and credentials that are necessary to a successful and productive adulthood. Making good on this promise requires public policies that will give dropouts a second chance within a 9–14 integrated education system.

RISING ASPIRATIONS / STAGNANT ATTAINMENT

Analysis of longitudinal data on the persistence patterns of dropouts offers a window into a set of issues that deserves a more central place within the developing interest in a more integrated 9–14 educational system. The "dropout problem" has long been viewed as confined to a very small—and particularly troubled or unmotivated—group of young people. A recent analysis of data from the National Educational Longitudinal Survey tells a very different story (Almeida, Johnson, & Steinberg, 2006). More than half of the young people who do not graduate from high school on time demonstrate through their behavior that they understand the importance of education and are willing to work hard to get a diploma and proceed to postsecondary education, despite the lack of options offered to them by the school system. These young people may have given up on their high school, but most do not give up on their education.

Only a small percentage of those who do not graduate in four years complete high school in a fifth or sixth year. However, close to 60 percent of dropouts do earn a high school credential within 12 years of starting high school—in most cases by passing the tests for a GED certificate. These young people do not stop there; they persist in seeking education beyond high school. Unfortunately, this persistence does not pay off the way young people might hope. Although nearly half of these GED holders enroll in a two- or four-year postsecondary institution, fewer than 10 percent of those who enroll will ever earn a degree, leaving them with limited career prospects at best.

As the data show, the considerable number of young people who drop out of high school are not more likely to reject the value of school than their peers. Yet once off track, these young people find that they are not offered alternative pathways to a successful future. Insofar as dropping out has been a concern of policymakers, they have focused on who drops out, why they do so, and what remediation or intervention programs help these individuals get a diploma and/or a job. A longitudinal analysis shifts the emphasis to two sets of questions:

- How and why do current educational options fail so many of our young people, and then subsequently fail to effectively recapture so many of them who get off track or drop out altogether; and
- How can our education system put them back on a pathway to earn both secondary and postsecondary credentials?

The answers to these questions are central to changing the life circumstances of the many young people who exit (and try to reenter) the education pipeline and struggle in today's economy.

TAKING ADVANTAGE OF BREAKTHROUGH RESEARCH

Fortunately, a growing base of evidence is helping to provide answers. In a series of groundbreaking studies of large urban districts with low graduation rates, researchers have identified leading indicators of dropping out that reliably identify students who, absent a school-based intervention, are unlikely to graduate from high school. Recent studies conducted by Elaine Allensworth and colleagues at Consortium on Chicago Schools Research, using data from the Chicago public schools, showed that an on-track indicator that signals when ninth graders are falling seriously off the track to earning a diploma is 85 percent predictive of future dropping out (Allensworth & Easton, 2005).[3]

Using its own definition of "over-aged and under-credited" high school students, the New York City Board of Education worked with researchers at the Parthenon Group and found that just under 20 percent of the high school students who are off track from a potential on-time graduation graduate within six years from their entry into high school (Lynch, 2006). Robert Balfanz of Johns Hopkins University and Liza Herzog of the Philadelphia Education Fund, using data from the Philadelphia public schools, have shown that school-based factors (e.g., behavior reports, poor grades) have predictive value for identifying future dropouts as early as sixth grade (Balfanz & Herzog, 2005).

This research, while offering discouraging data on the scope of the problem, also opens up the hope and possibility of new and much more effective approaches to policy and programming. Previous generations of research had identified a range of risk factors associated with dropping out, but none of these factors, alone or in combination, were strong predictors of whether a particular student would graduate. In fact, the best they yielded was about a 30 percent rate of predictability: that is, 70 percent of young people with the factor or combination of factors would have graduated anyway.[4] As a result, dropout prevention programs often served many students who would have graduated without the benefit of the program, and they probably failed to reach many of the students who most needed support. This problem, combined with the usual placement of dropout programs on the margins of daily school life, made it unlikely that schools, districts, or states would ever address the problem at scale.

The new research challenges the common misperception that dropping out is a one-time event, a decision made by individuals at one moment in time and largely influenced by personal or social circumstances beyond the school's influence or control. Far from being idiosyncratic, dropouts seem to follow identifiable patterns of performance and behavior in school—patterns that schools, districts, and states can and should analyze and address (Jerald, 2006). The knowledge yielded by leading indicators, such as those identified in this new research, appropriately focuses attention on the currently high rates of ninth-grade course failure, and it allows school leaders to take action before it is too late.

GROWTH IN EVIDENCE-BASED PRACTICE

Improved early warning systems are necessary but not sufficient. Successful action also involves having credible and consistent information on what works to ensure high school completion while also improving academic performance. The perception has long been widespread that "we do not know what, if anything, works" in dropout prevention or reentry. Here, too, recent research offers reasons for optimism. Policy and practice leaders can now design interventions based on a growing body of evidence about highly effective practices and strategies for addressing early academic difficulty in high school. This research further advances the possibility, and the obligation, to address these issues at scale.

Notably, evidence analyzed in MDRC's study of the ninth-grade Success Academy component of the Talent Development Comprehensive School Reform model, as well as district-based research in Chicago, show strong results from particular practices to improve students' skills in the first six months of ninth grade (Quint, 2006). Specifically, researchers have validated the efficacy of such practices as:

- more-intensive focus on literacy and mathematics in the early months of ninth grade, with a focus on helping students catch up to where their skills need to be in order to deal with high school–level texts and assignments;
- extended learning time in the after-school hours, as part of the catch-up and acceleration strategy; and
- quick response to academic failure, even before the reporting of first-semester grades.

Researchers have shown that the use of such strategies in the ninth grade has resulted in significantly more students passing "gateway" academic courses, such as Algebra, and in higher promotion rates from ninth to tenth grade. That, in turn, is highly predictive of whether a student graduates from high school.

The recent breakthroughs of actionable knowledge described here are already leading to breakthroughs in policy and practice. Challenged by low graduation and high dropout rates, a growing number of districts has begun to apply the new knowledge. Districts such as Philadelphia, New York City, Boston, and Portland, Oregon, are using predictive factors and research on effective practices to put in place systemic strategies directed at making substantial improvements in the high school graduation rate, without compromising their simultaneous push on raising the level of academic performance to the standard of college and career readiness.

These evidence-based strategies include both improved programming to ensure that students stay on track in high schools—especially in the ninth grade—and developing new schooling models and options for students who need a substantially different and more flexible form of programming. Perhaps the most ambitious effort, the design of "multiple pathways to graduation" in New York City, is a determined attempt to offer a differentiated range of options to students at very different points (in terms of age and credits) in the academic trajectory to graduation. Program designs recognize the potentially different strengths and needs of several different groupings of students:

- students who are 16 and have not completed ninth grade;
- older students (ages 17 to 20) who have accumulated many of the necessary credits before dropping out of high school; and
- older students with few credits and low skill levels.

Although this is a relatively recent effort, New York City officials are beginning to see a positive trend in graduation rates. Transfer schools—small, academically rigorous high schools specifically designed to help students get back on track to a diploma—consistently graduate two to three times more students who are overaged and under-credited than do the comprehensive high schools (Lynch, 2006).

These and other districts are combining various resource streams to develop options and pathways that help dropouts attain a high school diploma and college degree or certificate that leads to economic self-sufficiency. They are finding that there is no dearth of 17- to 21-year-olds willing to commit to diploma-granting high schools, *if* the programs are designed with the flexible schedules and curricula needed to address older learners' interests and family and economic responsibilities. These cities are also exploring "GED plus" models as an alternative for older students who have so few high school credits that returning to a diploma-granting program is really not feasible. Rather than simply preparing students to pass the GED exams, these programs directly take on preparing them to be successful in college.

BRINGING STRUGGLING STUDENTS AND DROPOUTS INTO THE CENTER OF A 9–14 INTEGRATED SYSTEM: THE ROLE OF POLICY

The growing evidence base of research and practice in regard to struggling students and dropouts yields insights as to the role of policy in creating a more integrated and aligned 9–14 system. A primary goal should be to produce far more high school graduates than currently emerge from our K–12 system, while also maintaining high standards of academic performance that ensure the success of this expanded pool of graduates in completing at least two years of postsecondary education. Three policy areas are emerging as particularly central to achieving that goal:

- Make graduation rates count in state accountability.
- Ratchet up dropout prevention through early warning systems.
- Support multiple pathways to and through a postsecondary credential.

State Accountability for Graduation Rates

A key conversation in K–16 efforts has centered on policies to enable greater integration of secondary/postsecondary accountability for student outcomes, encompassing the transition from high school to college, as well as college completion rates. But, as the research shows, for many young people, transition problems begin much earlier—particularly in the transition into and through ninth grade. States can and should address this problem by counting and accounting for dropouts in their accountability systems.

Schools, districts, and states currently have little, if any, incentive to pay continuing attention to the students they are losing. As the framers of the No Child Left Behind law recognized, there can be serious unintended consequences to emphasizing academic proficiency without a concomitant focus on ensuring that all students graduate from high school. While NCLB took a first step in establishing the graduation rate as a key element for measuring school and district performance, it created little real accountability for this at the state or district level. Unlike accountability for academic achievement, the federal government has not required graduation rates to be reported according to subgroups. And states have been allowed to propose their own methods for calculating graduation rates and to set their own—generally quite low—improvement goals.

The recent commitment of all 50 governors to using a common, four-year cohort rate graduation measure offers an important opportunity to make progress on these issues. Sixteen states have taken the lead and will publicly report cohort graduation rates by the end of 2007 (Curran, 2006).

While making cohort graduation rates public is a significant first step toward increased accountability for graduation, states and districts need to go further and recalibrate their educational accountability systems to ensure that every student does count, and to create incentives for schools to pay attention to struggling students. For example, Louisiana has framed a policy that will take effect in 2007 to provide incentives for high schools to encourage struggling students to stay in school and to tackle challenging course work that fully prepares them to succeed in college and work. The plan calls for awarding points in the accountability system not just on the basis of how well schools are doing in helping students reach proficiency targets, but also on their success at getting students across the finish line with a high school diploma (Steinberg, Johnson, & Pennington, 2006).

Early Warning Systems

A second key focus of state and district policy within a 9–14 system should be the strategic use of early warning indicators to identify potential noncompleters and ensure that students get back on track to graduation as quickly as possible. Being "off track" during the first year of high school is a strong predictor of school dropout. Addressing this problem early in high school is consistent with the best current research on ways that students disconnect from school and what schools can do to respond quickly to early signs of such disconnection.

In comprehensive dropout legislation enacted in 2006, Indiana has taken a first stab at this problem by requiring schools and districts to report the number of ninth graders who do not have enough credits to be promoted to tenth grade, and to advise such students of ways to recover missing credits and/or obtain remediation. Such a policy calls attention to the school-based factors that contribute to low graduation rates and creates a demand for more credit recovery and acceleration programs that will interrupt these factors and help students get back on track quickly.

Multiple Pathways to and through a Postsecondary Credential

Fashioning policies that create multiple pathways to take students through grade 14 is a third key area of policy. As described earlier, a number of school districts have begun to develop multiple pathways to high school graduation, in partnership with community and youth development organizations, school development organizations, and postsecondary institutions. Some are also starting to launch options and pathways that bridge directly into postsecondary. States could do a great deal more to enable such work.

Forty-two states have dual enrollment legislation that allows high school students to take credit-bearing college courses during their junior and senior years, but very few extend this opportunity to students who are off track to graduation or offer it as a pathway for returning dropouts to a high school diploma and postsecondary credential.

Indiana's dropout prevention legislation positions the state as one of few in the country leveraging dual enrollment to jump-start attainment for young people who have left high school without a credential. The legislation specifies the use of state dual enrollment funds to support "Fast Track to College Programs," which are high school and college "blends" that offer older dropouts—over 18—a way to earn both a high school diploma and an associate's degree. In an effort to open access to college courses to students who were not achieving in traditional high schools, dual enrollment in Massachusetts has included a specific set-aside for alternative education students.

The accessibility and relative affordability of community colleges make them a potentially powerful bridge into the education system or labor market for older adolescents who have dropped out of high school. But very few dropouts succeed in such institutions. Community colleges that offer GED programming on campus and community-based GED programs linked to community colleges are better positioned than are stand-alone GED programs to help completers make a smooth transition into appropriate college pathways. In implementing a 9–14 system, states can create incentives for providing GED programs at or linked to community colleges, and for the development of programs that combine developmental education with vocational or other credit courses, so that students without diplomas can accelerate their learning program and advance quickly.

CONCLUSION

It has long been assumed that the vast majority of young people will complete high school in four years, prepared to move directly to postsecondary study and/or work. We now know that 30 percent of all young people in the United States and roughly half of all black and Latino youth do not reach the milestone of an on-time graduation. Many flounder for years, trying to find or construct a pathway to the skills and credentials they need for full participation in civic and economic life.

State leaders today have an unprecedented opportunity to draw public attention to leakages in the education pipeline. Specifically, it is a moment to gain traction for policies that are based on new research on what works in dropout prevention and recovery and that take advantage of and reward the persistence demonstrated by so many older adolescents and young adults as they try to find pathways to the skills and credentials they need.

As long as the "dropout problem" was viewed as confined to a small, and perhaps troubled or unmotivated, group of young people, the proposed remedies could also be marginal—a program here, a policy waiver there. The current moment creates an obligation and an opportunity to embrace a more strategic and systemic approach. Fortunately, many states already have a platform for doing so, in the form of an active K–16 Council, or an Education Roundtable, or a Governor's Blue Ribbon Task Force on college and career success or economic competitiveness. Such bodies provide an appropriate forum for a systemic review of grades 9 through 14, with the goal of helping all young people—including those who are struggling or have left school altogether—to obtain the postsecondary skills and credentials for a productive adulthood.

19

State Policies that Support the Integration of 9–14

The Case of Early College High Schools

Joel Vargas

State policy is instrumental in promoting schools, programs, and partnerships that integrate grades 9–14. One way to grasp how state policies must adapt to support and expand these approaches is to examine their effect in several states on implementing one popular integrated school design: the early college high school. With over 130 early college high schools in over 20 states, a good understanding has emerged of what state policymakers can do to initiate, support, and sustain these small schools of 400 or fewer students. This understanding, in turn, can inform the development of policies to support related models.

Because early college high schools combine high school and college, they put into sharp relief the gaping disconnect between secondary and postsecondary education—in both practice and policy—even as they try to bridge that divide for underserved students. However, several types of state policy can support early college high schools and other models sharing their key practices. That is, the fledgling early college high school movement points to challenges and opportunities states have in building more robust dual enrollment programs, expanding Advanced Placement opportunities, and promoting other approaches that integrate high school and college work.

Early college high schools are autonomous schools that can improve college attainment for students who are underrepresented in postsecondary education, including low-income students, Latinos, African Americans, Native Americans, and English-language learners. Created by collaborations between local education agencies and colleges, they are designed so that underserved students can simultaneously earn a high school diploma and an associate's degree, or up to two years of transferable college credit.

The early college high school movement is still too young to make definitive judgments about its efficacy. However, early evidence from the oldest of these schools is very promising. Of 115 students starting at the first three early college high schools four years ago, over 95 percent graduated with a high school diploma, over 57 percent earned an associate's degree, and over 80 percent were accepted at a four-year college.[1] If results from this small initial group is any indication of future school success, early college high schools will be an important state strategy for improving high school and postsecondary attainment. Currently, there are nearly 16,000 students in early college high schools nationally; as the number of schools expands to over 240 by the end of the decade, total enrollment is projected to grow to over 80,000 young people.

While no state has adopted a full set of the policies needed to support early college high schools, some already had favorable policies on which to build or have reshaped key policies to meet early college goals. Changes to date are modest, but they suggest that some states are open to harmonizing dissonant policies—or, at least, to finding enough latitude within existing rules—to have established over 130 early college high schools nationally.

EARLY COLLEGE HIGH SCHOOL FEATURES AND THE ROLE OF STATE POLICY

Based on research and practice about what helps underrepresented young people move into and through postsecondary education, early college high schools have several key features that may or may not be supported by state policy.

- Students are motivated to work hard in school by the opportunity to accelerate into college-level work as soon as they are academically ready for it, sometimes as early as the ninth grade.
- Students are rewarded for hard work with the opportunity to earn two years of college credit, tuition-free.
- Learning takes place in small, personalized learning environments that demand rigorous, high-quality work and provide extensive support so that students can meet that demand.
- The physical transition between high school and college is eliminated—and with it the need to apply for college and for financial aid.
- Early college high schools are located on or near a college campus, so that young people experience the academic and social environment of college from an early age.
- Because they prepare students early for college-level work and must align curricula from grades 9–14, high school faculty better understand the skills and knowledge students must possess for success in college. The postsecondary institution, by dealing directly with high school–aged students, gains knowledge about how to improve both the transition to college and retention rates in the first years of college.

The policies affecting early college high schools and their development of these features lie primarily in seven areas: dual enrollment/dual credit, transfer rules, college eligibility requirements, teacher qualifications, funding formulas and structures, state accountability systems, and school-level autonomy. Early college high schools have found that some policies are likely to be in place already or are relatively easy to change. Other policy changes have been harder, if not intractable.

Easiest

Dual Enrollment / Dual Credit

Early college high school students should be able to count college courses simultaneously for high school graduation and college credit, as well as to satisfy high school day/minute requirements. In early college high schools or in an integrated system, student advancement should be based on demonstrations of proficiency according to aligned 9–14 standards, not according to seat time (the amount of time students spend in a high school class). If a student passes a college course covering content that meets or surpasses that of a high school course, it should count toward high school graduation even as it has the added advantage of allowing students to advance toward a postsecondary degree.

Many states already permit dual crediting, but some do not and are leery of doing so, perceiving that it is tantamount to "double dipping" if high schools and colleges claim state per-pupil funding for the same student. Rare states, like Florida, actually require high school students taking college courses to do so for dual credit, even while providing state funding to both the student's high school and college. The assumption is that students will shorten their time to a postsecondary degree and achieve savings for students and the state. Encouraging more states to allow or mandate dual crediting will probably require evidence that the resulting return on the state's investment would be greater than that from investments in traditional high schools or integrated 9–14 models that are restricted by dual crediting and seat-time rules.[2]

College Eligibility Requirements

If early college students are to advance to college courses as they are ready, admission should be based on performance criteria, not age or grade level. Because students at any given time may be ready for higher-level learning in one academic domain yet not in another, advancement to college courses should be made on a subject-specific basis corresponding to subject-specific performance.

Some states limit the number of college courses high school students can take or restrict enrollment to students of a certain age or grade. Others restrict enrollment to those with minimum cumulative grade point averages or combined SAT scores. Policymakers generally will consider exempting early college high schools from these restrictions. Texas restricted college course–taking to eleventh- and twelfth-grade students and to a limited number of courses per semester, but upon initiating early college high schools, the state allowed the schools to determine eligibility for any number of courses based on subject-specific assessments under the Texas Success Initiative. The University System of Georgia allows early college high schools to use a framework of P–14 competencies being developed by the state for determining each student's college-course readiness, rather than the typical minimum combined GPA and SAT score requirements.

Teacher Qualifications

In early college high schools, college and high school teachers must have the flexibility to teach according to their expertise and qualifications at any level within the school. The collaboration of high school and college faculty helps eliminate repetition, promotes the alignment of course content and standards, and better prepares students for the college environment.

Teacher unions may have concerns about nonmember professors teaching courses at high schools for credit. However, when included in the planning for early college high schools, they are generally amenable to allowing college professors to teach dual-credit courses. Some early college high schools have instituted team-teaching arrangements, with a high school teacher and a college professor collaborating, an approach that both instructors find rewarding.

States can offer incentives for this kind of collaboration. For example, Utah authorizes colleges to grant adjunct status to instructors of dual enrollment courses, and high school partners can nominate teachers. Also, dual enrollment partnerships can use state funds to develop joint professional development activities.[3] States should also offer incentives to state postsecondary institutions that encourage faculty to engage in high school improvement and instruction.

Harder

Transfer Rules

Early college high schools attempt to make transitions into and through college more seamless for students who are currently underrepresented in postsecondary education. Clear, formal, statewide articulation agreements would ensure that graduates of early college high schools could transfer their college-course credits easily to a four-year postsecondary institution, shortening the time to a bachelor's degree and resulting in savings to students and states. Transfer rules in support of early college high school or an integrated system would add transparency to both the prerequisites for transfer into general education and the major requirements for degree programs. Such rules would require public higher education institutions to accept dual-credit courses as equivalent to courses transferable under articulation agreements.

Many states have long struggled to build systemic transfer and articulation agreements to help students transfer from two- to four-year postsecondary institutions. Moreover, it is a challenge for postsecondary institutions to interpret and accept dual-credit courses for transfer. They sometimes question the quality of college courses that contain high school students, especially if those courses are taught on high school campuses.

In Ohio, the "transfer module" is a useful policy vehicle for early college high schools. The module is a transparent set of postsecondary courses articulated to general education requirements at the state's four-year colleges. Early college high schools can align their curricula with the transfer module to help ensure that college credits earned by graduates can be applied toward a bachelor's degree. Ultimately, states must encourage colleges to create and honor course-transfer agreements, whether or not the approved college courses are dual credit.

School-Level Autonomy

An early college high school needs autonomy to design an integrated, highly supportive education environment. This requires latitude in the design not only of curricula but also of joint professional development for secondary/postsecondary faculty. It also requires the assignment to personnel of multiple responsibilities—

particularly in small schools like early colleges—including those that provide supplemental support to students and foster high school–college collaboration.

Charter school laws can generally grant the flexibility required for early college high schools, and this approach works well in some states. California's charter school laws helped to resolve some barriers in initiating an early college high school serving high school dropouts and near-dropouts. Community college instructors can deliver a fully integrated high school–college curriculum, supported through Average Daily Attendance (ADA) funds, without having to be supervised by an employee from the sending school district.

However, not all states have charter school laws. Moreover, even in those that do, charter schools often do not receive maximum per-pupil state or district allocations. They also may not be able to tap into local bond funding for capital needs.

A promising policy alternative is North Carolina's Innovations Initiatives Act of 2003–04. It established a process for waiving state rules for districts and colleges engaged in "cooperative efforts between secondary schools and institutions of higher education," including those that "provide flexible, customized programs of learning for high school students who would benefit from accelerated, higher-level course work or early graduation," such as early college high schools. In fact, this waiver process is critical as North Carolina creates 75 such high school–postsecondary partnerships, known as "Learn & Earn" schools.

State Accountability Systems

No Child Left Behind requires states to report on the Annual Yearly Progress of their schools, including an accounting of graduation rates for high school students. Some states with a number of early college high schools, like New York, have provided for the special, accelerated features of early college high schools in the design of their accountability systems for reporting AYP, which include graduation rates. Doing so avoids inadvertently penalizing high schools that, rather than offer the traditional four-year program, offer a fifth year so that students can complete a high school diploma *and* a college degree. However, many states have yet to make such provisions, even though the U.S. Department of Education has shown a willingness to consider them in reporting AYP for redesigned high schools.

Hardest

Funding Formulas and Structures

Funding arrangements for schools and students should allow high schools to incorporate college course work at no cost to students—especially those for whom college cost precludes postsecondary access. In part, this can help students subsequently avoid remedial classes in college, creating more-efficient uses of financial aid and other state postsecondary funding. High schools and colleges should receive state support for the instructional and support costs of educating early college students. They should also have the flexibility to use various funding streams for these purposes, such as permitting some K–12 ADA funding to pay for college courses while also adequately funding high schools for the costs they still assume for those students.

There have been modest but notable steps to help finance early college high schools. Georgia and Tennessee, states that provide their own, nonfederal sources of funding for financial aid and scholarship programs, have made aid accessible to high school students for college courses. Some states, like Texas and North Carolina, allow both the college and high school to claim state per-pupil funding for dual enrollees. Overall, though, the ability of state finance systems to fund an integrated secondary-postsecondary curriculum remains quite limited. In most states, high school students are ineligible for college financial aid largely because the funding is usually tied to federal aid rules that restrict students enrolled in high school from receiving aid for college courses. Also, in many states, K–12 districts automatically lose funding when students enroll in college courses. This can discourage high schools from entering into partnerships with postsecondary institutions to start early college high schools. Moreover, as noted about dual crediting, some policymakers are suspicious of what they perceive to be any "double" funding of high schools and colleges for dual enrollees.

Ohio illustrates one way that state policymakers have been forward-thinking about investments in the early college approach to integration. They have committed $8+ million over two years to supplement existing per-pupil allocations for early college high schools, under the budgets of both the Department of Education and Board of Regents. Under this demonstration, the state is exploring whether earlier investments in early college students—using funds that would have otherwise been allocated later for postsecondary work—can translate into students' more efficient completion of a postsecondary degree.

STIMULATING MORE INTEGRATION

Early college high schools provide a way of gleaning what it would mean for a state to create an education system that integrates grades 9–14. In this respect, it is important that states take measures to ensure that the most-promising early college practices are not only sustained but also replicated more broadly. Such measures would include:

Coordinate P–16 education policies with the development of early college high schools

Efforts to promote coordinated education policies across K–12 and postsecondary systems—through P–16 councils or other means—can both provide benefits to and benefit from schools, like early college high schools, that manifest the envisioned coordination in practice. Georgia's ongoing development of P–14 standards, for example, complements the implementation of early college high schools. These efforts at P–16 coordination can enhance efforts to ease credit transfer and develop appropriate eligibility requirements for high school students taking an integrated 9–14 curriculum. If early college student outcomes are positive, a state's P–16 council could consider whether such policies should be applied more broadly.

Study the state's return-on-investment in financing an integrated course of study

It is important to examine and make explicit both the benefits of integrated secondary-postsecondary education—in terms of improving educational attainment—and the financial costs of creating these ties. If early college high schools are found to yield a greater return on investment than traditional high schools, then states might reconsider their unease about funding dual credit for any dual enrollee. Instead, enacting "hold harmless" funding that provides an incentive for high school and colleges to work together in powerful ways would be a good investment given the likely returns. Ultimately, to judge the validity of these or other hypotheses, early college outcomes must be tied to state finance implications.

Ask and answer key research questions

Evidence about the efficacy and cost benefits of early college and related strategies is essential for rational policymaking. Policy needs to take into account the following considerations, based on solid research and measurement of outcomes, requiring longitudinal data systems that can track individual students across the secondary and postsecondary sectors:

- Who are early college high schools serving, in terms of both demographic background and academic profile?
- Are these schools achieving results with students who traditionally lag in postsecondary attainment? At what rates do students graduate high school? How many college credits or associate's degrees do they earn? Do students go on to bachelor's degree programs, require fewer remedial college courses, and persist to a postsecondary credential more easily and more quickly than do nonearly college high school graduates from similar backgrounds?
- What elements of the early college high school design appear to be essential?

To the degree that early college high schools succeed in raising student outcomes in terms of both completing high school and a postsecondary credential, they can serve as critical evidence in support of expanding—perhaps making permanent—policies that fundamentally alter the transition from high school to college through integration.[4]

20

Return on Investment Analysis of Integrating Grades 9–14

Robert Palaich, John Augenblick, and Margaretha Maloney

Greater integration of secondary and postsecondary education systems will require not only new ways of structuring education finance but also an investment strategy to pay for the transition. Over time, state education attainment rates should rise, yielding a return on such investments.

Although the benefits of education to individuals and society are many, our analysis focuses on the financial benefits to states. In an environment of limited resources, policymakers considering moving toward an integrated grade 9 through 14 system need to understand the financial implications of any change. One way to gain insight into whether these investments are worthwhile is to analyze the costs and benefits of existing integrated programs. Here we apply cost-benefit analysis to one particular model of integrating grades 9–14—the early college high school—and use the results to understand the costs and benefits that could be expected from a more systemic integration of secondary and postsecondary systems.

Early college high school is one of a number of integrated secondary-postsecondary approaches in which students earn college credit while still in high school. Such programs—also known as "accelerated-learning options"—are a promising strategy to increase the number of young people obtaining college degrees, especially those young people at risk of struggling in today's economy.

Because establishing integrated programs requires increased state investment up front, as well as some duplicative spending by secondary and postsecondary institutions, policymakers will need to justify these added expenditures. The fundamental questions are: Does an integrated approach yield educational and financial payoffs, and if so, how long would it take to be realized? What are the projected long-term benefits of early college high schools in areas such as college degree attainment, individual financial gain, and economic contributions to society? How do these compare to the immediate and long-term expenses of early college high school?

Answering these questions makes it possible to determine the return on investment—the ROI—for each constituency involved. Short-term and long-term implications for state financing and other policies also emerge that can help lead to the expansion of these integrated approaches.

RETURN ON INVESTMENT ANALYSIS OF EARLY COLLEGE HIGH SCHOOLS

Early college high schools are a relatively new but fast-growing model of integrated secondary and postsecondary education. By integrating the first two years of college into high school, early college high schools make it possible for students to earn both a high school diploma and an associate's degree (or up to two years of credit toward a bachelor's degree). Early college high schools target at-risk and first-generation college-goers, usually low-income and minority youth, offering a challenging curriculum in a small-school environment.[1]

Currently, early college high schools are financed through an array of strategies. The one constant is that students and families do not have to pay college tuition. In most cases, the host school districts and the partner postsecondary institutions shoulder the costs associated with incorporating two years of college into the high school curriculum. The district and postsecondary institution often receive additional grant support from the state or from contributing foundations. Over the long term, funding is expected to come exclusively from state, local district, and postsecondary institution sources.

Recently, Augenblick, Palaich, & Associates, Inc., working with Jobs for the Future, developed a financial analysis model designed to determine the return on investment for early college high schools (Augenblick, Palaich, & Associates, Inc., 2006). The model is a cost-benefit analysis that can be used to determine the long-term ROI for a cohort of students experiencing a particular school program. Cost-benefit analysis uses financial estimates to provide the equivalent monetary value of a project in order to determine whether, on balance, the project is worth the investment.

In identifying costs and benefits and calculating a ROI for early college high schools, costs are calculated in terms of the expense of running the school and providing the postsecondary and other needed services. The estimate of the total cost of developing, producing, and delivering the program encompasses expenditures for personnel, program support services, overhead, supplies, and materials. It also includes an estimate of the state and local K–12 expenditures per pupil, plus added postsecondary and other public expenditures. Benefits are identified in terms of quantifiable benchmarks (e.g., student attendance, student persistence, graduation rates, and college credits and degrees earned). The estimate of the total financial benefit of the program includes money saved (additional social costs avoided[2]), money earned (including increased tax revenue from increased earnings due to higher levels of educational achievement), and anything else that adds to the bottom line, directly or indirectly. The estimates of costs and benefits are then used to calculate the ROI.[3]

For the early college high school study, we calculated the ROI for both early college and traditional high schools, using finance data from California and New York.[4] The difference in benefits between the early college and the traditional high school determined the "marginal" benefit of the integrated, accelerated-learning program.

Because early college high schools are too young to have a critical mass of graduates, key assumptions were made about student outcomes based on national data.

The model used data on actual outcomes for low-income students for the traditional high schools, reflecting the income composition of the students that early college high schools target within their respective districts. These graduates have traditionally low rates of college preparedness, and therefore low postsecondary enrollment and completion rates—only 20 percent eventually earn an associate's or bachelor's degree.[5]

Given the college orientation of the early college high schools and the fact that students earn college credit by graduation, the model assumes that early college low-income students will graduate qualified for college, and it projects their level of education attainment based on national data for similarly qualified students. The projection is that 20 percent of students will eventually earn an associate's degree, and that an additional 28 percent will earn a bachelor's degree. Although we use these figures in the ROI calculation, they appear to be conservative when compared to actual attainment rates from two early college high schools that have been in existence long enough to have graduates. Of the first cohort graduating from Harbor Teacher Prep Academy in California, 70 percent earned associate's degrees; 67 percent of graduates from the Middle College High School at LaGuardia Community College earned associate's degrees.

The results suggest that if early college high schools achieve student outcomes even approaching those of these two forerunner schools, they can be expected to generate an ROI greater than the comparable return for the traditional high school. The longer the time frame considered, the greater the return on investment. This finding holds true for individual school sites, for the states supporting them, and for individual students.

Specifically, the study projects that over a 15-year time frame, an early college high school can generate $25.3 million more worth of benefits than comparable traditional schools, while over 25 years they can generate $50.4 million more in benefits (Augenblick, Palaich, & Associates, 2006). In terms of the ROI for states, over the course of 15 years, policymakers could expect $1.33 to $2.11 more for every dollar invested in early college high schools than in traditional high schools. Over the course of 25 years, the states' return on investment could be $2.51 to $3.95 more for every $1.00 invested.

The greater ROI in this example is due to having more students attain higher levels of educational achievement, and earn incomes associated with higher educational attainment. It is also due to having students take fewer years to attain a given education level when compared to students in a traditional high school. Because traditional high school students spend more time in school and less time in the workforce than an early college high school student, their entrance into the job market is delayed. However, the most notable factor in the increased ROI for early college high schools versus traditional schools would be the higher postsecondary preparedness and degree-attainment rates of early college graduates.

The analysis also shows that the state ROI goes up when more students participate in early college high schools. When student participation reaches critical mass—approximately 15 percent of a state's students participating—the state will cease treating the investment in early college high schools as an exception or special program and be able to invest more effectively and efficiently in these programs. At this point, perhaps a decade from now, the state will see a boost in its return on investment for these schools, and this return will continue as the percentage of students participating increases over a 25-year period.

IMPLICATIONS FOR SYSTEMIC SECONDARY-POSTSECONDARY INTEGRATION EFFORTS

Many education reforms target the boundary between secondary and postsecondary education. Such efforts raise questions as to whether better coordination between these previously distinct levels of education might benefit all parties involved—students and families, schools, school districts, postsecondary institutions, and the states—by turning out better educated students at a lower overall cost. The ROI analysis of early college high schools, which is one way of addressing these questions, suggests affirmative answers.

Early college high schools are structured and funded today as a specialized project, as are other important efforts to span the secondary-postsecondary boundary (e.g., the federal outreach opportunity programs known as TRIO, Advanced Placement, and International Baccalaureate). This occurs because the finance systems of traditional K–12 and postsecondary education are discrete and are not designed in a coordinated manner that would naturally support what early college high schools are designed to do. This also places structural limitations on state support for dramatically increasing the number of early college high schools.

What costs and benefits would be involved in moving from a project orientation toward a fully integrated statewide financing system? In answering that question, it is helpful to distinguish between short-term and long-term financing policies. The short term centers on the proliferation of early college high schools and other accelerated-learning options. A long-term funding strategy would seek to make public college-level classes available to all public high school students who are academically ready and to enable more low-income students to enroll in them.

Short-Term Financing

Because an integrated reform strategy calls for increased up-front costs in the short term, it is unlikely that a state will redesign its secondary and postsecondary funding systems to support a move toward accelerated-learning options until a critical mass of students and institutions participate. Indeed, the state initially may choose to subsidize these options, spending money (often between 10 and 20 percent) beyond the usual education allocation to encourage secondary and postsecondary institutions to collaborate and set up integrated programs, such as early college high schools.

Such subsidies may result in "double paying" for a period of time, with the state funding secondary schools and postsecondary institutions to serve the same students. One way to do this would be to allow public colleges to claim state reimbursements based on the enrollment (i.e., full-time equivalents, or FTE) of dual enrollees, without reducing the state's per-pupil allocation to the high school (reducing the allocations would provide a disincentive for high school staff to encourage students to take college classes).[6]

Other incentives for accelerated-learning options might include payments for training high school staff to teach Advanced Placement, International Baccalaureate, and eventually college classes, or providing bonuses for teachers and schools to reward them for student performance on AP, IB, or dual enrollment classes (Arkansas, Texas, and Florida). A state might also consider providing incentives for postsecondary institutions to award college credit for high scores on AP and IB exams, or for students to finish high school with an associate's degree (Utah) (Long, Anthes, and Griffith, 2004).

The financial costs and benefits of these short-term expenditures can be examined from the perspectives of the five stakeholders in integrated high school reform:

- *Students:* Students and their families reap many benefits. Choices of enrolling in advanced and postsecondary courses expand; counselors assist students in locating and enrolling in appropriate courses both at the high school and the college. Significant financial assistance is provided in the form of free tuition for up to two years of college courses.
- *Secondary school partner:* Because the high school maintains FTE allocations for dual enrollment students, and may be rewarded based on the number of college credits a student has earned at graduation, the high school encourages students to take college classes and assists them in the enrollment process.
- *School district:* There is little financial impact on the school district. The state, foundations, or other outside sources of funding pay the additional costs of staff training, rewards to schools or students for high performance, and tuition. The district is not penalized for students taking college courses.
- *Postsecondary institutions:* Postsecondary institutions benefit in the short term as they see an increase in the number of high school students enrolling in their classes and receive the regular state allocation to pay for this full-time equivalent enrollment. Postsecondary institutions have an incentive to collaborate with high schools and make the process as easy as possible.
- *State:* In the short term, the state faces additional costs. It will double pay for the education of some students by funding the high school under the typical FTE school finance formula, paying for incentives, and, either directly or through reimbursement policies, by paying the higher education tuition or allowing the state universities to claim FTE dollars for students enrolled.

Long-Term Financing

The long-term ROI argument is a strong justification for appropriating funds to cover additional up-front costs. As long as state policymakers recognize the long-term return from integrated high school reforms, they should be willing to make the short-term investments to produce that return. Then, when participation reaches critical mass, the state can transition to a long-term funding solution, permanently changing the structure of secondary-postsecondary financing. These changes in the financing mechanism would eliminate state payments to both the secondary school and the postsecondary institution. Also, to the extent that more high school students take more college courses and use those courses to jump-start a postsecondary education or advanced certification, the total spent by the state on secondary and postsecondary education will be less.

In other words, a new method of education financing will need to emerge. Discussions of education systems where students advance seamlessly from prekindergarten through postsecondary (P–16) envision a time when high school per-pupil allocations, postsecondary per-credit allocations, and state aid/incentive dollars are combined and optimized (Long, Anthes, and Griffith, 2004). If the funding streams can be merged into a single system, many of the disincentives and barriers to enrolling high school students in college classes will disappear.

For example, to realize the additional savings gained from eliminating "double payments," the state must restructure the governance and financing of secondary and postsecondary education, creating a P–16 system. This would require the state to develop common methods of counting students at the secondary and postsecondary levels (including accounting for part-time status), as well as to analyze all associated instructional costs, such as the cost of a high school course, the cost of a postsecondary course, and whether those vary by course content or other factors.

To ease the immediate impact of lowered enrollments on a particular school district, and to give the district time to adjust to having fewer students in upper-secondary education, states should consider a declining enrollment adjustment in its formula funding. Such an adjustment would cushion the financial impact on schools losing enrollment by smoothing the loss of enrollment over a specified number of years.

As in the short-term analysis, the financial costs and benefits of long-term expenditures can be examined from the perspectives of the same five stakeholders of integrated high school reform:

- *Students:* The long-term program is at least as financially valuable to students and their families as the short-term program. Students will benefit from greater choices of courses at no additional cost. However, decisions about certain details will affect participation. For example, if the program required students to prepay college tuition, participation from low-income families would diminish, even if they were fully reimbursed at the end of the course. If tuition reimbursement were tied to obtaining a certain grade in the college class, fewer marginally qualified students might participate.
- *Secondary schools:* Under the long-term program, high schools will compete with postsecondary institutions for students. Depending on how many students participate and to what extent, a high school may lose state enrollment-based funding for instructional costs, which would mean a reduction in available teachers. High schools could retain a portion of the per-pupil cost through agreements to provide noninstructional services (e.g., counseling, extracurricular activities) to students taking courses at postsecondary institutions.
- *Postsecondary institutions:* Student FTEs for postsecondary institutions will increase, resulting in additional state aid. On the other hand, the institutions will spend more on overhead, for example, to forge agreements with districts and the state about how to cover tuition for participating secondary students. In addition, an institution, perhaps through an office (such as the Division of Continuing Education), would have to dedicate personnel to administering the program and helping students register for it.

- *School districts:* School districts will lose money due to decreased student FTE counts. The districts will need to calculate per-course costs and develop ways of counting the loss of FTE students. School districts will also need personnel to administer the program.
- *State:* Certain state costs will increase, depending on the approaches to integration a state chooses. This can range from creating and administering a gateway test, to developing a longitudinal system to track student progress, to administering a district allocation or student tuition-reimbursement program. The state will realize substantial economic benefit over time if it succeeds in promoting the program as larger numbers of students select this option, and as larger numbers of secondary schools enter into agreements with postsecondary institutions and become integrated high schools. The state will no longer double-pay for students who are in high school and taking college classes; a single payment per course will go to either the high school or the postsecondary institution. Time to completion for both high school and postsecondary degrees should decrease, so that the state may pay for fewer years of schooling for each student. The need for remedial courses in postsecondary institutions should decrease. Ultimately, as more students obtain not only high school diplomas but also associate's and bachelor's degrees, the state will benefit from the increased tax revenue, generated by the higher salaries that students earn.

A TRANSITION WORTH MAKING

Current efforts at integrated high school reform point states toward considering the long-term benefits of developing more integrated, cost-effective education finance systems. The early college high school concept—a successful recent configuration of integrated high school reform—combines many aspects of high school reform into a coherent, accelerated-learning program whose graduates leave high school with the skills necessary to enter the workforce or continue school toward a college degree. ROI analysis suggests that both the state and students and their parents benefit from the investment made in these integrated high schools. If states' leaders take a long view of the benefits of expanding these and similar efforts, they could potentially leverage larger economies of scale that break through the boundary separating their K–12 and postsecondary systems.

21

Using Dual Enrollment to Build a 9–14 System

Nancy Hoffman

> It's like I'm so much more important to the teachers now that I'm [taking college courses]. They pay attention to me because they know I'm serious and I'm not going to fool around in class and miss assignments and stuff like that. I'm college-bound now.
>
> —Rhode Island high school student, 2006

The future economic well-being of our young people might be predicted by a two-sided chart. One side (table 1) presents recent data showing the "hollowing out" of U.S. society over the last 40 years. The middle-income deciles have diminished, pushing the well educated (those with a bachelor's degree or higher) up toward the top of the income scale, and those with only a high school diploma into the bottom.[1]

On the other side of the chart (table 2) is a model high school/college-degree program that begins in the sixth grade at an early college high school affiliated with the City University of New York (CUNY). The curriculum includes all high school requirements, including preparation for and completion of the five state Regents examinations required for a high school diploma and the credit requirements of the associate's degree (to be completed in seven years, or by the twelfth grade). College courses replace some high school courses, and hybrid "stretch" or "bridge" courses help students gain the intellectual maturity and habits of mind necessary for college success (see table 2).

The message from the chart: We sell students short by celebrating high school graduation unless we send a very clear additional message: "some college" or the associate's degree is a minimum for achieving reasonable financial success. One side of the chart is the answer to the other.

If high school graduation is not enough today, how do we reshape our education system so that more young people get the postsecondary skills and knowledge required for economic stability and civic participation? Integrating the curricular requirements for grades 6 through 14 into a single, seven-year program can assure young people the minimum education—tuition-free—that will give them a chance at a decent income. But the group of CUNY early colleges under

Table 1. A Percentage Distribution of Households by Education and Class: The Changing Ability to Attain Middle-Class Status

Education and class[a]	1967	1969	1979	1989	1999	2003
Less than high school						
% low income (<$28,000)[b]	48.8	45.4	49.2	55.6	59.1	60.7
% middle income ($28,000–$81,000)[c]	48.5	50.7	45.9	40.0	36.8	35.2
% upper income (>$81,000)[d]	2.7	3.9	4.8	4.3	4.1	4.1
High school						
% low income	24.5	22.4	27.5	32.2	36.6	36.9
% middle income	69.0	68.5	61.9	56.9	52.8	52.1
% upper income	6.5	9.0	10.6	10.8	10.5	11.0
Some college						
% low income	20.5	19.0	22.9	22.6	24.8	26.4
% middle income	68.4	66.4	62.4	60.3	55.9	55.6
% upper income	11.1	14.6	14.8	17.1	19.3	18.0
Bachelor's						
% low income	12.3	11.9	14.2	12.8	11.6	13.4
% middle income	65.8	61.0	58.6	54.3	50.6	50.2
% upper income	21.9	27.1	27.1	33.0	37.8	36.4
Graduate						
% low income	10.7	8.0	10.1	8.6	5.5	6.8
% middle income	57.0	55.6	51.5	43.5	37.7	36.7
% upper income	32.3	36.4	38.5	47.9	56.7	56.6

Source: Data provided by Anthony Carnevale and Jeff Strohl, based on CPS March Supplement (1968, 1970, 1980, 1990, 2000, 2004).

[a] *Household education* is defined by the highest attainment in the household. *Class* is defined by deciles of household income in 2004 dollars.

[b] *Lower income* is the end point for the bottom two deciles in family income, or $28,000 in 2004 dollars.

[c] *Middle income* includes the middle five deciles in the family income distribution, and ranges from $28,000 to $81,000 in 2004 dollars.

[d] *Upper income* includes the top three deciles in the family income distribution and begins at $81,000 in 2004 dollars.

development represent an extreme remaking of the education system, and depend on conditions that are difficult to reproduce for the great mass of high schoolers in need of such interventions. CUNY's small, autonomous early college schools give students and teachers access to a college campus and its resources, and students as young as 12 or 13 years old can have minicourses with college professors. Indeed, the 17 campuses of the City University of New York located within the 5 boroughs of New York City are linked with 280 of the city's 375 high schools through an academic enrichment and dual enrollment program called College Now.

Nonetheless, dual and concurrent enrollment opportunities provided by state legislation or local agreements between public schools and postsecondary institutions have long existed. While dual enrollment rarely ensures the integration of two full years of college into high school, it does have the potential to be redesigned, systematized, and extended as a sturdy bridge between high school and college. Rather than serving only as a mechanism to advance the gifted and

Table 2. New York City Early College Academy Typical Course Sequence Grades 6-12. The chart outlines what a typical path through the New York City Early College Academy looks like. The courses highlighted in bold carry college credit (and often will count toward high school graduation requirements, too). The ® symbol indicates a Regents exam is associated with that course. An additional six to nine college credits will be offered to students during summer sessions.

						Grade 12	
Grade 6	Grade 7	Grade 8	Grade 9	Grade 10	Grade 11	Fall Semester	Spring Semester
Advisory	Advisory	Advisory	Advisory	Advisory	Advisory	Advisory	Advisory
Extended Humanities (Integrated English Language Arts and World Cultures)	Extended Humanities (Integrated English Language Arts and American History)	Extended Humanities (Integrated English Language Arts and American History)	English American History®	English®	**Eng 110: College Writing**	Choose 1 of the following *each* semester: **Comp Lit 102: Great Books** *or* **Eng 152: Works of American Lit** *or* **Eng 155: Great Works of Fiction**	
Math	Math	Algebra®	Geometry®	Trigonometry® *or* **Math 122: Precalculus**	Precalculus *or* **Math 110: Intro to College Math** *or* **Math 151: Calculus**	**College-level electives/ concentration course**	**College-level electives/ concentration course**
Integrated Sciences	Integrated Sciences	Life Science	Living Environment®	Physics/Chemistry: 2-year integrated high school course [Chemistry® at conclusion]		**College-level electives/ concentration course**	**College-level electives/ concentration course**
	Spanish	Spanish	**Span 111: Elementary Spanish I**	**Span 112: Elementary Spanish II**	**Span 203: Int. Span. I** *and* **Span 204: Int. Span. II**		
Music	Art	Music		**Hist 125: World Civilization to 1715**	**Hist 126: World Civilization 1715 to Present** [Global History® at conclusion]	**Econ 101: Intro to Macroeconomics**	Participating in Government
PE/Health	PE/Health	PE/Health	PE/Health	PE/Health	PE/Health	PE/Health	PE/Health
Technology	Technology	Technology			**Arts 151: Drawing 1**		
Inquiry Project	Inquiry Project	Inquiry Project	Inquiry Project	Inquiry Project	Inquiry Project	Inquiry Project	Inquiry Project

Notes: Students start off in college-level courses in the school building with other Academy students as classmates. They also start with college courses stretched over an entire year (rather than just one semester as they are in college) to give students more time to understand what's required to be successful. Then, as they gain more confidence and skill, they have an opportunity to take courses on campus at NYC College with other more-typical college students.

talented, dual enrollment can provide a substantial head start on the requirement of some postsecondary education for all. In recent years, policymakers and educators have turned to dual enrollment for just that purpose—as a strategy to increase the number of underrepresented students gaining postsecondary credentials, a means to integrate high school and college so that students can acquire a semester's worth or more of college-level learning while still entitled to public education without cost.[2] Dual enrollment can give students practice at doing college work while they are supported by collaborating high school and college instructors. At least nine states, including Florida, Maine, Minnesota, North Carolina, Tennessee, Texas, Rhode Island, Utah, and Virginia, either already have or are considering policies that share some characteristics of the CUNY model—that is, they are making the attainment of college credit in high school an opportunity, or a requirement, for all high school students.

This chapter considers *the potential of dual enrollment to serve as a transition-to-college strategy for a wide range of students, not just the gifted and talented. But it goes beyond this idea to show that dual enrollment can be a powerful tool for integrating high school and postsecondary education into a single system.* Serving about 20 percent of high school students today, dual enrollment can become the laboratory for aligning, integrating, and sequencing secondary and postsecondary curricula, standards, assessments, academic demands, and pedagogy. At the systems level, dual enrollment provides a skeleton for the cross-sector governance required to align high school exit with college entry, fund tuition, provide college credits for high school students taking college courses, and certify teacher and professor qualifications. It raises questions about the need for a single accountability and finance system across P–20.

WHY BUILD FROM DUAL ENROLLMENT?

At a New York City early college high school, instructors discovered that the problem-solving skills and content knowledge required for the Regents exam in physics were more inquiry-based and advanced than those required of first-year physics students in a CUNY senior college. After discussion with the high school physics teacher and the high school/college liaison, the chair of the physics department gave college credit to the high school students who had passed their high school physics course and the Regents exam. While still in high school, the students jumped over first-year college physics to a more-advanced course. They had college credits, college transcripts, and were on the pathway into a college major.

This anecdote raises familiar issues: the importance of alignment of standards and content across high school and college, and the related issue of course sequencing. For, as David Conley argues, high school teachers must cultivate in their students the habits of mind and foundational knowledge that enable young people to prepare for and master college-level content.[3] Course sequencing must attend not just to *what* but to *how* students learn. Yet the anecdote raises an additional sticky issue: If schools and colleges are going to do a better job of getting high school and college physics to follow one another sensibly, teachers and professors in partner institutions must come together for collaborative conversations and decisionmaking about course design and content, pedagogy, academic support, and the like. They must form what some educators call "vertical teams."

The last several decades have not produced many sustainable mechanisms for such systematic high school–college collaboration. Indeed, the cheerless history of a road paved with good intentions is that few partnerships extend beyond a period of initial goodwill generated by external funding for teacher-professor collaboration. The college physics department reviewed the Regents exam only because early college high school students must take college courses, and these new schools are designed to reduce the time to degree.

As the physics anecdote suggests, dual enrollment provides a laboratory already in place for collaborative course sequencing, including and going beyond curricular alignment. There are several reasons for this:

- Dual enrollment students from a public high school are taking credit-bearing courses in a neighboring college, and that college must ensure the quality of its credits.
- A structure must be in place to link the high school and college (e.g., a renewable partnership agreement; a person serving as liaison between high school and college to work out issues related to scheduling, transportation, transcripting, etc.).
- Both the high school and the college require feedback on student success—students either pass their college courses and get credit or they do not, and the high school and college transcripts both reflect their grades.
- If high school students are in regular college classes on campus, professors will notice their presence and make some judgments about how well their high school has prepared them for postsecondary education.
- Leaders in both sectors share responsibility (financial and otherwise) for the continued collaboration.

CUNY College Now works to adjust high school courses to meet Regents and college course standards and content, and partners review student data regularly. Other examples of ongoing partnerships built through dual enrollment come from the National Alliance of Concurrent Enrollment Partnerships (NACEP) founded in 1999. NACEP accredits programs in which "high school instructors teach . . . college courses during the normal school day. Such programs provide a direct connection between secondary and postsecondary institutions and an opportunity for collegial collaboration." Under NACEP guidelines, "[I]nstructors teaching the [Concurrent Enrollment Partnership] sections are part of a continuing collegial interaction, through annual professional development, required seminars, site visits, and ongoing communication with the postsecondary institutions' faculty and CEP administration. This interaction addresses issues such as course content, course delivery, assessment, evaluation, and professional development in the field of study."[4]

The NACEP structure points to the potential power of dual enrollment to link high school and college teachers. For example, Syracuse University's Project Advance has long used this model, albeit not as a strategy to increase college credential attainment rates or to provide college credits to students at no cost. Rather, Project Advance seeks to enable well-prepared students to earn credits early. Many local dual enrollment partnerships also attend to course sequencing, although they may consider such collaboration good program management rather than steps in building an aligned system. And some state legislation requires dual enrollment partners to make formal agreements for working together. The bottom line is that failure is expensive; if colleges offer courses at no cost, not only do they want the students to succeed, but many also see themselves as investing in a pool of young people who will enter their institutions with a leg up.

THE "SKELETON" OF A 9–14—OR P–20—SYSTEM

In addition to course sequencing, the physics anecdote points to a less-visible—but no less important—set of collaborative arrangements. To put dual enrollment in place, either through state legislation or through local agreements, some group must do the preliminary work to integrate grades 9–14. To set up the physics course, and the early college high school that offers it, representatives of the two sectors had to make joint decisions about:

- criteria specifying school student "readiness" for college work;
- equivalency of college credits and Carnegie units;
- qualifications for high school and college teachers to teach college-level courses;
- how public school per-pupil funding and college instructional and/or financial aid can support the costs of high school student participation;
- how governance works across sectors (e.g., who has decisionmaking authority, how quality is assured, how access is regulated, how conflicts are resolved);
- how data is collected and shared; and
- smaller issues that force recognition of incompatibility (e.g., scheduling, costs of texts and labs, support services, transportation).

In addition, in the typical dual enrollment program, and in early college high schools as well, the rules about what constitutes the end point of high school are unsettled. Because most students take only one or two dual enrollment courses during high school, school systems and postsecondary institutions generally admit students based not on the successful completion of "all or nothing" high school exit examinations, but rather on "readiness" criteria, such as a specified GPA in math or a counselor's recommendation that the student can manage an advanced art or biology course.

That is, dual enrollment opens the possibility that students can move across the line separating high school and college in increments, rather than all at once. Dual enrollment lowers the college-admissions stakes for students who might otherwise be intimidated by the application process. Simply put, it blurs the boundaries between high school and college.

ENVISIONING THE FUTURE

If that assessment of the potential of dual enrollment is on target, what policies should states put in place to systematize and exploit this potential? To answer that question, several states are considering the following policies or similar ones promoting the restructuring of dual enrollment into a better aligned and integrated 9–14 system:

- All students are encouraged to do some college-level work as part of high school in their areas of academic or career-based strength and interest.
- All students have an opportunity to receive up to a semester of college credit (i.e., four or five courses).
- The state offers incentives, in the form of scholarships or tuition and fee remission, for low-income dual enrollees to encourage their participation.
- To be eligible for free tuition, students must replace core high school courses with general education or concentration requirements of state public postsecondary institutions or with courses required to receive an industry certificate or associate's degree in a career area.
- A limited number of college courses may be taken on college campuses to save on costs.
- High school–required courses are replaced by equivalent or more-advanced college courses. (For example, calculus is a course that is likely to be equivalent at the high school or college level.)
- Dual enrollment is recognized in the state's data and accountability system and weighted in the state's high school diploma system (as are honors, AP, and International Baccalaureate courses).

STATES OFFERING BROAD ACCESS TO INTEGRATED 9–14

As noted, at least nine states have or are considering policies that share some characteristics of the CUNY model—that is, they are making the attainment of college credit in high school an opportunity for all high school students. These states are moving dual enrollment from its marginal status as an "opt out of high school" program for advanced students to a *central experience* of high school. With the passage of House Bill 1 in 2006, Texas now requires all students to have the opportunity to complete up to 12 college credits while in high school, *and* the legislation expressly targets students at risk of not completing a postsecondary credential. Proposed Maine legislation would require each high school to provide all students with free, college-level courses that also fulfill high school graduation requirements.[5] Virginia's Early College Scholars program allows students pursing an "advanced study diploma" to earn one semester of free college credits; in addition, students who begin industry certification in high school may complete the work without cost even after they graduate. Florida, Illinois, Kentucky, Utah, and Washington State have dual-credit opportunities that are so extensive—especially through community colleges—that substantial percentages of students, including those in career and technical education, graduate with college credit. In Utah, high school students who earn associate's degrees are eligible for scholarships worth 75 percent of upper-division college tuition.[6]

Several states are building networks of early college high schools (autonomous dual enrollment schools) designed so that students graduate with up to 60 college credits. Established for students most at risk of quitting school at or before high school graduation, early college high school networks with more than ten schools either open or in the planning stage exist in North Carolina (75 "Earn and Learn" schools), Michigan, Georgia, Texas, Maine, New York, and California. Smaller networks exist in Ohio and Washington State.

Under pressure to find mechanisms to augment their college success rates, these states and others are asking questions about the possibilities within dual enrollment in reviewing their college-access approaches. Research has not caught up with practices, so key questions remain to be answered (although preliminary data is encouraging).[7] Reenvisioning dual enrollment is not central to any state's efforts to improve high school, but in the characteristic churn that passes for planning in many states, these efforts are taking place side by side with large-scale, widely publicized, national and state initiatives to make college and work readiness the goal of high school graduation. The alignment of standards, assessments, and curriculum across the divide in order to lower college remediation and dropout rates is generally disconnected from dual enrollment, but making this connection could contribute to a new conception of how to make the border between high school and college more permeable (rather than better policed).

Two states—Rhode Island, our smallest, and Texas, the second-largest—are taking the lead in building dual enrollment into the core of an integrated 9–14 system. Referring back to the practices and policies already in place as specified above, these brief case studies point to the ways in which each state's current dual enrollment approach could provide a foundation for a 9–14 system.

Rhode Island: Building Bridges from the Ground Up

Over the last several years, the Governor's Statewide PK–16 Council has been discussing how Rhode Island can meet the needs of a state economy that has lost over 93,000 jobs in manufacturing in the last 20 years but has gained 89,000 jobs requiring some college education. While Rhode Island ranks near the top in the percentage of its population with postsecondary credentials, a closer look shows a bifurcation. Those who are very well educated with high incomes are benefiting from and, indeed, creating the new economy, while a large population of poor people—many of whom are immigrants from Cape Verde, South and Central America, the Caribbean, and Southeast Asia—who have little education and weak English skills are shut out. Education is the answer, but Rhode Island's bachelor's degree completion rates have declined in the last several years (The National Center for Public Policy and Higher Education, 2006). As a department manager from Rhode Island Hospital put it, "We are . . . surrounded by all these kids who want to work here [at the hospital], right across the street practically from the college that can train them, and we can't get our act together as a state to move them from high school through college and into the good jobs that are waiting right here for them."

In this context, the PK–16 Council is assessing the status of dual enrollment programs and exploring the development of a dual enrollment policy that would be the "college bridge" component of the new performance-based Diploma System the state is implementing beginning with the 2007–08 school year.[8] As imagined, the new system would allow students to use college courses as a demonstration of high school proficiency in the six designated areas of core learning. These six areas would also align with the postsecondary learning outcomes for key college courses. College courses could replace high school courses without concern for high school seat time, so students could move ahead in the core areas as soon as they are ready. Eligibility criteria tied to a new performance-based assessment system will be discipline-based and transparent.

Already, about 4,000 students—roughly 16 percent of Rhode Island juniors and seniors—take a dual enrollment course offered through their local high school or on the campus of one of the three public institutions of higher education. However, the highest levels of dual enrollment are in high schools with the *lowest levels* of free and reduced lunch (under 10 percent), while high schools with indicators of high poverty have almost no dual enrollment opportunities. A fee of $50 per credit in the largest program may be one cause of this inequity. Thus, dual enrollment now serves the students whose families are already benefiting from the new economy.

Rhode Island has multiple, long-term, secondary-postsecondary partnerships upon which to build a more equitable and open program, including:

- 12 different programs offered through the three public institutions of higher education;
- Partnerships with 55 of Rhode Island's 59 high schools, including 41 comprehensive public high schools, 9 career and technical schools, and 5 private high schools; and
- Over 100 different courses for high school students that transfer to associate's and bachelor's degree programs. (Jobs for the Future, 2006)

The PK–16 Council members, it is fair to say, were surprised when they learned of the extent of dual enrollment. Like most people concerned with the high school-to-college transition, they thought of dual enrollment as a program for the gifted, and had never considered its potential as a bridge to college. They were unaware that so many students had been signaling that they wanted an accelerated track to college, and that institutions had developed collaborative practices that were cost-effective and relatively simple to implement. In other words, secondary and postsecondary institutions had been transferring money, credit, students, and personnel over the long term; some were collecting data about students as well as participating in a feedback loop including high school and college teachers. The next step, then, is to modify this infrastructure and experience to serve the goals of a seamless PK–16 system.

As Rhode Island puts in place the financing, governance, and accountability structures required to build an equitable dual enrollment program to act as a college bridge, it will be able to build on the course sequences that already cross from high school to postsecondary, as well as to marry dual enrollment with the standard setting of the American Diploma Project, a coalition of 29 states dedicated to aligning K–12 curriculum, standards, assessments, and accountability policies with the demands of college and work.

As in other states, however, those working on developing college- and work-ready high school standards seem not to have benefited from the laboratory for alignment that already exists in the dual enrollment programs of the University of Rhode Island, Rhode Island College, and Rhode Island Community College. The state could learn a great deal from teachers and professors who taught over 2,000 high school students in Rhode Island College's dual enrollment courses in the 2004–05 academic year. Questions posed by David Conley (2005) would be right on the mark:

- How does this course help develop the intellectual maturity of students?
- How does this course connect with the courses that came before and will come after it? How does it identify and reinforce key concepts and knowledge that were previously learned? How does it anticipate skills that have yet to be mastered?
- Is the pace of the work and the expected student production on a trajectory to have students ready for what will be expected of them in college?

Texas: Policies and Practices Underlying Dual Enrollment

The high-visibility state of Texas presents a very different policy, practice, and political climate than tiny Rhode Island in pursuing improved PK–16 pathways and building on current dual enrollment structures to integrate grades 9–14. Where Rhode Island has built a performance-based system from the bottom up—eschewing high-stakes tests and using an inspector system for school-level accountability—Texas has sought to change its educational outcomes with policy levers—bold, top-down mandates with heavy accountability measures.

These moves are commensurate with the commitment of resources and attention required to address a high dropout rate, a wide achievement gap, and postsecondary completion rates that are among the most intractable in the nation.[9] In 2002, Texas ranked 43rd nationally in the percentage of its high school graduates who enrolled in college directly after receiving their high school diploma.[10] Texas received low grades in a number of categories in Measuring Up 2006, the report card of the National Center for Public Policy and Higher Education, particularly in college participation and completion. Only 30 percent of 18- to 24-year-olds are currently enrolled in college, while the percentage of students with the chance for college by age 19 is 33 percent. Texas received a C+ for college completion. Only 51 percent of full-time college students attain their degree within six years of entering college. For African American and Latino students, this percentage is even lower: 13 percent complete their degrees (National Center for Public Policy and Higher Education, 2006).

Texas has experience with widespread dual enrollment: In the last year for which data is reported (2000–01), more than 38,000 high school students took 80,000 college semester courses in high school.[11] Incentives for schools, teachers, and students to participate in dual enrollment are among the most encouraging in the nation. Students can get credit for high school and college courses simultaneously; high schools do not lose funding for students who participate; and colleges may count participating students. The criteria for enrollment are moderately restrictive: eleventh and twelfth graders can enroll on the basis of passing the tenth-grade, state-mandated Texas Assessment of Knowledge and Skills (TAKS) exam in the relevant subject area or by attaining an acceptable score on one of the college readiness tests accepted by the Texas Success Initiative. Colleges can impose additional standards. In regard to equity, however, until the passage of House Bill 1, high schools were not required to provide opportunities for dual enrollment, and postsecondary institutions could waive tuition or require it. As in Rhode Island, dual enrollment is serving primarily advanced students, reaching low-income students only where no tuition is required.

In 1999 and 2000, the state adopted rules into the Texas Education Code for community colleges and universities engaged in partnerships with school districts that resulted in dual credit. These rules specify student eligibility requirements, faculty qualifications, the location and composition of classes, the provision of student learning and support services, eligible courses, grading criteria, the transcripting of credit, and funding provisions. Thus, like Rhode Island, to sustain dual enrollment, communication across the divide was required. Some set of adults had to make decisions together across the sectors, an advantage of dual enrollment.

Texas has addressed the high school-to-college transition in practice as well as policy. As of 2006, the Texas High School Project in partnership with the Texas Education Agency had invested $261 million in a public-private initiative committed to increasing graduation and college enrollment rates in every Texas community. Dollars, strategic planning, technical assistance, and professional development services are flowing to new and redesigned high schools—including 15 early college high schools partnered with higher education institutions. Implementation of these schools required the negotiation of changes in dual enrollment rules—again, reason for adults to work together across 9–14.

In April 2006, the Texas legislature passed House Bill 1, the most pointed yet of the state's attempts to raise the college readiness and postsecondary degree-attainment rates of low-income, underachieving students. The measure requires high schools to make up to 12 college credits available for free to all high school students. HB 1 was heavily influenced by dual enrollment and the early college strategy: to create a college-going culture by blending high school and college so that students are in effect headed to college the day they start ninth grade. The rules state that HB 1 provides "$275 per high school student to districts to prepare students to go on to higher education, encourage students to take advanced academic course work, increase the rigor of academic course work, align secondary and postsecondary curriculum and support promising high school completion and success initiatives in grades 6 though 12."[12]

House Bill 1 thus sets the stage for integrating grades 9 (if not 6) through 14 at scale. From this perspective, HB 1 is an exciting move and a true entitlement to some college for all. That said, implementation of widespread, equitable opportunities for dual enrollment will require that Texas strengthen partnerships—and form new ones—between high schools and higher education institutions. It will force a second look at alignment, and at eligibility requirements for taking college courses. A mechanism to account for the dollars, credits, and students across high school and postsecondary will need to be put in place, and dual enrollment will have to be noted on transcripts. In regard to joint decisionmaking, local K–16 councils or other governance bodies will have to monitor the quality and design of expanded dual enrollment, but given the existence of a K–16 data system, a default college preparation curriculum, and membership in the American Diploma project—all of which support a better aligned and integrated system—Texas, like Rhode Island, can harvest the data and experience from early college and dual enrollment to build its system.

A WORK IN PROGRESS

Rhode Island and Texas point the way to more integrated 9–14 systems, but as I have argued here, both could use the structures and experience of dual enrollment to reorganize a fragmented, jerry-built set of connections. Policy wonks might prefer that alignment and integration take place through a set of comprehensive policy mandates, but given the troubled history of K–16, building up from the ground is less likely to fail. After all, it would be a step forward if deeper alignment takes place and dual enrollment merely expands to serve a wider group of students—those who might not have had a chance to accumulate free college credits in high school, and others who needed to "try out " college—even if 9–14 do not actually blend.

If the number of participants in dual enrollment continues to increase at the current rate, though, the chore of integration may take place organically. Cases in point: North Carolina and Tennessee are already positing that every high school graduate should have access to an associate's degree built into high school, and more states could soon begin such conversations. Is this a case of seeing a half-empty glass as three-fourths full? Can dual enrollment, indeed, be pushed beyond its current limits? The answer could come within only a few years.

22

Evolution of an Innovation

A Commentary on the State of Accelerated Learning

Travis Reindl

The emergence of accelerated learning offers a prime example of an adaptive innovation in American education. *Adaptive innovation* refers to the development of alternative program-delivery mechanisms in response to barriers arising from the existing delivery system. In the case of accelerated learning, a cluster of diverse programs—Advanced Placement, International Baccalaureate, dual/concurrent enrollment, early college high schools, and Tech-Prep—have been established to make the border between high school and college or the workforce more navigable by providing college-level work in high school.[1]

As with many adaptive innovations, the creation and evolution of many (if not most) accelerated-learning options have outpaced the development of a policy infrastructure to support and evaluate the expanding menu of options. On the whole, accelerated learning has matured to the point where local, state, and national stakeholders must be prepared to make critical decisions regarding whether and how these programs are integrated into their policy agendas. Faced with these decisions, policymakers and practitioners seek a more comprehensive understanding of accelerated learning, as well as a culture based on evidence and the resources to support these options.

The fiscal and policy environments surrounding accelerated learning present significant opportunities for and potential obstacles to further experimentation and development. At all levels of government, funding remains limited, with increasing pressure for maximum return on investment. Evidence is also mounting that the United States is lagging in human capital formation, which is increasing scrutiny of leaks in the education pipeline. Both of these factors are causing policymakers to focus more attention on educational transitions and to ask tough questions about priorities and policy options. In addition, families are attracted to accelerated-learning options because they see them as a way to combat the increases in college tuition that can make a postsecondary degree appear out of reach.

As adaptive and innovative as accelerated-learning approaches might be, though, they still present more questions than answers at a time when budgets are tight, time is short, and global competition is increasingly fierce.

THE ISSUES: GROWING PAINS FOR A MATURING MOVEMENT

Four primary issues must be addressed as the development of accelerated-learning options continues: mission and purpose, culture of evidence, quality and rigor, and finance. These issues are highly interrelated and present a combination of philosophical and practical questions for educators and policymakers alike.

Mission and Purpose

It is clear that there are varying—and sometimes conflicting—viewpoints regarding what accelerated learning is supposed to accomplish, even among stakeholders from the same state. Some approach accelerated learning from a "completion" perspective, arguing that increasing academic productivity and shortening the time-to-degree are and should be major objectives for these programs. This perspective is especially prevalent among elected leaders and national observers, who cite graduation-rate statistics and international comparisons on educational attainment in arguing for a more-efficient education pipeline.

Closely related to this is the idea that accelerated learning should be used to maximize return on the public's educational investment. This is also a viewpoint commonly associated with elected leaders, although a number of school, district, campus, and system leaders also subscribe to this school of thought. Debate in this area has been stimulated by research from Augenblick, Palaich, & Associates, showing positive financial returns from investments in Early College High Schools in selected states.[2]

Others place more emphasis on the enrichment potential of accelerated-learning options, holding to the belief that closing the "expectations gap" for historically disadvantaged and underrepresented populations should claim priority. Advocates for this perspective make the point that at-risk students are more responsive to challenge than to remediation, and cite early college high schools as an example. Institutional leaders such as Freeman Hrabowski, president of the University of Maryland, Baltimore County, urge stakeholders to look beyond throughput and output questions when thinking about accelerated learning, declaring, "I have a problem with acceleration only." Many practitioners also stress, however, that acceleration is not just going faster but also structuring the learning experience and teaching in a more-effective way.

These differences surface throughout the national discussion of accelerated learning. Such a diversity of perspectives strongly underscores the need for convening and communication mechanisms that cross educational sectors and focus on accelerated learning. Also on the horizon is a broader philosophical question: Does accelerated learning represent a step on the way to "what's next" in education pipeline reform, or is it, in fact, what's next? Some argue that "accelerated" is a misnomer because the general push for higher standards for college and workforce readiness should make accelerated learning the rule rather than the exception. It is merely a way station on the road to a more-demanding high school diploma.

Mission and purpose are among the less explored and debated dimensions of accelerated learning. State and local policymakers and practitioners seek tools and insights to make sense of accelerated learning and fit it into their policy agendas.

Culture of Evidence

Questions surrounding the robustness of a culture of evidence in accelerated learning are stimulating rich and sometimes contentious debate in the field. From this perspective, it appears that stakeholders, especially researchers and practitioners, are too often talking past one another rather than with one another. While analysts (and some policymakers) emphasize the dearth of comprehensive, comparable information regarding accelerated learning's impact and results, practitioners stress that significant data are, in fact, being gathered. The difference turns out to be less about whether a true culture of evidence exists and more about how to strengthen such a culture and bring it to scale.

Conversation in this area frequently starts from the assumption that the existing body of evidence on accelerated learning is weak and uneven. *The College Ladder*, a two-year research project that evaluated 22 postsecondary transition initiatives, was able to identify some signs of positive performance, but concluded that the initiatives collected insufficient data for a thorough analysis of outcomes, due to lack of longitudinal data and an inability to disaggregate.[3]

At the same time, a range of prospective tools and approaches are emerging that offer real promise. The most significant of these align with the primary evidence-related recommendations from the Western Interstate Commission for Higher Education (WICHE) (2006):

- *Through legislation, lawmakers should require their state departments of education and postsecondary institutions and systems to collaborate in the design, collection, analysis, and reporting of data that will provide the essential elements to examine student participation in accelerated-learning options.*
- *A national effort is needed to establish consistency in collecting, analyzing, and reporting across states on student participation in accelerated-learning options.* The research community should collaborate with the federal government, state departments of education, and postsecondary education to design and conduct studies that will provide the evidence-based research needed to help policymakers and others understand the effectiveness of accelerated-learning options on access and success for all students.

In addition to the work done by the National Youth Policy Forum on *The College Ladder*, there have also been research advances in the area of finance. The most recent example of this is an analysis of return on investment for early college high schools conducted by Augenblick, Palaich, & Associates, Inc.[4] Working with a combination of state, federal, and school data, APA found that early college high schools in New York and California would provide a positive return on investment ($1.33 to $2.11 more for every dollar invested over 15 years; $2.51 to $3.95 more per dollar invested over 25 years), provided that their cost structures did not differ too greatly from those of traditional high schools.

- *Philanthropic organizations, state governments, and the federal government should commit enough resources to support a robust, targeted agenda for research on accelerated-learning options, including longitudinal cohort studies that can track students through secondary school and into higher education and the workforce.* The need for a sustained commitment to data gathering, dissemination, and application is a real and pressing issue for the accelerated-learning movement, and the role of philanthropies should be acknowledged in addressing it. Entities such as the Bill & Melinda Gates Foundation, Lumina Foundation for Education, and the Spencer Foundation are substantively engaging the question of how to support and sustain a culture of evidence, specifically, by creating a convening capacity across educational sectors and evaluation frameworks. These and other philanthropies must be encouraged to continue their work in this area.

Building and maintaining a robust, intentional infrastructure of performance and value-added metrics for accelerated learning represents an area of considerable promise, with ample opportunities for experimentation and innovation. The challenge is to establish leadership and coordination at all levels—local, state, and national. Absent that, an "anarchy of innovation" will continue in accelerated learning, guided by educated hunches and case studies rather than hard data. Organizations that are deeply engaged in the promotion and analysis of accelerated learning, such as Jobs for the Future and the Western Interstate Commission for Higher Education, must seriously consider their respective roles in advancing these issues.

Quality and Rigor

Some of the most consequential—and controversial—questions surrounding accelerated learning are those related to the quality and rigor of the accelerated-learning experience. Such questions are consequential because the legitimacy of accelerated-learning options as policy levers depends in no small part on solid evidence and clear protocols to ensure true acceleration—and controversial, because conceptions of rigor can and do vary according to sector, purpose, and site of delivery. Some of the liveliest debates in the field center on these issues, as policymakers and practitioners clash over the *what* and the *who* of quality assurance.

The quality debate hinges in part on courses that are taught for college credit only to high school students by a high school teacher, an adjunct, or a visiting faculty member at the high school, opening the possibility that there may be one standard for a class of college students on campus and another for high school students. Some cite instances of "blended" environments, where the same course is taught (by the same instructor) to some students for secondary credit and to others for postsecondary credit, although in the second case, the course may not be equivalent to what would be offered on campus. Conversely, some cite instances where students find that an introductory college course is less rigorous than their high school course work in the same area.

Ongoing assessment and program evaluation is a promising—and needed—development for high school–based programs. A new organization, the National Alliance of Concurrent Enrollment Partnerships, accredits programs in which "high school instructors teach . . . college courses during the normal school day." Under NACEP guidelines, "[I]nstructors . . . are part of a continuing collegial interaction, through annual professional development, required seminars, site visits, and ongoing communication with the postsecondary institutions."

Along those lines, state experiences emphasize the value of explicit conversations and formal agreements between K–12 and postsecondary education systems regarding program purpose and content standards. For example, Florida and South Dakota attribute their successes in accelerated learning to a governing philosophy of rigorous quality control on the front end (for example, syllabus and instructor credential audits), reinforced by rigorous student assessments on the back end.

On the national front, accreditation of accelerated-learning programs, specifically dual and concurrent enrollment programs, is developing as a quality-assurance mechanism. NACEP promotes a statement of standards that it has established for recognition of dual and concurrent enrollment programs. The statement covers:

- curriculum (approval through the regular course-approval process);
- faculty (proper training and orientation of high school faculty);
- students (official status at a postsecondary institution);
- assessment (equivalent standards for secondary and postsecondary students); and
- evaluation (annual program assessment and evaluation).

While this framework does offer promise, it would require adaptation to fit the spectrum of accelerated-learning options, particularly those such as Advanced Placement or International Baccalaureate. Additionally, there is the question of what leverage will be necessary to make accreditation an industry standard for accelerated learning.

Given the fact that issues surrounding the quality and rigor of accelerated-learning options have been the subject of debate for the better part of a generation, policymakers and practitioners must be realistic about timelines and achievable objectives. Moreover, advances in gauging the adequacy of accelerated-learning initiatives are inextricably linked with the development of a robust, comprehensive culture of evidence. With these cautions in mind, accelerated learning's advocates must be prepared to move forward on multiple levels with respect to quality—or risk the credibility of these programs as a means to seal cracks in the education pipeline.

Finance

Of the primary issues facing accelerated learning, finance is most frequently cited as an area where practice is ahead of a cohesive policy framework. This point is underscored by policymakers' observations that states' funding for accelerated-learning options lacks intentionality. One national observer commented that these options are operating on "budget dust."

There are several fundamental issues that policymakers and practitioners must address as they strive to build a coherent fiscal framework for accelerated learning, including ownership, adequacy, and relationship to objectives. Also needed is further vetting of new analytical tools, such as the "return on investment" approach tested in the early college high school environment. Moreover, state-level case studies that point toward more rational and streamlined border crossing with respect to funding should be broadly disseminated and discussed.

Much of the challenge stems from the fact that two primary philosophies have developed around the fiscal aspect of accelerated learning: a *public good* viewpoint, focusing on social goods, such as expanded opportunity; and an *efficiency and return-on-investment* perspective, which emphasizes maximization of public investment. These philosophies, while not mutually exclusive, can and do collide in the worlds of state and local education policy.

These differences most immediately come into play in discussions about the relationship of funding to mission and purpose. Debate continues over whether the goals for accelerated-learning investments should be increased postsecondary access or greater financial leverage and reinvestment potential through reduced remediation, shortened time-to-degree, or both.

Also contributing to the largely ad hoc state of accelerated-learning finance are weaknesses in data and evidence, as discussed above. Findings from *The College Ladder* point out that many stakeholder intuitions about accelerated learning (e.g., the idea that it reduces remediation or time-to-degree) may not be borne out by more-robust data. For example, do the credits accumulated by accelerated-learning students ultimately speed the path to a credential or significantly improve postsecondary performance?

WICHE's report, *Moving the Needle,* is one of the few comprehensive attempts to answer some of the questions surrounding the financing of accelerated-learning options. The report describes the financial questions raised by various stakeholders involved in four types of accelerated-learning options, examines financing strategies that are used in selected states, and describes how financial analysis tools can be used to answer financial questions concerning the different options.

Equity in finance stands as another hurdle that accelerated learning must clear. Because a good deal of the resource base for accelerated learning is locally based, and because school districts present wide resource disparities, access to accelerated-learning opportunities (especially to Advanced Placement and the International Baccalaureate) tends to be uneven. To the extent that promoting access to postsecondary education is a key objective for a state's accelerated-learning program, experts consistently caution that equity concerns must be substantially addressed.

The observations coalesce around a handful of core principles:

- *Policymakers and education leaders must view a state's accelerated-learning programming as a whole, not as a collection of individual parts.* While this can be difficult because of multiple (and often disparate) constituencies and funding streams, seeing each program as part of a broader strategy is essential for promoting equity and efficiency. One entity, preferably at the state level, should be the "keeper of the vision."
- *States must have a plan to address funding equity issues pertaining to accelerated-learning options across schools and districts.* Sustainable funding from a variety of sources (local, state, and federal) should be identified and tapped, particularly in the form of incentives for disadvantaged schools and students.
- *Working together, stakeholders must build a robust system of results measurement into their accelerated-learning framework.* This includes financial metrics, such as return on investment, cost of completion, and net cost. Responsibility for this function—as with such matters as defining purpose and promoting equity—should be vested in a specific agency or entity (preferably at the state level), with annual reporting that links resources to results.

Case studies from Texas and Minnesota provide timely, concrete examples of policy initiatives that aim to fulfill these core principles. In both states, K–12 reform legislation served as the vehicle for promoting a stronger focus on accelerated learning. Through House Bill 1, Texas lawmakers have allocated up to $275 per year for each eligible K–12 student to participate in accelerated-learning programs. The legislation also extends state postsecondary student-aid eligibility to these programs.

In Minnesota, the governor and legislators launched "Get Ready, Get Credit," an initiative that adds significant state funding assistance for students participating in Advanced Placement, International Baccalaureate, and the College Level Examination Program, as well as for the ACT's college readiness assessment, the Educational Planning and Assessment System. The ACT initiative supplements a state's existing Postsecondary Education Options program, one of the oldest and most-robust dual- and concurrent enrollment programs in the nation.

Looking ahead, the biggest challenge for practitioners and policymakers alike will be to move the focus of finance conversations from the question of "How much?" to the question of "How?"

THE ROAD AHEAD

Given the challenges and opportunities recounted here, a simple question remains for the advocates of accelerated-learning options: What next? Following are a few recommended directions:

- *Build on the existing body of knowledge regarding the various accelerated-learning approaches, developing primers and menus of policy options for political and education leaders and practitioners.* This is most effectively tackled by organizations with a national reach, supported by constituents and the philanthropic community.
- *Establish a "culture of intentionality" that more fully integrates accelerated learning into state education policy agendas.* The heavy lifting here must be done at the state and local levels, catalyzed and supported by national policymaking organizations, such as the National Governors Association, the National Conference of State Legislatures, the State Higher Education Executive Officers, and the Education Commission of the States.
- *Continue experimentation with and the development of a culture of evidence, widely disseminating new models and metrics in areas such as return on investment and program quality.* This work will be done at the local, state, and national levels, and support will require a coordinated, collaborative approach, led by a national organization or a coalition of national organizations (policy or philanthropic).
- *Develop and promote a cohesive set of regionally and nationally recognized quality assurance standards for all accelerated-learning options.* Entities such as NACEP and the regional accrediting agencies are the most appropriate leaders here, supported and encouraged by national policymaker organizations.

Accelerated learning, like many other policy innovations, holds considerable promise as a means of bridging gaps in a decentralized educational system. As other movements have shown, progressing from "promise identified" to "promise fulfilled" requires a commitment to experimentation (and the acceptance of some failure), continuous learning, and the will to challenge the status quo and entrenched interests. If accelerated learning is to evolve from a loosely defined concept illustrated by an anarchy of exemplars, this is the path that policymakers, practitioners, researchers, and funders must be prepared to take. It is the road ahead, and the next steps await us.

23

Exploring Education Reform Systemically

The United Kingdom's Nuffield 14–19 Review

Geoff Hayward

In England and Wales, young people end compulsory schooling in the academic year they reach 16 years of age. Historically, only a minority of young people remained in full-time education after that age. However, the proportion staying on increased massively in the 1980s, reaching a maximum of 92 percent of 16-year-olds in 1992. This was the result of a complex amalgam of social and economic factors; for example, the sharp decline in the demand for unskilled youth labor following recessions in the 1980s changed parental aspirations and reforms to the system for qualifying for higher education. Since 1992, participation rates in post-compulsory secondary education have stagnated, so that currently only 75 percent of 16- to 19-year-olds are participating in education and training. This is far below the levels reached in the majority of other OECD countries, and it is a major source of policy concern in the United Kingdom where education, as is the conventional wisdom in most other countries, is seen as the key ingredient for maintaining individual employability and economic competitiveness in a globalizing economy.

As a consequence, we have experienced over the last decade a whirlwind of educational reforms. These efforts have largely centered on trying to make the education and training system more attractive to young people, by offering alternative qualification pathways such as apprenticeship; changing school governance; sharpening accountability measures through standards-based reforms and goal-setting; using public funding to widen participation in higher education; and, most recently, providing financial inducements to learners to remain in education and training at the end of compulsory schooling. Participation rates in higher education have increased substantially over the last decade as more young people achieved the level of qualification needed to matriculate.

The most recent evidence, however, suggests that these measures have had, at best, only a minor impact on participation rates in postcompulsory education and training. Indeed, the proportion of 16- to 19-year-olds who are not in employment, education, or training has increased from 9 percent to 11 percent over the last three years.

Given the amount of money, time, and effort invested in the reform agenda, this minor gain in a key metric of the performance of the postcompulsory education and training system suggests that there is a system failure in terms of those young people who stubbornly refuse to participate in education and training once they reach 16 years of age. It was the recognition of the systemic nature of the problems that led the Nuffield Foundation, a charitable body based in London, to commission a fundamental review of the 14–19 education and training system.

THE ORGANIZATION OF THE NUFFIELD REVIEW

The foundation launched the Nuffield Review in October 2003 and funded it until September 2009. The review is led by a directorate from the University of Oxford; the Institute of Education, University of London; the Universities and Colleges Admissions Service; and the University of Warwick Business School, and assisted by three research officers and a project manager. Subsequently we were joined by a new director from Wales.[1] The review, which I direct, comprises an extensive network of people from schools, further-education colleges,[2] higher education institutions, teachers' unions and professional associations, employers, private training providers, voluntary organizations, and government departments and agencies.

The review is not a conventional research project. Rather, it commissions work from experts in areas such as assessment, funding, governance, and mentoring to produce briefing papers. These briefing papers then form the basis for a series of expert group meetings, with a detailed record kept of the discussions. The discussions form the starting point for even more questions and lines of inquiry. In addition, we have undertaken more systematic reviews of the literature in areas such as disengagement from schooling, the transition into higher education and the labor market, and comparative analyses. Finally, we have also begun some small-scale research projects; for example, into the perceptions of higher education admission tutors of the reforms in 14–19 education. All reports are freely available on our website, www.nuffield14–19review.org.uk, which in turn promotes further rounds of comment and discussion.

Each year, the outcomes of the various lines of inquiry pursued during the course of the year are summarized in an *Annual Report* (also available on the website). The first three years of our inquiry have focused on developing a better understanding of the nature of the problems that the system is experiencing in terms of attracting and enabling the attainment of all learners. In the next three years, our aim is much more that of advocacy; for example, arguing for specific changes in policy direction and working with practitioner groups to disseminate the findings of the review about good practice.

The Education "System"

One of the challenges of undertaking a systemic review is to identify exactly what the system is that we should be investigating. Traditionally, the education system

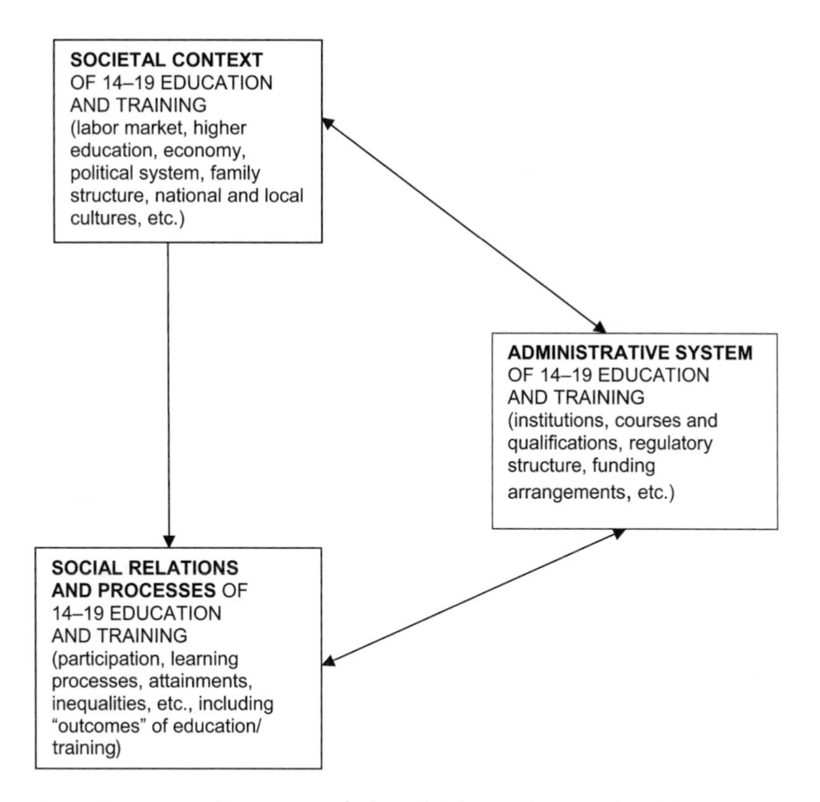

Figure 1. A Conceptual Framework for Thinking about Education and Training Systems in a Comparative Context

has been viewed in isolation from other institutions and systems. However, from the beginning the review recognized the need to frame the problems more broadly (see figure 1).

Thus, we have drawn upon two distinctions. The first is between the education and training system on the one hand and the wider societal context within which it is embedded; for example, we examined the operation of the youth labor market, the economy, legal frameworks, political system, welfare support, family structures, local and national cultures, and widening participation in higher education.

The second distinction is between education and training as a set of social relations and processes that are framed by an administrative system. The social relations and processes would encompass participation, learning processes, attainments, inequalities, and so on, including the outcomes of education and training. The administrative system comprises educational institutions, courses and qualifications, regulatory structure, funding arrangements, etc. The evidence suggests that there is no simple connection between the external social context and the dynamics of the education and training system, which has an inherent internal dynamic that is remarkably persistent in the face of social change.

For example, a persistent pattern in participation rates in postcompulsory education is that white, working-class boys with few qualifications are the most likely to leave the system at the earliest opportunity. This is particularly pronounced in the older manufacturing centers of northern England. The evidence suggests that these young men are aiming to enter the labor market and will search for traditional blue-collar jobs in industries such as shipbuilding, steelmaking, or coal mining, even though such jobs have dwindled rapidly in recent years.

CHANGES IN THE ADMINISTRATIVE SYSTEM OF EDUCATION AND TRAINING

Adopting this broader perspective on the system has enabled us to follow a number of different routes of inquiry to unravel the relationship and impact of the three components in our simple model on outcomes for young people. Sometimes this leads to counterintuitive results. Typically the ultimate targets for education and training policy are located in the set of social relations and processes, such as improved participation rates, better outcomes, and reduced inequality. In England and Wales, at least, such targets are to be achieved largely through the use of policy instruments aimed at changing the administrative system; for example, through qualification reform and more-demanding regulatory and accountability systems. In addition, the institutions offering 14–19 education and training—schools, colleges, private training providers, and, to some extent, employers—will need to be alert to the demands, needs, and beliefs of "actors" in the wider societal context, such as parents, higher education, the labor market, and demographic change. In a system of education and training where money follows the learner, downturns and upturns in the supply of young people may have a major impact on institutional behavior under a given set of administrative circumstances.

Consider my colleague Ewart Keep's analysis of the impact of widening higher education participation, which is generally accepted as a "good thing" in the context of a changing youth labor market and demographic change (Keep and Mayhew, 2004).

This has two dimensions. First, due to demographic changes, the 14–19 cohort will get smaller over the next few years. This may mean that young people will be in a seller's market, and therefore, employers who traditionally recruit young people may have to compete harder with each other in a dwindling labor pool, thereby driving up youth wages. This in turn may serve to undermine the impact and appeal of England's Education Maintenance Allowances (to young people) and Learning Agreements (to employers of young people in jobs without training).

Second, labor market projections of the structure of job growth in England point to a polarizing labor market. This means that while high-skilled occupations will expand, so, too, will a number of low-wage, low-qualification occupations. The middle of the labor market is expected to continue to "hollow out" as polarization increases. This development, coupled with the cumulative impact of the mass expansion of higher education, may create a polarization of the incentive structures facing young people. If a degree becomes the essential entry qualification to the vast bulk of higher-level, better-paid jobs, then the incentive to participate post–age 16 for those who are unlikely to gain access to higher education may be reduced.

The combination of these two factors could have a seriously deleterious effect on postcompulsory participation rates. Far from cruising toward the English government's target of 90 percent participation by 17-year-olds, policy may find itself struggling to maintain current levels of participation among relatively low-achieving youngsters.

The administrative system of education and training and the wider societal context represent an external environment to which institutions offering education and training to 14- to 19-year-olds need to adapt if they are to survive in a marketized education and training system. In so adapting, institutionally based actors will need to make decisions about the sorts of learning opportunities and experiences they will provide and the type of learners they will aim to recruit. These are likely to change as the external environment alters; for instance, through demographic change or the provision of new types of qualifications. Such institutional behavior, conditioned by adaptation to the external environment, will produce a "decision field" for young people, consisting of a range of learning opportunities distributed across different types of institutions and a schedule of incentives for young people to participate.

Figure 1 leads to a consideration of the incentives and disincentives that push and pull young people into and out of the education and training system, and distribute them within the system, where they will be set against changes in institutional behavior induced by changes in both the administrative system of education and training and the broader societal context. For example, school-by-school attainment tables, quasi-markets, and funding mechanisms, all elements of a growing managerialism in educational governance, are powerful incentives that may make institutions wary of taking on certain types of learners whom they consider to be "risky."

As a consequence, such learners are pushed out from certain forms of provision and into others; for instance, from general into weakly vocational provision or from schools into general further-education colleges, or out of the system altogether. The availability of alternative forms of provision, such as "weakly vocational qualifications," which provide a relatively cheap type of course provision, may be adopted to retain learners in one type of institution when their needs may have been better served by moving to alternative provision in another institution.

Sometimes the outcomes that result from such adaptive changes in the behavior of institutional actors seem to be positive, such as the continuing improvement in examination scores. At other times, they seem to be perverse. There is some evidence to suggest that current accountability systems lead teachers of vocational courses to adopt an inventory approach to assessment. This, it is argued, can damage relationships between teachers and learners and so result in an increased dropout rate from such courses. This is then reflected in the lower retention rates for vocational courses.

THE DECISIONMAKING OF YOUNG PEOPLE

Another major area where we need improvement is our ability to understand how young people make decisions. This provides the foil of agency for the more-structural analysis undertaken above. Young people should not be seen as cultural dupes but as knowledgeable actors making decisions, albeit with often only partial and biased information, within a complex decision field.

Young people interpret the incentives and disincentives to participate and progress in the 14–19 phase differently, depending on a variety of historical, social, and cultural factors. They actively construct the decision field and their position within it using a variety of locally, historically, and culturally situated resources to imagine their futures, interpret the opportunities available to them, and develop their aspirations and motivations. Some young people can make choices and succeed against the odds. The review aims to understand much more about the sorts of resources they can mobilize that enable them to do so. It is also very important to understand the processes through which young people define and express their identities in the process of becoming adults, through or against the education and training system, the labor market structures, and incentives.

A characteristic feature of the literature in this area is the lack of certainty and consensus about what is happening during the decisionmaking process. There does, however, seem to be a consensus that adolescent decisionmaking is an ongoing process of identity and attitude formation—and in some cases, information gathering—that is not necessarily linear in nature. The education and training system focuses on particular decisions and particular points in time.

So, as young people approach the end of compulsory schooling, they are engaged in making decisions within a complex decision field of possibly poorly perceived incentives and opportunities. Within this decision field, there are a range of opportunities that could be pursued and a schedule of incentives and disincentives that will affect the propensity to act in particular ways. These incentives and disincentives can be conceptualized as factors that pull and push young people into or out of the system. For the more academically successful, these processes probably operate at a subliminal level; there is no real choice being made about whether to stay on (because that is assumed to be the correct thing to do), but rather, they are making decisions about *what* to study. For young people with lower levels of attainment at age 16, there is a need to weigh up (albeit in a manner that at best approaches bounded rationality) the relative merits and opportunity costs, both economic and personal, of staying on and participating in different ways. Such young people are more likely to feel the weight of factors that operate to push or pull them out of the education and training system than their academically more successful peers. These include historically and locally constructed social and cultural resources (cultural capital), and the networks of adults and peers that young people interact with (social capital).

At least four factors seem to be at work here: delayed transitions and restructuring of the life course; destandardization and individualization of transitions; individualized perceptions of risks and opportunities; and multidimensional, dynamic identities.

MOVING FORWARD

Much of the work of the Nuffield Review to date, as the examples above illustrate, has been to develop our understanding of the dynamics of the 14–19 education and training system through examining the research literature, engaging in an ongoing dialogue with experts from a range of fields. We now have a good understanding of how the system works for some but is also dysfunctional for too many. Such understanding is crucial for the design of case-sensitive policy.

However, to make progress with helping more young people complete their education requires far more than a mere analysis of the issues. Within the English and Welsh system, failure is enshrined at 16. A number of policy levers are being used to overcome this and ensure that a greater proportion of young people continue their education beyond the end of compulsory schooling and access higher education. These levers include paying young people to stay on in full-time education, and continual reform of the vocational education system. Nevertheless, I increasingly despair of suggestions for achieving social justice through changes to qualification systems, a particularly English obsession. For example, we search continually for parity of esteem between vocational and general qualification pathways, but elite universities recruit from the latter not the former, and employers value academic over vocational qualifications when recruiting for all but the most specialized trade jobs.

It seems to me that the key to a solution of our poor participation rates in post-compulsory education and training is to ensure equal access to attainment in academic qualification pathways. The challenge is how to produce an attitude that all can succeed, while establishing the right balance of incentives for teachers and schools to ensure that more *do* succeed. This, I suggest, means striking an appropriate balance between teacher autonomy and accountability, and developing alternative performance-management systems. It is to the design of such systems and the development of more collaborative teaching and learning arrangements that the Nuffield Review will turn its attention over the next three years. In addition, we will turn increasingly to advocacy as well as research in our attempts to further influence policymakers.

PART VI

What Comes Next? Accountability, Data Systems, Financing

The least developed—and, some would say, most important—structures needed to sustain a 9–14 integrated education pipeline are state-level data and accountability systems and financing. These final essays present either a unique state example of a significant advance in policy or, in the absence of proven practices, seed the conversation with provocative and untested ideas about what should come next.

In Texas, one of the few states that sets and reports progress on postsecondary goals, such goals "force strategic collisions" between sectors, explains Michael Collins. To reach the state's education goals, he writes, postsecondary must collaborate with K–12, and especially around the transition to postsecondary.

Getting the data needed to gauge progress toward state goals remains a major challenge, although a number of states have systems under design. Also citing Texas, Chrys Dougherty and Lynn Mellor illustrate how such data systems can be constructed and then used to answer essential policy questions related to integrating grades 9–14. Looking at Florida, with the nation's best-developed data system, Jay Pfeiffer describes how education and workforce data can be merged—and how such data systems can become a public resource.

Peter Ewell notes that many states have been improving their K–12, longitudinal data-tracking capabilities, yet only a fraction of the states can follow students from K–12 into their postsecondary years. Looking ahead, Ewell presents the challenges to data systems for tracking students moving on multiple pathways among varied postsecondary providers.

Education finance and financial aid systems must also be rethought and restructured. As Jill Kirk, John Tapogna, and Duncan Wyse note, state budgets and finance data are based on separate funding for the K–12 and postsecondary systems, and thus, policymakers have little insight into how instructional costs and student services across K–16 could be funded equitably and effectively. Working in Oregon, they have developed a K–16 budget tool that provides the state with a promising way of constructing a single finance system. Arthur Hauptman and

Edward St. John, in separate chapters, note that financial aid systems are not constructed to motivate students to prepare for and succeed in college. Yet financial aid is a critical factor in promoting access to higher education. Hauptman and St. John propose controversial finance policies that could get better results for low-income students.

The book says little except retrospectively about the additional big levers: governance and accountability across P–20. Kirst and Usdan's historical essay in Part II, focusing on New York, presents the sole example of a state with combined governance but without significant P–20 integration. As for P–20 accountability, because most states lack policies incorporating rewards and sanctions that measure the performance of higher education, and the accountability systems of No Child Left Behind do not translate well into the postsecondary level, there is as yet little to say.

24

Postsecondary Numerical Goals as Catalyst for P–16 Reform

Texas Sends a Message

Michael Collins

If the economic competitiveness of the United States is on the verge of decline because we are not educating Americans fast enough to remain on top, and if the nation is falling behind in educational attainment, practicality suggests that the first thing we should do is determine the "knowledge production level" needed to remain in the lead, and then set goals to meet that standard.

In 2006–06, I conducted a 50-state study with my colleagues at Jobs for the Future to begin to find out how well the nation is addressing this need (Collins, 2006). Specifically, we sought to learn about goals each state had established for higher education attainment. The research revealed that, in fact, few states have quantifiable goals for higher education enrollment, retention, and graduation.[1] And of those states with quantifiable goals, even fewer disaggregate their data to account for the progress of students of color and low-income students. Despite real threats to our global economic primacy by advances in educational attainment by other nations, the states—and the nation as a whole—have placed a low priority on setting numerical goals for postsecondary attainment.

Moreover, among the states that do have goals, there is great variation in the quality of the goals and the reasoning behind them. In the best cases, states have defined the goals clearly and tied them directly to high-priority needs. In the worst cases, the goals are opaque and disconnected from real state needs; rather, they refer to generic notions of excellence or lack any explicit logical underpinning.

National education reform efforts, which focus on P–16 governance, standards and alignment, longitudinal data tracking, and accountability, have done little to advance efforts to set state goals for postsecondary attainment. Granted, the organizations advocating reforms do call on states to set goals for high school graduation and postsecondary participation, but such goals receive relatively little attention compared to the four areas of primary concern.

By ascribing a lower priority to attainment goals, though, states may be missing an opportunity to use them as a lever to speed progress toward those higher-priority reforms. Setting realistic yet challenging numerical goals can act as a catalyst to speed P–16 reform. Reaching challenging numerical goals requires a cross-sector approach to fixing the education pipeline, culminating in an integrated set of P–16 policies that not only removes barriers at the borders between the K–12 and postsecondary sectors, but also builds bridges across them.

While we found that few states have rational goals tied to specific state needs, if they have set any goals at all, Texas is one among a handful of states that has initiated comprehensive goal-setting efforts. Its experience with setting state-level numerical attainment goals suggests how goals can accelerate the pace of meaningful P–16 reform.

CLOSING THE GAPS: TOWARD COMPREHENSIVE P–16 REFORM

Texas arrived at its goals after reviewing dramatic projections made by the state demographer. Like other states, Texas was concerned about its future economic competitiveness in the global economy, and troubling demographic trends were threatening the state's ability to compete. The rapid growth of Texas's Latino population was creating a scenario where, without intervention, the largest part of the state's population would be concentrated at the lowest levels of education attainment. Clearly, this would have a devastating social and economic impact (Murdock, S. H., White, S., Hoque, M. N., Pecotte, B., You, X., & Balkan, J., 2003).[2]

The impact of demographic changes and the resulting grim economic forecast served as the backdrop while Texas higher education officials and P–16 stakeholders began a process to reverse the historical trends. The state responded through a planning process that culminated in statewide numerical goals to increase the higher education participation and success rates of all Texans. The goals specifically emphasized closing the attainment gap between the state's white population and its Latino and African American populations.

Goal-setting brought together a diverse group of disconnected P–16 stakeholders, culminating in the creation of an integrated set of policies connecting K–12 and higher education. Just as important, the specter of challenging goals sped state-level policy reforms precisely in each of the four areas of prime concern among the nation's education reformers: P–16 governance; standards and alignment; longitudinal data tracking; and accountability.

P–16 Governance

Historically K–12 and higher education have operated separately. This was the case in Texas as of 1999, at the outset of the higher education planning process that ultimately established numerical goals. Even though the legislature had signaled its expectation for cross-sector collaboration as early as 1985 by creating the Joint Advisory Committee to advise the state's K–12 and higher education governing boards on cross-sector issues, the state board of education and the Higher Education Coordinating Board continued to work largely independently of each other. This changed, however, in 1998, when the staff of the sister agencies began meeting informally to address cross-sector issues, including college readiness and teacher education.

The next year, as the state moved forward in its higher education planning process, it became clear that the scope of the goals, and the commensurate challenges of reaching them, necessitated a deliberate collaboration between K–12 and higher education. To accomplish this, the legislature approved a rider to the state's budget appropriation act requiring this collaboration, and the informal public education and higher education working group officially became the P–16 Council.

In 2000, the Coordinating Board adopted the state's higher education plan, *Closing the Gaps by 2015*, which contained numerical goals, and the P–16 Council became an even more important venue for developing strategies that would bring P–16 stakeholders together. However, the P–16 Council lacked the authority to set policy, and it struggled to be more than a place where the sectors came together to hear reports. The legislature agreed that the current P–16 structure was inadequate to the challenges presented by the demographic shifts and the consequences of not reaching the state goals, and it wrote the P–16 Council's authority into law, mandating interaction between K–12 and higher education.[3]

While there was fledgling collaboration between the sectors prior to establishing goals, it was informal and sporadic. The sense of urgency presented by not reaching agreed-upon state goals served as a catalyst for the creation of the formal P–16 Council to own the transition space between the sectors.

Standards and Alignment

Just as goals catalyzed a breakdown of the wall between K–12 and higher education, they had a similar impact on narrowing the alignment gap between the standards for graduating from high school and those for entering college. In 2000, there was a large gap between high school exit-level standards in Texas and the state's college entrance standards. Only 27 percent of high school graduates who took the Texas Academic Skills Program (TASP), the state's college readiness exam, passed all three sections: reading, writing, and math (Texas Higher Education Coordinating Board, 2003).

Part of the problem was that too few students took a rigorous college preparatory curriculum. Only 40 percent of the 1999–2000 public high school graduates completed a college prep curriculum (Texas Higher Education Coordinating Board, 2003). The result was that large numbers of high school graduates needed remediation upon entering college. In fact, by 2000, developmental education contact hours were generating $185 million in general revenue appropriations, a 376 percent increase over general revenue appropriations in the 1988–89 biennium when TASP was implemented (Texas Higher Education Coordinating Board, 2002).

In recommendations to the Higher Education Planning Committee, the staff of the Coordinating Board explicitly identified the misalignment of the standards for K–12 and higher education as a barrier to reaching the state goals. As a result, increasing the rigor of the high school diploma became the first state-level strategy to reach the participation goal. The strategy called for making a college prep curriculum the standard high school diploma for all high school students, and the P–16 Council served as a venue to rally support from relevant stakeholders to support that objective. Representatives from the higher education systems, K–12 districts, and the business community, particularly the Texas Business and Education Coalition, worked to get the support of the legislature.

Legislation supporting increasing the rigor of the high school diploma was enacted in 2001. Beginning with freshmen entering high school in 2004, a college preparatory curriculum is the standard for graduation at Texas public high schools.

The specter of the goals in *Closing the Gaps* permeated the cross-sector discussions leading to the development of a more-rigorous high school diploma to equip students with the academic skills needed to perform college-level work and avoid costly remediation. And the catalytic effect of the goals has continued to affect other areas of reform.

Longitudinal Data Tracking

At the time Texas was developing its goals for educational attainment, data for the K–12 and postsecondary systems was stored in separate databases that did not exchange information with one another, which prevented a comprehensive overview of the education pipeline. This fractured view was a barrier to reaching the goals, so state higher education officials partnered with K–12 to integrate the two separate databases into a user-friendly, interagency, longitudinal database that would make it possible to track student progress across sectors and into the workforce.

Again, the P–16 Council was the platform for discussions on creating a data-tracking system that would allow information to be exchanged across the respective agencies. It was under the Council's auspices that the Higher Education Coordinating Board, the Texas Education Agency, and the State Board for Educator Certification came together to develop the new system.

In 2001, the legislature demonstrated its support for a P–16 longitudinal data-tracking system by funding the Information Access Initiative. The result was the creation of the Texas P–16 Public Education Information Resource, a database that links K–12, higher education, and workforce data. Without this capability, it would be difficult, if not impossible, to determine whether the state's education pipeline is on the trajectory to success.

Accountability

When Texas set the goals for higher education attainment, the state did not have a formal higher education accountability system. This meant there was no official way to measure progress toward the goals. The Coordinating Board took the lead in developing a simple and clear system to measure progress toward or away from the state goals.

The system to measure progress has two main components: individual institutional performance and statewide performance. At the request of the Coordinating Board, each higher education institution submitted targets that represented its respective share of the overall statewide goals, and both the individual and collective reports are evaluated and calibrated annually.

The legislature required the Coordinating Board to report on progress toward the goals annually. The board's report contains simple charts and tables that illustrate institutional and statewide performance, and these are accessible to the public through a website.[4] This clear and concise system to measure progress was a precursor to the state's current higher education accountability system, which is organized by goals in the state's higher education plan, *Closing the Gaps*.

PUTTING IT ALL TOGETHER

Setting a small number of goals that are tied directly to state needs, and then measuring progress in achieving them, demonstrates a true commitment to raising educational attainment. It also sends a powerful message to stakeholders, particularly to the different sectors of education: Collaboration is the only way to achieve success. Numerical goals potentially force strategic collisions between sectors, and they create an incentive for collaboration across sectors and for measuring the value-added of different actions and, ultimately, for measuring student progress. Numerical goals themselves will not cause progress. Framed correctly, though, they can send a powerful signal about a state's desired future and the consequences of falling short on what it takes to get there.

25

Assessing and Reporting Progress

Florida's Integrated Data Systems

Jay Pfeiffer

Florida's public education system, recognized for the breadth and depth of the data resources that the state's department of education maintains, is a leader in collecting information on the performance of secondary and postsecondary education and other systems and programs that receive public funding. In addition, Florida has established notably effective record-linkage policies across the many agencies that govern K–12, employment security, adult education, and other public services.

In cooperation with public school districts, technical centers, community colleges, and universities, a wide variety of Florida agencies collect program and administrative data that describe the educational progress of students and the efficacy of education-related policies. This information is used to meet federal and state statutory requirements for reporting and accountability, as well as to monitor and manage educational programs in classrooms and at the local and state levels. The data are also fundamental to exchanging transcripts and other information between students and educational institutions and in providing the public, including parents and students, with information that assists them in making informed decisions.

One cornerstone of Florida's approach to the collection and use of data is the Florida Education and Training Placement Information System. FETPIP was established by the Florida legislature in 1984, making it the nation's oldest such system. This interagency system collects not only data on current students but also follow-up data on former students and participants in other types of education training, such as welfare recipients, prisoner releases, adult learners, and GED earners.

Particularly innovative for efforts to integrate grades 9 through 20 is the PK20 Education Data Warehouse, a cross-delivery sector and time-integrated system maintained by the Florida Department of Education. Known as the EDW, it integrates data from 26 state-level operational source systems and provides a view across systems reflecting the PK–20 public education environment. It was initially developed over a three-year period, from January 2001 through May 2003.

EDW data comes from, and is shared among, student information systems for public schools (K–12), adult and career and technical centers, community colleges, and universities; finance and accounting information systems for each delivery sector; and student assessment databases, including the Florida Comprehensive Assessment Test and the College Placement Test. Also included are databases on student financial aid for postsecondary education, databases on student financial aid for K–12 scholarships, facilities information, and data used in career information and guidance systems.

These data largely deal with the enrollment characteristics and academic progress of students as they move through the public school system, into postsecondary institutions and the labor force. The data originate with school districts, community colleges, and universities. They are compiled from student registrations, classroom performance information, and local finance and accounting systems.

Each of the information systems includes data dictionaries, comprehensive sets of data elements, edits, transmission management reports, and other tools that facilitate the provision of consistent and accurate data at the state level. Various kinds of reports are generated from these databases to meet local, state, and federal reporting needs. These reports are made available in various forms, including hard copy and electronic formats.

THE FLORIDA EDUCATION AND TRAINING PLACEMENT INFORMATION SYSTEM

The Florida Education and Training Placement Information Program provides its services to and includes data from a variety of agency applications. The term *applications* refers to the programs and organizations for which FETPIP provides follow-up data-collection services. Currently, FETPIP encompasses over 30 applications, including records on all public high school graduates and dropouts, all community college associate's degree and vocational students, all school district-sponsored secondary and postsecondary vocational students, all state university system graduates, and Florida's department of education adult education and GED students. Through cooperation with individual institutions and their licensing boards, the applications also encompass students from selected private vocational schools, colleges, and universities.

FETPIP is not limited to the agencies under the purview of the state department of education. It also encompasses all Workforce Investment Act programs (through the Agency for Workforce Innovations), welfare reform participants (from the Department of Children and Families), unemployment insurance claimants (from Florida's Department of Revenue), and all correctional system releases (from the Department of Corrections and the Prison Industries). Also included are smaller operations, such as adult migrant worker education, apprenticeships, and certain longitudinal collections, such as annual follow-up on a cohort of students who left Florida public high schools in 1990–91.

Organizations representing each application provide FETPIP with individual student or participant files from their management information system units. The files include individual identifiers (name, social security number), as well as demographic, socioeconomic, and programmatic data. In the most recent data collection cycle, conducted in fall 2006, these applications provided FETPIP with nearly 10 million program-level records, representing about 4 million individuals.

FETPIP collects follow-up data that describe the employment, military enlistment, incarceration, public assistance participation, and continuing education experience of the participants being followed. It accomplishes its collection electronically, linking participant files to the administrative records of other state and federal agencies.

In addition, Florida has contracted with the National Student Clearinghouse for information on out-of-state students. The NSC, established to help lending institutions verify postsecondary enrollments for loan-repayment scheduling, maintains current enrollments files covering about 90 percent of the nation's postsecondary institutions, public and private. It also includes data on the credentials obtained by students in its database. NSC enrollment data enable FETPIP to identify the postsecondary experiences of Florida students who leave the state.

On an annual basis, records are electronically linked with a number of other agencies. For example, the department of corrections provides data on new incarcerations and recidivism. Additional linkages are conducted through agreements with federal agencies. For example, the U.S. Department of Defense provides data on military enlistments, and the federal office of personnel management provides data on federal career service employment.

FETPIP also conducts record linkages against employment records on a quarterly basis. This process is essential to the performance measures required of programs funded under the Workforce Investment Act. FETPIP conducts a variety of ad hoc record linkages as well. These are tailored to requests from users who may include representatives from the participating agencies or from researchers, national organizations, state organizations, and others.

Once data are collected and reviewed, FETPIP provides a variety of reports and files. Thus, FETPIP data become integral elements in the accountability reporting of public schools, vocational institutions, community colleges, universities, and workforce programs.

PK20 EDUCATION DATA WAREHOUSE

Florida has excellent operational systems for collecting data from all education and workforce delivery systems, at the student or employee level. Until recently, though, the large quantities of comprehensive data amassed by each system were not stored in a manner that allowed for timely and cost-efficient longitudinal or historical analyses.

Addressing this challenge is the mission of the PK20 Education Data Warehouse. Based on a common set of business rules and definitions, data from the diverse source systems are loaded into the EDW, where the records are matched and entered into a single database, making it is possible for data-based products to be generated quickly.

Still in its early phases of operation, the EDW already encompasses a wide variety of data on students (e.g., demographics, enrollment, educational programs, promotion, attendance, test scores); educational institutions (e.g., types, location, graduation rates); financial aid (e.g., loans/grants, disbursement); student employment (e.g., industry, military, wages); courses (offerings, student and teacher participation, instruction type, grades); educational staff (e.g., demographics, certification, instruction type); and educational awards (type, program, institution).

The EDW will represent the department of education's revised foray into providing deep, broad access to information. In arenas that have numerous large operational data systems, such as the department, management often has access to only a small fraction of the available information. Typically, this is because data are collected by separate operational systems optimized for processing transactions rather than for analyses. Without effective tools to facilitate analysis in addressing stakeholder questions, too little information will be gleaned from the potential inherent in the abundance of data collected—or even paralyze the use of the data.

In contrast, the EDW offers integrated, *one-stop shopping* for relevant data elements. Having a single source for accurate, longitudinal data strengthens the department's reporting. Moreover, warehousing protects entities that collect enormous amounts of data, like the department of education, from the potential pitfalls of having hundreds of reports and analyses or several key employees with personal Excel or Access databases.

The EDW continues to evolve. For example, it is now characterized by monumental databases and desktops accessed by a small number of department employees. The next steps will take Florida education data, including K–12, postsecondary, and workforce data, to a more-open portal for public consumption.

LESSONS LEARNED

Today, Florida has a well-established system for collecting and sharing student-level data among education sectors for the purposes of accountability, research, evaluation, and funding. Its approach to collecting and using data has become a model, cited by national education-reform efforts, including the Data Quality Campaign, which supports the efforts of state policymakers to improve the collection, availability, and use of high-quality education data.

Florida's experience in building key education data systems, with its emphasis on integrating diverse data resources, suggests a number of lessons about the data systems with special attention to integrating grades 9 through 20.

Secure and maintain executive leadership and commitment

Leadership commitment is an important starting place as states, or educational organizations within states, consider developing systems that involve data collection by local education agencies. This commitment may come in the form of legislative initiative, as was the case with FETPIP and the EDW; executive-level commitment, as was the case with applications and with the EDW and FETPIP; or "groundswell" support, where local organizations recognize the value-added of state-level data collection and reporting.

Articulate the long- and short-term goals and purposes of a state-level education information system, and revisit those as necessary

While a long-range vision is important, it also is important to realistically manage expectations. This requires clearly outlining short-range, achievable goals. It is never a bad idea to exceed short-term goals; it *is* a bad idea to not meet them. For example, the short-range goal for the EDW was to serve the immediate needs of education decisionmakers in participating agencies, while the long-term vision is to continuously add new data and create seamless forms of public access.

Publicly articulate the benefits and risks for everyone involved

The benefits of FETPIP and the EDW for Florida's state-level education systems, including integrated ones, consist of reducing and managing the impact of changing federal or state reporting requirements on local entities; assuring consistent and accurate reporting and analysis; providing a means of reporting state or federal data on behalf of local organizations; and providing comparative information statewide. There are significant risks and costs as well. For example, start-up expenses must be borne and accounted for. Moreover, as both FETPIP and the EDW recognize, data that are often sensitive must be collected and protected in a fashion that precludes untoward release or improper use. Also, there may be political and ownership resistance to both the collection and the release of some data.

Build on existing systems and expertise

School districts, community colleges, and universities have significant investments and expertise in defining, designing, collecting, maintaining, and reporting data on students, staff, facilities management, and finance. Florida's state-level development has built on this knowledge and expertise.

Pursue opportunities to provide service and share information

The data collected are useful beyond federal and state reporting and accountability processes. The data can serve consumers in making decisions about institutions and academic paths. They can assist in the management of student learning and achievement. They can support research on best practices and promising new policies. These opportunities must be actively sought as a part of a system's ongoing operation. Thus, the same agencies that participate in collecting education-related data in Florida can not only request reports from FETPIP and the EDW, but also receive assistance in its use as well.

Publicize products, services, and capabilities

All potential and actual reports, analyses, research documents, and other services must be known to users so that they will peruse available information and request additional information needed for their purposes. In Florida, the department of education website (www.fldoe.org) provides windows into the data collected by FETPIP and the EDW.

Establish and maintain a culture of integrity around data and information

Timeliness and accuracy are critical to any data system. In systems development, implementation, and maintenance, this requires the use of a variety of processes and tools to ensure quality, such as reporting edits, data dictionaries, technical assistance, and data audits. In Florida, inputs from all databases are updated on a regular, preestablished basis; for example, community colleges report detailed student and staff data eight times each year. Once edited and cleansed, these data are loaded into operational databases unique to community colleges and sent to the EDW.

Exceed all requirements dealing with confidentiality and restricted release

State and federal laws address the collection and dissemination of individually identifiable student data. The best known is the Family Educational Records Protection Act (FERPA). In integrated systems, the legal requirements are complicated by laws governing other sources of information. All provisions must be observed and exceeded. However, it would be wrong to consider the laws and requirements as barriers that preclude *any* form of data collection or data exchange involving individually identifiable data.

The EDW does not store personally identifiable data. During the matching process, a randomly generated unique identification number is assigned, and personally identifiable data (e.g., the source student identification number, name, birth date) are not loaded. Only EDW staff accesses the warehouse database, and any request for data at the detail level received from outside the department of education must go through a high-level approval process before release of data.

Recognize that change is constant and ongoing

Government leadership is constantly changing. Elected and appointed officials change as elections occur. Staff changes below leadership levels change as well. Technology changes, data needs change, and requirements change. To the degree that changes should be anticipated, they should be addressed. Data system professionals need to be prepared to react to changes as they occur.

Ongoing, reliable support is necessary to maintain the investments in time and money that were made in initial development. Ongoing support should be secured from regular state sources, supplemented from time to time by federal or foundation grants or participation in funded research.

All of these kinds of lessons are constant necessities. They do not end after a system is successfully implemented, nor do they end with the passing of an administration or with turnover in key staff. With its 20 years of experience and evolution in collecting and using data for improving its education systems, Florida illustrates that the lessons learned must be constantly addressed.

26

Data Requirements for a Coherent P–16 System

Chrys Dougherty and Lynn Mellor

Policymakers and educators are exploring the goal of making a broad, challenging, intellectually rich curriculum available as the standard for all students, not just the most educationally advantaged young people. Effectiveness in accomplishing this goal requires that each level of education—preschool, elementary, middle school, high school, and postsecondary education—prepare students well for the next level. Failure to do so has the greatest impact on disadvantaged students, who are likely to have fewer alternative ways to make up the missing academic preparation.

For many students, transitions between levels are difficult because they are told they are performing satisfactorily in one level, when in fact they are poorly prepared for the next one. This is like relay runners failing to agree on handoff points. In the case of ill-prepared students, the baton is dropped off well short of that point.

Preventing this coordination failure requires the alignment of curricular content standards and performance standards across levels—including between high school and postsecondary education—so that teachers and students are clear about what is expected of students at the next level.[1]

Ensuring that students leaving one level are indeed well prepared for the next requires a longitudinal data system that makes it possible to follow students and report back on how they performed in the next level, course, or grade, based on the condition they were in when they left the prior level. Specifically, the data system should make it possible to answer such questions as:

- What performance levels on state exams indicate that a student is prepared for higher education?
- Are recommended college preparatory courses preparing students for college?
- What is the relationship between students' eighth-grade performance on state exams and their readiness for college after high school?
- Which school systems best prepare economically disadvantaged students for postsecondary education?

TEN ESSENTIAL ELEMENTS OF A LONGITUDINAL DATA SYSTEM

To follow students over time, and to analyze such issues as academic growth, student mobility, graduation rates, course quality, and teacher quality, many states are building longitudinal data systems incorporating "Ten Essential Elements" identified by the National Center for Educational Accountability and the Data Quality Campaign (2005):

1. *A unique statewide student identifier,* making it possible to follow students over time as they move from grade to grade and from district to district, from prekindergarten through grade 12, and ideally into postsecondary education;
2. *Student-level enrollment, demographic and program participation information,* to identify where and for how long students are enrolled, to account for student mobility, and to ensure that test data are disaggregated correctly;
3. *The ability to match individual student test records from year to year,* to measure academic growth, assess student progress toward reaching challenging college- and career-readiness standards, and identify whether students who have reached those standards are still making progress;
4. *Information on untested students,* so that states can ensure that students from all groups are participating in state tests, and they can account for students who were exempted from the tests;
5. *A teacher identifier system with the ability to match teachers to students,* to help educators and policymakers understand the connection of student academic growth to specific teacher training and qualifications;
6. *Student-level transcript information,* including information on courses completed and grades earned, to make it possible to analyze the relationship between course-taking patterns and student success on state assessments and readiness for college and work;
7. *Student-level college readiness test scores,* such as performance on the ACT, SAT, SAT II, Advanced Placement, International Baccalaureate, and state exams designed to assess college readiness, to use as early indicators of whether students are prepared to succeed in postsecondary education and work;[2]
8. *Student-level graduation and dropout data,* which along with elements 1, 2, and 10, enable states to calculate longitudinal graduation rates as defined, for example, in the National Governors Association compact;[3]
9. *The ability to match student records between the P–12 and higher education systems,* without which the relationship between student preparation in P–12 and their success in postsecondary education cannot be evaluated; and
10. *A state data audit system,* to assess data quality, validity, and reliability, because the decisions made in education are only as good as the information on which they are based.

USING LONGITUDINAL DATA

Several brief examples illustrate the use of longitudinal data to address the first two questions that introduced this chapter.

Question One: What performance levels on state exams indicate that a student is prepared for higher education?

To address this question, the Texas Higher Education Coordinating Board, in collaboration with the Texas Education Agency, merged student-level scores on the Texas Assessment of Knowledge and Skills (TAKS) with data on the same students' results from the SAT and ACT exams and the Texas Higher Education Assessment (THEA), the exam most commonly used by Texas public colleges and universities to assess whether students require remediation before taking credit-bearing courses. Table 1 summarizes the Coordinating Board's analysis.

Thus, a student scoring at the state passing standard of 2100 on the English Language Arts TAKS had a predicted ACT reading score of 17.7, a predicted SAT score of 461, and a 57 percent probability that he or she would not need remediation after enrolling in a Texas public college or university. Using this and other information, Dougherty, Mellor, and Smith (2006) recommended that school systems target a benchmark eleventh-grade TAKS score of 2300 in order to have a high assurance that students will be college-ready. The authors then backward-mapped this benchmark to grades 3 through 10 to provide school systems with targets to indicate that students are on track to college readiness in earlier grades.

Question Two: Are recommended college-preparatory courses preparing students for college?

Many states encourage students to enroll in advanced and college preparatory courses in high school in order to increase their readiness for college and the workplace. Texas and Louisiana have made a college prep curriculum the default high school graduation plan for all students, and Indiana is phasing in a similar requirement. Twelve states now have "State Scholars" programs, generally sponsored by business organizations such as the state chamber of commerce, that encourage students to take college prep courses in high school.[4]

Table 1. Relationship of Eleventh-Grade TAKS Scores to College Readiness Measures

	TAKS Score	Predicted ACT Score	Predicted SAT Score	Approximate Probability of a THEA Score[a]	
				>230	>270
English[b]	2100	17.7	461	57%	n/a
	2200	20.1	502	77%	n/a
	2300	22.5	543	90%	n/a
	2400	24.9	584	100%	n/a
Mathematics	2100	19.5	472	67%	5%
	2200	21.9	521	90%	26%
	2300	24.3	570	100%	77%
	2400	26.7	618	100%	100%

[a] A THEA score of 230 is the cutpoint for indicating that a student is ready to take credit-bearing college courses; a math THEA score of 270 has been identified as the indicator of readiness for college algebra.
[b] The eleventh-grade TAKS English language arts test covers reading and writing.

But have students mastered the academic content implied by the labels of the courses they have taken and for which they received credit? Data from the Texas Higher Education Coordinating Board and other sources suggest that this is often not the case for low-income and minority students (Dougherty, Mellor, and Jian, 2006). For example:

- 63 percent of low-income students, 61 percent of African American students, and 59 percent of Hispanic students who graduated under the state's Recommended High School (college preparatory) Program in 2000 needed remediation in one or more subjects when they enrolled in Texas public higher education institutions. For white and non–low-income students, the figures were 27 percent and 33 percent.[5]
- 60 percent of Texas low-income students, 65 percent of African American students, and 57 percent of Hispanics who received course credit for geometry and Algebra II failed a state exit exam covering those subjects. The corresponding figures for white and non–low-income students were 32 percent and 36 percent, respectively.[6]
- In a study by the Texas Education Agency, 58 percent of Texas low-income students, 67 percent of African American students, and 57 percent of Hispanics who received course credit for Algebra I in 1999 failed the corresponding end-of-course exam. The percentages for white and non–low-income students were 35 percent and 39 percent.[7]
- Fewer than one in four low-income students in the 2002 Texas high school graduating cohort who took one or more Advanced Placement exams passed any of those exams. This amounted to fewer than one low-income student in seven who received credit in an AP course, because many students receiving credit for the course did not take the exam.[8]

The practice of awarding college preparatory course credit to poorly prepared students can be termed "orange drink labeled as orange juice": transcripts indicating that the students were college-ready frequently reflected faulty information. Pretending that students are college-ready when they are not is a disservice to current students, who find out soon enough that they are poorly prepared, and to future generations of students, as school systems misled by faulty data do not improve their practices.

A NOTE ON DATA AVAILABILITY TO RESEARCHERS

Even if the data exist, state and local educational agencies may lack the research capacity to address these questions. One cost-effective approach, adopted by the Florida Department of Education, among others, is to make the data available to third-party researchers for analysis at no cost to the state. This requires the state to adopt data-sharing guidelines and agreements with researchers to comply with the provisions of the federal Family Educational Rights and Privacy Act. Without such guidelines, enabling researchers to access student-level micro-data under appropriate confidentiality agreements, the data may remain locked and unused in state education agency vaults.

CONCLUSION

Students are likely to encounter difficulty in any educational transition between levels (elementary, middle, high school, or postsecondary education) unless:

- the curriculum is aligned across the two levels, so that the "handoff points" are agreed upon; and
- longitudinal data systems make it possible to follow students across levels so that educators in each level can see that smooth handoffs occur.

The transition between high school and postsecondary education is especially problematic because these two key features of an integrated, coherent system are lacking. Adding them, and promoting research to track success of these policies with students, belong at the top of states' policy agendas if they wish to promote not only access to postsecondary education, but also the likelihood that students will be prepared to succeed once they get there.

27

Seamless Data Systems to Promote Student Progression

Peter T. Ewell

To achieve the goal of a postsecondary credential for every high school graduate, we need a new conceptual approach to designing and implementing state-level, student unit record (SUR) data systems. Of course, data systems only compile and organize figures and "facts." They tell us what has happened, not why; nor do they tell us how to achieve the desired advances in educational attainment, which cannot occur without the alignment of standards for high school to those for the first two years of college, without appropriate governance and policy frameworks, and without greatly increased investments in student-support structures.

To track the far greater numbers of students who should be flowing through the upper ends of the education pipeline, we need comprehensive student databases to:

- handle the transactional task of managing the vastly increased workload involved in transitioning students across discrete educational steps; and
- support the increasingly sophisticated research that will be needed for states and systems to discover and foster the most effective and efficient educational pathways for students of various types and in varying conditions.

BACKGROUND

The current situation with regard to managing information in elementary-secondary and postsecondary education represents in microcosm many of the challenges associated with integrating these systems themselves. On both sides of that educational divide, capacity is impressive and growing—but with little linkage across the divide that reflects a common vision or objective. In K–12, states are moving quickly—often with significant federal funding—to develop longitudinal data systems in response to the reporting requirements of No Child Left Behind. With vigorous leadership from the national Data Quality Campaign, their designs include linkages to colleges and universities as a key element of database design.[1] However, few of these designs are finalized, and far too often college and university officials are unaware of their existence. In postsecondary education, the National Center for Education Statistics has proposed a nationwide unit record data system, but that proposal is mired in the politics of privacy—at least in part because the system's architecture is linked fundamentally to the use of social security numbers—at a time when state K–12 database designers are developing unique student identifiers. Meanwhile, among the 40 states that have developed postsecondary SUR systems, only 10 have experience in linking college and high school records (Ewell & Boeke, 2007). Indeed, a comparison of the list of state postsecondary unit record systems so identified by higher education leaders overlaps, but does not entirely correspond to, a similar list of states whose K–12 leaders identify as capable of linking high school records with college attendance.

For a variety of reasons, these conditions cannot stand. Stakeholder demands, embodied by the recommendations of the Secretary's Commission on the Future of Higher Education, see longitudinal information on student progress as necessary for monitoring and improving student success.[2] Meanwhile, in both the K–12 and postsecondary educational arenas, emerging forms of educational provision challenge the designs of existing data systems. These new forms of delivery include modular curricula that do not fit easily into curricula designed around fixed-length programs, "asynchronous approaches," which are not time-based, and electronically delivered or blended technology approaches that fundamentally alter the notion of attending class. Other rapidly growing instructional delivery approaches—for example, middle college and early college high schools—create entire institutions that sit on the boundary between the two sectors (Hoffman, 2004). Finally, the student population is increasingly diverse—demographically in terms of race/ethnicity and age, and educationally in terms of educational experience and learning style.

Such changes challenge the established design of student data systems and will inevitably cause schools and colleges—as well as the state agencies that coordinate and govern them—to change what they do. Yet the problem goes further. The goal of a postsecondary credential for every high school graduate will mean unprecedented increases in the numbers of students flowing through the education pipeline. Increases of this magnitude cannot be achieved by simply doubling the capacity of traditionally organized schools and higher education institutions. Many of the new forms of provision will need to be harnessed in order to "double the numbers."

More importantly, they must be coherently integrated if students are to avoid the difficulty of migrating across educational environments seamlessly and without the inefficiencies and loss of momentum associated with repeating content already mastered elsewhere. This, too, will demand good information systems to track student progress, respond to the need for rising levels of student support, and develop and evaluate new policies.

PLANNING ASSUMPTIONS: THE FUTURE HIGHER EDUCATION ENVIRONMENT

To describe the needed data systems, imagine the educational environments within which they will operate.[3] Based on trends already apparent, we can envision a number of probable features of the environment for higher education in about 2020.

A considerable increase in postsecondary capacity at the lower-division level

Under current operating conditions, the existing array of postsecondary providers will be unable to accommodate the numbers of students necessary to achieve the goal (National Center for Higher Education Management Systems, 2006a). Higher education's unprecedented expansion in the 1960s and 1970s was accommodated by vast increases in the size and number of institutions, but except for innovations in the community college sector, expanded enrollments did not result in new kinds of institutions. Nor, for the most part, did they change the way classes were taught or the governance and organization of postsecondary providers. Modes of instruction remained largely traditional, with economies of scale providing the only potential for gaining efficiencies.

The limits of expansion in this manner—especially if mass postsecondary education is to remain cost-effective—have probably been reached. Instead, expanded capacity will likely be in part accommodated by new kinds of postsecondary providers. Examples include regional service centers offering established degree programs (e.g., those recently established in Oklahoma), distance-delivered programs offered by both independent and public providers, and a host of proprietary or "charter" institutions. The exact character of these new providers is less important for estimating future data system requirements than the likelihood that there will be many of them and that they will take many different forms.

Greater student mobility across modes of instruction

As the number of providers grows, student mobility among them will also likely increase. Student movement among postsecondary providers in search of credentials is already at a record high (Adelman, 2005). As various modes of delivery, such as asynchronous technology-based programs, proliferate among established providers, it will become easier for students to access them sequentially or simultaneously in search of best prices or convenience.

At the same time, consumer information to support such enrollment decisions will become ubiquitous. Catalogs of degree-program offerings are already online in some states, and efforts to expand such resources for potential students to include individual course offerings will grow as institutions become more entrepreneurial. As pioneered by such institutions as Western Governors University, moreover, course offerings may increasingly be "mapped" in terms of content and associated competencies to a variety of degree programs so that students can choose appropriately—a property common to online consumer databases in other kinds of markets.

A future environment with many new providers, added to the mix of postsecondary education, will greatly increase the complexities of managing credit transfer and other handoffs of student records from one provider to another. This, in turn, will considerably strain institutional registration and records systems.

Competency standards defining basic student skills at various levels

It seems unlikely that an array of new and existing providers can accommodate increases in capacity without paying some attention to aligning skill standards at different levels, ultimately expressed in terms of student competency, rather than credit hours completed. Alignment of this kind will be especially needed in light of increased multi-institutional attendance, and it is receiving increasing attention in two-year to four-year transfer, its most obvious current manifestation. Illustrating this growing phenomenon are the Quality in Undergraduate Education initiative and recent efforts in Missouri, Utah, and other states to establish an underlying competency framework to govern statewide general education transfer requirements (Henry, 2006).

The established credit frameworks in secondary or postsecondary institutions are not doomed to disappear, however. Instead, new ways to map student achievement (e.g., credit by examination, assessment of prior learning) onto these established frameworks will likely grow, perhaps through mechanisms pioneered by the American Council on Education and the Council for Adult and Experiential Learning. One way to manage this complexity is to establish a "qualifications framework." Qualifications frameworks, which are evident in much of the English-speaking world, including Australia, New Zealand, South Africa, Ireland, and Hong Kong, align standards at various levels across a growing array of education providers. Extending this concept further might be third-party certification authorities. The United States has already experienced an explosion of credentialing in vocational areas (Adelman, 2000), established to make individual "packages" of learning short of a degree more meaningful and marketable. These challenges will likely require new kinds of record-keeping capabilities positioned toward documenting competencies, as well as for recording the traditional array of classes and credits (Johnstone, Ewell, & Paulson, 2002).

FUTURE STATE DATA SYSTEMS: DESIGN SPECIFICATIONS

Developments like these, if they occur, will significantly change the way individual higher education institutions structure and manage student records, but for a number of reasons, state data infrastructures will also be increasingly salient.[4] First, state funding will continue to be critical for higher education. Although much of the needed expansion in capacity may come through new kinds of institutions, economies gained by expanding enrollments, or efficiencies at established institutions, fulfilling the promise of a postsecondary degree for every high school graduate will surely require more money. As in the past, increased investment will bring with it increased accountability for student success—and the consequent need for states to track progress and outcomes.

Even more important, as states embrace the goal of increasing postsecondary attainment, the *manner* in which they invest new resources may simultaneously shift. Currently, underserved student populations face formidable affordability barriers, requiring significant, need-based financial aid. To meet increases in demand, states will increasingly have to mobilize the capacity of *all* educational providers, not just public institutions. Consequent shifts in mechanisms of financial support will probably raise state policy questions centered on how to obtain maximum returns from the investment of state aid. And states will be increasingly interested in investigating complex policy questions centered on identifying which paths through the education pipeline are optimal for which kinds of populations under different sets of circumstances.

All this points to several properties that will likely characterize state SUR data systems of the future.

Capability to track individual students longitudinally and across many kinds of providers

The capability to track individual students as they move through the early stages of the education pipeline through high school is already a minimum requirement in most states because of the reporting requirements of No Child Left Behind. With this stimulus, many states are building unit record databases that will eventually include the capability of tracking students from high school into postsecondary settings. Community college systems in a number of states have recently experienced a similar impetus to upgrade their longitudinal tracking capacities because of major foundation-supported policy projects, such as Ford Foundation's *Bridges to Opportunity* and the *Achieving the Dream* initiative of Lumina Foundation for Education (NCHEMS, 2006b).[5] Yet another motivation for enhancing state-level longitudinal tracking capability comes from workforce development, where, again, one objective is to identify the most cost-effective investments in worker training. All of these stimuli demand a seamless data environment in which individual student records can be easily linked to enable a given student's educational activities to be tracked over time and across different educational settings.

It is important to stress that none of this will necessarily require a single "data warehouse" built from scratch in each state. Many states have already invested heavily in building their postsecondary information resources, and, given recent advances in secure records linking, it may make sense for a state to pursue a more-decentralized strategy. But whatever course is taken, establishing such a capability will require two things: agreed-upon national standards for assigning and using unique student identifiers to link individual enrollment records at all levels; and consistent national definitions for a common core of data elements that describe student demographics and behaviors at all levels.

A flexible data architecture

Current SUR designs in higher education are organized conceptually around traditional modes of delivery, based on fixed terms and credits. Only about half of the state and system SURs record transcript-level detail for every student, and very few contain data on noncredit educational activity (Ewell & Boeke, 2007). Whether credit or noncredit, the way workforce training settings deliver instruction often differs substantially from traditional term-based, fixed-duration classes. Often they are delivered in accelerated or compressed course formats in which program starting and ending times do not correspond to established beginning and end-of-term dates. Community colleges are already experiencing difficulties with reporting and analyzing data as they attempt to fit these classes into traditional registration and records systems.

Such developments demand a data architecture that more resembles the way medical records are kept. In contrast to current educational records systems that are organized around a single, relatively rigid, definition of an "encounter" (a class), medical records are based on a definition of an encounter that begins with a diagnosed condition, includes treatments of varying lengths and types, and leads to an exit condition related to the original diagnosis. In postsecondary records systems of the future with comparable capabilities, each educational "encounter"—whether a traditional class or a nontraditional training event—would be documented for each student by a "diagnosis" in the form of a pretest, a "treatment" (learning that might be delivered by multiple providers), and an "exit condition" based on assessed competencies. There are no technical reasons why such a data system could not be built today, but substantial work would be required to develop the data definitions and procedures to use it effectively.

Multiple access and update capability

The task of populating today's state SUR database systems is straightforward. Constituent public colleges and universities, increasingly supplemented by nonprofit institutions participating in state financial aid programs, submit student record data directly, governed by a defined, term-oriented schedule and using a standard set of formats and data element definitions. Because many of these institutions use a common student registration and records system, moreover, standard data processing routines can be established to regularly upload the required information. States maintaining SURs have established sophisticated procedures for detecting errors in data entry and transmission—one of the most important (if least understood) requirements of a workable common database.

A complex network of nontraditional providers challenges this way of operating. Students may rapidly amass instructional experience from a wide range of providers coordinated through a common program—perhaps established by the state itself as a way of multiplying attainment. And they may be enrolled simultaneously at more than one institution. This requires an efficient way for institutions to update shared student records—and in real time—so that advisors can track student progress and intervene where necessary.

At the level of state policy, all this requires a database that can be appropriately accessed and manipulated by researchers, and they may also want to supplement student records with a range of specially collected evaluative information (e.g., student portfolios). These requirements imply a database that can receive information about the same student from multiple providers simultaneously and that gives multiple providers access to obtain information about the educational activities and attainments of a given student.

Modularity

Different states will likely have quite different capacities to develop data systems. As a result, data system designs will need to be modular, with the overall architecture established early; also, users must be able to add other components as the state's capacity to integrate and coordinate multiple providers evolves. This may mean first developing research databases, where the stakes associated with maintaining records for individual students are lower. It also implies that states building such systems should devote their earliest efforts to critical tasks that will govern the entire implementation process, such as drafting and agreeing on common data element definitions. Further, the autonomy of major university systems is likely to continue, which may mean the evolution of multiple parallel—though compatible—databases in many states.

Because of the substantial investments of both funds and expertise entailed in developing new data systems, future efforts may involve consortia of states acting in concert with a common set of designers and vendors. Indeed, it is surprising that this has not yet happened, although there is some interest in acquiring data systems wholesale from states that have recently implemented a new state-of-the-art SUR.[6]

A core of commonly defined data elements

Underlying all these properties is the fundamental need for a core of commonly defined data elements applied to students, educational encounters, and outcomes. At a minimum, these data elements must encompass:

- *A unique student identifier.* This should be consistent with the unique identifiers being developed by all states in connection with No Child Left Behind. While postsecondary SURs will always carry the social security number, which is needed for linking to employment records and other external databases, the SSN should not be the primary student identifier.
- *Demographic descriptors for students.* These should include all current Integrated Postsecondary Education Data System (IPEDS) identifiers, plus appropriate descriptors to identify research populations relevant to state policy (e.g., state scholarship recipients, special service populations).[7]
- *Competency descriptors.* These should be established nationally to be compatible with an eventual qualifications framework. They should include credentials or degrees awarded at various levels, as well as the competencies themselves, and indicate the means used to establish competency (e.g., a test score, a learning assessment, a demonstration, a portfolio).
- *Descriptors of a considerably expanded array of educational encounters.* These should include traditional classes taken for credit in traditional formats, but they may also include nontraditional experiences, such as distance learning, accelerated learning opportunities, service learning experiences, internships, asynchronous mastery-based work, and mastery demonstrated through test-out or credit awarded for prior learning. As postsecondary instruction gradually migrates toward a competency framework, these data elements will become less important for managing decisions about individual students because competencies will have taken their place; however, they will remain extremely important for longitudinal policy research directed toward establishing the most efficient and effective "paths" for different kinds of students.

APPLYING THE NEW STATE STUDENT UNIT RECORD DATABASES

Whatever the eventual shape and contents of future state SUR databases, they must support two quite different, but equally important, functions: managing individual student transitions; and supporting detailed policy research.

Managing Individual Student Transitions

Up to now, student transitions from one institution to another have been a matter for individual institutions to manage. Operating with its own curricular requirements, and with a computerized student registration and records system tailored to meeting this unique environment, each institution determines what counts for what. So long as the number of these transactions remains limited, this is a workable system. In a distributed and greatly expanded system of postsecondary education, expecting individual providers to manage transitions using established course-equivalency frameworks will become increasingly inefficient and impractical.

Far better, under these circumstances, would be more centralized data resources. A key new function of state SUR data systems might be to allow postsecondary education providers of many kinds to simultaneously access information about an *individual* student to add to or verify the student record as needed. This capability would also need to be able to manage *simultaneous* enrollments on the part of a particular student in multiple institutions. A rudimentary but illustrative example of such a database is the National Student Clearinghouse.[8] Participating institutions supply the Clearinghouse with a few pieces of data about all current students several times each year. The Clearinghouse, in turn, can generate reports for participating institutions to verify which institutions their students may have previously attended or what credentials they may have earned—or even to determine where former students subsequently enroll.

The Clearinghouse is an independent nonprofit, but there are compelling reasons for states to directly support the development of these resources. One intriguing possibility here is outsourcing. Multiple states could underwrite the development of such a capacity and provide ongoing support for it, under clear contractual relationships that require regular reviews of performance by state authorities.

Supporting Detailed Policy Research

At the same time, there will be a need for data resources to support policy research. A basic task here is simply to keep track of how a state's postsecondary education assets—traditional public and private institutions, as well as a growing array of nontraditional providers—are being accessed, for what purposes, and by whom. Answers to such questions may decisively affect state funding decisions about postsecondary education, and they may well stimulate the evolution of quite different models of support than traditional credit-based formula allocation.[9]

Other research questions might focus on a particular statewide issue—for example, the effectiveness of state investments in scholarships in terms of students who earn credentials in high-need fields and who remain employed in the state. In addition, policy research might pursue longitudinal inquiries into the relative effectiveness of different educational paths or treatments for particular kinds of students. This is already a major application for the most sophisticated P–16 state data resources.

Once again, much of the needed research capacity might be effectively discharged by outsourcing to an established third-party entity, perhaps housed at one of the state's major research universities. An interesting example is the Illinois Education Research Council at Southern Illinois University Edwardsville, which houses unit record data provided by institutions throughout the state and uses it to conduct policy research on behalf of the state as a whole.[10] A similar "semipublic" venture in P–16 education is the National Center for Educational Accountability, housed at the University of Texas at Austin.[11] Such contractual arrangements may allow greater research flexibility than conducting the work inside higher education agencies, and would help insulate state policy research capacity from budget cuts when funds for state agencies get tight.

CONCLUSION

State and system student unit record systems with such expanded capabilities will require significant investments to develop and a good deal of forward planning. Whatever their eventual contents and character—and these may be quite different from the properties described in this chapter if the environment for postsecondary education evolves differently—they will be an essential tool for achieving ambitious policy goals for student attainment.

The development of data systems may seem mundane compared to other substantial issues entailed in increasing postsecondary attainment. However, data collection capacity must stay in sync with and inform the inevitable and innovative expansion of postsecondary opportunities that will result from integrating grades 9–14.

28

Developing a P–20 Budget Tool

Giving Direction to Oregon Public Education

Jill Kirk, John Tapogna, and Duncan Wyse

Advanced economies are increasingly propelled by knowledge-based manufacturing and services—not only electronics, software, and electronic commerce but also new products, process innovation, and sophisticated business practices now common in long-established traditional industries. For a state, competing with economies in other states and nations demands a skilled workforce that can only be developed through rigorous and increasingly advanced education. Moreover, people at many levels of work must now have such knowledge and skills.

These requirements place enormous demands on education systems throughout the PreK–20 education continuum. In order for people to enter well-paying, upwardly mobile jobs, schools must now educate *all* students in skills and knowledge previously reserved for a small percentage of leaders and managers. The implication of these changes is that states need education systems vastly different from those of 50—even 30—years ago. They must educate more students to a higher level than ever before, and they must educate them better than ever before.

In Oregon, a transparent, performance-driven budget would give state policymakers a necessary first step for substantive reforms to the PreK–20 education continuum. Armed with better information about how scarce resources are allocated, policymakers can create a more-integrated system (including the critical grades 9–14) that supports each student in acquiring essential skills at their best pace, provides a wide range of learning options that makes transitions from grade to grade easier, and responds quickly to the needs of employers for skilled and innovative people. We first provide a context for PreK–20 reform in Oregon, and then focus on the development of a transparent, performance-driven budget.

BUILDING THE CASE FOR PREK–20 IN OREGON

Recognizing the global economic trends, as well as their implications for public education, members of Oregon's Education Roundtable have established the goal of having the best-educated and trained workforce in America. To achieve that goal, the business and philanthropic leaders who compose the Oregon Education Roundtable have advocated for a seamless education enterprise that starts in prekindergarten and extends through graduate school. They argue that the unified PreK–20 system must improve access to learning that is personalized, connected to the demands of work and citizenship, and relevant to the student's life experience and goals. The system must prepare students at each stage to move to the next. At the postsecondary level, the system must afford every student access to as much learning as they desire. That education must be affordable and offer smooth pathways, capacity, and personal support to help students complete their studies.

In January 2005, Governor Ted Kulongoski and other Oregon elected officials pledged support for sweeping PreK–20 education improvements. Describing education and economic development as "one and the same," the governor endorsed the Roundtable's initiative, calling for greater education attainment by more Oregonians and substantial overhaul in education systems to achieve that objective. Oregon Senate President Peter Courtney and House Speaker Karen Minnis promised to support these measures in the 2007 session of the legislature.

TRANSFORMING THE SYSTEM

The Roundtable identified three "bedrock" infrastructure transformations that are required to meet students' needs and achieve a new vision for Oregon's public education system.

Oregon's disparate education systems must be organized as a continuum of educational experiences and services designed around the needs of students, with the late teen years serving as the fulcrum of the design.

The continuum should be designed so that all education leading up to the late teen years is excellent preparation for postsecondary learning, careers, and citizenship. Course curricula through the grade levels must unfold logically so that students learn what they should know at each level and then proceed smoothly to the next, even if the next level is at a different institution.

This progression through the education levels should be supported by several principles that apply to the postsecondary level as much as to the K–12 years.

- Curricula, assessments, and high school exit and postsecondary entry and placement criteria must be vertically aligned so that students advance efficiently and without institutional barriers.
- Students must have access to an assessment system that provides them with feedback about their performance that will inform their next levels of instruction and help them to manage their own learning.
- Students' progress should be motivated and measured by performance related to proficiencies rather than by time spent in classes. Those who can advance quickly should not be held back by the artifacts of time-based credit systems; those who require more time to learn some or all subjects should be afforded as much as they need to become proficient.

The system must use information technology sufficiently integrated and aligned over the PreK–20 continuum to track and manage the educational progress of students and the operational performance of institutions.

The data system would do this in many ways. An immediate need is to show both students and institutions where students are on their education paths and how well they are progressing. For example, the K–12 system does not have the capability now to determine whether a student who withdraws from a high school has dropped out or simply transferred to another school system. At the postsecondary level, we currently cannot track the persistence and completion of students who do not finish at the institution where they initially enroll. We do not know whether a student who does not return the next fall has left higher education or simply gone to another institution. A comprehensive PreK–20 data system with confidential student identifiers would yield feedback useful for analyzing and addressing large patterns and problems in student progress and system performance.

But before either of the first two steps can occur, Oregon must adopt a budget and funding distribution system that is predictable, that invests for educational results, and that encourages the system to work in an integrated manner in support of students.

It will take a sturdy instrument of change to create a true PreK–20 continuum. A budget is such an instrument. Budgets drive and therefore can change behavior in virtually all organizations, public or private, education or commerce. Developing a single unified and transparent budget for the education enterprise will be a powerful lever of change. This is the critical first step to the PreK–20 transformation, and it has several components:

- Creating a budget that drives the policy debate;
- Unpacking the education continuum; and
- Developing and testing performance outcomes for each program.

SPENDING ADRIFT: FUNDING EDUCATION IN THE ABSENCE OF GOOD INFORMATION

In 2004, both the Oregon Business Council and the Chalkboard Project—a foundation-led effort to reform K–12—examined historic spending throughout the PreK–20 continuum. Through complementary, but separate, analyses, they found that only four categories of Oregon's state and local education per-student spending had grown in real terms since 1991: prekindergarten, regular education for middle school students, special education for K–12 students with physical and mental disabilities, and developmental education for community college students (Oregon Education Roundtable, 2006). Over that time period, per-student spending has fallen at the high school level and all levels in the Oregon University System (see figure 1).

While many policymakers and business leaders were generally aware of spending declines in higher education, few knew the magnitude of disinvestment, and none had seen the per-student trends displayed so clearly.

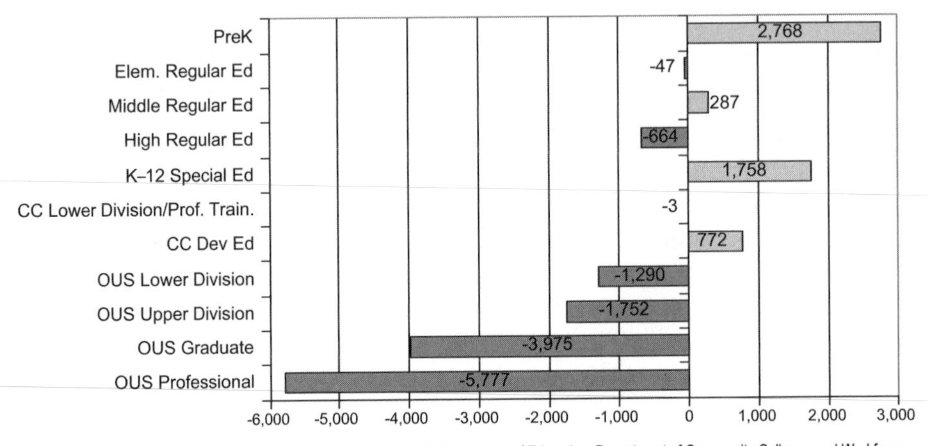

Source: ECONorthwest calculated using data from the Oregon Department of Education, Department of Community Colleges and Workforce Development, and the Oregon University System

Figure 1. Change in Per Student Spending, 1991–2003, Expressed in 2003 Dollars

What quickly became clear through the Oregon Business Council and Chalkboard Project analyses is that policymakers, business leaders, and other stakeholders lacked a clear understanding of how the state invests its education dollars and what it gets—or should expect—in return. State and local policymakers would be hard-pressed to measure how their recent investments in K–12 special education have improved the educational outcomes of students with disabilities, or to what degree the disinvestment in higher education has limited college access. Put simply, Oregon's educational investments drifted between 1991 and 2005, with some areas gaining and others declining. A key point for the work described here is that a transparent budget can ensure that gains or reductions in certain areas of education spending will be deliberate and that policymakers and the public will know exactly what changes are occurring.

KEY QUESTIONS: CREATING A BUDGET THAT DRIVES THE POLICY DEBATE

Lacking timely and clear information on investment trends, state and local policymakers essentially traded one education sector against another, without knowing they were doing it and with no good sense of the consequences. When it comes to making critical education investments and weighing trade-offs, Oregon's budget process leaves policymakers in the dark. They know only that one appropriation level will maintain programs roughly as they exist, while deviations from that amount will either expand or contract them.

Responsible policymakers and their constituents should know more. Oregonians should break out of the existing educational "silos," look across the entire PreK–20 continuum, and begin to understand how investments at one level affect another. Rather than debating education investments at the billion-dollar level per system, Oregonians could be asking such questions as:

- How much do we spend *for each student* at various levels of PreK–20 education? How has it changed over time?

- Is per-student spending adequate and, if not, what additional resources are needed and what would they buy us?
- What are the key noninstructional inputs to a quality education? How much do we spend on them? Could we get a better return on our investment?
- What drives labor costs (e.g., salaries, retirement benefits, health care benefits, contracted labor)? What share of labor expenses fall in instructional and noninstructional categories?
- What programs are we delivering through the continuum? What are their goals, and are we meeting them? Does an investment or disinvestment at one level of the continuum directly impact spending or outcomes at another level?
- Where do we ask students and parents to share in the cost of education? Where don't we, and why?
- How does a change in spending in higher education affect enrollments at Oregon public colleges and universities? When tuition levels rise, how many students opt out of the Oregon system? What are their characteristics, and where do they go?
- Across the higher education system, do different institutions provide some comparable programs at different costs? If so, are students attending lower-cost institutions rewarded uniformly with lower out-of-pocket costs?

This abbreviated list of questions begins to illustrate the type of information that a revamped budget system could provide education stakeholders. Yet despite having strong, clear advantages over the existing process, any overhaul of the budget will have to overcome opposition from nearly all of the existing funded districts, institutions, and agencies. The current system, despite its flaws, is familiar and predictable to them. While these stakeholders may be dissatisfied with recent funding trends, the year-to-year outcomes have nonetheless been easy to foresee.

UNPACKING THE EDUCATION CONTINUUM

If it is executed well, an overhaul of the budget process will radically alter Oregon's budget debates. Clear, concise presentations will inspire sharper questions. Given the magnitude of the change, implementation of the transparent, performance-based budget should proceed in multiple steps, beginning with the first two questions in the above list. Those questions involve unpacking the education continuum into a list of distinct educational programs and then developing and testing performance outcomes (results) for each selected program.

A reformed budget presentation would span the PreK–20 continuum and isolate the largest programs and those that have unique purposes. For example, for children younger than five years old, the budget would track separately prekindergarten (e.g., Head Start) and early intervention programs for those with special needs. The budget would separate regular education in K–12 schools into programs delivered to elementary, middle, and high school students. While this separation makes some sense today, future research might suggest other combinations (e.g., the integration of elementary- and middle school–aged students or the integration of grades 9 through 14). The state would appropriate specific amounts for English as a Second Language (ESL), alternative education, and two categories of special education (i.e., programs targeted to students who remain in regular classrooms and programs for students in separate programs). Student transportation, which has distinct goals from most other K–12 activities, would receive a separate appropriation.

At the higher education level, today's community college activities could be separated into two categories: developmental/remedial programs and those that lead to an associate's or, ultimately, a bachelor's degree. The state could divide funding of the Oregon University System into separate appropriations for lower-division, upper-division, graduate, and professional schools. The state could also track spending on student scholarships.

Analyses sponsored by the Oregon Business Council and the Chalkboard Project (table 1) show what a transparent budget would have looked like for the 2002–03 school year. Tracking spending from all relevant sources (federal, state, local, and private), Oregon educational institutions and agencies spent a total of $4.1 billion.

The budget analysis in table 1 distinguishes between "stand-alone" and "supplemental" programs. A student can participate in a stand-alone program (e.g., elementary regular education) without participating in any other program. By contrast, students enrolled or participating in the supplemental programs are simultaneously enrolled in a stand-alone program. For example, many English-language learners participate in forms of mainstream, regular K–12 education in concert with their ESL course work.

For each program, the table shows the number of full-time equivalent students, per-student expenditures by major source, and the total state and local government investment (that is, the number of FTE students multiplied by the sum of the state and local per-student spending amounts). We look just at the state and local total because that is the focus of the budget debate at the state capitol and at universities, colleges, and school boards across the state; however, totals for federal, private, and total spending could also be calculated.

The advantages of a transparent, unified budget are manifold.

- *It sheds light on important programs that state policymakers have glossed over in the past.* By organizing the system into manageable and related enterprises, policymakers, administrators, and stakeholders can better identify opportunities for overhaul and reinvention. For example, spending on special education for K–12 students accelerated during the 1990s without routine and clear reporting on the number of students served, the per-student cost of services, or the students' performance on reading and math relative to students without special needs.
- *It consolidates the education investment debate.* High-quality preschool, lower K–12 class sizes, expanded college aid, and other reforms all contribute to Oregon's overarching goal of developing a world-class workforce. Nonetheless, they compete for limited resources. In a unified budget environment, the programs, and their advocates, will go head to head in the policy arena.
- *Over time, it will expose duplication and encourage efficiency across what are now fractured systems.* The greatest opportunities for change appear where the existing systems intersect, particularly grades 9 through 14. High schools,

Table 1. Unpacking the Oregon PreK–20 Budget, 2002–2003 School Year

Program	Number of Full Time Equivalent Students Served	Estimated Expenditures per Full-Time Equivalent Student Served: State	Local	Federal and Other Grants	Tuition and Fees	Total	Total State and Local Government Investment
PreK–20 Stand-Alone Programs							
Prekindergarten/Head Start	10,026	$3,287	$0	$4,683	$1	$7,971	$32,951,819
Early intervention for children ages 0–5 years	7,158	$4,196	$2,171	$1,030	$10	$7,407	$45,574,948
Grades K–5 regular instruction, administration, and support	241,344	$3,341	$1,729	$696	$254	$6,020	$1,223,620,032
Grades 6–8 regular instruction, administration, and support	131,443	$3,162	$1,636	$665	$287	$5,750	$630,757,207
Grades 9–12 regular instruction, administration, and support	166,162	$3,429	$1,774	$762	$493	$6,458	$864,494,052
Alternative education programs	7,363	$3,747	$1,939	$1,510	$80	$7,276	$41,865,695
Special education outside the regular education setting	8,862	$10,635	$5,503	$4,663	$289	$21,090	$143,017,714
Remedial programs/ developmental ed	18,613	$1,697	$703	$529	$901	$3,831	$44,678,297
Community college lower-division and professional training	74,084	$1,951	$809	$628	$1,036	$4,424	$204,497,342
OUS lower-division baccalaureate	23,058	$2,923	$0	$306	$3,560	$6,789	$67,402,920
OUS upper-division baccalaureate	33,072	$4,080	$0	$468	$4,776	$9,324	$134,919,418
OUS graduate programs	13,413	$6,319	$0	$782	$7,131	$14,233	$84,754,666
OUS professional programs	1,136	$9,377	$0	$1,212	$10,347	$20,936	$10,652,286
PreK–20 Supplements to Regular Education							
Special education in regular education settings	63,010	$2,745	$1,420	$929	$62	$5,157	$262,465,097
English as a Second Language	49,580	$860	$445	$119	$16	$1,440	$64,698,630
K–12 student transportation (regular students)	467,077	$194	$100	$13	$6	$313	$137,288,868
K–12 student transportation (special education students)	71,872	$366	$189	$22	$4	$580	$39,876,441
Oregon Student Assistance Commission undergraduate need grant[a]	17,340	$960	$0	$0	$0	$960	$16,646,400
GRAND TOTAL							**$4,050,161,832**

Source: ECONorthwest calculation using Oregon Department of Education, Office of Community College, and Oregon University System data

[a] Spending for this category is from the 2000–01 fiscal year

community colleges, and universities all deliver remediation for students who have fallen behind, as well as accelerated course work for high achievers. In a unified budget and system, policymakers will quickly ask: Who does that work best, and at what price?

BENCHMARKING: DEVELOP AND TEST PERFORMANCE OUTCOMES FOR EACH PROGRAM

Under current practice, spending on sizable programs is buried within the larger accounting framework. The state makes no attempt to determine whether spending supports a program's goals. In some cases, no distinct goals exist except to support overall education achievement or attainment.

Table 2 lists illustrative performance benchmarks for each of the recommended PreK–20 programs. As with the programs themselves, this list of benchmarks represents a proposal that education stakeholders should amend and expand. In some areas, the benchmarking exercise would shed light on programs that have received little scrutiny to date. For example, state and local governments spent $65 million on English as a Second Language in 2002–03 and only recently have released reports on how many students enter the system each year, how many complete, and how their English skills improved over time (Tareen, 2005).

Universities and colleges already track the shares of incoming students who persist year to year, advance through the system on schedule, and ultimately graduate. However, these key indicators rarely enter the budget debate. Oregon's higher education list of indicators also could be expanded to include less-common but useful ones related to quality and efficiency. For example, the University of Florida tracks "excess credit hours," which is the number of credits students take beyond those necessary to complete a degree. Officials expect some excess credits as students change majors or drop/fail classes. Too many excess credit hours impede access for other students at a university with limited physical and staff resources.

WHO WINS, WHO LOSES?

The creation of a transparent, performance-driven budget creates unprecedented challenges for everyone involved. For example, developing and testing appropriate performance expectations for each program will take considerable time and effort. Before any indicator is adopted, it must be thoroughly vetted and measured over time. Most importantly, the indicator must have acceptance and relevance at the classroom, department, and school levels.

Just as important, the education system will have to perceive, manage, and measure itself differently in order to serve students as they need to be served. The way funds are distributed and spent will have to be organized around students, not institutions.

Changing the budget and distribution process will threaten many who are comfortable in the system as it is. To achieve transformation of vision, mission, and infrastructure on the scale anticipated will require the relentless focus of policymakers in education; government, business, and philanthropy; the assistance of experts in and beyond Oregon; and the engagement of front-line educators,

Table 2. Illustrative Performance Expectations for Selected PreK–20 Programs

Program	Performance Expectation
PreK–20 Stand-Alone	
Prekindergarten/Head Start	XX% of students showing learning gains in literacy, language, mathematics, science, creative arts
Early intervention for children under five years old	XX% reduction in the proportion of K–12 students identified as needing special education
Grades K–5 regular instruction, administration, and support	XX% of students with math and reading learning gains in grades 3–5; XX% of students proficient in reading, math, and writing in grades 3 and 5
Grades 6–8 regular instruction, administration, and support	XX% of students with math and reading learning gains in grades 6–8; XX% of students proficient in reading, math, and writing in grade 8
Grades 9–12 regular instruction, administration, and support	% of students with math and reading learning gains in grades 9–10; XX% of students proficient in reading, math, and writing in grade 10; percentage graduation rate among starting ninth-grade cohort
Alternative education programs	Alternative schools held to grade-specific outcomes described above
Special education outside the regular school setting	Reduced achievement gap between students with and without severe disabilities by XX%, with raised achievement by both groups
Remedial programs/ developmental education	XX% of students moving out of remediation and moving to lower-division or professional training; XX% of adult basic education students earning literacy completion points
Community college lower-division and professional training	XX% of entering AA students completing degree; XX% of AA graduates earning >$XX/hour; XX% of students graduating within two years and transferring to a four-year college or entering the workforce
OUS lower-division baccalaureate	XX% second-year retention of incoming freshmen
OUS upper-division baccalaureate	XX% freshman cohort graduation rate within six years; XX% graduating within four years; XX% of graduates with starting employment paying at least $XX per hour
OUS graduate programs	XX,000 master and doctoral degrees within four years
OUS professional programs	XX% of first-time entrants graduated; XX% of graduates obtaining professional licenses
PreK–20 Supplements to Regular Education	
Special education in regular school settings	XX% reduced achievement gap between students with and without disabilities, with raised achievement of both groups; XX% of special education students graduated
English as a Second Language	XX% making progress on ACTFL; XX% of Level X students exiting from ESL within X months
K–12 student transportation (regular students)	Provision of safe and reliable access to school while improving student attendance
K–12 student transportation (special education students)	Provision of safe and reliable access to school while improving student attendance
Oregon Student Assistance Commission undergraduate need grant	XX% of low-income students attending OUS institutions

Source: ECONorthwest

parents, and students. And, as with any sizable reform, all the stakeholders in education will be eager to know who would win and who would lose in a unified budget environment.

To that question we answer: who knows? Clear, concise budget information will drive the debates and shape resource allocations in ways that cannot be predicted, but we can say this much: Programs that support the state's education goals at good value will likely expand, while those that do not will contract. Unfortunately, at this point, a weak and fractured budget process makes it nearly impossible to distinguish the good programs from the bad.

29

Financing Higher Aspirations and Better Preparation

Arthur M. Hauptman

Financial barriers are a key factor that may prevent the effective integration of grades 9 through 14, particularly for students from low-income families. Traditionally, the primary policies for reducing these financial barriers are to keep postsecondary tuition low at public institutions and to increase the availability of student financial aid. But these twin policies by themselves often are not enough to overcome the substantial obstacles to ensuring a smooth transition from high school to college, especially for impoverished students who are most at risk.

It is now generally recognized that it is at least as important to improve the preparation of students most at risk and to raise their aspirations early in their schooling. It has also become increasingly clear that more support services, such as mentoring and counseling, are key components in improving the academic preparation of students, and thus reducing their need to take remedial courses once they enroll in a postsecondary program. Moreover, the available evidence suggests that many of these students are more likely to make a commitment to work hard in school if they get early and reasonable assurance—when they are still in grade school or middle school—that enough financial resources will be available when they reach college age.[1]

These conclusions, which are just as true for programs that seek to integrate grades 9–14 as they are for more traditional transitions from high school to college, lead to several important questions:

- How can public policies be better utilized to raise the aspirations and improve the preparation of students, particularly those students who are most at risk?
- What are the effects on aspiration and preparation levels of traditional policies, such as low tuition at public institutions and various student aid programs?
- What are the potential effects of less-traditional financing approaches, such as the range of publicly and privately financed early commitment programs that have mushroomed in the past two decades?

To answer these questions, this chapter examines why traditional financing approaches have not had the desired effect of raising the aspirations of typically underserved groups of students or improving their readiness to do college-level work. If anything, it seems that preparation levels for these groups of students have declined over time. On the other hand, publicly and privately funded early intervention efforts seem to be doing a much better job of raising aspiration and preparation levels. Might expansion of these efforts be sufficient to address these problems of low aspirations and insufficient preparation?

WHY REDUCING FINANCIAL BARRIERS IS IMPORTANT

In any postsecondary educational venture, it is critical to reduce the financial barriers that may prevent a broad range of students from enrolling in and completing a postsecondary program. However, lowering the financial barriers to participation is probably just as or even more important for the innovative integrated 9–14 approaches, such as dual enrollment, accelerated learning, or early college programs, than it is for more traditional high school-to-college transitions.

Throughout most of American history, discussions of the importance of reducing financial barriers have focused on ways to reduce the price that students pay at the time they enter college, either by subsidizing tuition at public institutions or by increasing the amount of financial aid students are eligible to receive. In recent decades, however, it has become clear that the issue extends well beyond reducing the price that students or their families pay at the point of enrollment. For policies to be effective, they must reach students *before* they are in high school to convince them that enough resources will be available to them when they are ready for college. There are two reasons:

- *Raising the educational aspirations of at-risk students while they are still in grade school or middle school is critical to improving their preparation, participation, and performance in postsecondary education.* This assertion is based more on intuition and observation than on systematically collected empirical results, which do not really exist yet.[2] One observation is that recent public and privately funded efforts that seek to ensure sufficient funds will be available to at-risk students have achieved participation and completion rates that far exceed what might otherwise have been anticipated.
- *Students who are better prepared to do college-level work are more likely to succeed in completing their degree.* This may seem so obvious that the point need not be made. Perhaps, but with the focus on improving access, relatively little attention has been paid to whether students are prepared to do the work or whether they are likely to complete their degree. This is particularly true for students most at risk.

Many of those involved in these debates have tended to treat the issues of preparation, participation, and performance as separable issues that should be addressed through separate policies. This chapter is based on a different premise: that better preparation is a key predictor—perhaps the most important one—of better performance, measured in terms of both year-to-year retention and degree completion.

THE EFFECTS OF TRADITIONAL FINANCING ON STUDENT ASPIRATIONS AND PREPARATION

Low tuition at public institutions and a broad range of student financial aid programs at the federal and state level have been this country's primary policies to increase college participation rates and to improve educational opportunities for disadvantaged groups of students. In many respects, these policies have been very successful: U.S. college participation rates are among the highest in the world and have been for a number of decades. Roughly 18 million students now enroll in postsecondary education every year; in previous generations, it would have been hard to imagine that so many students would have had this opportunity. In this respect, policymakers in many other countries look to the United States as a model to emulate.

In other important respects—particularly chronic equity differences among groups of students—the picture is less rosy. Although the participation rates of low-income students are indeed at their highest level ever, the gap between poor and rich students is just about as large as it was when the federal government first created student aid programs in the 1960s. Despite the fact that tuition remains highly subsidized at most public institutions and the availability of aid has grown, many low-income students remain convinced that they will not be able to afford tuition and other expenses that have grown at twice the rate of inflation for more than two decades. Perhaps equally as important, low-income students are much more likely to be unprepared to do college-level work, which severely undermines their ability to succeed academically if and when they do enroll.

These issues of raising aspirations and improving preparation are probably even more critical for integrated 9–14 approaches. Without high aspirations, students are even less likely to be willing to make the additional effort entailed in demanding programs such as accelerated learning. And without sufficient preparation, students in accelerated enrollment or other nontraditional arrangements are much less likely to succeed.

These results of current policies should not be surprising. Keeping tuition low at public institutions does not address the living expenses and opportunity costs of withdrawing from the labor force to become a student, and these are much larger than the tuition expense per se. Students typically do not know how much financial assistance they will be eligible for until, in the twelfth grade, they apply for aid and colleges admit them. Neither low tuition nor most traditional student aid programs do much good in raising aspirations because they provide students or their families with little if any assurance that enough aid for college will be available when students are still in grade school or middle school.

Similarly, few states have even minimal standards that students must meet in order for institutions to receive state funding. And very few of the federal or state student aid programs contain requirements that students demonstrate competencies at a certain level in order to receive aid.[3] So neither low-tuition policies at public institutions nor student financial aid encourage more-adequate preparation.

This is not to say that federal and state policymakers have ignored the need to raise aspirations or improve preparation. The federal Higher Education Act of 1965, in addition to creating a number of student aid programs, also established the so-called TRIO programs of Upward Bound, Talent Search, and Special Services. Those legislators responsible for enacting these programs obviously recognized the importance of identifying poor but promising students early in the their educational careers, and then providing a range of counseling and other support services throughout the education pipeline in an effort to improve the capacity of disadvantaged students to do college-level work. Student support efforts also were created in several states during this time period, including in New York, where such programs were established at both the City University of New York and the State University of New York.

The notion of using student aid to raise aspirations also has been an ongoing concern. A key intent of the original Basic Grant legislation in 1972 (renamed Pell Grants in 1980) was to raise the aspirations of the most economically disadvantaged students. Senator Claiborne Pell and other key legislative sponsors sought to do this by ensuring that all eligible students would receive an award, moving away from the practice of having financial aid officers choose which federally eligible students would benefit from limited funding. The legislative intent was to make students aware of award levels at least several years in advance, perhaps while still in grade school or middle school. This would help convince disadvantaged students and their families that going to college was a financial reality.

Neither TRIO programs nor Pell Grants, however, have achieved their well-intentioned goals. The TRIO programs have never grown beyond a demonstration effort involving a limited number of institutions. Less than 10 percent of eligible students benefit from services provided under the TRIO programs. Moreover, the support services they provide often occur after the student has enrolled, so they may have a negligible effect on preparation levels before the student enrolls in college. State efforts along these lines are too few and far between to be effective. The limitations of the federal budget process, which prohibits the reservation of federal funds for use many years in the future, has effectively blunted the critical purpose of raising awareness.

Private efforts seem to have been much more effective than public ones in meeting the goal of providing financial assurance to the most-at-risk students. This trend began in the early 1980s, when Eugene Lang, an industrialist who had been active in a variety of educational activities, addressed the graduates of the New York public school that he had attended a half century earlier. Throwing away his prepared remarks, Lang spontaneously promised that students would receive sufficient aid to enroll in and complete college if they were prepared to do college-level work when they graduated from high school. He also promised to provide mentoring, counseling, and other services that would greatly increase the chances of student success.

The first class of Lang graduates had remarkable results: Nearly all completed high school, and most enrolled and successfully completed a postsecondary educational program. By 1986, Lang had established the "I Have a Dream" foundation to promulgate this privately driven model in communities across the country.[4]

In the quarter century since Lang first made his promise, many philanthropists and corporations have made similar guarantees to classes of grade school and middle school students who attend tough schools. These private efforts tend to follow the Lang model of combining a promise to students of enough money to go to college if they are prepared to do the work with mentoring, counseling, and other supports that help ensure their better preparation.

A key question is how federal and state governments might build on the success of these privately funded, early commitment activities, thereby expanding the number of at-risk students who can benefit from the full range of postsecondary opportunities. The federal program, Gaining Early Awareness and Readiness for Undergraduate Programs (GEAR UP), enacted in 1998, sought to make this promise a reality by guaranteeing that enough funds would be available to students, in addition to promoting university–middle school partnerships and other interventions. But again, the vagaries and restrictions of federal legislative and budget processes and an unwillingness among policymakers to move against these restrictions have led to watered-down provisions that prevent GEAR UP from achieving the promise of a financial guarantee. In the final legislation, participating students receive a symbolic certificate saying they had earned the right to receive enough aid, but they do not get the real guarantee necessary to achieve higher levels of preparedness and rates of participation and degree completion. Perhaps the most successful aspect of GEAR UP has been the creation of hundreds of university–middle school partnerships that expand the horizons of at-risk students through a wide range of support services and more information about education opportunities.

A number of states have enacted programs that have important elements of early commitment, but most of these lack a critical feature, such as a guarantee of aid or limits within which students are eligible to benefit. However, at least three states have stepped up to the plate and enacted programs of aid and student support services that have the potential of raising aspirations and improving preparation levels:[5]

Indiana's Twenty-first Century Scholars Program was enacted in 1990 and then greatly expanded in 1999, spurred by a GEAR UP grant to ensure more adequate geographical distribution of services to urban and rural areas. Seventh and eighth graders whose families are eligible for free or reduced-priced lunches and who make a pledge of good citizenship can participate. In exchange for graduating from an Indiana high school with at least a 2.0 GPA, applying on time for state and federal student aid, and several other related promises, the program agrees to pay for up to eight semesters of college tuition at participating state public institutions. Benefits are also provided to eligible students who attend a wide range of private and proprietary institutions.[6]

Oklahoma's Higher Learning Access Program was created in 1992 to improve the chances of success for eighth, ninth, and tenth graders whose family income is $50,000 or less. OHLAP provides scholarships and a range of support services to students who qualify on the basis of completing certain high school services, achieve a 2.5 GPA, and remain drug- and alcohol-free. Scholarships may be used at public two- and four-year colleges, accredited private institutions in the state, and public technology centers.

Rhode Island's Children's Crusade for Higher Education, founded in 1989 as a partnership between public and private officials, is still another example of how states can create or promote early commitment aid programs. Funding comes from a variety of public and private sources. The goal is to "[e]nroll all third graders in the state and provide them with a mentor to guide them on the path to college."[7] In 1995, Rhode Island shifted funds in the direction of providing support services, in recognition that scholarship funds by themselves were not sufficient to meet program goals. Also since 1995, efforts have targeted schools with high concentrations of low-income students in a limited number of Rhode Island cities.

While these three programs demonstrate how much states can contribute to increased aspirations and better preparation of at-risk students, they represent a small fraction of the funds states devote to student aid and a much smaller proportion of total state spending for higher education. And, although the results of these efforts have been encouraging, their effectiveness in raising aspirations of at-risk youth is yet to be fully evaluated.

According to an analysis that synthesized the results of four papers, the following characteristics seem to be critical in improving access for low-income and minority students (Martinez & Klopott, 2003):

- *Raising Expectations for Students*—including working with parents, teachers, and other staff to help students understand and achieve their full educational potential;
- *Providing Academic Support*—including making available a wide range of mentoring and tutoring services, particularly in math, science, and language skills, that seem especially critical in improving college-level preparation;
- *Improving Social Support for Students*—including helping students develop strong social networks and ensuring that students and their families have adequate information to make decisions that are in their best interests; and
- *Achieving Better P–16 Alignment*—including linking curricula and expectations from grade to grade, as well as aligning high school graduation rates with college admission standards.

All of these are critical components in many early intervention and commitment efforts.

PARTICULAR CONCERNS RELATING TO INTEGRATED 9–14 APPROACHES

Little hard data has yet been collected that would help to address the question of whether the financing structure encourages, discourages, or is neutral with regard to greater integration of grades 9 to 14. While such approaches are still quite new, the Western Interstate Commission for Higher Education (2006) has conducted a survey to investigate whether the rules used in making admissions decisions and determining financial aid eligibility gave advantage or disadvantage to students enrolling in accelerated-learning programs.[8] Most of the surveyed states and institutions indicated that accelerated learners were treated no differently than other students; those that said there was a difference suggested that accelerated learners would be at a disadvantage relative to traditional learners in three ways:

- Students seeking to enroll in accelerated programs may find that the admissions process at many institutions does not take into account their particular status.
- Students participating in accelerated programs may enroll for fewer semesters than more-traditional learners, but in most cases they will still be responsible for paying for the same amount of tuition as students enrolled longer.

- Students in accelerated-learning programs may be enrolled in yearlong programs, but federal, state, and institutional student aid programs are in most cases unlikely to provide more aid on an annual basis to reflect the longer term of enrollment for students who are learning on an accelerated basis.

Proponents of accelerated programs and other 9–14 integrated approaches would say that admissions, tuition setting, and aid programs should recognize the special circumstances of students seeking to take advantage of such options. Looked at from the other side, it certainly would be worthwhile to enact policies that do not disadvantage students in 9–14 integrated approaches compared to more-traditional transitions from high school to college.

THREE SUGGESTIONS FOR IMPROVEMENT

Undoubtedly, progress has been made in recent decades in developing policies and programs that raise the aspirations and improve the preparation of students who traditionally have been underserved in postsecondary education. A growing number of federal and state policymakers and institutional officials are increasingly aware of the importance of motivating students to be ready to do college work, and a number of programs have been established. But it is also clear that we have a long way to go to meet the objective of making students more secure in the knowledge that enough resources will be available if they are ready to do the work. The following three steps would promote further progress along this dimension:

Expand the scope and funding of the federal GEAR UP program to promote the creation of effective partnerships between universities and middle schools

Since its creation in 1998, GEAR UP has proved to be effective, particularly in establishing relationships between universities and middle schools to expand the availability of a wide range of support services and to make students more aware of their postsecondary possibilities. Although no comprehensive evaluation has studied the question, GEAR UP seems to have been less effective in raising aspirations, given that it has never fully provided the assurance of financial resources.

It is unrealistic to expect that such a financial guarantee could be provided anytime in the near future, in light of federal budget deficits and continued resistance among many policymakers and others central to the appropriations process to making federal spending commitments many years in advance of when checks would be written. However, it is not unrealistic to suggest, and even expect, that GEAR UP might be provided with additional funding so that the number of university–middle school partnerships might be multiplied and the number of students benefiting from such arrangements increased substantially.

Provide federal incentives that encourage the expansion of state and private early commitment programs

A number of private and state early intervention, student aid efforts have succeeded in raising the participation and degree-completion rates of at-risk students through providing both a range of support services and sufficient financial resources to raise the aspirations of students who otherwise would be unlikely to enter and complete postsecondary education programs. The chief problem is that these efforts cover only a very small percentage of the young people who could benefit from them. Is there a way to "go to scale?"

One way is for the federal government to provide substantial additional funds that would encourage more states and more private organizations and individuals to establish early intervention programs of this sort. To do this, the existing Leveraging Educational Assistance Partnership program could be modified so that the federal government would match only those state programs that qualified as early commitment, rather than use much-broader definitions in which virtually all state aid programs qualify for the match. The LEAP program assists states in providing student aid programs for students who demonstrate financial need and are pursuing a postsecondary education. The aid can be delivered in the form of grants or community service work-study employment.

Establish savings accounts for low-income students while they are still in grade school, giving them greater assurance that funds will be available when they reach college age

Given the difficulties in using traditional financing approaches to raise aspirations and improve preparation, different approaches for addressing the chronic problem of how best to raise educational aspirations among students most at risk should also be considered. One idea is to establish savings accounts that could be funded through a combination of public and private contributions. These savings accounts, which could be established when students are still in grade school, would represent a funding source for college for those who lack the family resources and savings that many middle- and upper-income students can draw upon. Just as federal tax policies now encourage savings for college among wealthier families by reducing their income tax liabilities for investments in designated accounts, the proposed savings accounts would seek to make savings a reality for students much further down on the income ladder. Students would be able to use funds from these accounts only at properly accredited postsecondary education programs. Public and privately donated funds not utilized after students reach a certain age would be made available for use by others.

The role of state and local governments would be to identify students who qualify for these accounts on the basis of their family circumstances and possibly to provide seed money for their establishment in the name of individual children. The role of the federal government would be to provide tax incentives for corporations and private individuals to make contributions into these accounts. The role of the private sector would be to make contributions to the accounts and continue to help provide the counseling, mentoring, and support services that allow students to be properly prepared to take advantage of the funds put aside in their name.

WHAT WE KNOW

In sum, we now know a lot more about what works when it comes to raising aspirations and improving preparation of the most at-risk students than when the student aid programs were begun in earnest some four decades ago. We know, for example, that adequately funded student aid programs are necessary but not sufficient to do the job. What is needed now is the commitment to fund additional state, local, and private efforts that provide support services and financial guarantees to targeted groups of students. And establishing and funding savings accounts for poor but promising students early in their educational career would represent another large step forward in improving equity.

30

Integrating Public Finance into Strategies for Improving Preparation, College Enrollment, and Persistence

Edward P. St. John

The goals of improving academic preparation, college access, and degree attainment are now well established nationally and in most states. Therefore, it is important to consider how to integrate the financing of K–12 and higher education in ways that make it easier for prepared students to enroll in college.

Conceptually, there are diverse strategies for integrating K–12 and higher education, including:

- Integrating high school with the first two years of college, enabling students to graduate high school with two-year degrees;
- Using no (or low) tuition for the first two years of college, enabling all students to enroll at a lower cost of attendance;
- Providing guarantees of student financial aid for low-income students to reduce concerns about costs, encourage preparation, and directly support enrollment and degree attainment;
- Using merit-based grants, possibly even student accounts, to subsidize college costs for students who take steps to prepare and meet standards;
- Coordinating state finance strategies (funding institutions, tuition, and student grants) to equalize educational opportunities for equally prepared students across income groups.

It is not possible to assess any of these strategies unless we consider evaluative research that examines the impact of related policies on college enrollment and educational attainment, rather than research that considers only intermediate variables like high school courses completed or net prices. This is necessary because policies often do not influence critical intermediate variables in the ways policymakers intend.

In *Refinancing the College Dream*, I developed the "balanced access and attainment model" to help build an understanding of the ways in which both education policies and public finance strategies influence educational outcomes, rather than using narrow assumptions that consider only one approach or the other (St. John, 2003). This chapter presents the balanced access model and summarizes what has been learned from research literature that has used this model to build an understanding of how K–12 reforms and public finance policies link to critical outcomes, and to help us assess the probable effects of the five strategies for integrating K–12 and higher education.

THE BALANCED MODEL OF PREPARATION, ACCESS, AND ATTAINMENT

Research that explicitly examines the impact of education and public finance policies on these outcomes has been limited (e.g., Musoba, 2006; St. John, 2003, 2006). Moreover, this research illustrates the contradictory nature of current policies. These really are both the best and worst of times with respect to access and degree attainment:

- The percentage of high school graduates going on to college increased in the 1980s and 1990s, but there was also a dip in the percentage of students completing high schools (St. John, 2003, 2006).
- Students who are academically well prepared for college have higher odds of graduating and going on to college, but well-prepared low-income students are less likely to enroll, persist, and graduate than their wealthier peers with similar preparation (St. John, 2006).
- The inequalities across income and race/ethnic groups were greater for both college access and degree attainment in the 1990s than they were in the 1970s. That is, the benefits of educational progress were not equally distributed for either high school preparation or college enrollment (St. John, 2003, 2006).
- In 2005, the college enrollment rate for high school graduates was 69 percent, but the gap in the rates for African Americans compared to whites has grown since 1999, and Hispanics still have the lowest enrollment rates (Mortenson, 2005).

To understand how policy actually links to these findings about preparation, access, and attainment, it is necessary to consider the roles of both education policies and public finance strategies. In the past few years, there has been substantial progress in research that has used the balanced model (see figure 1) to: review the literature on policy linkages to preparation and postsecondary attainment; and explicitly examine these linkages in well-designed studies that meet generally accepted statistical standards for research on access and attainment (Becker, 2004; Heller, 2004).

Using this model reveals that current efforts to improve opportunity for students to complete an integrated 9–14 education have great potential to reduce inequality. The primary focus of these efforts is on improving preparation programs in high schools and strengthening the links between high school and the first two years of college. Such reforms are crucial, but they should not ignore the role of finances. Low-income families have deep, and in most cases reasonable, concerns about college costs, given the substantial debt burden for low-income

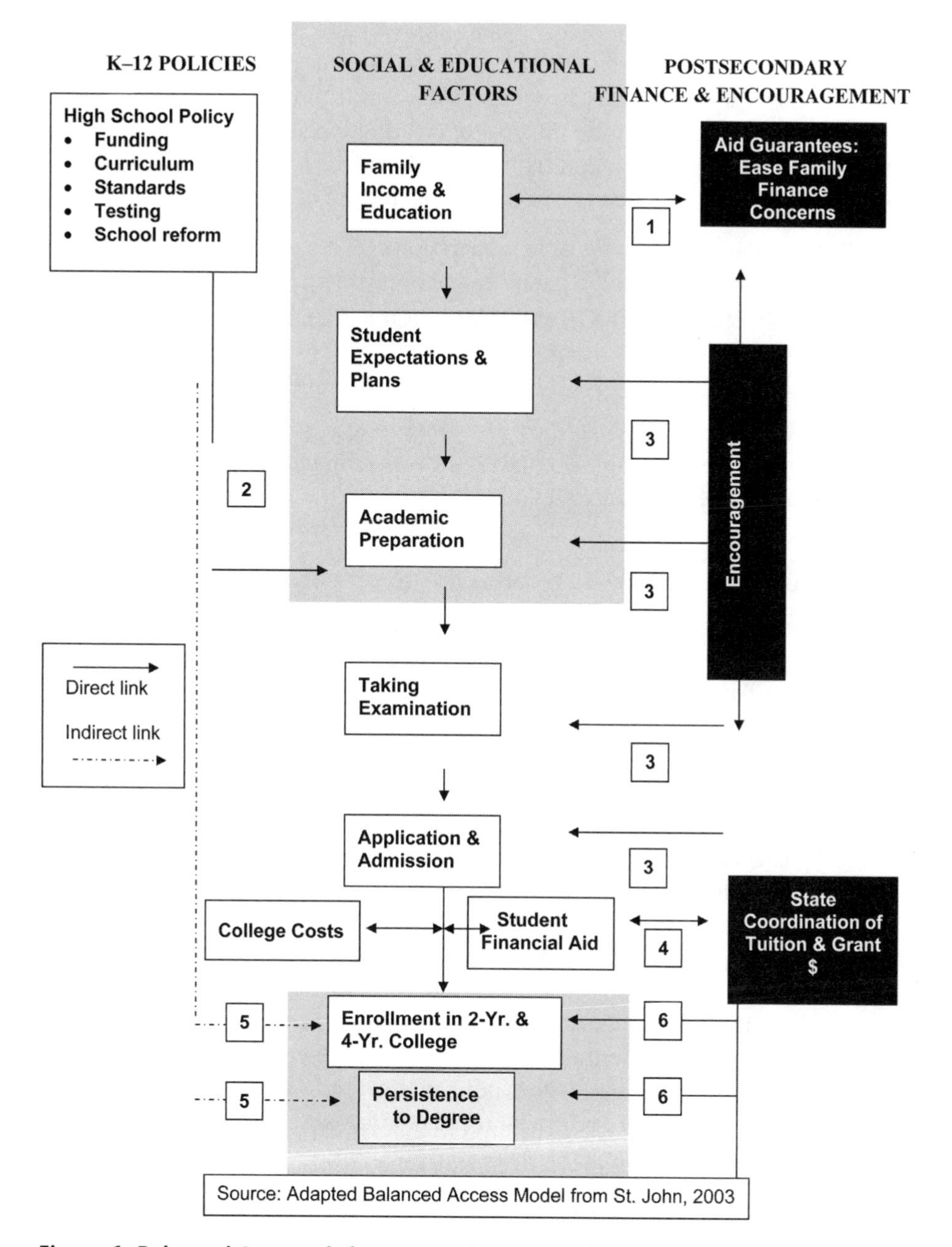

Figure 1. Balanced Approach for Integrating Public Finance with Education Policies to Improve Preparation, College Enrollment, and Degree Attainment

college graduates (Advisory Committee on Student Financial Assistance, 2002; Hartle, Simmons, & Timmons, 2005). Even if families do know the actual costs of enrollment, their fears of paying for college can still be well founded. In fact, the net price after grants for the average students with zero expected family contribution is more substantial than the allowable borrowing limits for federally subsidized loans, so parents must borrow against uncertain future family earnings. Thus, college costs can be a deterrent to preparation, as well as to access.

Given the substantial differences in autonomy of K–12 schools and public colleges and universities, along with the variations in the methods of funding in each sector, it will be necessary to achieve integration through coordination and incentives, along with pursuing the goal of creating a new, integrated public education system. The research that has used the balanced approach for integrating finance and education policies reveals evidence related to five linkages:

- High school policies can enable preparation;
- Encouragement links to preparation and application;
- State finance policies link to aid packaging;
- K–12 reforms indirectly link to access and attainment; and
- State finance policies link to enrollment and attainment.

Figure 1 and table 1 illustrate how the five program strategies for integrating the financing of K–12 and higher education connect to various policy linkages to preparation and postsecondary attainment.

Both school finance and K–12 reforms link to preparation.

To a very large extent, the current wave of high school reforms is based on research that examines: the correlation between completion of advanced high school courses and college success; and the alignment of high school curricula and admissions standards in states. State requirements for graduation link to college access through student preparation (see figure 1, Linkage 2). Preparation—an intermediate outcome—can also be influenced by family expectations and concerns about college costs. In addition, there are substantial variations in high school contexts (e.g., levels of funding, the availability of advanced courses) across schools within states, which also mitigate the effects of state policies.

It is often assumed that because there is (*A*) a correlation between completing advanced math courses in high school and attainment (e.g., Adelman, 2006) that (*B*) requiring more math courses will (*C*) result in more access. However, just because *A* is true, it is not necessarily true that *B* (requiring an advanced curriculum) will improve *C* (increased enrollment rates). The problem is far more complex than is often assumed, because *B* does not cause *A*. Findings from research on the policy effects of high school reforms on preparation and college enrollment include the following (St. John, 2006):

- Increased math requirements for high school graduation in the 1990s were associated with improvements in state test scores (e.g., average SAT scores), controlling for other factors, but they were negatively associated with high school graduation rates and not significantly associated with college enrollment rates by high school graduates.
- Some accountability reforms (e.g., exit exams for graduation) had positive links to high school graduation rates when the role of funding for instruction was also considered. Linking funding with accountability may be an important step, but funding is important independent of accountability measures (e.g., better pay attracts better teachers).
- Raising state math requirements for graduation was not significantly associated with the completion of advanced courses (beyond Algebra II) upon graduation

Table 1. How 9–14 Financing and Education Strategies Link to Gains in Preparation, Access, and Degree Attainment

	Strategies				
Linkages	1: Integrate high school and first two years of college	2: No or low tuition for first two years of college	3: Provide a guarantee of grant aid	4: Use merit-based awards (or accounts)	5: Coordinate state finance & information
1: Easing family concerns about college costs encourages preparation	Could remove concerns about paying for the first two years, encouraging preparation	Could ease, but not remove, concern about cost of first two years	Eases concern about cost of two- or four-year colleges, improves preparation	Could ease concern for students who meet merit (or earn awards); could discourage others	Eases concerns about costs if students learn about options; not as direct as Strategy 3
2: High school policies can enable preparation	Early college programs enable more students to prepare	Efficacy of low tuition depends on quality of information	Efficacy depends on tight links to high school reforms and quality of reforms	Merit aid increases dropout rate; tight links and earned credit merit testing	Efficacy depends on the types and quality of reforms by high schools
3: Encouragement links to preparation and application	Improve two-year attainment, but access to four-year colleges remains a challenge	No direct link; can be built into parallel high school reforms	No direct link; can be built into parallel high school reforms	No direct link; can be built into parallel high school reforms	No direct link; can be built into parallel high school reforms
4: State finance policies link to aid packaging	Opportunities for two-year access expanded; no assurance of access to four-year colleges	High-cost strategy for states, especially when demand increases	Provides incentives for colleges to recruit low-income students	Provides incentives for colleges to recruit students meeting criteria	Expands opportunities in public and private colleges
5: K–12 reforms indirectly link to access and attainment	Improves opportunity, to the extent that new courses are of high quality	Dependent on high school preparation; no direct link	Dependent on high school preparation; no direct link	Merit grants have mixed effects; Individual accounts merit testing	Dependent on high school preparation; no direct link
6: State finance policies link to enrollment and attainment	Improves attainment of two-year degrees; limited effect on four-year attainment	Improves two-year attainment; limited effect on four-year attainment	Improves attainment of two- and four-year degrees	Improves attainment for awardees, but inequality persists	Improves educational attainment within states

for the entire 1992 cohort in a reanalysis of the National Educational Longitudinal Study (NELS) or for either high-income students or low-income students. Further, implementation of higher requirements after 1992 did not result in higher rates of high school graduation or college enrollment, controlling for other factors.

- However, for middle-income students in the 1992 cohort, there was a positive association between raising graduation requirements and access to advanced math courses (e.g., trigonometry and calculus).

This research indicates the need for a consistent, high-quality, and integrated approach to improving high school preparation, especially in schools serving mostly low-income students. Improving preparation within high schools requires adequate financial resources, as well as high-quality curricula. The old myth that requirements and not money matter has been proven false once again (see also Musoba, 2006).

Guarantees of aid tend to reduce family concerns about college costs and links to preparation.

While improvements in high schools can make a better education more accessible, there is no guarantee that students will take advantage of opportunities provided to them. Research evidence confirms the link between family concerns about costs and dropping out of high school. For example, state funding for merit grants in the 1990s was associated with higher dropout rates, as well as with the retention of more students in state (St. John, 2006).

Some of this evidence comes from Indiana's Twenty-first Century Scholars Program, which provides low-income eighth-grade students with a guaranteed grant equaling public tuition if they take the steps to prepare for and apply to college (St. John, Musoba, Simmons, Chung, Schmidt, & Peng, 2004). Students pledge to complete high school, stay drug-free, and apply to college and for student aid. Historically, these students were encouraged to complete a preparatory curriculum; recently, the student part of the contract made that a requirement.

Research confirms that the Twenty-first Century Scholars program is associated with improvements in enrollment rates and that it equalizes the odds for degree attainment. Key findings include:

- Students in the Indiana high school class of 1999 who took the Scholars pledge were more likely than the otherwise average student to apply for student aid and enroll in college (St. John, et al. 2004).
- Students in the high school class of 1999 who took the Scholars pledge had higher odds than the otherwise average student of enrolling in two- and four-year colleges, including private colleges (St. John, et al., 2004).
- Students in the 1999 cohort who took the Scholars pledge and enrolled in college had the same odds of persisting during the first four years as the otherwise average student (St. John, Gross, Musoba, & Chung, 2006).

Additional evidence comes from the Washington State Achievers Program, which couples high school reforms with early scholarships for students in 16 low-income high schools. This five-year program awarded scholarship guarantees to high school students using noncognitive criteria for selection among low- and middle-income applications. In addition, the schools received large grants to implement school reforms, including implementation of small schools with larger schools.

Key findings include:

- During the first year of implementation, students in the Washington State Achievers program had higher odds of enrolling in college than did average students in high schools that were comparable in terms of the socioeconomic status of their students (St. John & Hu, 2006).
- After three years of implementation, schoolwide effects were evident in Washington State Achievers schools (Herting, Hirschman, & Pharris-Ciurej, 2006).
- By 2004, students from Washington State Achievers schools who received WSA scholarship awards had substantially improved rates of enrollment in advanced courses and college enrollment (St. John & Hu, in press).

These examples illustrate that linking reforms with strategies that ease concerns about college cost represents a viable approach for enabling preparation, access, and degree attainment for students from low-income families. However, these programs improve access because of the money provided, not because they provide information. Not only do we need to learn more from the programs that have been implemented, but this growing research base also can (and should) be used to inform the development of new, integrative strategies in states, communities, high schools, and colleges.

Encouragement programs link to aspirations and preparation.

There is a great deal of information about intervening variables (e.g., completion of advanced math courses) related to the intent of encouragement programs (Linkage 3). Substantial research shows associations of variables like aspirations and parental involvement to eventual college enrollment and success (Perna, 2005). This research can be used to rationalize encouragement, just as research on high school courses is used as a rationale for increasing graduation requirements and research on net price is used to rationalize spending on student aid programs.

The recent reanalysis of NELS (the 1992 cohort) found substantial numbers of students who aspired to go to college yet who did not prepare for or enroll in a postsecondary institution (St. John, 2006). In addition, several analyses have found that large numbers of prepared, low-income students never had the opportunity to enroll in four-year colleges (Fitzgerald, 2004; Lee, 2004). Thus, encouraging more students to apply for college and for student financial aid could raise aspirations, but if students who aspire to go to college are left behind, it is possible that encouragement could result in an unfulfilled promise by increasing aspirations but not enrollment.

Research on these linkages is limited but compelling (e.g., Hossler, Schmit, & Vesper, 1999; Perna, 2005). The studies cited above of the Washington State Achievers Program and the Twenty-first Century Scholars Program provide additional evidence that when information and mentoring are integrated into a program with aid guarantees, the programs enable more preparation and college enrollment.

However, in these cases there is explication of the role of finances, a topic often left out of some studies that focus on encouragement (e.g., Perna, 2005). Thus, the comprehensive approach works, but it is not easy to isolate the effects of encouragement and information.

Coordination of state finance strategies links to packaging and enrollment.

There are research findings relating public tuition and funding for merit- and need-based grants to student aid packages (Linkage 4) and enrollment. In particular, enrollment by low-income students is related to their ability to pay for college (Heller, 1997; Leslie & Brinkman, 1988; St. John, 2003). Coordination of state finance strategies involves balancing subsidies to institutions and students with tuition charges so that inequalities in opportunity are not increased. Well-coordinated strategies can improve access, equalize opportunity, and maintain institutional quality, all at less cost for taxpayers than poorly coordinated strategies.

K–12 reforms link to access and college completion.

High school reform can indirectly influence access and degree attainment through improvement in preparation (Linkage 5). The research that examines statistical correlations between math courses and degree attainment (e.g., Adelman, 1999, 2006) typically overlooks the role of policy. Rationalizing new policies on research on the class of 1992 that did not even consider policies in place in 1992 seems shortsighted, so we needed research that considered the role and influence of public policy.

The reanalysis of NELS indicates that high school policies (e.g., requiring more math courses) had an association with attainment of calculus for middle-income students, confirming the first part of the linkage structure; in addition, math courses were associated with degree attainment (St. John, 2006; St. John, Gross, Musoba, & Chung, 2006). Controlling for test scores and high school math, low-income students were more likely to be currently enrolled after eight years than to have dropped out of college. Thus, increasing high school graduation requirements increased, rather than reduced, inequalities in the opportunities to attain college degrees. This reinforces the need for reforms that focus on high schools serving low-income students.

Coordination of state finance policies links to degree attainment.

In addition to the indirect effects of student financial aid on enrollment and college choice, financial aid and college prices have a direct effect on both whether students attain college degrees and how long it takes to attain a degree (Linkage 6). A substantial research base confirms this relationship (Leslie & Brinkman, 1988; St. John, 2003; St. John, Cabrera, Nora, & Asker, 2000).

The fact that low-income students take longer to attain degrees, controlling for preparation, should be a source of concern to policymakers, including advocates of 9–14 reform, just as they are to parents of low- and middle-income students. It is clear that the average low-income student must borrow about $8,000 to pay for enrollment in a four-year college (ACSFA, 2002; Hartle, et al., 2005), an amount that requires unsubsidized loans that accrue interest during college. These debt loads are especially problematic for families earning less than $30,000 per year, given that many students with zero expected family contribution must take out parental loans. This packaging practice results in more hours of student work during college.

ASSESSING ALTERNATIVE APPROACHES TO INTEGRATION

Research using the balanced approach can inform policy aimed at integrating the five academic and financial strategies for improving attainment of 9–14 education (see table 1). The integration of high school with the first two years of college (Strategy 1) can potentially provide a means of reaching the 9–14 goals. To the extent that the costs of these strategies are achieved through doubling up courses (or advancing their content) during high school, this option would also be less costly than other options.

However, the options of providing collegiate courses during high school and of low tuition for community colleges (Strategy 2) do not resolve the financial access problem after high school, especially for students going on to, or transferring into, college. Providing guarantees of grant aid for low-income students (Strategy 3) has confirmed linkages to improved preparation, access, and persistence. Merit aid (Strategy 4) has some advantages because it enables alignment of support with admission standards, but it also has some disincentives for students who do not meet the merit criteria. The option of constructing individual accounts for students who earn academic credits during high school (a variation on Strategy 4) merits further testing, but there is not yet evidence on this type of targeted approach.

Coordinating finance strategies (Strategy 5)—and especially providing more funding for need-based grants when college tuitions rise—represents the best means for equalizing enrollment opportunity for equally prepared students across income groups. This approach also provides incentives for preparation, but it is crucial to provide information and encouragement. In fact, none of these strategies, by themselves, fully addresses the challenges we face in efforts to improve and equalize educational opportunity.

CONCLUSIONS

Informed decisions about public investments in education require the consideration of taxpayer costs along with the financial and academic aspects of achievement and educational opportunity. After nearly three decades of increased inequality in opportunities to prepare for college and in the opportunities to enroll in college and attain degrees, it is time to think about the challenges in ways that integrate concern about finances and preparation. In the middle 1970s, the federal government and states had a balanced approach to educational policy and finance that equalized education opportunity. However, the excellence movement increased inequality, shifting resources from programs that had an equalizing influence to new programs that served wealthier students. The push to improve 9–14 attainment could reduce this gap.

Several different approaches for advancing the 9–14 agenda have been introduced and documented, often tried out and funded by foundations and public agencies. While more evaluative evidence is needed to build a more-complete understanding of the efficacy of these strategies, it is important to interpret research on these new ventures using a balanced understanding of the financial and academic aspects of educational opportunity. This research confirms that strategies that reduce family concerns about college costs, especially for low-income students, are crucial to improving preparation, just as advances in high school curriculum can enhance college achievement. Both the academic and financial aspects of educational improvement merit attention as new strategies are crafted and tested. Integrating finances into the reform process also provides a means of considering taxpayer costs in relation to the goals of expanding and equalizing educational opportunities across income groups.

Notes and References

INTRODUCTION

1. Based on high school graduating class of 1992.
2. Source: Preliminary data from the National Center for Higher Education Management Systems for Making Opportunity Affordable, an initiative supported by Lumina Foundation for Education.
3. From personal correspondence with Anthony Carnevale.
4. Based on high school graduating class of 1992.
5. Source: U.S. Census Bureau. Current Population Survey.
6. See chapter 2, "Doing the Math: What It Means to Double the Number of Low-Income College Graduates."
7. See chapter 3, "Common Ground."
8. See http://nces.ed.gov/pubsearch/pubsinfo.asp?pubid=2005008.
9. If a student took multiple courses, schools counted the student for each course in which he or she was enrolled. Thus, enrollments may include duplicated counts of students.
10. In fall 2001 (the last year for which data are available), over 15 million students were enrolled in public and private high schools in the United States (U.S. Department of Education, 2003).
11. See http://www.utahsbr.edu/acad01f.html#NCS.
12. Source: Personal communication with Stuart Cochran, director of research and evaluation for Collaborative Programs, CUNY, 2006.
13. Early college high schools in operation or planned have a projected capacity of over 95,000 students. See www.earlycolleges.org.
14. From personal correspondence with David Conley.
15. In the 2005–06 academic year, only 7.6 percent of undergraduates at the flagship University of Virginia received federal Pell Grants—the lowest proportion among the nation's elite public colleges, according to a *Chronicle of Higher Education* analysis in January 2007. Pell Grants typically are awarded to students from families with incomes of $40,000 or less. A university survey found that more than 60 percent of last year's undergraduates came from families with annual incomes of $100,000 or more (Keller, 2007).

References

Advisory Committee on Student Financial Assistance. (2001). *Access denied: Restoring the nation's commitment to equal educational opportunity*. Washington, DC: Author.

Andrews, H. S., & Barnett, E. (2002). *Dual credit/enrollment in Illinois: A status report.* Champaign: University of Illinois at Urbana Champaign, Office of Community College Research and Leadership.

Balfanz, R., & Legters, N. (2004). *Locating the dropout crisis—Which high schools produce the nation's dropouts? Where are they located? Who attends them?* Baltimore: Johns Hopkins University.

Honawar, V. (2005, July 27). To maintain rigor, College Board to audit all AP courses. *Education Week*, p. 10.

Keller, J. (2007, January 26). Virginia lawmakers consider bill to encourage students to start at 2-year colleges. *Chronicle of Higher Education*, p. A22.

Kentucky Council on Postsecondary Education. (2006). *The dual enrollment of high school students in postsecondary education in Kentucky, 2001–02 to 2004–05.* Frankfort, KY: Author.

Kleiner, B., & Lewis, L. (2005). *Dual enrollment of high school students at postsecondary institutions: 2002–03* (NCES 2005–08). Washington, DC: National Center for Education Statistics.

U.S. Department of Education. (2003). *Digest of Education Statistics, 2003.* National Center for Education Statistics. Retrieved February 24, 2005, from http://nces.ed.gov/programs/digest/d03

Venezia, A., Kirst, M. W., & Antonio, A. L. (2003). *Betraying the college dream.* Stanford, CA: Stanford Institute for Higher Education Research.

Western Interstate Commission for Higher Education. (2006). *Accelerated learning options: Moving the needle on access and success. A study of state and institutional policies and practices.* Boulder, CO: Author.

CHAPTER 1 CONFESSIONS OF AN EDUCATION FUNDAMENTALIST
Anthony P. Carnevale

1. For a well-written review of Turkheimer and related work, see Kirp (2006).

References

Clark, T. N., & Lipset, S. M. (Eds.). (2001). *The breakdown of class politics: A debate on post-industrial stratification.* Baltimore: Johns Hopkins University Press.

Grubb, W. N., & Lazerson, M. (2004). *The education gospel: The economic power of schooling.* Cambridge, MA: Harvard University Press.

Kirp, D. (2006, July 23). After the bell curve. *The New York Times Magazine*, Section 6, pp. 15–16.

CHAPTER 2 DOING THE MATH, *Susan Goldberger*

1. See figure 1 on page 29.
2. The percentage of 18- and 19-year-olds who were enrolled in postsecondary education in 1993 was 44.4 percent, compared to 47.8 percent in 2004, the most recent year for which data are available (The Condition of Education 2006, NCES, Table 1-1. Percentage of the population ages 3–34 enrolled in school, by age group: October 1970–2004. Available online at http://nces.ed.gov/programs/coe/2006/pdf/01_2006.pdf). The bachelor's degree completion rates of 25- to 29-year-olds grew less than 1 percent, from 27.8 percent to 28.6 percent, between 1997 and 2005, the most recent year for which data are available (The Condition of Education, 2000–2006, Table 31-3. Percentage of 25- to 29-year-olds who completed a bachelor's degree or higher, by race/ethnicity and sex: March 1971–2005. Available online at http://nces.ed.gov/programs/coe/2006/section3/table.asp?tableID=494).

   Overall degree attainment also remained flat through the 1990s. Only 35 percent of students who entered college for the first time in the fall of 1995 earned an associate's or bachelor's degree within five years, compared to 37 percent of students who began college in the fall of 1989 (The Condition of Education, 2000–2006, Table 19-1. Percentage distribution of 1989–90 and 1995–96 beginning postsecondary students by their status at the end of five years. Available online at http://nces.ed.gov/programs/coe/2004/section3/table. asp?tableID=61).

3. Both the NELS data set and our analysis of the NELS data use "socioeconomic status," or SES, as the indicator of poverty. Socioeconomic status is a composite variable that takes into account family income, education, and occupations. SES is widely accepted by researchers as a more-accurate indicator of poverty or lack of opportunity than a point-in-time measurement of income. (In this chapter, the term "low-income" is used synonymously with "low-SES" for readability.) In the NELS data set, SES is constructed using questionnaire data about the mother's and father's highest level of education, their occupations, and family income. For the purpose of this analysis, the NELS students were divided into five socioeconomic "quintiles" of equal size. The 20 percent with the lowest SES scores are in quintile one; the 20 percent with the highest SES scores are in quintile five.
4. The measure of college preparation used in this chapter is a composite measure adapted from code provided by NCES on the NELS 88/2000 data analysis system (DAS). This composite, based on the "CQCOMV2" variable from the DAS, combines information from the student survey record and high school transcript data sets. It accounts for several measures of high school performance:

    - High school senior year rank in class percentage
    - Cumulative grade point average for academic courses
    - SAT combined test scores
    - ACT composite scores
    - NELS 1992 math and reading composite test score percentiles

    Following the variable code provided by the DAS, this variable classifies students based on their overall ranking on these five criteria. The resulting composite produced five categories of student preparation for college:

    - *Highly qualified:* Those whose highest value on any of the five criteria would put them among the top 10 percent of college students for that criterion.
    - *Very qualified:* Those whose highest value on any of the five criteria would put them among the top 25 percent of college students for that criterion.
    - *Somewhat qualified:* Those whose highest value on any of the five criteria would put them among the top 50 percent of college students for that criterion.
    - *Minimally qualified:* Those whose highest value on any of the five criteria would put them among the top 75 percent of college students for that criterion.
    - *Not qualified:* Those who had no value on any criterion that would put them among the top 75 percent of college students.

    The chapter translates these qualification categories into "Academic Preparation" levels and combined the top two categories into the single "Very/Highly Prepared" category. Due to subtle differences between the NELS data set available on the DAS and the NELS restricted data set used for this chapter, there will be slight differences between the measure of college qualification or academic preparation used here and those used by other authors who use the DAS public files to calculate this variable. For example, one of the criteria used in the CQCOMV2 variable was "Cumulative grade point average for academic courses." This variable was not available on the restricted data sets, so it was necessary to construct this average from the raw transcript data.
5. The estimated number of 4 million students enrolled in the eighth grade in the fall of 2001 was calculated by adding together public and private school enrollment figures from the U.S. Department of Education's National Center for Education Statistics (NCES). According to NCES, there were 3.619 million public school students and 338,000 private school students enrolled in the eighth grade in the fall of 2001, for a

total of 3.957 million students. That number was rounded up to 4 million for the purposes of this report (Sources: Table 40. Enrollment in public elementary and secondary schools, by level and grade: Fall 1987 to fall 2001. Available online at http://nces.ed.gov/programs/digest/d03/tables/dt040.asp; U.S. Department of Education, National Center for Education Statistics, Private School Universe Survey [PSS], 2001–2002).

6. College enrollment rates have increased only slightly since the early 1990s, when the eighth graders in the NELS study first were eligible to attend college. The percentage of 18- to 19-year-olds who were enrolled in postsecondary education in 1993 was 44.4 percent, compared to 47.8 percent in 2004, the most recent year for which data are available (The Condition of Education 2006, NCES, Table 1-1. Percentage of the population ages 3–34 enrolled in school, by age group: October 1970–2004. Available online at http://nces.ed.gov/programs/coe/2006/pdf/01_2006.pdf). College degree completion rates grew even less than enrollment rates since the eighth graders in the NELS study first were eligible to earn a four-year degree. The bachelor's degree completion rates of 25- to 29-year-olds grew less than 1 percent, from 27.8 percent to 28.6 percent, between 1997 and 2005, the most recent year for which data are available (The Condition of Education, 2000–2006, Table 31-3. Percentage of 25- to 29-year-olds who completed a bachelor's degree or higher, by race/ethnicity and sex: March 1971–2005. Available online at http://nces.ed.gov/programs/coe/2006/section3/table.asp?tableID=494).
7. Rounded to nearest thousand.
8. C. Adelman, *The Toolbox Revisited: Paths to Degree Completion from High School through College* (Washington, DC: U.S. Department of Education, 2006); C. Adelman, *Answers in the Tool Box: Academic Intensity, Attendance Patterns, and Bachelor's Degree Attainment* (Washington, DC: U.S. Department of Education, 1999); K. Akerhielm, J. Berger, M. Hooker, and D. Wise, *Factors Related to College Enrollment: Final Report Prepared for Under Secretary U.S. Department of Education* (Princeton, NJ: Mathtech, 1998).
9. Rounded to nearest hundred.
10. Florida Department of Education website; available online at http://www.fldoe.org/CC/OSAS/DataTrendsResearch/dt20.pdf; Successful Completion Rates in College Preparatory Programs Increase.
11. The estimate of 1,500 high-performing small high schools yielding 17,000 new low-income college graduates was calculated by estimating how many additional college graduates would be generated if these new schools could raise the high school graduation rates of low-income SES students from 65 percent to 90 percent and raise the college readiness rates of these graduates from 20 percent somewhat/very prepared to 80 percent somewhat/very prepared for college. The estimate did not assume any difference in the college enrollment and completion rate of low-SES high school graduates from existing versus new small schools. It applied the enrollment and completion rates of low-SES students by qualification level presented in this chapter. The calculation further assumed that each new small school enrolled 100 ninth graders a year, and that 50 percent were members of the lowest SES quintile. Applying the increased graduation and college readiness rates to this incoming group of 50 low-SES ninth graders in each school yielded a total of 17 college graduates (e.g., 34 percent success rate), compared to an estimated success rate of 5.5 college graduates per 50 low-SES ninth graders (i.e., 11 percent success rate). Thus, these 1,500 schools would each yield 11.5 more college graduates than untransformed high schools per 50 incoming ninth graders, for a total of (11.5 × 1,500) 17,250 more eventual college graduates a year.

    The estimate of 500 early colleges yielding 12,000 more low-income college graduates a year was based on the same assumptions about enrollment numbers of low-

SES students (50 percent of incoming ninth graders) and high school graduation rates (90 percent) and college readiness rates (80 percent at somewhat/very prepared levels) used to calculate the impact of 1,500 new small high schools. However, the estimate of early college's impact on college success rates makes the additional assumption that the integration of significant college course work into the high school experience will raise the college enrollment and completion rates of low-income early college graduates to rates comparable to their middle- and upper-class peers graduating from traditional high school programs. This additional assumption raises the estimated number of 50 entering low-income ninth graders expected to complete college to 24, for a college success rate of 48 percent compared to 34 percent at the average new small school and 11 percent at an untransformed high school.

CHAPTER 3 COMMON GROUND, *Andrea Venezia, Joni Finney, and Patrick M. Callan*

1. *Claiming Common Ground* identified four policy dimensions. For purposes of discussion in this chapter, the third and fourth policy dimensions have been collapsed into statewide data systems and accountability.
2. College and postsecondary education are used interchangeably in this chapter and encompass the range of educational opportunities beyond high school, including professional certificate and degree programs offered at public, private, for-profit, and not-for-profit two-year and four-year colleges and universities.
3. See http://www.act.org/activity/winter2004/survey.html.
4. For this and other examples of promising practices in this area, see chapter 11, "The California Early Assessment Program: Implications for States in Developing Readiness Agendas."
5. See chapter 28, "Developing a P–20 Budget Tool: Giving Direction to Oregon Public Education."
6. For more information, see www.dataqualitycampaign.org.
7. See www.fldoe.org/news/2006/2006_02_02-2.asp.
8. See http://cpe.ky.gov/NR/rdonlyres/04F25118-4FBB-4C8A-8D1B-4197EA4CEAEA/0/SummaryHB1-20050401.pdf.
9. See http://cpe.ky.gov/planning/5Qs/default.htm.
10. See www.highereducation.org/crosstalk/ct0405/news0405-kentucky.shtml.
11. For example, Georgia passed legislation mandating that a statewide P–16 council meet on a regular basis. This worked under former Governor Barnes, but the council has not met since Governor Perdue took office in January 2003.
12. See chapter 7, "Alignment of High School Expectations to College and Work."

References

Callan, P. M., Finney, J. E., Kirst, M. W., Usdan, M. W., & Venezia, A. (2006). *Claiming common ground: State policymaking for improving college readiness and success* (National Center Report #06-1). San Jose, CA: National Center for Public Policy and Higher Education.

Education Trust. (1999). Ticket to nowhere: The gap between leaving high school and entering college and high performance jobs. *Thinking K–16, 3*(2), 26.

Evenbeck, S., Seabrook, P. A., St. John, E., & Murphy, S. (2004). Twenty-first Century Scholars: Indiana's program of incentives for college-going. In R. Kazis, J. Vargas, & N. Hoffman (Eds.), *Double the numbers: Increasing postsecondary credentials for underrepresented youth* (pp. 169–175). Cambridge, MA: Harvard Education Press.

Institute for Educational Leadership. (2002). *Gathering momentum: Building the learning connection between schools and colleges.* Washington, DC: Author.

Kirst, M., & Venezia, A. (Eds.). (2004). *From high school to college: Improving opportunities for success in postsecondary education.* San Francisco: Jossey-Bass.

Mortenson, T. (2004, November). *Postsecondary Education Opportunity, 149.* Retrieved from www.postsecondary.org

National Center for Education Statistics. (2002). *Enrollment in postsecondary institutions.* Washington, DC: U.S. Department of Education.

National Center for Higher Education Management Systems. (2005). *As America becomes more diverse: The impact of state higher education inequality.* Boulder, CO: Author.

National Center for Public Policy and Higher Education. (2004). *Measuring up 2004* [Electronic version]. San Jose, CA. Retrieved from www.highereducation.org

National Center for Public Policy and Higher Education. (2005, November). *Income of U.S. workforce projected to decline if education doesn't improve* (Policy Alert Series). San Jose, CA: Author.

U.S. Department of Education. (2001).*The condition of education.* Washington, DC: National Center for Education Statistics.

Venezia, A., Kirst, M. W., & Antonio, A. L. (2003). *Betraying the college dream* (Stanford University's Bridge Project Final Report). Stanford, CA: Stanford Institute for Higher Education Research.

Wyse, D. (2005, September 13). *Should states budget for K–16? What difference would it make?* Paper presented at conference, State Policy Dimensions for K–16 Reform, Racine, WI.

CHAPTER 4 SEPARATION OF K–12 AND POSTSECONDARY EDUCATION

Michael W. Kirst and Michael D. Usdan

1. This section is derived from research and field visits undertaken in 2004 for a publication of the National Center for Public Policy and Higher Education, the Stanford Institute for Higher Education Research, and the Institute for Educational Leadership (Venezia et al., 2005). The report also included case studies of Florida, Georgia, and Oregon. For more details on New York and the other three state case studies, see www.highered.org.
2. For a more-detailed analysis of how a number of policy levers can potentially overcome this disjuncture, see Callan et al. (2006).
3. For example, Jobs for the Future, under whose aegis this volume is being written, has become another relatively new and significant voice for bridging inter-level separation. JFF's efforts to improve the credential attainment rates for low-income students and its concerns about the lack of alignment between K–12 and postsecondary standards, assessments, curricula and expectations, student transitions, workforce preparation, and other issues pertaining to developing a more-integrated education system have made it an important catalyst in projecting awareness of the significance of K–16 among policymakers and business leaders.

References

Bailey, S. K. (1974). Education and the state. *Educational Record,* 55(1), 5–6.

Callan, P. M., Finney, J. E., Kirst, M. W., Usdan, M. D., & Venezia, A. *Claiming common ground: State policymaking for improving college readiness and success* (National Center Report No. 06-1). San Jose, CA: National Center for Public Policy and Higher Education.

Chronicle of Higher Education. (2006, March 10), School and college. Section B.

Dunham, A. (1969). *Colleges of forgotten Americans.* Berkeley, CA: Carnegie Foundation for the Advancement of Teaching.

Hurwitz, E., Minar, W. D., & Usdan, M. D. (1969). *Education and state politics: The devel-*

oping relationship between elementary-secondary and higher education. New York: Teachers College Press.

Immerwahr, J. (1999). *Doing comparatively well: Why the public loves higher education and criticizes K–12.* San Jose, CA: National Center for Higher Education and Public Policy.

Ravitch, D. (2000). *Left back: A century of failed education reforms.* New York: Simon and Schuster.

Tyack, D., & Cuban, L. (1995). *Tinkering toward utopia: A century of public school reform.* Cambridge, MA: Harvard University Press.

Venezia, A., Callan, P. M., Finney, J. E., Kirst, M. W., & Usdan, M. D. (2005). *The governance divide: A report on a four-state study on improving college readiness and success.* San Jose, CA: National Center for Public Policy and Higher Education.

CHAPTER 5 A COLLEGE-READY NATION, *Kristin D. Conklin and Stefanie Sanford*

1. See chapter 6, "Raising Expectations for Academic Achievement," and chapter 30, "Integrating Public Finance into Strategies for Improving Preparation, College Enrollment, and Persistence."

CHAPTER 6 RAISING EXPECTATIONS, *Stan Jones*

1. See, for example, Horn and Nunez (2000) and Choy (2002).

References

Achieve, Inc. (2006). *Closing the expectations gap 2006.* Washington, DC: Author.

Adelman, C. (1999). *Answers in the tool box: Academic intensity, attendance patterns, and bachelor's degree attainment,* Washington, DC: U.S. Department of Education.

Choy, S. P. (2002). *Access and persistence: Findings from 10 years of longitudinal research on students.* Washington, DC: American Council on Education, Center for Policy Analysis.

Horn, L., & Nunez, A.-N. (2000). *Mapping the road to college: First-generation students' math track, planning strategies and the context of support* (NCES 2000-153). Washington, DC: National Center for Education Statistics.

Mortenson, T. (2006, June). College continuation rates by family income for recent high school graduates 1987–2004. *Postsecondary Education Opportunity, 168.* Retrieved from www.postsecondary.org

St. John, E. P., Musoba, G. D., Simmons, A. B., & Chung, C. G. (2002). *Meeting the access challenge: Indiana's Twenty-first Century Scholars Program* (New Agenda Series, Vol. 4, No. 4). Indianapolis: Lumina Foundation for Education.

CHAPTER 7 ALIGNMENT OF EXPECTATIONS, *Christine Tell and Michael Cohen*

1. Achieve was created by the nation's governors and business leaders in 1996 to help states raise academic standards and achievement so that all students graduate ready for college, work, and citizenship.
2. For more information on the summit, see www.achieve.org/node/301.
3. A group of Achieve studies documenting the lack of rigor in high school graduation requirements (Achieve, 2004) and high school exit exams (American Diploma Project, 2004a), as well as the skills colleges and employers want (American Diploma Project, 2004b), may be found on the Achieve website at www.achieve.org.
4. In general, prior to ADP, most states allowed districts to set their own graduating requirements, mandating only that students have a specific number of credits or such subjects as civics or physical education.
5. Achieve conducted additional alignment studies with positive reports on alignment in Indiana, Kentucky, Ohio, and Rhode Island.

6. For reports on the various activities of the Colorado Education Alignment Council, see www.fund4colorado.org/events.php.
7. For the final report of the Lt. Governor's Commission on Higher Education & Economic Growth, see www.cherrycommission.org.
8. See chapter 9, "Challenges in the Transition from High School to College."

References

Achieve, Inc. (2004). *The expectations gap: A 50-state review of high school graduation requirements.* Washington, DC: Author.

American Diploma Project. (2004a). *Do graduation tests measure up? A closer look at state high school exit exams.* Washington, DC: Achieve.

American Diploma Project. (2004b). *Ready or not: Creating a high school diploma that counts.* Washington, DC: Achieve.

Peter D. Hart Research Associates/Public Opinion Strategies. (2005). *Rising to the challenge: Are high school graduates prepared for college and work? A study of recent high school graduates, college instructors, and employers.* Washington, DC: Achieve.

CHAPTER 8 THE PROMISE OF O*NET, *Anthony P. Carnevale*

1. Employers will need workers with robust competencies, but they are unlikely to take on greater human resource development responsibilities at a time when they are shedding long-term commitments and are overburdened with the world's highest labor costs. In addition, as the global labor market for college-educated labor grows and job tenure declines, employers will increasingly become buyers—not developers—of skilled labor.
2. Of the 1,399,542 bachelor's degrees conferred in 2004, 42,106 were conferred in the liberal arts and sciences, general studies, and humanities. In 2004, there were 13,327 bachelor's degrees awarded in math, but 307,149 in business; 22,164 in parks, recreation, leisure, and fitness studies; 70,968 in communications; and 77,181 in the visual and performing arts. The same pattern is reinforced in the expansion in applied associate's degrees, certificates, certifications, and customized training. Of the 665,301 associate's degrees conferred in 2004, 227,650 were conferred in the liberal arts and sciences, general studies, and humanities, and only 801 were conferred in mathematics.
3. See www.onetcenter.org.

CHAPTER 9 CHALLENGES IN THE TRANSITION, *David Conley*

References

Achieve, Inc. (2004). *Do graduation tests measure up? A closer look at state high school exit exams.* Washington, DC: Author.

Achieve, Inc., Education Trust, & Thomas B. Fordham Foundation. (2004). *The American Diploma Project: Ready or not: Creating a high school diploma that counts.* Washington, DC: Achieve.

Adelman, C. (1999). *Answers in the tool box: Academic intensity, attendance patterns, and bachelor's degree attainment.* Washington, DC: U.S. Department of Education.

Adelman, C. (2006). *The tool box revisited: Paths to degree completion from high school through college.* Washington, DC: U.S. Department of Education.

Brown, R. S., & Conley, D. T. (2007). Comparing state high school assessments to standards for success in entry-level university courses. *Journal of Educational Assessment, 12,* 137–160.

City University of New York. (1992). *The City University of New York: College preparatory initiative.* New York: Author.

Competency-Based Admission Pilot Project. (1995). *Admission competencies: Competencies, standardized reporting profile, and rating scale for competency-based admission pilot project.* Madison: University of Wisconsin System.

Conley, D. T. (1994). *Proficiency-based admission standards study.* Eugene: Oregon State System of Higher Education. (ERIC Document Reproduction Service No. ED367213).

Conley, D. T. (1996). Oregon's Proficiency-Based Admission Standards System (PASS). In *Responding to school reform: Higher education defines new roles in Oregon, Wisconsin, and Florida, 7–18.* Denver: Education Commission of the States.

Conley, D. T. (2003). *Understanding university success.* Eugene: University of Oregon, Center for Educational Policy Research.

Conley, D. T. (2005). *College knowledge: What it really takes for students to succeed and what we can do to get them ready.* San Francisco: Jossey-Bass.

Conley, D. T., Aspengren, K., Gallagher, K., & Langan, H. (2006). *College Board curriculum study for science.* Eugene, OR: Educational Policy Improvement Center.

Conley, D. T., Aspengren, K., & Stout, O. (2006). *Advanced placement best practices study: Biology, chemistry, environmental science, physics, European history, U.S. history, world history.* Eugene, OR: Educational Policy Improvement Center.

Conley, D. T., & Ward, T. (2006). *Aligned courses project annual report to the Fund for the Improvement of Post-Secondary Education (FIPSE).* Eugene, OR: Center for Educational Policy Research.

Garb, F. (1998). *University of Wisconsin competency-based admissions pilot project spring 1998: Final report.* Madison: University of Wisconsin System.

National Commission on Writing in America's Schools and Colleges. (2003). *The neglected "R": The need for a writing revolution.* New York: College Board.

Tell, C. A., & McDonald, D. (2003, November 12–16). *The first year: Students' performance on 10th-grade standards and subsequent performance in the first year of college (2001–02).* Paper presented at the annual conference of the Association for the Study of Higher Education, Portland, OR.

University of Nebraska. (1993). *University of Nebraska subject matter competencies: Preparation of students for admission to the university.* Unpublished manuscript, University of Nebraska.

Venezia, A., Kirst, M. W., & Antonio, A. (2004). *Betraying the college dream: How disconnected K–12 and postsecondary systems undermine student aspirations.* San Francisco: Jossey-Bass.

CHAPTER 10 SENDING SIGNALS TO STUDENTS, *Bridget Terry Long and Erin K. Riley*

1. Data requested from Early Mathematics Placement Testing by the author on historical participation by high school; received January 23, 2006.
2. See www.empt.org, accessed January 9, 2006.
3. See www.calstate.edu/eap, accessed March 26, 2006.
4. See www.calstate.edu/eap, accessed March 26, 2006.
5. See http://mdtp.ucsd.edu/OnlineTests.shtml, accessed May 7, 2006.
6. See www.calstate.edu/eap, accessed March 26, 2006.

References

Adelman, C. (1999). *Answers in the toolbox: Academic intensity, attendance patterns, and bachelor's degree attainment.* Washington, DC: U.S. Department of Education, Office of Educational Research and Improvement.

Adelman, C. (2006). *The toolbox revisited: Paths to degree completion from high school through college.* Washington, DC: U.S. Department of Education.

ACT. (2003a). *Educational planning and assessment system case study: Preparing Oklahoma students for the future.* Iowa City, IA: Author.

ACT. (2003b). *Educational planning and assessment system case study: Measuring Illinois students' progress toward state learning standards.* Iowa City, IA: Author.

Bernhardt, R., & Hilgoe, E. (2005). *The North Carolina Early Mathematics Placement Testing Program final report 2004–2005 to the North Carolina high schools.* Mimeo. Greenville, North Carolina.

Breneman, D. W., & Haarlow, W. N. (1998). Remedial education: Costs and consequences. *Fordham Report, 2*(9).

California State University. (2006). Early assessment program. Retrieved March 28, 2006, from www.calstate.edu/eap

Early Mathematics Placement Testing. (2006a). Retrieved January 9, 2006, from www.empt.org

Early Mathematics Placement Testing. (2006b). Data requested by the author on historical participation by high school. Received January 23, 2006.

Greene, J., & Foster, G. (2003). *Public high school graduation and college-readiness rates in the United States* (Education Working Paper No. 3). New York: Manhattan Institute, Center for Civic Information.

Kentucky Early Mathematics Testing Program. (2005). *2005 annual report.* Retrieved January 10, 2006, from www.mathclass.org/kempt-info/AnnualReport2005.htm

Laughbaum, E. (2003). *State of the Ohio Early College Mathematics Placement Testing Program.* Mimeo.

Mathematics Diagnostic Testing Project (MDTP). (2006). Retrieved May 7, 2006, from http://mdtp.ucsd.edu/OnlineTests.shtml

McCabe, R. H. (2001, February). Developmental education: A policy primer. *League for Innovation in the Community College, 14*(1).

Mills, K. (2004, Fall). Preparing for success in college. *National Cross Talk, 12*(4).

National Governors Association. (2005). *Getting it done: Ten steps to a state action agenda.* Washington, DC: Author.

Ohio Board of Regents. (2002). *Making the transition from high school to college in Ohio 2002.* Columbus: Ohio Board of Regents.

Venezia, A., Kirst, M., & Antonio, A. (2003). *Betraying the college dream: How disconnected K–12 and postsecondary education systems undermine student aspirations.* Stanford, CA: Stanford Bridge Project.

Zuiker, M. A. (1996). *The Ohio Early College Mathematics Placement Testing Program: Program evaluation.* Unpublished doctoral dissertation, Ohio State University.

CHAPTER 12 LESSONS FROM THE FIELD, *Cecilia Cunningham and Roberta S. Matthews*

1. For more information on the Early College High School Initiative, see chapter 19, "State Policies that Support the Integration of 9–14: The Case of Early College High Schools."

CHAPTER 13 ANOTHER ROUTE TO COLLEGE, *Terry Grobe*

1. Holyoke's Early College model is supported through the Diploma Plus network.
2. CommCorp designed Diploma Plus to increase the number and quality of educational alternatives for vulnerable youth. Diploma Plus schools exist in Massachusetts, New

York, Rhode Island, and Connecticut. Diploma Plus schools are being planned in California. The model is being replicated nationally with support from the Bill & Melinda Gates Foundation.

3. See www.commcorp.org/diplomaplus/dp-outcomes.html.
4. See www.commcorp.org/DP/outcomes/html.

References

Brigham Nahas Research Associates. (2004). *2002–2003 graduate study.* Unpublished paper, Cambridge, MA.

Massachusetts Department of Education. (2004). *MCAS retest results show students are requiring fewer tries to pass.* Boston: Author.

CHAPTER 14 COMBINING TO IMPROVE COLLEGE SUCCESS, *Dan Restuccia*

1. Data available online at http://schools.nyc.gov/daa/2005ela48/pdf/Highlights.pdf.
2. See chapter 15, "CUNY College Now: Extending the Reach of Dual Enrollment."
3. For the *Newsweek* list, see www.msnbc.msn.com/id/12532678?s=0&np=13& sort=raa.

References

Jonas, M. (2007). The new math. *Commonwealth, 12*(1), 56–69.

CHAPTER 15 CUNY COLLEGE NOW, *Tracy Meade and Eric Hofmann*

1. We define "traditional dual enrollment" as participation in college-level courses by high school students.
2. The College Now program is part of the educational canvas of two enormous systems. In a given year, CUNY enrolls 190,000 undergraduates in 17 colleges (six two-year community colleges, seven four-year senior colleges, and four comprehensive colleges that offer both associate's and bachelor's degrees). The New York City Department of Education enrolls 300,000 high school students.
3. Much of this success in college-credit course completion is due to a rigorous application process (e.g., interviews, essays) and student support during course-taking.
4. The category of race/ethnicity is optional on the College Now registration form and accounts for the large number of unknowns in this area of our data. The New York City Department of Education does not include the category "other." We have recently reached an agreement with the department to match our registration data with its student records in order to fill in the demographic picture of College Now.
5. College Now programs at the community colleges offering remedial course work decide eligibility requirements for credit-course enrollment. Some, such as Kingsborough Community College, use grade point average as the main criterion for credit-course enrollment. Kingsborough uses a GPA of 80 as the cutoff for enrollment in college-credit courses and a GPA of 65 to 80 for enrollment in its developmental courses.
6. The authors thank Ljubica Depovic for her contribution to this section of the essay.
7. See chapter 9, "Challenges in the Transition from High School to College," for more information on Standards for Success.

References

Kleiner, B., & Lewis, L. (2005). *Dual enrollment of high school students at postsecondary institutions: 2002–03.* Washington, DC: U.S. Department of Education, National Center for Education Statistics.

Understanding university success: A report from Standards for Success (a project of the Association of American Universities and The Pew Charitable Trusts). (2003). Eugene, OR: Center for Educational Policy Research.

CHAPTER 16 ACADEMIC IDENTITY DEVELOPMENT, *Michael J. Nakkula and Karen C. Foster*

1. See chapter 19, "State Policies that Support the Integration of 9–14: The Case of Early College High Schools."

References

Chavous, T. M., Bernat, D. H., Schmeelk-Cone, K., Caldwell, C. H., Kohn-Wood, L., & Zimmerman, M. A. (2003). Racial identity and academic achievement among African American adolescents. *Child Development, 74,* 1076–1090.

Markus, H., & Nurius, P. (1986). Possible selves. *American Psychologist, 41,* 954–969.

Mickelson, R. A. (1990). The attitude-achievement paradox among black adolescents. *Sociology of Education, 63,* 44–61.

Ogbu, J. (1986). Class stratification, racial stratification, and schooling. In L. Weis (Ed.), *Class, race and gender in American education* (pp. 163–82). Albany: State University of New York Press.

Yowell, C. M. (2002). Dreams of the future: The pursuit of education and career possible selves among ninth-grade Latino youth. *Applied Developmental Science, 6*(2), 62–72.

CHAPTER 17 SECONDARY-POSTSECONDARY LEARNING OPPORTUNITIES *Jennifer Brown Lerner and Betsy Brand*

1. Other terms used to describe many of these approaches include accelerated-learning options and credit-based transition programs.
2. AYPF recognizes that AP could be considered a unique SPLO but did not find any evaluations that assessed AP by itself. For this reason, we categorized AP with dual enrollment. AP provides opportunities for high school students to take college-level classes in high school settings that culminate in a nationwide exam aligned with college-level content and expectations. Depending both on the examination score received and on the college attended, these courses may lead to advanced placement or credits awarded for entry-level courses.
3. For more information on the Early College Program at Wells, see: www.earlycollege.me.edu.
4. For more information on Middle College High School at San Joaquin Delta College, see http://sites.lodiusd.net/schoolcity/ssb/content.cfm?si=0&fi=0&siteID=0x365D0422C38AD611&ptc=/0x365D0422C38AD611/0x33660422C38AD611&CFID=980402&CFTOKEN=29357738.
5. For more information on Gateway to College, see www.gatewaytocollege.org.
6. For more information on Mott Middle College, see http://mmc.geneseeisd.org.
7. For more information on the Early College High School Student Information System, see www.partners.earlycolleges.org/ECHSResources2.php?R1ID=20.

References

Churchill, W. D., & Iwai, S. I. (1981). College attrition, student use of campus facilities, and a consideration of self-reported personal problems. *Research in Higher Education, 14,* 353–365.

Cross, K. P. (1985). Education for the 21st century. *National Student Affairs Administrators in Higher Education Journal, 23*(1), 7–18.

Jekielek, S., Moore, K., Hair, E., & Scarupa, H. (2002, February). *Mentoring: A promising strategy for youth development* (Child Trends Research Brief). Washington, DC: Child Trends. Retrieved August 31, 2006, from http://www.mentoring. ca.gov/pdf/MentoringBrief2002. pdf#search =%22mentoring%3A%20a%20promising%20strategy%20for%20%20 youth%20development%22

McKeachie, W. J., Pintrich, P., Lin, Y., & Smith, D. (1986). *Teaching and learning in the college classroom: A review of the research literature*. Ann Arbor: University of Michigan, National Center for Research to Improve Postsecondary Teaching and Learning.

National Academy of Sciences-National Research Council. (1977). *Retention of minority students in engineering: A report of the Retention Task Force, Committee on Minorities in Engineering, Assembly of Engineering, National Research Council*. Washington, DC: National Academy of Sciences. (ERIC Reproduction Service No. ER152467)

Smith, J. B., Walter, T. L., & Hoey, G. (1992). Support programs and student self-efficacy: Do first-year students know when they need help? *Journal of the Freshman-Year Experience, 4*(2), 41–67.

Swail, W. S. (2004). *Value added: The costs and benefits of college-preparatory programs*. Washington, DC: Educational Policy Institute. Retrieved from http://www.educational policy.org/pdf/value_added.pdf#search =%22value%20of%20pre-college%20success% 20class%22

CHAPTER 18 CREATING PATHWAYS FOR STRUGGLING STUDENTS

Adria Steinberg and Cheryl Almeida

1. The term "keen economists" comes from Roderick (2006).
2. See, for example, Miller (2006) and National Research Council (2001).
3. A student is considered on track at the end of ninth grade if he or she has earned at least five full-year course credits and no more than one F (based on semester marks) in a core academic course.
4. As cited by Jerald, Gleason, and Dynarski (2002).

References

Allensworth, E., & Easton, J. Q. (2005). *The on-track indicator as a predictor of high school graduation*. Chicago: Consortium on Chicago School Research.

Almeida, C. A., Johnson, C. O., & Steinberg, A. (2006). *Making good on a promise: What policymakers can do to support the educational persistence of dropouts*. Boston: Jobs for the Future.

Balfanz, R., & Herzog, L. (2005, March 18). *Keeping middle grades students on track to graduation*. Paper presented at the Regional Middle Grades Symposium, Philadelphia.

Curran, B. (2006). *Implementing graduation counts: State progress to date*. Washington, DC: National Governors Association Center for Best Practices.

Jerald, C. (2006). *Identifying potential dropouts: Key lessons for building an early warning data system—a dual agenda of high standards and high graduation rates*. Washington, DC: Achieve.

Jerald, C., Gleason, P., & Dynarski, M. (2002). Do we know whom to serve? Issues in using risk factors to identify dropouts. *Journal of Education for Students Placed at Risk, 7*, 25–41.

Lynch, J. (2006, June). *Office of Multiple Pathways to Graduation: Developing and strengthening schools and programs that lead to high school graduation and postsecondary opportunities for over-aged, under-credited youth*. Paper presented at the CCSSO Secondary School Redesign Conference, Atlanta.

Miller, P. (2006, June 22). GED battery no substitute for diploma. In Diplomas count: An essential guide to graduation policy and rates [Special issue]. *Education Week*, p. 8.

National Research Council. (2001). *Understanding dropouts: Statistics, strategies, and high-stakes testing*. Washington, DC: National Academies Press.

Olsen, L. (2006, June 22). The down staircase. *Diplomas count: An essential guide to graduation policy and rates*. Washington, DC: *Education Week*, pp. 5–6, 10–11.

Quint, J. (2006). *Meeting five critical challenges of high school reform: Lessons from research on three reform models*. New York: MDRC.

Roderick, M. (2006). *Closing the aspirations-attainment gap: Implications for high school reform*. New York: MDRC.

Steinberg, A., Johnson, C., & Pennington, H. (2006). *Addressing America's dropout challenge: State efforts to boost graduation rates require federal support*. Boston, MA: Jobs for the Future.

Taylor, J. C., & Liebowitz, M. (2004). *Breaking through: Helping low-skilled adults enter and succeed in college and careers*. Boston: Jobs for the Future.

CHAPTER 19 STATE POLICIES THAT SUPPORT INTEGRATION OF 9–14
Joel Vargas

1. Early college high schools are a recent development—the first ones opened in 2002. Thus, the percentages of students graduating, earning associate's degrees, and being accepted to four-year colleges are likely to rise in one more year.
2. See chapter 20, "Return on Investment Analysis of Integrating Grades 9–14," for more information.
3. See Hoffman (2005). Also see Utah concurrent enrollment regulations at http://www.rules.utah.gov/publicat/code/r277/r277-713.htm.
4. One way that states are addressing these and related questions is by participating in the national Early College High School Student Information System, a highly secure system that provides data to support the Early College High School Initiative. The SIS collects aggregated data and unidentifiable, student-level data for the period beginning at least two years prior to enrollment in the early college high school through graduation or departure from the school. Schools and school districts supply data related to a number of broad categories: staffing, student demographics, student longitudinal information, early college high school courses, student GPA, transcripts, student enrollment, student discipline, student attendance, and graduation. The SIS will document students' post–early college high school enrollment in higher education through the National Student Clearinghouse.

Reference

Hoffman, N. (2005). *Add and subtract: Dual enrollment as a state strategy to increase postsecondary success for underrepresented students*. Boston: Jobs for the Future.

CHAPTER 20 RETURN ON INVESTMENT ANALYSIS, *Robert Palaich, John Augenblick, and Margaretha Maloney*

1. The Early College High School Initiative has established over 130 schools thus far, serving over 20,000 students in 24 states nationwide. Over 250 schools serving over 100,000 students are planned nationwide by the end of the decade. For more information, see chapter 19, "State Policies that Support the Integration of 9–14: The Case of Early College High Schools," and www.earlycolleges.org.
2. Social costs include the cost of remedial programs, court and prison costs that are a consequence of criminal behavior, and income maintenance programs such as TANF and Food Stamps.

3. Program ROI = [(total benefit − total costs)/total costs] × 100.
4. The modeling used a combination of sampled cost data from early college high schools and typical traditional high schools, as well as projected outcomes extrapolated from the National Education Longitudinal Study (NELS, 1988) in order to supplement the limited data available from early college high schools, which are still too young to have many graduates.
5. Source: JFF analysis of data from the National Educational Longitudinal Study for students from the two lowest-income SES quintiles.
6. In Washington State's Running Start, a concurrent enrollment program where qualified high school juniors may take college classes at a local community or four-year college, school districts receive the full basic education per-pupil amount and then must pass 93 percent of the funds to the college; 7 percent is retained for administrative purposes. After initial growth, expansion of the Running Start program has been slow (Palaich et al., 2006). Because the high schools lose money when students attend college classes, there is a disincentive for schools to encourage students to participate in the Running Start Program.

References

Augenblick, Palaich, & Associates. (2006). *Return on investment in early college high schools*. Boston: Jobs for the Future.

Baum, S., & Payea, K. (2005). *Education pays: Update 2005* (Trends in Higher Education Series). Washington, DC: College Board.

Long, A., Anthes, K., & Griffith, M. (2004). *P–16 education in Oregon: Finance* (ECS Policy Brief). Denver: Education Commission of the States.

Palaich, R., Blanco, C., Anderson, A. B., & Silverstein, J. S. (2006). Financing accelerated-learning options: Understanding who benefits and who pays. In *Moving the needle on access and success* (pp. 57–72). Boulder, CO: Western Interstate Commission for Higher Education.

CHAPTER 21 USING DUAL ENROLLMENT TO BUILD A 9–14 SYSTEM

Nancy Hoffman

1. See also chapter 1, "Confessions of an Education Fundamentalist: Why Grade 12 Is Not the Right End Point for Anyone."
2. The term "dual enrollment" here describes options for college course-taking for high school students, whether delivered in high schools or on college campuses. These options include such programs as Tech-Prep, middle college, and early college high schools. States and institutions also use the terms concurrent enrollment, accelerated learning, postsecondary education, and credit-based transition options to describe college-level learning in high school.
3. For more information, see chapter 9, "Challenges in the Transition from High School to College." Additional insight into these questions comes from Achieve's technical work in the American Diploma Project (see chapter 7, "Alignment of High School Expectations to College and Work") and various state projects to align high school exit and college entrance standards.
4. See www.nacep.org.
5. Maine's legislation builds from the state's implementation of early college high school programs at 10 sites that encompassed 14 public and private postsecondary institutions and 40 or more high schools as of 2006.
6. For more information, see Hoffman (2005).

7. See chapter 17, "Secondary-Postsecondary Learning Opportunities: Some Promising Practices," for a summary of research on these questions.
8. The council has retained Jobs for the Future to conduct this assessment and provide recommendations for changing dual enrollment policies. Currently, a single sentence in Board of Regents for Elementary and Secondary Education policy directs high schools to develop dual enrollment programs.
9. See chapter 24, "Postsecondary Numerical Goals as Catalyst for P–16 Reform: Texas Sends a Message."
10. See http://higheredinfo.org.
11. See www.cpa.state.tx.us/comptrol/fnotes/fn0302/doing.html.
12. Both dual enrollment and early colleges are mentioned in the Commissioner's Rules for Expenditures, available online at http://www.tea.state.tx.us/rules/tac/chapter061/ch61ii.html.

References

Conley, D. T. (2005). College knowledge: Getting in is only half the battle. *Principal Leadership, 6*(1), 16–21.

Hoffman, N. (2005). *Add and subtract: Dual enrollment as a state strategy to increase postsecondary success for underrepresented students.* Boston: Jobs for the Future.

National Center for Public Policy and Higher Education. (2006). *Measuring up 2006.* San Jose, CA: National Center for Public Policy and Higher Education.

Vargas, J., & Hoffman, N. (2006). *Dual enrollment in Rhode Island: Opportunities for state policy.* Boston: Jobs for the Future.

CHAPTER 22 EVOLUTION OF AN INNOVATION, *Travis Reindl*

1. This chapter draws on a wide-ranging conversation about accelerated learning among participants in Accelerated Learning: Shaping Public Policy to Serve Underrepresented Youth, a first-of-its-kind national conference held in 2006. Here I attempt to capture major themes and controversies from the conference and offer personal reflections regarding the next stages of development of accelerated learning. For more information on the conference, see www.jff.org.
2. See chapter 20, "Return on Investment Analysis of Integrating Grades 9–14."
3. See chapter 17, "Secondary-Postsecondary Learning Opportunities: Some Promising Practices."
4. See chapter 20, "Return on Investment Analysis of Integrating Grades 9–14."

Reference

Western Interstate Commission for Higher Education. (2006). *Accelerated learning options: Moving the needle on access and success.* Boulder, CO: Author.

CHAPTER 23 EXPLORING EDUCATION REFORM SYSTEMICALLY *Geoff Hayward*

1. The directorate is composed of Geoff Hayward (Oxford University), Anne Hodgson (Institute of Education), Jill Johnson (Universities and Colleges Admissions Service), Ewart Keep (Warwick and Cardiff Universities), Richard Pring (Oxford University), Gareth Rees (Cardiff University), and Ken Spours (Institute of Education).
2. There is no real American equivalent to a further-education college, although they are in some ways England's community-college counterparts. They cater to learners from the age of 14 up and offer a range of vocational, academic, and adult provisions.

Reference

Keep, E., & Mayhew, K. (2004). The economic and distributional implications of current policies on higher education. *Oxford Review of Economic Policy, 20,* 298–314.

CHAPTER 24 POSTSECONDARY NUMERICAL GOALS, *Michael Collins*

1. Twenty states have quantifiable goals for enrollment and graduation, ten for retention, and only nine for all three.
2. Texas state demographer Steve Murdoch projected that by 2040, despite gains in the percentage of the total number of the workforce at all educational levels compared to levels in 2000, Latinos would be concentrated in lower education-attainment categories of the workforce. Consequently, the attainment levels were projected to be lower in 2040 than in 2000 (Murdock et al., 2003).
3. In 2005, the legislature further strengthened the role of the P–16 Council.
4. See www.txhighereddata.org/Interactive/accountability.

References

Collins, M. (2006). *By the numbers: State goals for increasing postsecondary attainment.* Boston: Jobs for the Future.

Murdock, S. H., White, S., Hoque, M. N., Pecotte, B., You, X., & Balkan, J. (2003). *The new Texas challenge: Population change and the future of Texas.* College Station: Texas A&M University Press.

Texas Higher Education Coordinating Board. (2003). *Annual Texas Academic Skills Program/ Alternative (TASP/A) test: Report on student performance, initial pass rates (with/without exemptions) by test area, ethnicity, gender, high school curriculum, economically disadvantaged 1998–2002 high school graduating class.* Austin, TX: Author.

Texas Higher Education Coordinating Board, Division of Finance, Campus Planning, and Research. (2002). *Appropriations for developmental education in Texas public institutions of higher education.* Austin, TX: Author.

Texas Higher Education Coordinating Board, Planning and Information Resources Division. (2003). *Student performance and the recommended high school program: In Accordance with Texas Education Code, Chapter 56 Subchapter M.* Austin, TX: Author.

CHAPTER 26 DATA REQUIREMENTS FOR A COHERENT P–16 SYSTEM *Chrys Dougherty and Lynn Mellor*

1. The importance of this alignment has been discussed by Achieve (2004), pages 14 and 15.
2. Creating an integrated K–14 assessment system requires states to make an assessment of the college readiness part of their statewide testing program.
3. The National Governors Association signed the compact, *Graduation Counts: A Compact on State High School Graduation Data*, on July 17, 2005. It includes the commitment to "report annual progress on the improvement of their state high school graduation, completion and dropout rate data."
4. The states with State Scholars programs are: Arizona, Arkansas, Connecticut, Indiana, Kentucky, Maryland, Mississippi, New Jersey, New Mexico, Oklahoma, Rhode Island, Tennessee, Texas, and Washington. See www.centerforstatescholars.org.
5. E-mail communication from James Dilling, Texas Higher Education Coordinating Board, March 3, 2005. An earlier analysis by Lopez (2000) using data on 1997 high

school graduates found that about half of students receiving "Advanced" or "Advanced with Honors" diplomas needed remediation in one or more subjects when they entered Texas public higher education institutions.

6. The analysis, using longitudinal student-level data acquired from the Texas Education Agency, covered students taking the 11th grade TAKS exam in 2003 who had received credit for Geometry and Algebra II.
7. See Texas Education Agency, "A Study of the Correlation between Course Performance in Algebra I and Algebra I End-of-Course Test Performance," accessed November 8, 2006, at www.tea.state.tx.us/student.assessment/resources/studies/correlation.pdf.
8. Source: Research analyses at the National Center for Educational Accountability.

References

Achieve, Inc. (2004). *Ready or not: Creating a high school diploma that counts.* Washington, DC: American Diploma Project.

Data Quality Campaign. (2005). *Creating a longitudinal data system: Using data to improve student achievement.* Washington, DC: Achieve.

Dougherty, C., Mellor, L., & Jian, S. (2006). *Orange juice or orange drink? Ensuring that "advanced courses" live up to their labels.* Austin, TX: National Center for Educational Accountability.

Dougherty, C., Mellor, L., & Smith, N. (2006). *Identifying appropriate college-readiness standards for all students.* Austin, TX: National Center for Educational Accountability.

Lopez, O. (2000). *The relationship of the Texas High School Curriculum to college readiness: An update—implications for increasing student college participation and success.* Unpublished paper.

National Governors Association. (2005). Graduation counts: A compact on state high school graduation data. Washington, DC: Author.

CHAPTER 27 SEAMLESS DATA SYSTEMS, *Peter T. Ewell*

1. See www.dataqualitycampaign.org.
2. See www.ed.gov/about/bdscomm/list/hiedfuture/index.html.
3. A planning horizon of 15 years maximum seems appropriate for this exercise: not so far as to make predictions impossible, yet far enough to plan significant changes in established ways of operating.
4. For a variety of reasons related to funding and assigned responsibility, the state remains the unit of analysis in this imagined scenario for constructing future SUR systems, although cooperative common data systems might profitably be established in some regions with established patterns of substantial interstate student migration, such as lower New England and urban areas that straddle state boundaries.
5. For more information on these initiatives, see http://www.communitycollegecentral.org/AboutUs/ProjectDescription.pdf and www.achievingthedream.org.
6. For example, Idaho recently explored acquiring the Web-enabled comprehensive SUR system implemented at considerable expense by the Ohio Board of Regents. One reason why such opportunities have not been pursued is the fact that state postsecondary structures have evolved differently, requiring different definitions and operating procedures to be accommodated. If the trends forecast for the future of postsecondary education unfold as outlined earlier, the need for common standards and requirements will become paramount, providing increasingly favorable opportunities for common system development.
7. See http://nces.ed.gov/ipeds/for information on the Integrated Postsecondary Education Data System, established as the core postsecondary education data collection

program for the National Center on Education Statistics. It is a system of surveys designed to collect data from all primary providers of postsecondary education.
8. See www.studentclearinghouse.org.
9. For example, Oklahoma's regional service centers are based on a funding model that awards educational development funds to a regional council, which then purchases instructional programs from multiple providers based on what it needs.
10. See http://ierc.siue.edu.
11. See www.nc4ea.org/index.cfm?pg=home&CFID=177603&CFTOKEN=55077634&jsessionid=6a30eb3d15900$B5$98$7.

References

Adelman, C. (2000). *A parallel postsecondary universe: The certification system in information technology*. Washington, DC: U.S. Department of Education, Office of Educational Research and Improvement.

Adelman, C. (2005). *The toolbox revisited: Paths to degree completion from high school through college*. Washington, DC: U.S. Department of Education, Office of Educational Research and Improvement.

Ewell, P., & Boeke, M. (2007). *Critical connections: Linking states' unit record systems to track student progress*. Indianapolis: Lumina Foundation for Education.

Henry, R. J. (2006). *Faculty development for student achievement: The QUE Project*. Bolton, MA: Anker.

Hoffman, N. (2004). Challenge, not remediation: The Early College High School Initiative. In R. Kazis, J. Vargas, & N. Hoffman (Eds.), *Double the numbers: Increasing postsecondary credentials for underrepresented youth* (pp. 213–220). Cambridge, MA: Harvard Education Press.

Johnstone, S. M., Ewell, P. T., & Paulson, K. (2002). *Student learning as academic currency*. Washington, DC: American Council for Education.

National Center for Higher Education Management Systems. (2006a). *Containing costs in higher education: Making the case*. Boulder, CO: Author.

National Center for Higher Education Management Systems. (2006b). *Achieving consensus on common indicators*. Boulder, CO: Author.

CHAPTER 28 DEVELOPING A P–20 BUDGET TOOL, *Jill Kirk, John Tapogna, and Duncan Wyse*

References

Oregon Education Roundtable. (2006). *Raising the bar for PreK–20 education in Oregon: 6 White papers*. Retrieved from www.oregonedroundtable.org/studies&reports_white papers.html

Tareen, S. (2005, October 27). English mastery goal hard to master. *The Oregonian*.

CHAPTER 29 FINANCING HIGHER ASPIRATIONS, *Arthur M. Hauptman*

1. Timpane and Hauptman (2004) review available research and analysis on how preparation levels and aspirations affect rates of participation and persistence.
2. See chapter 30, "Integrating Public Finance into Strategies for Improving Preparation, College Enrollment, and Persistence" for a discussion of research that supports the related claim that families' concerns about college costs affect student academic preparation.
3. This is notwithstanding the federal "ability to benefit" provisions that allow students without a high school diploma or GED to qualify for federal aid. But these largely self-administered tests do not provide much of a real standard to measure whether students are truly prepared to do college-level work.

4. For a description of the Lang and other private early interventions efforts, see Blanco (2005).
5. See Blanco (2005) for details on state programs.
6. See chapter 6, "Raising Expectations for Academic Achievement," and chapter 30, "Integrating Public Finance into Strategies for Improving Preparation, College Enrollment, and Persistence" for more information on the Twenty-first Century Scholars Program.
7. Source: Rhode Island Children's Crusade website, as reported in Blanco (2005).
8. For the survey reports, see Western Interstate Commission for Higher Education (2006).

References

Blanco, C. (2005). *Early commitment financial aid programs: Promises, practices, and policies.* Boulder, CO: Western Interstate Commission for Higher Education.

Martinez, M., & Klopott, S. (2003). *Improving college access for minority, low-income, and first generation students.* Boston: Pathways to College Network.

Timpane, M., & Hauptman, A. (2004). Improving the academic preparation and performance of low-income students in American higher education. In R. Kahlenberg (Ed.), *America's untapped resource: Low-income students in higher education* (pp. 59–101). New York: Century Foundation Press.

Western Interstate Commission for Higher Education. (2006). *Accelerated learning options: Moving the needle on access and success.* Boulder, CO: Author.

CHAPTER 30 INTEGRATING PUBLIC FINANCE, *Edward P. St. John*

References

Adelman, C. (1999). *Answers in the tool box: Academic intensity, attendance patterns, and bachelor's degree attainment.* Washington, DC: National Center for Education Statistics.

Adelman, C. (2006). *The toolbox revisited: Paths to degree completion from high school through college.* Washington, DC: U.S. Department of Education.

Advisory Committee on Student Financial Assistance. (2002). *Empty promises: The myth of college access in America.* Washington, DC: Author.

Becker, W. E. (2004). Omitted variables and sample selection in studies of college-going decisions. In E. P. St. John (Ed.), *Readings on equal education: Vol. 19. Public policy and college access: Investigating the federal and state roles in equalizing postsecondary opportunity* (pp. 65–86). New York: AMS Press.

Fitzgerald, B. (2004). Federal financial aid and college access. In E. P. St. John (Ed.), *Readings on equal education: Vol. 19. Public policy and college access: Investigating the federal and state roles in equalizing postsecondary opportunity* (pp. 1–28). New York: AMS Press.

Hartle, T. W., Simmons, C. A. M., & Timmons, B. H. (2005). *What every student should know about federal financial aid.* Washington, DC: American Council on Education.

Heller, D. E. (1997). Student price response in higher education: An update of Leslie and Brinkman. *Journal of Higher Education, 68,* 624–659.

Heller, D. E. (2004). NCES research on college participation: A critical analysis. In E. P. St. John (Ed.), *Readings on equal education: Vol. 19. Public policy and college access: Investigating the federal and state roles in equalizing postsecondary opportunity* (pp. 29–64). New York: AMS Press.

Herting, J. R., Hirschman, C., & Pharris-Ciurej, N. (2006). *The impact of the promise of scholarships on college ambitions, preparation, and enrollment: A preliminary evaluation of the Washington State Achievers Program.* Paper presented at the 2005 meeting of the Association for Public Policy and Management.

Hossler, D., Schmit, J., & Vesper, N. (1999). *Going to college: How social, economic, and educational factors influence the decisions students make*. Baltimore: Johns Hopkins University Press.

Lee, J. B. (2004). Access revisited: A preliminary reanalysis of NELS. In E. P. St. John (Ed.), *Readings on equal education: Vol. 19. Public policy and college access: Investigating the federal and state roles in equalizing postsecondary opportunity* (pp. 87–96). New York: AMS Press.

Leslie, L. L., & Brinkman, P. T. (1988). *The economic value of higher education*. New York: Macmillan.

Mortenson, T. (2005). *College continuation rates for recent high school graduates in 2005*. Retrieved from http://postsecondaryopportunity.blogspot.com/

Musoba, G. D. (2006). Aptitude v. adequate funding: What policies influence adequate preparation? In E. P. St. John (Ed.), *Public policy and educational opportunity: Vol. 21. School reforms, postsecondary encouragement, and state policies on postsecondary education. Readings on equal education* (pp. 223–270). New York: AMS Press.

Perna, L. W. (2005). A gap in the literature: The influence of the design, operations, and marketing of student aid programs on the formation of family college-going plans and resulting college-going behaviors of potential students. *Journal of Student Financial Aid, 35*(3), 7–15.

St. John, E. P. (2003). *Refinancing the college dream: Access, equal opportunity, and justice for taxpayer*. Baltimore: Johns Hopkins University Press.

St. John, E. P. (2006). *Education and the public interest: School reform, public finance, and access to higher education*. Amsterdam, Netherlands: Kluwer.

St. John, E. P., Cabrera, A. F., Nora, A., & Asker, E. (2000). Economic influences on persistence reconsidered: How can finance research inform the reconceptualization of persistence models? In J. M. Braxton (Ed.), *Reworking the departure puzzle: New theory and research on college student retention* (pp. 29–47). Nashville: Vanderbilt University Press.

St. John, E. P., Musoba, G. D., Simmons, A., Chung, C.-G., Schmidt, J., & Peng, C.-Y. (2004). Meeting the access challenge: An examination of Indiana's Twenty-first Century Scholars Program. *Research in Higher Education, 45*, 829–873.

St. John, E. P., Gross, J. P. K., Musoba, G. D., & Chung, A. S. (2006). Postsecondary encouragement and academic success: Degree attainment by Indiana's Twenty-first Century Scholars. In E. P. St. John (Ed.), *Readings on equal education: Vol. 21. Public policy and equal educational opportunity: School reforms, postsecondary encouragement, and state policies on postsecondary education* (pp. 257–291). New York: AMS Press.

St. John, E. P., & Hu, S. (2006). The impact of guarantees on financial aid on college enrollment: An evaluation of the Washington State Achievers Program. In E. P. St. John (Ed.), *Public policy and educational opportunity: Vol. 21. School reforms, postsecondary encouragement, and state policies on postsecondary education. Readings on equal education* (pp. 223–270). New York: AMS Press.

St. John, E. P., & Hu, S. (in press). School reform, scholarship guarantees, and college enrollment: A study of the Washington State Achievers Program. In E. P. St. John (Ed.), *Confronting educational inequality: Vol. 22. Reframing, building understanding, and taking action, Readings on Equal Education*. New York: AMS Press.

About the Editors

Nancy Hoffman is vice president of youth transitions at Jobs for the Future. She leads JFF's work on dual enrollment, directs the Early College High School Initiative (funded by the Bill & Melinda Gates Foundation), and works with Making Opportunity Affordable, a major initiative of Lumina Foundation for Education. Dr. Hoffman came to JFF from Brown University where she was a senior lecturer in education. She has served as vice provost for undergraduate studies at Temple University, as academic services dean at the Harvard Graduate School of Education, and as a professor in several other institutions. She is the author most recently of *Women's True Profession: Voices from the History of Teaching* (Harvard Education Press) and, with Richard Kazis and Joel Vargas, coeditor of *Double the Numbers: Increasing Postsecondary Credentials for Underrepresented Youth* (Harvard Education Press).

Marc S. Miller, PhD, is director of publications at Jobs for the Future.

Joel Vargas works with the Early College High School Initiative at Jobs for the Future, examining the district and state policy implications related to the initiative and exploring how state and federal policies can improve the postsecondary attainment of underserved students. He has directed, initiated, and studied a variety of middle school and high school programs designed to promote college-going for underrepresented students. He also has been a teacher, editor, and research assistant for the Civil Rights Project at Harvard University. Dr. Vargas is coeditor of *Double the Numbers: Increasing Postsecondary Credentials for Underrepresented Youth* (Harvard Education Press, 2004).

Andrea Venezia is senior policy associate with WestEd. Her work examines education policy, particularly as related to access to postsecondary success and the transition from K–12 to postsecondary education. Dr. Venezia has worked for a variety of state, federal, and not-for-profit entities, including the National Center for Public Policy and Higher Education, the Stanford Institute for Higher Education Research, the Texas Higher Education Coordinating Board, and the National Education Goals Panel.

About the Authors

Cheryl Almeida directs Jobs for the Future's research on improving options and outcomes for struggling students and out-of-school youth. She has over 20 years of experience in research and evaluation, as well as in policy and program development in education and child development. Recent publications have focused on the education persistence of dropouts and state policy that supports improved outcomes for struggling students and out-of-school youth.

John Augenblick serves as president of Augenblick, Palaich, & Associates, Inc. (APA), a Denver-based consulting firm founded in 1983. APA works primarily with state-level policymakers on education issues, particularly those concerning finance.

Betsy Brand has served as director of the American Youth Policy Forum since 2004; she joined the organization as codirector in 1998. Brand oversees the projects and staff of AYPF and specializes in high school reform, career preparation, and college access and success. Brand's education policy career started in 1977 when she became a legislative associate for the House Committee on Education and Labor. She subsequently served on the Senate Labor and Human Resources Committee and as assistant secretary for vocational and adult education at the U.S. Department of Education under President George H. W. Bush. Brand currently chairs the Center for Occupational Research and Development, the National Child Labor Committee Board of Directors, and the National High School Alliance Steering Committee, and serves on other boards and advisory committees.

Patrick M. Callan is president of the National Center for Public Policy and Higher Education, an independent, nonpartisan organization, created by national foundations to ensure educational opportunity, affordability, and quality higher education. He has previously served as executive director of the California Higher Education Policy Center, the California Postsecondary Education Commission, the Washington State Council for Postsecondary Education, and the Montana Commission on Postsecondary Education, and as vice president of the Education Commission of the States.

Anthony P. Carnevale is a research professor at Georgetown University. Dr. Carnevale has served as vice president for public leadership at the Educational Testing Service, director of human resource studies at the Committee for Economic Development, president of the Institute for Workplace Learning, director of political and government affairs for the American Federation of State, County and Municipal Employees, and a senior staff member in both houses of Congress. In 1993, President Clinton appointed Dr. Carnevale as chairman of the National Commission for Employment Policy, and in 1994, secretary of commerce Ronald Brown appointed Dr. Carnevale to the Board of Overseers for the Malcolm Baldrige National Quality Award. Dr. Carnevale coauthored the principal affidavit in *Rodriguez v. San Antonio*, a landmark U.S. Supreme Court case that resulted in significant reforms to promote equal educational opportunity in most states.

Michael Cohen, president of Achieve, Inc., since January 2003, oversees the organization's efforts to ensure that the quality of standards-based reforms that states undertake remains high. Prior to joining Achieve, Cohen was a senior fellow at the Aspen Institute, focusing on high school reform. From 1993 to 2001, he served in several senior educational policy positions in the Clinton administration, helping to make the federal government a supportive partner in state education reforms.

Michael Collins is a program director at Jobs for the Future, where he focuses on state policy issues for the Early College High School Initiative, Achieving the Dream: Community Colleges Count, and Double the Numbers, JFF's campaign to dramatically increase the number of young people from low-income and minority families who attain postsecondary credentials. Mr. Collins has worked in multiple capacities on education reform and higher education policy, helping improve public education at the local and state levels. He served as assistant commissioner for participation and success at the Texas Higher Education Coordinating Board, where he led the agency's efforts to increase the number of students enrolling and succeeding in higher education. He also oversaw implementation in Texas of "Education—Go Get It," the state's innovative, research-based public awareness and motivational campaign to increase student participation and success in the state's colleges and universities.

Kristin D. Conklin, formerly a program director with the National Governors Association's Center for Best Practices, launched and managed the organization's 26-state Honor States Grant Program. The grant program supports governors' leadership efforts to improve college-ready graduation rates. Conklin is the author of *Ten Steps to Getting It Done*, the signature product of Governor Mark Warner's initiative as chair of the National Governors Association. For six years, she led NGA's efforts to support governors and their key advisors on high school and higher education issues. Prior to NGA, she ran the Washington office for the National Center for Public Policy and Higher Education and provided analytic leadership for the development of the first comparative report card of state higher education performance, Measuring Up. Conklin currently serves as senior counselor to the undersecretary of the U.S. Department of Education.

David Conley is professor of educational leadership and policy at the University of Oregon. He is founder and director of the Center for Educational Policy Research (CEPR) and of the Educational Policy Improvement Center (EPIC). Through these centers, he conducts research on a range of issues related to the high school–

college transition. His most recent book, *College Knowledge: What It Really Takes for Students to Succeed and What We Can Do to Get Them Ready*, summarizes research that identifies the knowledge and skills necessary for student success in entry-level university courses. From 1994 to 2001, he served in the office of the vice chancellor for academic affairs of the Oregon University System as executive director of the Proficiency-Based Admission Standards System (PASS).

Cecilia Cunningham is executive director of the Middle College National Consortium at LaGuardia Community College. Dr. Cunningham served as the principal of Middle College High School at LaGuardia Community College for 22 years until 2002. She started her career as a math teacher and holds a doctorate in education from Teachers College at Columbia University.

Chrys Dougherty is director of research at the National Center for Educational Accountability. He is responsible for the design of the Just for the Kids School Reports and oversees procedures for selecting consistently high-performing schools and the center's research projects using longitudinal student data. He authored *Asking the Right Questions about Schools: A Parents' Guide* and has written extensively on the value of longitudinal student data and the Ten Essential Elements of statewide student information systems. After teaching science in an elementary school in Oakland, California, he received his MA in public affairs from the LBJ School of Public Affairs in 1985, and earned a PhD in economics from Harvard University in 1992. From 1992 to 1998, he taught statistics, economics, econometrics, and education policy courses at the LBJ School of Public Affairs. Dougherty joined Just for the Kids (later NCEA) in 1997 in order to improve the information that parents, educators, and community leaders have about schools.

Peter T. Ewell is vice president of the National Center for Higher Education Management Systems, an independent research and development organization on higher education policy. His primary research areas are the assessment of student learning in higher education and improving student success in postsecondary settings. He has undertaken major projects in these areas with support from Lumina Foundation for Education, the Pew Charitable Trusts, and the W. K. Kellogg Foundation. He has consulted with 23 state systems of higher education and with over 400 colleges and universities.

Joni Finney is vice president of the National Center for Public Policy and Higher Education, an independent, nonpartisan organization, created by national foundations to ensure educational opportunity, affordability, and quality higher education. Dr. Finney oversees the research, communication, and administration of the National Center. She directs research studies related to higher education finance, governance, and performance, including developing the nation's first state-by-state report card for higher education, Measuring Up.

Karen C. Foster is a visiting faculty member in research at the University of Dayton School of Education and Allied Health Professions, specializing in qualitative and ethnographic research methods. She is a former research associate from

Harvard University Graduate School of Education, where she collaborated with Michael Nakkula for ten years. Along with Dr. Nakkula and colleagues from Search Institute in Minneapolis, she is coauthor of the upcoming book, *Skateboard Parks, Schools, and Boardrooms: The Complexities of Collaboration in Community-Based Youth Development.*

Susan Goldberger is director of new ventures at Jobs for the Future. She is responsible for promoting the development, testing, and scaling of new school and program designs that expand educational and economic opportunity for low-income youth and adults. Dr. Goldberger's youth-related work focuses on the identification, documentation, and promotion of effective small schools designs for helping urban youth achieve college success. Her adult-related work focuses on development and expansion of effective program models for preparing and placing low-income adults in well-paying, career-ladder jobs.

Terry Grobe is a program director at Jobs for the Future, where she works on city and state initiatives directed at improving outcomes and options for low-income and out-of-school youth. She has extensive professional experience in school reform, alternative education, and youth systems development. Previously, Grobe worked for Commonwealth Corporation, where she was project director for Diploma Plus, a national alternative school model, and helped create and manage the Reaching All Youth (RAY) Coalition, a statewide network of alternative schools and youth programs.

Arthur M. Hauptman has been an independent public policy consultant since 1981. He is an internationally recognized expert in higher education finance and has written and spoken extensively on issues of student financial aid, college costs, tuition fees, and resource allocation. He has consulted on higher education finance issues with more than a dozen countries, as well as a number of federal government agencies, state agencies, and higher education institutions and associations in the United States.

Geoff Hayward is a university lecturer in educational studies, associate director of the ESRC Research Centre on Skills, Knowledge and Organisational Performance (SKOPE), and a fellow of Kellogg College, University of Oxford. He is a director of the Nuffield 14–19 Review. This body has six years of funding from the Nuffield Foundation, a charitable trust, to undertake a fundamental and independent analysis of the 14–19 Education and Training system in England and Wales, with the aim of influencing policy development.

Eric Hofmann, associate director of College Now, monitors program performance and is responsible for shaping professional and curriculum development activities to support CUNY college faculty and New York City high school teachers.

Stan Jones is the commissioner for higher education in Indiana. As the state's primary higher education agency, the Commission for Higher Education is responsible for planning and coordinating Indiana's state-supported system of postsecondary education. Throughout his professional career, Stan Jones has helped push important educational policy issues to the forefront of the Indiana political agenda, serving 16 years in the Indiana state legislature and more than five years as a top aide to then governor Evan Bayh. Jones is credited as a primary architect of several landmark education policy initiatives, including Indiana's Core 40 curriculum and the 21st Century Scholars program, a scholarship program aimed at increasing the number of low-income students attending and completing a postsecondary education.

Jill Kirk is a vice president of the Oregon Business Council, a private, nonprofit, nonpartisan organization consisting of chief executives from some of Oregon's largest businesses. Her primary area of responsibility is policy work relating to public education. Prior to joining OBC, Kirk was a human resources director for Tektronix, Inc., a high-technology firm headquartered in Beaverton, Oregon. Kirk served on Oregon's state board of education from 1995 to 2004.

Michael W. Kirst is professor emeritus of education and business administration, by courtesy, at Stanford University. As a policy generalist, Kirst has published articles on school finance politics, curriculum politics, intergovernmental relations, and education reform policies. He is the author of ten books, including *From High School to College* (2004), and *The Political Dynamics of American Education* (2005). Kirst was a member of the California state board of education from 1975 to 1982, and its president from 1977 to 1981. He was cofounder of Policy Analysis for California Education (PACE) in 1983, and is a member of the management and research staff of the Consortium for Policy Research in Education. Before joining the Stanford faculty, Kirst held several positions with the federal government, including staff director of the U.S. Senate Subcommittee on Manpower and Poverty.

Jennifer Brown Lerner is a program associate at the American Youth Policy Forum, where she identifies and researches education-related issues, policies, and programs for AYPF's publications and learning events, including Capitol Hill forums, site visits, and roundtable policy meetings. Prior to joining AYPF, Lerner was at Teachers College, Columbia University. There, she pursued a concentration in leadership, policy, and politics and drafted a policy brief for the National Center for Schools and Communities at Fordham University. Lerner has also worked as a teacher and development officer for two independent schools in the Boston area. Prior to that, she was active in creating a school-supplement program called Summerbridge (now Breakthrough Collaborative) in Atlanta, Georgia, which engages middle school students in year-round academic enrichment, with high school and college students serving as teachers and mentors. In 2005–06, she served as an education policy fellow at the Institute for Educational Leadership.

Bridget Terry Long, PhD, is an associate professor of education and economics at the Harvard Graduate School of Education. Using the theory and methods of economics, she studies the transition from secondary to higher education and beyond. Her work has focused on college access and choice, factors that influence college student persistence, and the behavior of postsecondary institutions. Several of her research papers examine the enrollment and distributional effects of financial aid programs. She has also examined the effectiveness of post-secondary remediation and the impact of class size and faculty characteristics on student persistence. Dr. Long received her PhD and MA from the Harvard University Department of Economics, and her bachelor's from Princeton University. She is a faculty research associate of the National Bureau of Economic Research and was a recipient of the National Academy of Education/Spencer Postdoctoral Fellowship.

Margaretha Maloney is an independent writer who focuses on preschool through postsecondary education policy issues. She has also worked extensively in the area of social services policy development.

Roberta S. Matthews is the provost at Brooklyn College. Prior to that, she served as the founding director of the CUNY Honors College, vice president for academic affairs at Marymount College, and in various academic and administrative posts at LaGuardia Community College (CUNY), including interim president. Her experience in higher education spans public and private, community and senior colleges. She has long worked in school-college collaboration initiatives.

Tracy Meade, university director for collaborative programs at the office of academic affairs of the City University of New York, manages and oversees all aspects of College Now and the university's affiliated schools.

Lynn Mellor is responsible for the implementation of research at the National Center for Educational Accountability. In addition to managing its Advanced Placement research grant, she oversees all research projects conducted at the center. Before joining NCEA, Dr. Mellor spent five years as director of research for a pharmaceutical research organization, and eight years at the Texas Education Agency, where she conducted research and evaluations on public school programs. Dr. Mellor earned her PhD in educational psychology from the University of Texas in 1995.

Michael J. Nakkula is a research associate at the Harvard Graduate School of Education, where he directs Project IF (Inventing the Future), an initiative that develops and studies innovative education and youth development models. He is also the past codirector of HGSE's Risk and Prevention master's program (1998–2006), which trains graduate students to work with children and adolescents in urban school and community settings. Nakkula has published widely on adolescent development in urban education settings, including his recent book with Eric Toshalis, *Understanding Youth: Adolescent Development for Educators* (Harvard Education Press).

Robert Palaich is a senior partner and vice president of Augenblick, Palaich, & and Associates, Inc. (APA). He has written articles on education reform, at-risk youth, teacher policy, school finance, district spending patterns, tax and expenditure limitations, state legislatures, and state teacher policy.

Jay Pfeiffer is deputy commissioner of accountability, research, and measurement at the Florida Department of Education. He began employment with the State of Florida in 1972, working with the State Manpower Council. Since then, his career in policy and evaluation research has focused on education, employment, and training programs. He has served in the department of education as director of education information and accountability, and as assistant deputy commissioner for accountability, research, and measurement. In 1984, he started developing the Florida Education and Training Placement Information Program as a legislative project. FETPIP, which he directed until 2002, became a first-of-its-kind program linking data from multiple administrative data resources for accountability purposes. He is the recipient of a Lifetime Achievement Award from the National Association of State Workforce Agencies for innovations in information technology.

Travis Reindl joined the staff of Jobs for the Future in 2006, where he leads Making Opportunity Affordable. Funded by Lumina Foundation for Education, this major national initiative focuses on improving college access and affordability. Mr. Reindl also contributes to other JFF initiatives that seek to ensure that all young people can obtain a quality high school and postsecondary education. Prior to joining JFF, Mr. Reindl served as director of state policy analysis and assistant to the president of the American Association of State Colleges and Universities.

Dan Restuccia is the training director of the University Park Campus School Institute, a partnership of the school, Clark University, and Jobs for the Future. The institute supports efforts to use UPCS as a national model for the Early College High School Initiative and the broader small schools movement. He has also taught math at the school and is a graduate of a grade 7–12 school himself.

Erin K. Riley is an independent research consultant who has worked extensively on numerous projects related to education policy and postsecondary institutions. Working with Dr. Bridget Terry Long, she has analyzed the impact of financial aid, examined student outcomes at community colleges, and researched state policies focused on improving academic preparation. They coauthored "The Demand Side of Student Loans: The Changing Face of Borrowers," a chapter in a forthcoming volume about private loans. Prior to working as an independent consultant, Riley worked for Eduventures, a private education research and consulting firm in Boston. She holds an EdM in educational policy and management from Harvard University's Graduate School of Education and a bachelor's in economics from Case Western Reserve University.

Edward P. St. John is Algo D. Henderson Collegiate Professor at the Center for the Study of Higher and Postsecondary Education, University of Michigan. His research focuses on public policy in both K–12 and higher education. Recent books include *Education and the Public Interest: Education Reform, Public Finance, and Access to Higher Education* and *Refinancing the College Dream: Access, Equal Opportunity, and Justice of Taxpayers*.

Stefanie Sanford is deputy director for national initiatives for the Bill & Melinda Gates Foundation, directing national policy development and advocacy grant-making in education. Prior to joining the foundation, Sanford served as deputy director of policy for Texas governor Rick Perry, and held a number of other senior positions in Texas state government. After taking leave from the state to pursue graduate study, she was selected to be a White House fellow, where she served in the White House Office of Cabinet Affairs. She has written extensively on a range of public policy topics, including her first book, *Civic Life in the Information Age,* drawn from her dissertation research and published in 2007. Sanford holds a bachelor of science from Texas Christian University, a master of public administration from the John F. Kennedy School of Government at Harvard University, and an interdisciplinary PhD in political communication and information technology from the University of Texas at Austin.

David Spence is president of the Southern Regional Education Board, the nation's first interstate compact for education. SREB was created in 1948 to help government and education leaders work together to improve education across the 16-state region. From 1998 to 2005, he was executive vice chancellor and chief academic officer of the California State University System. Among his accomplishments was the development of a systemwide initiative to increase graduation rates. Most notably, he coordinated the implementation of California's Early Assessment Program. For this work, he received the 2006 Virginia B. Smith Innovative Leadership Award from the National Center on Public Policy and High Education. He also has been executive director of the Florida Postsecondary Education Planning Commission, executive vice chancellor for the University System of Georgia, executive vice chancellor and vice chancellor for academic programs at the State University System of Florida, and SREB vice president for educational policies. He received his PhD in higher education from SUNY/Buffalo (now the University of Buffalo) in 1974.

Adria Steinberg, associate vice president at Jobs for the Future, leads JFF's work on expanding and improving educational options and outcomes for the large group of young people who are struggling to stay on or get back on the road to a productive adulthood. She has almost four decades of experience in the field of education as a teacher, administrator, researcher, and writer. Combining knowledge of practice, policy, and research, her articles and books have made her a key contributor to the national conversation about high school reform.

John Tapogna is a managing director at ECONorthwest, an Oregon-based economic consulting firm. He has provided economic, budgetary, and analytic support to national, state, and local governments, with an emphasis on education finance. Prior to joining ECONorthwest, Tapogna was a budget analyst at the Congressional Budget Office, where he forecasted the nation's welfare spending and estimated the budget impacts of mid-1990s welfare overhaul.

Christine Tell joined Achieve, Inc., in 2004 as director of the American Diploma Project to work with states on the alignment of high school exit standards and assessments with placement in postsecondary institutions and entry into the workplace. Prior to Achieve, Christine directed similar work for the chancellor's office of the Oregon University System and the design and implementation of the Proficiency-Based Admission Standards System. Since the National Education Summit in 2005, 29 states have joined the ADP Network and formally committed to P–16 alignment. Tell currently serves as the director of postsecondary outreach and alignment for these states.

Michael D. Usdan has extensive practical and academic experience in both K–12 and postsecondary education. He is a senior fellow at the Washington, D.C.–based Institute for Educational Leadership, where he has served as president for 20 years. He has served as a state commissioner of higher education, a college president, and a professor. At the K–12 level, he has been a public school teacher, an administrator, and a city school board member and president. Usdan has written frequently on problems relating to urban education, the relationship of government and politics to education, and inter-level issues. Among other affiliations, he is senior fellow at the National Center for Public Policy and Higher Education and the George Washington University.

Duncan Wyse is president of the Oregon Business Council and a member of Oregon's state board of education. Prior to his OBC position, Wyse was executive director of the Oregon Progress Board, where he developed Oregon Shines, Oregon's long-range strategy for economic growth, and Oregon Benchmarks, indicators measuring how Oregon is doing as a people, place, and economy.

Index

Note: Information contained in figures and tables are indicated by an italic *f* and *t*, respectively.

ability competencies, 89
Academic Competitiveness Grants program, 70, 77
Academic Standards for College and Work (Alignment Institutes), 83–86
accelerated learning. *See* dual enrollment
accountability
- data systems essential elements, 234, 245
- No Child Left Behind, 179
- and quality measures, 8
- secondary graduation rates, 171–172, 272
- and state data tracking systems, 46, 48–49, 51–54
- Texas, 224–225

Achieve, Inc. *See also* American Diploma Project Network
- about, 285*nn*1–5
- *Closing the Expectations Gap,* 73
- *Expectations Gap 2006,* 68
- *Getting It Done: Ten Steps to Improving America's High Schools,* 67–68
- secondary school curricula, 63

Achieving the Dream (Lumina), 243
ACT Educational Planning and Assessment System, 209
An Action Agenda for Improving America's High Schools (NGA), 63, 65–71
admissions, postsecondary
- aligning with high school standards, 63, 76, 82, 145
- competency-based admissions, 93–94, 177
- *Gratz v. Bollinger,* 66
- historical context of, 56–57
- Proficiency-Based Admission Standards System, 94
- selectivity of, 47
- *vs.* preparedness, 118

Advanced Placement program, 77, 143, 149, 290*n*2
advisory programs, 161
African Americans
- educational disparities, 45
- educational identity development, 156
- high school graduation rates, 66
- postsecondary enrollment rates, 270

Agendas, Alternatives, and Public Policies (Kingdon), 66
algebra, 97
Alliance for Excellent Education, 52
American Diploma Project Network, 63, 67, 71, 81–86, 94, 201–202
American Youth Policy Forum, 159, 290*n*2
Another Route to College, 133–138
Arkansas
- Academic Challenge Scholarships, 70–71
- Smart Core curriculum, 71

assessment
- aligning high school and college, 23, 46, 48, 49–50, 54, 76, 103, 106, 207, 250
- California Early Assessment Program, 49–50, 107*t*, 108, 110–111, 113–120
- early placement assessment policies, 105–112, 107*t*
- Illinois Prairie State Achievement Exam, 107*t*
- Kentucky Early Mathematics Testing Program, 107*t*
- North Carolina Early Mathematics Placement Testing Program, 107*t*
- Ohio Early Mathematics Placement Testing, 107*t*, 108, 109, 111
- Oklahoma Educational Planning and Assessment System, 106–108, 107*t*, 109–110

assessment (*continued*)
Proficiency-Based Admission Standards System, 94

Bantz, Charles, 27
Bill & Melinda Gates Foundation, 52, 63, 65
blue-collar economy, U.S., 15, 25
Blueprint for an Action Agenda (NGA), 68
Borough of Manhattan Community College, 146
Bridges to Opportunity (Ford Foundation), 243
Brooklyn College, 123–131

California
California Early Assessment Program, 49–50, 107*t*, 108, 110–111, 113–120
California Standards Tests, 114
California State University, 49–50
charter school laws, 179
Reading Institute for Academic Preparation, 115–116
San Joaquin Delta College, 161–162
University of California, 57
Wallace Annenberg High School, 152–158
Cardinal Principles of Secondary Education, 57
Carl D. Perkins Vocational and Technical Education Act, 159
Center for Educational Policy Research, 95–103
Charles Stewart Mott Foundation, 163
charter schools, 179
child care, 18
Claiming Common Ground, 46, 283*n*1
Clark University, 139–140
Closing the Expectations Gap (Achieve, Inc.), 73
Closing the Gaps by 2015 (Texas), 223
College Board Schools, 140
college education. *See* postsecondary education
College Examination Board, 57
The College Ladder: Linking Secondary and Postsecondary Education for Success for All Students (AYPF), 159, 205
College NOW (CUNY)
about, 139–141, 289*nn*1–7
Foundation Courses project, 147–149
origins, 143–144
results and participation, 144–146, 192
typical course sequence, 193*t*
college preparation. *See* preparedness, college
Colorado, 85
"Committee of Ten," 56–57
community college system, 19, 47–48, 173
competency-based admissions, 93–94, 177
content knowledge, 95
Core 40 curriculum (Indiana), 69–70, 73–75
costs, of education, 56, 261, 271

Data Quality Campaign, 52
data systems, educational
Achieving the Dream, 243
Bridges to Opportunity, 243
current national status, 239–240
essential elements of, 234, 245
Florida Education and Training Placement Information System, 227–232
focus of, 235–236
future design specifications, 242–245
importance, 46, 51–53, 68, 233
Kentucky, 53–54
managing student transitions, 246
National Student Clearinghouse, 229
O*Net database, 87–91
planning assumptions, 240–242
PreK–20 education system, 251
research uses of, 236, 246–247
state-level policies, 46, 51–54
Texas example, 224
Dayton Early College Academy (Ohio), 152–158
degree attainment rates, college, 4, 16
Diploma Plus network, 288*nn*1–2
District of Columbia, 27
Double the Numbers conference, 27
dropouts, secondary school, 167–173
dual crediting, 177
dual enrollment programs. *See also* early college programs
broad access to, 121, 143–150, 194–202
culture of evidence, 205–206
definition, 159
financing, 207–209
future prospects, 209–210
mission and purpose, 204
National Alliance of Concurrent Enrollment Partnerships, 195

quality and rigor, 206–207
state policies, 6–7, 172, 177

early college programs
about, 22–23, 70, 152–153, 159
advantages, 176
Another Route to College, 133–138
Early College High School Student Information System, 292*n*4
educational identity development, 155–157
financing, 179–180, 186–189
gradual development of, 125–126
Middle College Early College High School, 123–131
number and scope, 292*n*2
pedagogical lessons of establishing, 127–130
physical and logistical barriers, 126–127
psychological factors, 155
return on investment analysis, 183–189
Science, Technology and Research Early College High School, 123–131
self-responsibility needed in, 130–131
state policy support for, 175–181
student impressions of, 153–155
early placement testing
about, 105–106
California Early Assessment Program, 113–120
general implications concerning, 117–119
implications of design on success, 108–109
results of implementation, 111
variation in implementation, 106–108, 107*t*
economic value, of education, 23–25
education system, U.S.
consensus view of, 18–19, 25–26
economic, cultural, and political roles, 23–25
employability as standard outcome, 2, 15, 18, 87, 91, 211
intrinsic value of, 24
political life, and education, 24–25
politics, as source of reform, 58
professionalization of, 58
projected drop in overall attainment, 45
social pressures on, 55–56
as "unequalizer," 1, 19–21
Education Trust, 63, 66. *See also* American Diploma Project Network
educational fundamentalism, 19
Educational Policy Improvement Center, 98–103
employability, and education, 2, 15, 18, 87, 91, 211
employer-provided benefits, 16
employers, as stakeholder in education, 22–23, 81–86, 87–88, 286*n*1
Engler, John, 68
English education, 82, 83–84, 95–96, 170
Ewing Marion Kauffman Foundation, 63
Expectations Gap 2006 (Achieve, Inc.), 68

financing postsecondary education
Academic Competitiveness Grants program, 77
aligning with rigorous coursework, 76–77
dual enrollment programs, 205–206, 207–209
early college programs, 179–181, 183–189
effects of traditional systems, 261–264
federal incentives to early commitment programs, 265–266
and gains in preparation, access, and attainment, 272–277, 273*t*
GEAR UP, 263, 265
hybrid student financial aid programs, 70–71
importance of, 260
need for, 4
9–14 integrated programs, 264–265
P-20 education, 249–258
private philanthropy and, 262–263
promoting K–12 and postsecondary collaboration, 46, 48, 50–51
recent progress in, 63–64
savings accounts, 266
Florida
Florida community college system, 38
Florida Education and Training Placement Information System, 227–232
increasing degrees granted, 27
PK20 Education Data Warehouse, 227–232
Ford Foundation, 243
Fordham Foundation, 63

Gates, Bill, 65
GE Foundation, 63
GEAR UP (Gaining Early Awareness and Readiness for Undergraduate Programs), 263, 265
GED certificates, 29, 33–34, 33*f*, 167, 168, 171
gender inequalities, 20
Georgia, 84, 180
Getting It Done: Ten Steps to Improving America's High Schools (Achieve, Inc.), 67–68
global college workforce, 17
global knowledge economy, 15
Granholm, Jennifer, 85
Gratz v. Bollinger (2003), 66
Greene, Jay, 66, 68

high school education. *See* secondary education
Higher Education Act of 1965, 261–262
Hispanics. *See* Latinos
Holyoke Community College, 133–138
Honor States Grant Program, 68

"I Have a Dream" foundation, 262
identity development, educational, 152–153, 155–157
Illinois Prairie State Achievement Exam, 107*t*
immigration policy, 18
income and education connection, 22
Indiana
  college preparatory curriculum required, 69–70, 75
  dropout prevention, 172–173
  Indiana Twenty-first Century Scholars Program, 51, 77, 263, 274
  Indiana University–Purdue University Indianapolis, 27
  policies and practices, 73–78
interest competencies, 89

Jobs for the Future, 27, 66, 184, 284*n*3

Kentucky
  Kentucky Early Mathematics Testing Program, 107*t*
  Postsecondary Education Improvement Act, 53
Kindgon, John, 66
Kingsborough Community College, 146
knowledge competencies, 89

labor markets, dual, 87–88
LaGuardia Community College, 123–131, 147
Lang, Eugene, 262
Latinos
  educational disparities, 45
  educational identity development, 156
  high school graduation rates, 66
  low-attainment levels, 295*n*2
  postsecondary enrollment rates, 270
liberal education, 24
literacy education. *See* English education
low-income socioeconomic status. *See also* financing postsecondary education
  actual college graduation rates, 28–29
  college completion of, 29*f*, 30, 45
  college enrollment of, 29*f*, 30, 36–37, 37*f*, 261
  college preparation of, 30*f*, 33–35, 35*f*, 37–39, 38*f*, 236, 261, 282*n*11
  doubling college graduation rates, 27–28, 32–33, 40–41, 40*t*
  educational attainment rates, 192*t*
  estimating current degree earners, 31–32, 31*f*
  GED holders, 29, 33–34, 33*f*
  high school completion, 29–30, 29*f*, 33–34
  raising aspirations through funding options, 259–267
Lumina Foundation for Education, 52, 63, 243

Maine, 293*n*5
Maryland, 85
Massachusetts, 133–138
math education, 69, 82, 83–84, 170, 272
meritocratic ideals, 19, 26
Michigan, 27, 85
middle-class status
  college jobs to maintain, 17
  educational criteria for, 15–17, 192*t*
Middle College Early College High School (MCECHS), 123–131
Middle Colleges, 124, 159
middle schools, 139–141
Minnesota, 209
minorities. *See* African Americans; Latinos

Mott Middle College (Michigan), 163
Moving the Needle (WICHE), 205, 208

A Nation at Risk, 65, 66
National Alliance of Concurrent Enrollment Partnerships, 195, 206–207
National Council of La Raza, 140
National Education Data Summit, 52
National Education Longitudinal Study, 20, 28
National Education Summit (2005), 81–82
National Governors Association
  An Action Agenda for Improving America's High Schools, 63, 65–71
  Honor States Grant Program, 68, 71
National Science Foundation, 148
National Student Clearinghouse, 229
New Visions for Public Schools, 148–149
New York
  CUNY College NOW, 139–141, 143–150, 192, 193*t*
  Middle College Early College High School, 123–131
  Science, Technology and Research Early College High School, 123–131
  secondary-postsecondary integration, 59–62
No Child Left Behind, 171, 179
normal schools, 57
North Carolina
  Early Mathematics Placement Testing Program, 107*t*
  Innovations Initiatives Act, 179
Northern Virginia Community College, 27
Nuffield Review (UK), 211–217, 294*nn*1–2

occupational competencies, 87–91
O'Connor, Sandra Day, 66
offshoring, 17
Ohio
  Dayton Early College Academy, 152–158
  early college program funding, 180
  Ohio Early Mathematics Placement Testing, 107*t,* 108, 109, 111
  transfer module policy, 178
Oklahoma
  Higher Learning Access Program, 263
  Oklahoma Educational Planning and Assessment System, 106–108, 107*t,* 109–110
O*Net database, 87–91

Oregon
  funding P–20 education, 249–258
  Oregon Business Council, 50
  Oregon University, 94
  Portland Community College, 162
Owens, Bill, 85

peer support networks, 162–163
Pell Grants, 70, 262, 279*n*15
Pew Charitable Trusts, 63
political life, and education, 24–25
politics, as source of reform, 58
Portland Community College (Oregon), 162
postsecondary education
  access roads to, 21–22
  aligning high school and college, 46, 49–50, 74–75, 81–86, 93–95
  attainment rates and socioeconomic status, 1, 2, 20, 27–28, 192*t,* 270
  "college for all" strategy, 18–19, 25, 87
  as criteria for middle-class status, 15–17
  degree areas conferred, 286*n*2
  degree attainment rates, 4, 16, 280*n*2, 282*n*6
  demographics since 1980s, 4
  differences from secondary, 99–100
  enrollment rates, 29*f,* 30, 36–37, 37*f,* 261, 270, 282*n*6
  private institutions and, 59
  selective access to, 21
  separation from K–12, 55–64
  support system for attainment, 4
PreK–20 education, 249–258
preparedness, college
  access, attainment, and, 270–277, 271*f*
  aligning high school course work and assessments with, 48, 49–50, 63, 73–77, 81–86, 93–95, 100–101
  An Action Agenda for Improving America's High Schools, 63, 65–71
  biggest challenge, 47
  CEPR/EPIC recommendations for, 102–103
  college-ready standards inconsistent, 47–48
  college success courses, 162
  educational identity development, 152–153, 155–157
  finance and K–12 reform lead to, 272–274, 273*t*
  generals skills needed, 98

preparedness, college (*continued*)
improving, 33–35, 35*f*, 37–39, 282*n*11
of low-income individuals, 30*f*
math skills, 97–98
measuring, 281*n*4
nature and urgency of problem, 66–67
promising current practices, 159–163
reading and writing skills, 95–96, 114–115
remedial courses, 47, 48
problem-solving skills, 24
Proficiency-Based Admission Standards System, 94

racial inequalities, 20
readiness, college. *See* preparedness, college
reading proficiency, 95–96, 114–115
Refinancing the College Dream (St. John), 269–270
reform efforts, educational, 58
remedial education, 47–48, 82, 105–106, 145–147
retirement age, 16, 17
return on investment, early college programs, 183–189
Rhode Island
Children's Crusade for Higher Education, 263–264
PK–16 Council, 198–200
Rivera, Manuel, 140
Rochester, New York, 140

safety, of environment, 162–163
San Joaquin Delta College, 161–162
Science, Technology and Research (STAR) Early College High School, 123–131
secondary education. *See also* early college programs
academic rigor of, 4
African American graduation rates, 66
aligning career preparedness with, 22–23, 81–86, 87–91
aligning high school and college, 46, 49–50, 74–75, 81–86, 93–95
combining with middle school, 139–141
dropout problem, 167–173
general skills for college success, 98
graduation rates accountability, 171–172
historical view, 56–57
incoherence of program of study in, 99–100, 102
leaders wary of postsecondary influence, 62
linking to postsecondary education, 46–47, 74–75, 81–86, 93–95
math skills for college success, 97–98, 272
readiness for, 139
reading and writing skills for college success, 95–96, 114–115
reform efforts, 46, 272
requiring college preparatory curriculum, 69–70, 73–75, 223–224
rigorousness of, and college success, 73
senior seminar, 101
senior year programming, 114–115
teacher professional development, 115–116
urban school graduation rates, 1, 168–169
vocational tracks, 18
secondary-postsecondary integration. *See* dual enrollment; early college programs; separation of K–12 and postsecondary education
Secondary-Postsecondary Learning Options, 159–165
separation of K–12 and postsecondary education
about, 55–56
current status, 62–64
evolution of, 56–57
New York case study, 59–62
policy implications of, 62
recent trends, 58
Sinclair Community College, 153
skill competencies, 89
socioeconomic status. *See* low-income socioeconomic status; middle-class status
socioeconomic status, and college attainment rates, 1, 2, 20, 27–28, 192*t*, 270, 281*n*3
Special Services, 262
Standards for Success (CEPR), 95–98, 148
state-level policies
accountability systems, 179, 224–225
An Action Agenda for Improving America's High Schools, 67–72
aligning high school and college, 46, 49–50, 74–75, 81–86, 93–95
Claiming Common Ground, 46, 283*n*1

college eligibility requirements, 177
credit transfer rules, 178
dropout prevention, 171–173
dual enrollment, 6–7, 177, 197
early college programs, 175–181, 183–189
funding, 46, 48, 50–51, 179–180, 249–258, 276–277
Getting It Done, 67–72
leadership, 74, 84–85
monitoring reform efforts, 54
postsecondary attainment goals, 221–225
public reporting, 78
recent changes, 62–64
recommendations to guide, 71–72
replacing existing policy framework, 102–103
Rhode Island example, 197–200
school-level autonomy, 178–179
separation of K-12 and postsecondary education, 59–62
"State Scholars" programs, 235, 295*n*4
student data tracking through postsecondary, 46, 51–54
teacher qualifications, 177–178
Texas example, 200–202
Summit on High Schools (2005), 67
SUR data systems. *See* data systems, educational
Syracuse University Project Advance, 195–196

Talent Development Comprehensive School Reform, 170
Talent Search, 262
teacher education, 57, 177–178
technical prep, 159
Texas
data system use by, 235–236, 235*t*
dual enrollment policies, 200–202
financing accelerated learning, 209
postsecondary attainment goals, 222–225
Texas Assessment of Knowledge and Skills, 235
Texas Higher Education Assessment, 235
Thomas B. Fordham Foundation, 94
The Toolbox Revisited: Paths to Degree Completion from High School through College (U.S. DOE), 73
tracks, career and education, 22–23
TRIO programs, 262
tutoring support, 161–162
21st Century Scholars program (Indiana), 51, 77

Understanding University Success (Conley), 95
United Kingdom, 211–217
University of Virginia, 279*n*15
University of Wisconsin, 93–94
University Park Campus School, 139–140
Upward Bound, 262
urban school graduation rates, 1, 168–169
U.S. Department of Education, 52
U.S. job growth, 1, 16–17, 18

Virginia, 279*n*15
vocationalism, 18, 23–25, 57

Wallace Annenberg High School (Los Angeles), 152–158
Warner, Mark, 67
Washington
Running Start, 293*n*6
State Achievers Program, 274–275
Wells High School (Maine), 161
Western Interstate Commission for Higher Education, 205, 208, 264
Wisconsin, 93–94
work style and values competencies, 89
writing proficiency, 95–96